*Genetics and Education*

ARTHUR R. JENSEN

---

# *Genetics and Education*

1817

HARPER & ROW, PUBLISHERS
*New York, Evanston, San Francisco, London*

To my wife Barbara

# CONTENTS

# Acknowledgements

For permission to reprint articles in this volume the author and publisher would like to thank the following: the President and Fellows of Harvard College for 'How Much Can We Boost IQ and Scholastic Achievement?' (*Harvard Educational Review*, 1969, **39**, 1-123); the Academic Press, Inc. for 'A Theory of Primary and Secondary Familial Retardation' (*International Review of Research in Mental Retardation*, 1970, **4**, 33-105); the National Academy of Sciences for 'Estimation of the Limits of Heritability of Traits by Comparison of Monozygotic and Dizygotic Twins' (*Proceedings of the National Academy of Science*, 1967, **58**, 149-156); the Editor of *Behavior Genetics* for 'IQs of Identical Twins Reared Apart' (*Behavior Genetics*, 1970, **1**, 133-148); the Editor of *The Humanist* for 'Genetic Research on Human Mental Abilities: Ethical Issues' (*The Humanist*, January-February 1972, 5-6); the American Psychological Association for 'A Note on Why Genetic Correlations are not Squared' (*Psychological Bulletin*, 1971, **75**, 223-224).

Additional footnotes to the articles, made for this book, are distinguished from the original footnotes by an asterisk, instead of a numeral.

# Preface

A little more than three years have now passed since the original publication of my article 'How Much Can We Boost IQ and Scholastic Achievement?' in the *Harvard Educational Review* (Winter, 1969). The storm of ideologically, often politically, motivated protests, misinterpretations, and vilifications prompted by this article has by now fortunately subsided, with most encouraging signs of being displaced in professional journals and conferences (and now to a large extent even in the popular press) by rational and sober consideration of the educational and societal implications of the important issues raised in this article. The heat and smoke have largely abated, which is all to the good; yet the concerned interest of the kind I had originally hoped my article would stimulate has continued to grow. Since its publication, reprint requests numbering in the thousands have been received, which of course I could not personally fill; and they are still coming in, merely to be answered by a form letter. Judging from my mail, many college courses in education, psychology, biology, and genetics throughout the country have devoted a substantial part of their discussion to my article, and in a number of departments that have come to my attention whole courses and seminars have been built around it. I have in my files hundreds of term papers which students have written on the article in a variety of courses (including a few from high school classes), sent to me by the students who wrote them or by their teachers. The handling of the volume of mail resulting from this publication and its attendant publicity was for many months practically a full-time job for my wife, whose superior capabilities for organization and diplomacy have considerably

1

relieved the burden on me, making it possible, unstintingly, to continue my research on some of the problems that were highlighted in my article.

Because of the continued and growing interest in these topics among educators and workers in the biological, behavioral, and social sciences, I heartily welcomed the suggestion to reprint the article, making it more accessible to a wider, more international audience. Also, some of the most typical inquiries I have received from readers of the original publication, it turns out, are answered in detail in several of my other closely related publications. In attempting to answer these inquiries, I soon ran out of my supply of reprints of the most relevant articles. The few most germane and frequently requested of these articles have been included in the present volume. Two of them go into the study of twins in considerable detail. The first deals with the estimation of the heritability of intelligence (and other traits) by means of comparing identical and fraternal twins. The second is a re-analysis of all the existing major studies of the IQs of identical twins who were separated early in life and reared apart. Then, since most psychologists who have studied statistics as a part of their formal training were taught that the proportion of variance accounted for in one variable by another variable is given by the $r^2$, that is, the square of the coefficient of correlation between the two variables, many psychologists wrote to me in puzzlement as to why I had not squared the correlations between identical twins in order to obtain the estimate of the proportion of IQ variance attributable to genetic factors. This is a point which has never bothered geneticists, to my knowledge, probably because they have been brought up on it, so to speak, and have used correlations for somewhat different purposes than those for which psychologists typically think about the meaning of a correlation coefficient. The article 'Why Genetic Correlations Are Not Squared' is my answer to these inquiries. It is essential that the reader not be puzzled on this point if he is to understand the quantitative logic of heritability estimation based on kinship correlations. Also, I have received many inquiries from workers in the fields of special education and mental retardation concerning the relationship of problems in these fields to the so-called nature-nurture controversy and to the conspicuous connection between social class and the frequency of milder forms of mental retardation and scholastic backwardness. The problems here are so diverse that one cannot even begin to tackle all the questions that are posed. But the gist of the directions which my thinking and research have taken in this area, making no claim to comprehensive ness, are presented in 'A Theory of Primary and Secondary Familial Mental Retardation'. My research in the two years since this article originally appeared has led to some revisions of my theory, particularly regarding the degree of functional dependence of Level II (intelligence) ability upon Level I (memory and rote learning) ability, and these new points are summarized in the *Addendum* to the article on familial mental retardation. Finally, questions are frequently raised concerning the ethical and moral problems involved in the public discussion of the genetic aspects of individual and especially social class and racial group differences in socially and educationally valued traits such as intelligence. Major symposia have been devoted to discussion of these moral and ethical issues. The essence of my statements in two such symposia in which I was an invited participant is given in the last selection in this volume.

For readers who may wish to delve into commentary aroused by my *Harvard Educational Review* (henceforth abbreviated *HER*) article, I have included a bibliography of commentary on the *HER* article. The list is as complete as I can make it by the time this volume goes to press. Some of these items are quite worth reading, many are trivial, and some are plainly misinformed. I have made no attempt to select them, but have simply aimed to make the list as complete as possible. It would have been practically impossible and scarcely worth while for me to have responded individually to each of these items. I have replied to critics only in those instances where the criticism has dealt with scientific (rather than ideological) issues or when the facts have been seriously misrepresented in reputable scholarly journals with a large readership and therefore should not be allowed to go unchallenged. I have generally not bothered with articles in the popular press.

In all the published criticisms and in the personal correspondence I have received, several errors in the original publication have been turned up, all minor points and mostly typographical. These have all been corrected in this edition. In all but the most trivial instances, I have footnoted the changes. The claims of some of my overly zealous critics that there exists a large number of errors or misinterpretations in this work simply have not held up under examination. In a subsequent issue of the *HER*, for example, one critic stated:

> I should like to make it clear at the outset, however, that in Jensen's article I found many erroneous statements, misinterpretations, and misunderstandings of the nature of intelligence, intelligence tests, genetic determination of traits, education in general, and compensatory education in particular. A colleague reports coming across 17 such errors in a casual perusal. . . . Perhaps so large a number of errors would not be remarkable were it not for the fact that Jensen's previous work has contained so few, and, more malignant, all the errors referred to are in the same direction: maximizing differences between blacks and whites and maximizing the possibility that such differences are attributable to hereditary factors.

This critic was informed many months ago that all errors were to be corrected in this new edition of the article and that he could perform a service by specifically pointing out all the errors he claimed existed. But he has been unable to point to anything that by any stretch of the imagination could be called an error except one obvious misprint (which the printers had already corrected in all printings subsequent to the first, along with two other obvious typographical errors that occurred in the first printing). The attempts to discredit the main substance of my article have been most intemperate in some circles, ultimately to the discredit and embarrassment of the critics. On the other hand, I have corrected all actual errors in this edition that were noted by critics or were brought to my attention by various knowledgeable correspondents.

Another class of questioning that has often been addressed to me concerning the *HER* article has to do not with the substantive issues but with my reasons for writing the article – the history of the whole affair, including the tumultuous reactions that followed its publication. This is probably as appropriate a place as any to chronicle these events briefly and to set the record straight in those instances where attempts have been made to misrepresent the true chain of events.

As a psychological researcher, how did I go from the rather esoteric research on theoretical problems in serial rote learning to research on the inheritance of mental abilities and its implications for education? Up until about 1961, all of my psychological research was conducted in the laboratory, as is true of most investigators in the psychology of human learning, and all of my experimental subjects were university undergraduates. The details of the problems I was researching in an attempt to achieve an adequate theory of certain serial learning phenomena – one of the classical topics of human learning research – are unimportant in the present context. The point is that they were about as far removed from the topics of the present volume as one could get and still be working in the field of psychology. While I was engrossed in my research on serial learning, one of my graduate students who worked as a school psychologist brought to my attention what appeared to be a challenging problem for a researcher on human learning. Besides, it was a part of my personal philosophy that a scientist should try to bring his technical expertise to bear on practical as well as theoretical problems; and here, it seemed, was a worthy practical problem. My student said he was looking for a good culture-free or culture-fair test of intelligence and had not been able to find one. All the tests he used, whether they were claimed to be culture-fair or not, were in considerable agreement with respect to children diagnosed as educationally mentally retarded (EMR), by which they were assigned to special small classes offering a different instructional program from that in the regular classes. To qualify for this special treatment, children had to have IQs below 75 as well as lagging far behind their age-mates in scholastic performance. My student, who had examined many of these backward pupils himself, had gained the impression that the tests were quite valid in their assessments of white middle-class children but not of minority lower-class children. Many of the latter, despite IQs below 75 and markedly poor scholastic performance, did not seem nearly as retarded as the white middle-class children with comparable IQs and scholastic records. Middle-class white children with IQs in the EMR range generally appeared more retarded than the minority children who were in special classes. Using nonverbal rather than verbal tests did not appreciably alter the problem. I confirmed my student's observations for myself by observing EMR children in their classes and on the playground and by discussing their characteristics with a number of teachers and school psychologists. My student's observations proved reliable. EMR children who were called 'culturally disadvantaged', as contrasted with middle-class EMR children, appeared much brighter socially and on the playgound, often being quite indistinguishable in every way from children of normal IQ except in their scholastic performance and in their scores on a variety of standard IQ tests. Middle-class white children diagnosed as EMR, on the other hand, though they consituted a much smaller percentage of the EMR classes, usually appeared to be more mentally retarded all round and not just in their performance in scholastic subjects and IQ tests. I asked myself, how could one devise a testing procedure that would reveal this distinction so that it could be brought under closer study and not depend upon casual observations and impressions.

It appeared to me that most of the item content of traditional IQ tests called for information and skills that the testee was expected to have had the opportunity to acquire before taking the test. In short, most IQ tests assessed what the subject had learned outside the testing situation. If it could be assumed that all subjects had had roughly equal opportunities for learning prior to being tested, their scores could well be an accurate reflection of their learning ability. But in cases where this assumption could not be made, as in the case of children with a quite different cultural background, it struck me that perhaps the best way to assess a child's learning ability (which at that time I more or less equated with intelligence) was not to test what the child had learned at some time prior to the test situation but to measure his rate of learning something new, right in the testing situation itself. This I called a 'direct learning test'. I devised several such tests, using the simplest possible materials. What we found in our first studies was that EMR children who were 'culturally disadvantaged', meaning they were from low socioeconomic status (SES) homes, performed much better on our direct learning tests relative to middle-SES EMR children of the same low IQ. In short, direct learning tests reflected important behavioral and cognitive differences between low-SES and middle-SES EMR children which were not at all reflected in scores on the usual IQ tests or in scholastic achievement. In fact, on the learning tests many of the EMR children performed as well as children of average IQ and some even performed as well as children at the so-called 'gifted' level of IQ (i.e., IQs above 130 or 140).

What did it mean? At first I thought perhaps I had found the first culture-fair test that actually worked, for we found in testing representative samples of disadvantaged children, who generally score 10 to 20 points lower than middle-class white children on standard IQ tests, that there was practically no difference between the score distributions of low-SES and middle-SES children, or between racial minority and majority children, on the direct learning tests. My subsequent research along this line has led me to the theoretical interpretation of the phenomenon which I have spelled out in the present volume in 'A Theory of Primary and Secondary Familial Retardation' and its *Addendum.*

This work naturally led me to an interest in children's learning and cognitive processes in general, and more and more my laboratory experiments involved children rather than college students. This led me also to large-scale testing in the schools when some of our laboratory learning tests were adapted to group testing in the classroom. At the same time I inevitably became deeply immersed in the rapidly growing educational literature of the 1960s on the psychology of the culturally disadvantaged – at that time a new term for the children of the poor, especially racial minorities such as Negroes, Mexican-American, Puerto Ricans, and American Indians, as well as poor whites. Much of this literature was still in the form of unpublished research reports on projects supported by the federal funds that had been poured into attempts to understand and ameliorate the educational plight of the nation's poor. So much material was accumulating so rapidly (I soon had two filing cases full) that I felt a need to scan all these reports, winnow them to find the most substantial and methodologically sound studies, classify them, and digest and organize the results into a reasonably coherent body of knowledge which could be summarized in a book, along with my own research contributions in this area. My decision to begin this project coincided ideally with my being invited to spend a year as a Fellow at The Center for Advanced Study in the Behavioral Sciences at Stanford. This freed me for one year from teaching and the other academic chores of a professor, so that I could devote my full time to working on my projected book on the psychology of the culturally disadvantaged.

What struck me as most peculiar as I worked my way through the vast bulk of literature on the disadvantaged was the almost complete lack of any mention of the possible role of genetic factors in individual differences in intelligence and scholastic performance. In the few instances where genetics was mentioned, it was usually to dismiss the issue as outmoded, irrelevant, or unimportant, or to denigrate the genetic study of human differences and proclaim the all-importance of the social and cultural environment as the only source of individual and group differences in the mental abilities relevant to scholastic performance. So strongly expressed was this bias in some cases, and so inadequately buttressed by any evidence, that I began to surmise that the topic of genetics was ignored more because of the particular author's social philosophy than because the importance of genetic factors in human differences had been scientifically disproved. It seemed obvious to me that a book dealing with the culturally disadvantaged would have to include a chapter that honestly attempts to come to grips scientifically with the influence of genetic factors on differences in mental abilities.

At that time I was largely but not utterly ignorant of the research on the genetics of mental abilities. I would have been even more ignorant had I not gone to England as a postdoctoral research fellow some years earlier, for American psychology textbooks and the courses during the years of my education were, almost without exception, lacking any adequate account of findings in this field of research. But fortunately, while in London, I had had the privilege of attending the Walter Van Dyke Bingham Memorial Lecture, sponsored by the American Psychological Association, and delivered that year (May 21, 1957) by Professor Sir Cyril Burt, whose topic was 'The Inheritance of Mental Ability'. I did not go to the lecture out of any special interest in the topic but simply because Sir Cyril Burt, who was then in his seventies, was one of England's most famous psychologists, and I merely wanted to see him in person. His lecture was impressive indeed; it was probably the best lecture I ever heard, and I recommend it to all students of psychology and education. (It was published in the *American Psychologist*, 1958, **13**, 1-15). But at the time, the message of Burt's lecture met no immediate need in my thinking or research and was merely stored away in my memory for future reference.

So in preparation for writing the one chapter of my book on the culturally disadvantaged that was to deal forthrightly with the genetics of intelligence, rather than ignore the subject or dismiss it cavalierly as so many writings in this field had done, I began by reading Burt's masterful Bingham Lecture, which led me to all his other excellent articles in this area, and soon I found myself engrossed in reviewing the total world literature on the genetics of human abilities. One could not go far into this topic without getting into those branches of genetics called population genetics and quantitative genetics, and so I began to study these subjects in their own right. They were not entirely foreign territory to me, since they are based largely on statistical concepts, mainly the analysis of variance, of which I already had a good grasp. In the course of this study I wrote several articles about genetic research on intelligence and its relevance to the problems of individual differences in education.

My first public statement concerning the role of genetic factors in educational differences was made in an invited address, 'Social Class, Race, and Genetics: Implications for Education', at the annual convention of the American Educational Research Association (February 17, 1967). (This was published in the *American Educational Research Journal*, 1968, **5**, 1-42.) At that time I pointed out that present educational practices have been unsuccessful in providing a large segment of our population with the knowledge and skills needed for economic self-sufficiency in our increasingly technological society. Literal equality of education falls short of solving this problem. I said, 'If we fail to take account either of innate or acquired differences in abilities and traits, the ideal of equality of educational opportunity can too easily be interpreted so literally as to be actually harmful, just as it would be harmful for a physician to give all his patients the same medicine. One child's opportunity can be another's defeat' (p. 3). I voiced the opinion that failure to give due weight to the biological basis of individual and group differences in educationally relevant traits and abilities, as well as to social-environmental factors, may hinder efforts to discover optimal instructional procedures suited to a wide range and diversity of abilities. Inappropriate instructional procedures, often based on the notion that all children learn in essentially the same way except for easily changed environmental influences, can alienate many children from ever entering upon *any* path of educational fulfillment. My concerns in this area were strongly reinforced by the then recently published and now famous

Coleman report on *Equality of Educational Opportunity* (U.S. Department of Health, Education, and Welfare, 1966, 737 pp.). This landmark study in the history of American education, based on the testing of more than 645,000 pupils in 4000 of the nation's schools, presents massive evidence that discrepancies in educational achievement by different social class and racial groups are correlated to only a slight degree with inequalities in those variables over which schools traditionally have control. The data made it abundantly clear that biological and social environmental factors associated with social class, race, and family background accounted for most of the variance in intellectual ability and scholastic performance.

At the annual meeting of the AERA the following year (1968) I took part in a symposium on intelligence testing in which I presented my findings on the triple interaction among social class, intelligence, and rote learning ability (which I now call the Level I-Level II Theory).

I mention these two AERA addresses because they are what led to my being asked to write the article for the *Harvard Educational Review*. A member of the *HER* Editorial Board wrote me early in 1968 asking if *HER* could publish the paper I gave at the AERA symposium on intelligence testing. I sent them the paper, but since what I had to say in that paper was of quite limited scope, I decided to revamp it into a slightly larger paper that would put it into a broader context of problems concerning intelligence and education, the main outline for which I had already prepared as the basis of another invited address at an educational conference held that year in California. This larger paper (about 30 typed pages) I entitled 'How Much Can We Boost IQ and Scholastic Achievement?' I sent this, as well as the requested symposium paper, to *HER*. About a month later I received a three-page letter (dated April 26, 1968) from the co-chairman of the *HER* Editorial Board saying they wanted me to revise and expand the 'How Much Can We Boost IQ . . .' article. The letter stated: 'Your article would serve as a lead piece in a discussion which we are planning on the concept of intelligence, in which psychologists with diverse perspectives on the nature of intelligence would be asked to comment on your ideas.' And the letter listed half a dozen noted psychologists (and a geneticist) who would be asked to contribute commentaries on my article. Their stated aim was to invite an 'environmentalist', a 'cognitive psychologist hostile to the construct of intelligence', the 'Piagetian concept of intelligence', and a 'geneticist or psychologist with a strong genetic background'. The letter went further, to spell out an outline of the paper the editorial board hoped I would write. I think it worth reproducing this outline verbatim, since there were later public denials by *HER's* Editorial Board that all of these topics (particularly A.1.*b*) were a part of *HER's* solicitation of my article:

The Board has agreed to publish a revised manuscript which would take the following general form:
A. The question posed in the title of the article can be answered adequately only by looking at the notion of 'intelligence' and evaluating some of the major controversies that have surrounded it.
   1. Arguments against the extreme environmentalist position. This would include material from 'How Much . . .' and 'Social Class, Race and Genetics'. This section would include:
      *a*. A clear definition of 'genetic' and 'non-genetic' factors and of the notion of 'heritability.'
      *b*. A clear statement of your position on social class and racial differences in intelligence.
   2. Environment as a threshold variable.
   3. The two-factor theory of intelligence, including a clear explication of the hypothesized relation between the two factors and the differential distribution of learning in different social class groups.
B. Given this framework, what are the prospects for boosting IQ and what are the potential benefits and drawbacks?
   1. Why bother to do it at all?
   2. What are the most efficient ways of doing it?
      *a*. Genetic methods.
      *b*. Pre-, peri-, and postnatal intervention.
      *c*. Educational intervention: a misdirection, according to Jensen. (Comment here specifically on Bereiter's work.)
C. What then would educators focus on?
   1. Improvement of achievement.
   2. Development of children with high learning abilities but low IQ.
   3. Maximization of best abilities.
   4. Other ideas.

I thought this a quite good outline and I incorporated all of it into my revision. Because of previous writing commitments, I was not able to work on the *HER* article until the middle of the following September. I delivered the completed typescript to *HER* about the first week in November. The Board suggested a few changes, mostly deletions, totaling not more than about 15 pages, since the typescript was over 200 pages – the longest article ever published in the *HER*. Because of deadline problems, proofs were never sent to me. This resulted in a few minor obvious misprints which were corrected in all later printings of the article after the first.

The article appeared in the Winter 1969 issue of *HER*, published on February 28, 1969. The seven invited commentaries on my article (by Jerome S. Kagan, J. McV. Hunt, James F. Crow, Carl Bereiter, David Elkind, Lee J. Cronbach, and William F. Brazziel), along with my rejoinder to these commentaries, were published in the next issue of *HER* (Spring, 1969).[1]

The popular press in the United States picked up and broadcast their interpretations of my *HER* article with a speed and zeal that seems unprecedented in the publicity given to articles in academic journals. So swift was the press coverage that I was reading about the article in the newspaper at least two weeks before a copy of the journal had even reached me in California. I am often asked, how did all this publicity in the popular press come about? I can only tell what I know from my own experience of the events.

The very day of publication I received a long-distance telephone call from a reporter from the *Boston Globe*, who said he had received a pre-publication copy of my article from *HER* and had written a news story about it. He had wanted to check out some of his interpretations with me. I then phoned the editorial office of *HER* to ask if other news media had received copies and was informed that a press release had been sent to a number of popular magazines, in some cases with copies of the entire article.

[1] All of this has been made available by the *HER* (13 Appian Way, Cambridge, Mass. 02138) in three paperbound reprints. The first entitled *Environment, Heredity and Intelligence* ($3.75), includes the original paper, seven solicited discussions thereof, and a reply by Jensen. The second, titled *Science, Heritability and IQ* ($2.50), contains five more discussion articles. The third consists of 19 letters to the editor identified as pages 581-631 from Volume 39 (3) with the title, *Correspondence: Political, Technical, and Theoretical Comments* ($ 1.15).

Also, the solicited commentaries by the seven critics in the Spring issue were sent to the press. I had not seen any of these yet myself, and did not receive copies for at least another month, although I saw 'previews' of them in the popular press. By an odd coincidence, the same afternoon that I had spoken with the *HER* editorial office, I was visited in my office by a staff writer from the *U.S. News & World Report*, a widely read news magazine. He knew nothing of the *HER* article, but was on the Berkeley campus to interview various members of the University faculty concerning a story he was preparing on 'campus unrest', for which Berkeley became especially noted following the famous 'free speech movement' and campus riots of 1965. In the course of the interview, I told my visitor about the *HER* article and the fact that *HER's* editors had already released it to the press. He was interested and so I gave him a Xerox copy of my typescript. Within two or three days he visited *HER's* editorial office, interviewed members of the Editorial Board, and obtained copies of my critics' replies. Two weeks later, on March 10, *U.S. News & World Report* published his feature article about my *HER* article; it was the first of the feature articles to appear in a national magazine. (A follow-up article appeared in *U.S. News* on June 2, 1969.) It was much more accurate and comprehensive than any newspaper items that had previously appeared, and with the exception of the *New York Times*, the *U.S. News* was the only newspaper or magazine which checked their paraphrases of the main points of my article with me by phone prior to publication. Many other magazines and newspapers assured me in interviews that they would do this, but they never did, with consequent inaccuracies and misunderstandings. Several nationally syndicated newspaper columnists took up the debate and several other popular magazines ran stories on it. Easily the most thorough, thoughtful, and well-balanced story appeared in the *New York Times Magazine* (August 31, 1969). The *N.Y. Times* commissioned Lee Edson, one of the top popular science writers in the country, to write the article. He came to his first interview with me remarkably well prepared; not only had he carefully read and annotated my article but he had already collected story material at the *HER* editorial office in Cambridge and had interviewed a number of psychologists and geneticists for their opinions of my work. He spent several days in Berkeley; he had many hours discussion with me and with numerous other Berkeley professors who were known to have opinions on my work or on the issues in general. Edson had the popular science writer's gift of making technical problems simple and understandable to the intelligent layman without violating accuracy. His article, it seemed to me, was eminently fair and of meticulous accuracy in summarizing the whole debate up to that time.

I later learned from an editor of the *New York Times Magazine* that Edson's article brought more letters-to-the-editor than any other article they had ever published. A number of these were published in the two or three weeks that followed the Edson article. The editors' selection of letters for publication seemed to emphasize the more dissident ones, perhaps because they expressed views more typical of the majority of the letters received. As a sample of the full spectrum of opinions expressed, it may be worth quoting from some of the published and unpublished letters (which were turned over to Mr Edson and some of which were sent to me).

Most of the published letters were emotional protests rather than factual counter-arguments. But they indicated some of the sincerely and nobly motivated blocks and obstacles to rational consideration of the issues raised in the *HER* article, especially the sensitive question of racial genetic differences in mental abilities. One letter to the editor (September 21) states in part:

> The myth of white superiority has been around for a long time. It has since been quoted as justification for segregation, discrimination and for all manner of second-class treatment of blacks in the economic, social, and educational spheres. However much I may cry out for recognition as an individual black American, my initial identity is as a member of the group. If the group is to be labeled intellectually inferior, I, as a member of that group, am also inevitably and automatically labeled.

Another writer says:

> Those who would silence Jensen are challenging one of our most strongly held beliefs, i.e., that all knowledge is good. His opponents are emotional, confused, and irrational, but I think their position is fundamentally wise. Suppose Jensen continues his studies and is able to prove beyond question that there is substantial racial differences in ability to reason abstractly? What then? How will that knowledge be used? Is there any doubt that Americans will simply use proof of such

racial differences to justify oppression at home and abroad? . . . The wise scientist will not devote himself to research on the relation between races and ability; the wise university will not honor those who do, or disseminate their work.

A common response is to question intelligence tests, as did the correspondent who wrote:

It is possible that there is such a thing as inherited intelligence, but no testing conceived by man is valid in ascertaining this.

Some of the criticisms which appear to deal with technical arguments actually amount to misinterpretations of the data of well-known studies. One of the most commonly misinterpreted set of findings is the famous study by Skodak and Skeels (1949). Referring to this study as a refutation of the high heritability of intelligence, two assistant professors of psychology wrote:

Jensen also cites studies of children adopted in infancy, in which the children's IQ scores later correlate with the intelligence or education of their natural mothers, but do not correlate at all with the intelligence or education of their adopted parents. Thus, for example, adopted children whose natural mothers had relatively low IQ scores in comparison to the other mothers tended to have relatively low IQ scores in comparison to the other children. However, Jensen fails to mention the crucial fact that the IQ scores of the adopted children in these same studies averaged 20 to 30 points higher than those of their true mothers. Whereas, in general, the natural mothers came from the lowest strata of society, the adopted parents were from a higher socioeconomic status. This finding indicates that while heredity may play a role in individual differences in intelligence – reflected in the IQ correlation between adopted children and their natural mothers – environment can affect IQ scores by an average of 20 to 30 points. This is about the average differences in IQ obtained between children from low and high socioeconomic families.

However, the data referred to by these writers simply do not lead to this conclusion. Indeed the results are quite consistent with a heritability of 0·80 for intelligence (i.e., 80 percent of the population variance in intelligence is attributable to genetic factors). Let us take a closer look at these data in the study by Skodak and Skeels. This well-known study by Skodak and Skeels (1949) is often held up as an example of evidence which supposedly contradicts the high heritability of intelligence. The fact that the adopted children in the Skodak and Skeels study turned out to have considerably higher IQs than their biological mothers is thought to constitute a disproof of the conclusion from many heritability studies that genetic factors are more important than environmental factors (in the ratio of about 2 to 1) in the causation of individual differences in IQ. (Another way of saying this is that the heritability of intelligence is about 0·80, i.e., about 80 percent of the IQ variance is attributable to genetic factors. The 20 percent of the variance due to environmental differences can be thought of as a normal distribution of all the effects of environment on IQ, including prenatal and postnatal influences. This normal distribution of environmental effects has a standard deviation of about 7 IQ points since the total variance of IQ in the population is $15^2 = 225$ and the 20 percent of this which is attributable to environment is $0·20 (225) = 45$, the square root of which gives $SD = 6·71$.) Is there anything in the Skodak and Skeels data that would contradict this conclusion? Skodak and Skeels based their study on 100 children born to mothers with rather low IQs (a range from 53 to 128, with a mean of 85·7, $SD$ of 15·8). The children were adopted into what Skodak and Skeels described as exceptionally good, upper middle-class families selected by the adoption agency for their superior qualities. Of the 100 true mothers, 63 were given the 1916 form of the Stanford-Binet IQ test at the time of the adoption. Their children, who had been reared in adoptive homes, were given the same test as adolescents. The correlation between the mothers' and children's IQs was 0·38. Now, the *difference* between the mothers' IQs and the children's IQs is not really the relevant question. Yet it is on this point that the interpretation of this study has so often gone wrong. What we really want to know is, how much do the children differ from the IQs we'd predict from a genetic model? Using the simplest model, which assumes that the children represent a random selection of the offspring of mothers having a mean IQ of 85·7 and are reared in a random sample of homes in the general population, the children's average predicted IQ would be 96. In fact, however, their average IQ turns out to be 107, or 11 points higher than the predicted IQ. If 20 percent of the IQ variance is environmental, and if one standard deviation of environmental influence is equivalent to about 7 IQ points, then it might be said that the Skodak and Skeels children were reared in environments which averaged 11/7ths or about 1·6 standard deviations above the average environment of randomly selected families in the population. This would be about what one should expect if the adoption agency placed children only in homes they judged to be about one standard deviation above the average of the general population in the desirability of the environment they could provide. From what Skodak and Skeels say in their description of the adoptive families, they were at least one standard deviation above the general average in socioeconomic status and were probably even higher in other qualities deemed desirable in adoptive parents. So an 11-point IQ gain over the average environment falls well within what we should expect, even if environmental factors contribute only 20 percent of the IQ variance. But this 11 points of apparent gain is more likely to be an over-estimate to some extent, since these children, it should be remembered, were selected by the agency as suitable for adoption. They were not a random selection of children born to low IQ mothers. Many such children are never put out for adoption. (Most of the children were illegitimate, and as indicated in Leahy's (1935) study, illegitimate children who become adopted have a higher average IQ than illegitimate children in general or than legitimate children placed for adoption.) Even so, it is interesting that Skodak and Skeels found that the 11 adopted children whose true mothers had IQs below 70 averaged 25 points lower than the 8 adopted children whose true mothers had IQs above 105. There are also certain technical, methodological deficiencies of the Skodak and Skeels study which make its results rather questionable; these deficiencies were trenchantly pointed out many years ago in critiques by Terman (1940, pp. 462-467) and McNemar (1940). In summary, the Skodak and Skeels study, such as it is, can be seen to be not at all inconsistent with a heritability of 0·80 for intelligence.

Of the 15 letters published in the *New York Times Magazine* (September 18, 1961, p. 38), only one (by Harvard psychology professor S. S. Stevens) was not condemnatory:

It was good to read Lee Edson's first-rate story on 'jensenism, *n*. The theory that IQ is largely determined by the genes', August 31. Of course, to someone with a 40-year-long interest in IQ testing, the theory that the IQ derives mainly from the genes is generations old. I absorbed the theory in evening seminars at the home of L. M. Terman, the father of the Stanford-Binet test. Despite its age, the theory needs an eponym to serve as a handle in the rising debate, and the name of Arthur Jensen offers high credentials for the honor. With the care and integrity expected of a scientist, he has reviewed the recorded evidence and has undertaken studies of his own to unravel further the nature of the learning process in children of both high and low endowment. Unmindful of the hot blast of political credo, he has told the story clearly and calmly, and as it is.

The environmentalists have had the microphone in recent years and they have talked up an American brand of Lysenkoism, which holds that brain power can be taught. That notion draws much of its powerful appeal from the hope we all feel that somehow we can shake the world and make it better, right now. Practically everybody is trying to improve somebody. There is nothing particularly wrong with preaching and teaching; there is only the scientific question concerning what can and what cannot be altered. Stature, for example, responds very little to stretching; dexterity responds fairly well to training; and the language spoken, say, French or English, depends wholly on the environment.

But there is that stubborn IQ. Williams Stern's concept of the 'mental quotient', what Terman renamed the intelligence quotient, is the ratio of mental age to chronological age. That concept of the IQ has, I believe, proved itself the most important quantitative concept contributed thus far by psychology. As with many prime concepts in science, the importance stems directly from invariance. The IQ, competently measured, remains essentially constant over the child's growing years. If the IQ rose and fell, or wavered like the moods of joy and sadness, it would long since have lost its interest; and the psychometricians would have turned to other pursuits. Indeed, if the IQ should lose its constancy, the steam of frustration behind the move to abolish IQ testing would quickly blow itself out. On the other hand, if someone wants to find himself acclaimed as a benefactor of mankind, let him devise a sure and workable method of boosting the IQ. A quicker method, of course, than the long slow process of selective mating – the breeding process by which men have performed near miracles in the improvement of qualities in plants and animals.

In the meantime, it seems clear that we gain nothing by turning our backs on the process of biological inheritance which sets the design for our size and appearance, and for much of our behavior. Nature bends not a whit to our wishing. It is better to probe her secrets in open discussion than to try to shout her down, as some would shout down jensenism.

Some of the most interesting comments and observations, not even hinted at in any of the published letters, are found among those that were never published. A professor of computer sciences wrote:

> I am saddened by the fact that so many of my colleagues who bravely spoke up during the height of the McCarthy madness have chosen during the interim to identify with the aggressor. It would be an unfortunate assessment of the current academic scene if their objections a decade ago were not to the techniques involved, but only represented a defense of that which was being attacked.

A psychology professor wrote:

> It appears that another form of 'generation gap' has occurred within behavioral science. The massive tides in the climate of opinion that arose in slow but swelling reaction against the scientific resolutions in favor of the heritability of intelligence during the 1930s has swept aside these essentially sound conclusions, without the data *per se* having been reliably refuted. And a whole new generation of young behavioral scientists have been trained in void of history and in the light of illimitable but unjustifiable environmentalistic presuppositions as to potential effects of intervention in the human career. If Professor Jensen cannot be said to have set the record absolutely straight – for this is too much for single scientific acts – he has at least put the history of the problem back on course. In spite of the fact that at this time in the affairs of man his report is hard to accept, one's confidence in the rectification of immediate science by the more inexorable forces of history will stand in favor of his ultimate vindication. Meanwhile, this reviewer's judgment is that Jensen serves more honestly and with greater powers of observation and analysis, the social causes involved in his study than do many of his critics who simply decry the findings without refutation, and who thereby maintain dangerously the illusions which Jensen constructively attempts to dispel.

Another professor of psychology:

> Reporter Lee Edson deserves congratulations for treating Jensen's scholarly article as serious social *science*, rather than as the political document that other journalists and even many social scientists have misconstrued it to be. Whether or not one agrees with Jensen's

conclusions *after* studying the 123-page paper carefully, clearly Jensen is a master of his empirical and theoretical materials as few or no environmentalists are of theirs. Most of the critiques I have seen lean heavily on misinterpretations of Jensen's position and on presentation of possible but implausible alternative hypotheses.

A professor of biology:

In the last several months I have been quietly bringing Jensen's article to the attention of selected colleagues who have the statistical and biological background needed to evaluate it. I have encountered two responses. Some said that even if it were true they did not believe the subject should be scientifically investigated at this time. On the other hand, without exception those who said they had read Jensen's paper with care have thanked me for telling them about it. In some cases their response was one of emotional shock at facts hitherto unknown to them. To my mind, one of the most significant features of Jensen's article is the way it dichotomizes technically competent scientists into 'let's look' and 'let's hide' groups.

A professor of philosophy:

The attack on Jensen is one more sign, among many others that make some of us more and more uneasy, that on some issues we must as a group speak with one voice, no dissent or ambiguity permitted. It is increasingly heretical to dissent in any way not only from the proposition that all human groups are the same in every important respect, that our society is sick, that middle-class values are injurious not only to the society as a whole but to members of the middle class, and a growing list of other similarly dubious or badly supported propositions. . . . It is not merely that we must all be 'relevant', but we must be *correctly* relevant, on the right side of relevant issues. Jensen has committed the new sin of being, not irrelevant, but counter-relevant. He is academically with the significant in-thing, all right, but he is saying unforgivable things about it. It is my guess that the attacks by younger faculty on the scholarly associations, which have been so far mainly concerned with forcing them to take positions on 'relevant' issues, will soon shift to an insistence that the 'correct' positions be taken on those issues. I have a sad feeling that Jensen is a premature martyr in the long struggle to come within the universities.

In most accounts in the popular press most of the main points of my article were never mentioned, being completely displaced by the racial issue, which was often a grotesque parody of what I had actually written on this topic. The press usually preferred to cast the *HER* debate as the 'good guys' versus the 'bad guy'. This kind of writing, with all its stir and slur, aroused some persons who would not be expected to go to the original source to see what I had actually said, to write hateful letters or make threatening phone calls, sometimes in the middle of the night. These reactions could only be expected in view of some of the provocation in the popular press, which, though it may have sincerely expressed the emotional state of the writer, was highly misinformative both as to the letter and the spirit of my article. One nationally syndicated newspaper columnist, for example, wrote:

> What an affront this has been to millions of black people, just now manifesting a nationalistic pride, to feel they are being told, 'Forget it; some of your few highly intelligent members will make it, but on the whole the black man will remain second-class equipment!' Some of the more outraged souls, black and white, would like to settle the whole thing by proving that they have IQ enough to tie a noose that will fit Jensen's neck.

The generation of hate, rather than information, by the use of emotionally charged words and phraseology and the building of an impression of combative conflict among 'experts' are the chief ingredients of the kind of reporting on which a large segment of the press thrives, and when it is not applied sufficiently in a reporter's account, apparently it is injected at some higher editorial level. A magazine science writer wrote me apologetically about an article he was assigned to write about the '*HER* controversy', saying 'the printed version differs in numerous ways from the original one which I wrote. We always seem to come out on the short end in the perennial struggle with the editors.'

For several weeks, *The Daily Californian*, the student newspaper on the Berkeley campus, ran a number of articles and scores of letters-to-the-editor about the controversy. Six distinguished professors in the social sciences signed a letter claiming I was 'extremely naïve about the nature of cultural differences in test performances', and that 'we disagree strongly with many inferences he has made from his studies', etc. It turned out that none of the signers had even read the *HER* article and apparently were reacting only to the accounts in the popular press. A professor of philosophy at Berkeley whose interesting analysis of the reactions on the Berkeley campus was published in the *Review of Educational Research* (Scriven, 1970), described the attempts in leading articles in the student paper to summarize the debate as all 'totally incompetent by the standards of a good freshman Psychology 1 student'. A few of the headlines convey the tone of the commentaries:

Education Caucus Supports SDS in Jensen Firing
Teachers State Jensen's Theories Are 'Frightening, Damaging'
Suppression of Jensen Not the Answer
Inquisitional Tactics and the Jensen Case
Extremely Dangerous Attack on Arthur Jensen
   Should Be Called Off
On Exposing All Racists
For Firing Jensen, Having Read His Article

Some letters demanded I be fired from my professorship; others urged students to boycott my classes; still others defended my academic rights. The whole affair in the student paper was finally summarized in a commentary by a professor of English at Berkeley (R. W. Rader, *The Daily Californian*, May 6, 1969).

Robert Olton's crushing letter in Friday's *Daily Californian* provides a pleasingly perfect denouement to the little morality play in which Professor Arthur Jensen, the putative villain, is revealed as the triumphant hero, his destiny reversed, his enemies put to shame. But what a crude little drama! Not even Al Capp or Harold Gray would have dared put forth anything quite so crude; would have dared make the central figure so patly the hero by precisely those values used to judge him a villain; would have dared make the antagonists so blindly stupid, so rashly and improbably neglectful of their manifest duty to inform themselves before accusing; would have dared include on the fringes of the mob high-minded scholars from a great university fatuously trumpeting their ignorant righteousness.

Of course it was really a comedy from the beginning – no one ever feared that Jensen would be thrown to the wolves, however much he might have had to suffer their howls. But the story is comic not because of the intention to harm was not serious but only because the defenses are for the moment reasonably strong. When the defenses were down during the French Revolution, it was people very like the SDS – friends of liberty, equality, fraternity; enemies of the rotton establishment – who guillotined Lavoisier ('La République n'a pas besoin de savants') and forced Lafayette to flee for his life because they did not realize that these men were better friends of freedom than they.

Our little play is too full of poetic justice to make the true point clearly. The point is, of course, that Jensen did not need to be so resplendently right to be justified and that his attackers are not so simply reprehensible as they seem. The attackers were moved by humane ideals to what they conceived to be moral action. They forgot that morality without knowledge based on critical inquiry is not a virtue but a vice. 'Be not righteous overmuch' was a saying popular in the eighteenth century, the century of reason; and it remains the perpetually valuable counsel of reason. (Not the villainous but the righteous, Mill points out, put Socrates and Christ to death.) Because we need the counsel of reason and because we cannot know what it is until it has stood the test of free debate from all quarters (and even then not certainly), we do not persecute for opinion even those who appear as harmfully wrong as Professor Jensen was made to seem; more plainly – to repeat the truth which will always need repeating – we do not persecute for opinion at all.

Meanwhile, the editorial office of the *HER* was having unusual troubles. They were under attack from various individuals and organizations on the Harvard campus, such as the Black Students Union, for having solicited and published my article. The intimidated Editorial Board quickly took steps to make amends and appease their angry critics. The ensuing events are unprecedented in the history of scholarly publication in America and warrant a detailed account. It should be noted that the *HER* is managed entirely by graduate students under the sponsorship of the Graduate School of Education at Harvard. A new Editorial Board, made up of graduate students usually in Education and the Social Sciences, is elected each year. Over the many years of its existence, they have published, on the whole, one of the distinguished and influential journals on the American educational scene. Unfortunately, however, under the pressures of reactions stemming from my article, the Board's academic wisdom and adherence to traditional principles of scholarly publication were pathetically wanting.

The first came to my attention when I was sent a copy of the *Harvard Crimson*, the student newspaper, which carried articles and editorials condemning my article and in which a 'position statement' put out by *HER*'s Editorial Board was quoted as follows:

> The editors of the *Review* said in a written statement yesterday that they had solicited the Jensen article, but had not requested that it treat the racial problem. 'We committed ourselves to publish an article dealing generally with the topics in an outline we enclosed with our letter of commitment', the statement read. 'The outline made no mention of an analysis of racial differences in intelligence.' The editors refused to comment on why they decided to publish the [Jensen] article, saying that opinions on the issue were so disparate that they could not reach agreement on a joint statement. (*Harvard Crimson*, February 28, 1969.)

I set the record straight on this point simply by sending a copy of *HER's* solicitation letter, including the outline, to the editor of the *Crimson*. My letter was published in the *Crimson* two months later (April 29, 1969), and shortly I received an apology for the misstatement from one of the editors. In the meantime, however, the Board's misstatement was sent out in mimeographed form to apparently anyone who directed inquiries to the *HER* office. A number of my own colleagues received copies of this mimeographed position statement, which also blamed me for releasing my article to the press. But I myself was never able to obtain a copy directly, either by written request or by a telephoned request to one of the editors. It was most interesting, therefore, to see how very frequently some person in the audiences before which I appeared as a lecturer would stand up at the end waving the mimeographed disclaimer put out by *HER*. More interesting is the fact that some persons went on quoting *HER*'s disclaimer even after I had sent them copies of the solicitation outline and the editor's letter of apology for the false statement. Falsehoods apparently cannot be refuted even by conclusive factual evidence among those who have an overwhelming emotional need to believe them.

*HER* retreated further in the face of criticism by suddenly halting the sale of the Winter issue containing my article. It became virtually impossible to purchase a copy of this issue, not because the supply was exhausted but because the *HER* editors thought no one should be allowed to read it without also having to buy the rebuttals that were to follow in the Spring issue – the antidote to my article, as it were. The University bookstore on the Berkeley campus was refused their order for copies to be used in graduate seminar. (This refusal was later reversed.) A Nobel Laureate who wanted to buy copies to send to members of the Psychology, Anthropology, Sociology, and Genetics sections of the National Academy of Sciences (whose 700-odd members are regarded as the nation's scientific elite) was refused copies. The co-chairman of the Editorial Board wrote to this eminent scientist as follows: 'I can only convey to you the strong wish of the entire Editorial Board that the [Jensen] article be considered as *part* of a conversation (with other voices heard from), not the whole of it, and that you rethink any decision either to select passages out of context or to use the article alone' (March 27, 1969). All orders for the highly publicized Winter issue of *HER* were answered by a form letter which stated:

> The Jensen article, 'How Much Can We Boost IQ and Scholastic Achievement?', presents a view of intelligence that we feel must be read in the context of expert discussion from other psychologists and geneticists. The Spring issue will contain eight lengthy discussions of the Jensen article by . . . Since we feel that it is imperative that our readers be given access to the entire debate, we are offering the following options . . .

(All of these options required the purchasing of the rebuttals in the Spring issue.)

I protested this policy in phone calls to the editors only to find that things had gone even a bit further: they had decided not to sell me reprints of my own article (this was a complete reversal of previous policy) and there was a question of whether my rejoinder to the critiques in the Spring issue would be published, either in the same issue or the Summer issue. In other words, *HER* subscribers would get the rebuttals to my article, but not my rejoinder. A letter from the co-chairman of the Board followed, saying, 'I shall write you on April 8th after the Board has reached a decision whether or not to publish your reply in one of our issues'. At this point, the Associate Dean of the School of Education at Berkeley called the Dean of the Graduate School of Education at

Harvard to see if this unbelievable story could be true. Whether this call had any influence, I do not know, but I soon received word that the *HER* Board decided in favor of including my rejoinder in their Summer issue. But they still refused to sell me reprints, despite the fact that they had already sent me a routine order blank for the purchase of reprints. Checking with authors of articles in the *HER*, I learned that they had filled out the same form and were sent all the reprints they had ordered. It was clear that I had been singled out for special treatment. The letter from *HER* informing me of the denial of my reprint order said: 'We want to present both sides of the issues and feel it is imperative that the article and responses be distributed together.'

Fortunately, I was not the only one who protested against this highly irregular and suppressive policy. Others protested more effectively. Eight of the faculty of the Department of Educational Psychology at a large Eastern university signed a letter of protest to the *HER* Board and sent copies to the Dean of the Harvard Graduate School of Education, the President of Harvard, and the President and Executive Officers of the American Educational Research Association. The letter also found its way to the Trustees of Harvard University. The letter stated in part:

> While it might be desirable to have access to the commentary and criticism of Jensen's article when discussing it, it is not in the best scientific or academic tradition to insist, as a matter of policy, that a scholarly product must be ringed-about by 'interpretations' before it is circulated further within the scholarly community. You are seriously questioning an individual's intellectual integrity when you state that he must read several articles before he is capable of evaluating a particular article for himself. Scholarly debate and evaluation is not dependent upon the availability of 'approved' facts and viewpoints. Scholarly activity, as I am sure you realize, is the *seeking* of truth as represented by the facts which one has available, and it is a continuing process. Surely, you must realize that approximately four months intervene between the publication of the Winter issue and the expected publication date of *Environment, Heredity and Intelligence*. It seems unlikely that the Spring issue of *HER* will be available before the end of the current semester.
>
> Your policy concerning the interim distribution of the article appears to be at best anti-intellectual and at worst a form of censorship. By so

limiting the distribution of the article you are making it difficult for people to read the article and to evaluate it for themselves. In addition, you are encouraging people to depend upon the popular press as their main source of information about the article. Intellectual and scholarly debate is not best served by making one dependent upon second-hand information. A position such as the one you have taken is entirely alien to anyone who is dedicated to academic freedom and to freedom of the press and is entirely inappropriate for a scholarly journal with the reputation of the *Review*. (April 8, 1969.)

This letter received an answer from *HER*, which stated,' . . . may I commend to you the thought of St Teresa, who cautioned against complaining of the ills we have, not knowing those we have been spared'. The next word I got from *HER*, on April 24, was a telegram saying, 'Letter of explanation concerning reprints is being sent today – it offers you reprints at less than cost – we are sorry for any misunderstanding.' Thus *HER* reverted to its original standard policy. I received reprints of my article, and on May 1, *HER* formally announced that single copies of the Winter issue and reprints of my article were available to anyone ordering them.

Although *HER*'s editors originally planned to have four or five discussants in the Spring issue, the number was upped to seven. For the most part these commentaries were reasonably thoughtful, scholarly attempts to deal with the issues by my paper. But in view of the defensive and conciliatory position the editors of *HER* found themselves in after these commentaries had been solicited, submitted, and now published, the several discussants' generally moderate tone and lack of any essential disagreement with the main points of my article did little at all to 'put down' my article and assuage the 'guilt' of the Editorial Board. Evidently they felt they had not made sufficient amends to their attackers on the Harvard campus and elsewhere. To do so, apparently they thought it necessary to exceed the limits of responsible scholarly criticism. And thus the main contents of their Summer issue was conceived. A number of papers were solicited to accomplish the put-down that the seven discussions in the Spring issue had failed to do – in fact, had not even aimed to do. It is interesting that at least two of the solicited papers, although delivered on schedule by their authors, were refused publication. Why? Because they were not interesting or relevant? No. It was because they did not take a sufficiently 'put down' stance toward my article and, even worse, had dared to take a critical stance toward my critics – the ultimate offense. Both solicited contributors are distinguished scholars in fields relevant to their commentaries: Professor Ellis B. Page, an educational psychologist at the University of Connecticut and Professor Michael Scriven, a philosopher at Berkeley. Professor Scriven's interesting discussion, solicited but then rejected by *HER*, was later published by another journal ('The Values of the Academy: Moral Issues for American Education and Educational Research Arising from the Jensen Case,' *Review of Educational Research*, 1970, **40,** 541-549). Professor Page's article also was accepted and scheduled for publication in still another journal, but just as it was going to press it was suddenly scratched at the request of an official of the journal's sponsoring professional organization who had got wind of it.

But the Summer 1969 issue of *HER* remains of psychological and sociohistorical, if not of scientific, interest. It contains some twenty articles and letters, most of them only masquerading as serious critiques of my article. Likening me to Hitler (p. 592), for example, was apparently not beneath the Editorial Board's standards for a scholarly journal, while Scriven's and Page's articles, on the other hand, apparently were considered unacceptable. One author whose 'critique' appeared in the Summer issue evidently had some misgivings about its overly hasty publication in *HER*, for he later stated in a personal letter that his contribution was written over a weekend and that 'it will be published in that form, due to the inefficiency of *HER*, who accepted this preliminary draft without arranging for criticism and revision. I would have taken out the *ad hominem* attacks, corrected a couple of mistakes, and generally cleaned it up.' But he was never sent the proofs. He concludes, 'So that's why the first draft was so mean. I'm sorry that it will probably be the published draft.' This, I believe, is a typical characterization of the tone and quality of most of the contents of the Summer issue.

Some of these articles contained factual, methodological, and theoretical errors and unsubstantiated accusations against my article, such as Deutsch's claim that 'Perhaps so large a number of errors [in Jensen's article] would not be remarkable were it not for the fact that Jensen's previous work has contained so few, and more malignant, all the errors referred to are in the same direction: maximizing differences between blacks and whites and maximizing the possibility that such differences are attributable to hereditary factors' (p. 254). Though Deutsch has been repeatedly requested to do so, he has not been able to back up this charge of a 'large number of errors' all slanted in one direction. (His attempt to do so, finally forced by demand of the Committee of Scientific and Professional Ethics and Conduct of the American Psychological Association, is by any standard a pathetic document.)

Immediately after publication of the Summer issue, I telephoned *HER* to say that some of the statements, such as Deutsch's, should not be left unchallenged, but an editor told me that they would not publish any rejoinder that I might write at that point. I was most concerned about replying to the one article most likely to be taken seriously – by Richard J. Light and Paul V. Smith, a statistician and a sociologist at Harvard, entitled 'Social Allocation Models of Intelligence: A Methodological Inquiry'. Because of its highly technical nature, being based on a computer simulation from a mathematical model, only the quantitatively most sophisticated readers would be able to detect its serious shortcomings. What Light and Smith attempted to do, in brief, was to demonstrate that even if the heritability of intelligence is 0·80 (the average value I found in my review of all the evidence), the mean White-Negro IQ differences of one standard deviation (i.e., 15 IQ points) could be accounted for entirely by environmental differences in terms of a 'social allocation model' in which the two populations have identical distributions of genotypes for intelligence. In the first place, I had never claimed that the high heritability of intelligence *within* either or both racial groups was sufficient to prove that mean differences *between* the groups was attributable, in whole or in part, to genetic factors. It is axiomatic in quantitative genetics that *within* group heritability cannot prove *between* group heritability. The relationship is one of probability or likelihood, that is, the higher the heritability of a trait *within* each of two groups, the greater is the likelihood that a mean difference *between* the groups has a genetic component and the smaller is the likelihood that the group difference is attributable solely to environmental variation. This likelihood function can be expressed in terms of the definite mathematical relationship that exists between *within* group and *between* group heritability.[1] Light's and Smith's critique, therefore, is quite beside the point. It attempts to prove a theoretical point which no one ever disputed, which in fact is axiomatic in quantitative genetics. But Light and Smith were misunderstood by many as proving that the mean White-Negro differences was entirely attributable to environmental factors. A Nobel prize-winner in physics, Professor William Shockley, who is highly adept at mathematical analysis, took the Light-Smith model at face value to see what kinds of predictions it would lead to other than the particular one it was expressly devised to yield. Shockley's analysis proved most interesting. He found, for example, that the Light-Smith model could explain *any* size mean difference (e.g., 100 IQ points) between two groups strictly in terms of environment, and could do so even if the difference was in fact largely genetic. Secondly, he found that when the model's parameters are set to make the white mean equal to 100 and the variance (i.e., the square of the standard deviation) equal to 225 (the actual population values), the variance for the Negro group generated by the model as applied by Light and Smith lies between 340 and 617. This is highly discrepant with the fact that most studies show IQs to have a smaller variance in Negro than in white samples. The model also yields a Negro sibling correlation as high as those generally found for identical twins reared together, implying much higher heritability of IQ in Negroes than in whites. Finally, the model predicts that if there is no Negro-White genetic difference in a given generation, there will be one in the *next* generation. The model itself thus refutes the very point it attempted to demonstrate. From his analysis of the Light-Smith

[1] A quantitative geneticist, J. C. De Fries, has formulated the relationship between heritability *between* group means ($h_B^2$) and heritability *within* groups ($h_w^2$), as follows:

$$h_B^2 \cong h_w^2 \frac{(1-t)r}{(1-r)t}$$

where: $h_B^2$  is the heritability *between* group means.
$\quad\quad\quad h_w^2$  is the average heritability *within* groups.
$\quad\quad\quad t$  is the intraclass correlation among *phenotypes* within groups (or the square of the point biserial correlation between the quantized racial dichotomy and the trait measurement).
$\quad\quad\quad r$  is the intraclass correlation among *genotypes* within groups, i.e., the within-group genetic correlation for the trait in question.

model, Shockley, noting its serious shortcomings amounting prac-tically to absurdities, concludes, 'Thus their attempt to construct an environmental explanation constitutes in fact a reductio-ad-absurdum basis for rejecting their premises.' Shockley tried to have his analysis of Light and Smith published by *HER*, but without success. This is most unusual in scholarly publication. If the Shockley paper had been merely an expression of opinion, that would be one thing. But a journal's refusal to publish a critique which points out essential logical infirmities and wide discrepancies from well-known facts in an article previously published in that journal, is most unusual. Fortunately, Shockley's critique (followed by a reply and a rejoinder), after prolonged and thorough review by a number of referees, was finally published by a journal of the American Educational Research Association (Shockley, W. 'Negro IQ Deficit: Failure of a "Malicious Coincidence" Model Warrants New Research Proposals', *Review of Educational Research*, 1971, **41**, 227-248; Light, R. J. and Smith, P. V. 'Statistical Issues in Social Allocation Models of Intelligence: A Review and a Response', *RER*, 1971, **41**, 351-367; Shockley, W. 'Models, Mathematics, and the Moral Obligation to Diagnose the Origin of Negro IQ Deficits', *RER*, 1971, **41**, 369-377).

One of the discussants in *HER*'s Spring 1969 issue accused me of 'girding' myself for a 'holy war against "environmentalists" ' (p. 338). But there is nothing at all war-like in my original *HER* article or in my rejoinder (*HER*, Summer 1969) to the discussants in the Spring issue, as any reader can see for himself. If there was anything at all war-like in the aftermath of the *HER* publications it was surely on the part of those 'environmentalists' who publicly resorted to unusual exertions in their opposition to me for my having questioned their dogma.

Social scientists – anthropologists, sociologists, and social psy-chologists – were the most conspicuous. The Society for the Psychological Study of Social Issues (SPSSI), a Division of the American Psychological Association, issued a press release, signed unanimously by the members of the Council for SPSSI, which attempted to discredit many of the main points in my article. The SPSSI statement was published in part in newpapers across the nation and fully in several professional journals, including the

Summer 1969 issue of *HER* and the *American Psychologist*, (November, 1969, pp.1039-1041), which also published my reply in the same issue. The SPSSI statement is so typical of opinions and criticisms voiced by a large segment of the social science community that it is worth quoting in full:

'As behavioral scientists, we believe that statements specifying the hereditary components of intelligence are unwarranted by the present state of scientific knowledge. As members of the Council of the Society for the Psychological Study of Social Issues, we believe that such statements may be seriously misinterpreted, particularly in their applications to social policy.

'The evidence of four decades of research on this problem can be readily summarized. There are marked differences in intelligence test scores when one compares a random sample of whites and Negroes. What is equally clear is that little definitive evidence exists that leads to the conclusion that such differences are innate. The evidence points overwhelmingly to the fact that when one compares Negroes and whites of comparable cultural and educational background, differences in intelligence test scores diminish markedly; the more comparable the less the difference. There is no direct evidence that supports the view that there is an innate difference between members of different racial groups.

'We believe that a more accurate understanding of the contribution of heredity to intelligence will be possible only when social conditions for all races are equal and when this situation has existed for several generations. We maintain that the racism and discrimination in our country impose an immeasurable burden upon the black person. Social inequalities deprive large numbers of black people of social, economic, and educational advantages available to a great majority of the white population. The existing social structures prevent black and white people even of the same social class from leading comparable lives. In light of these conditions, it is obvious that no scientific discussion of racial differences can exclude an examination of political, historic, economic, and psychological factors which are inextricably related to racial differences.

'One of our most serious objections to Jensen's article is to his vigorous assertion that compensatory education has apparently failed. The major failure in so-called compensatory education has been in the planning, size, and scope of the program. We maintain that a variety of programs planned to teach specific skills have been effective and that a few well-designed programs which teach problem-solving and thinking have also been successful. The results from these programs strongly suggest that continuous and carefully planned intervention procedures can have a substantially positive influence on the performance of disadvantaged children.

'We point out that a number of Jensen's key assumptions and conclusions are seriously questioned by many psychologists and geneticists.

'The question of the relative contributions of heredity and environment to human development and behavior has a long history of controversy within psychology. Recent research indicates that environmental factors play a role from the moment of the child's conception. The unborn child develops as a result of a complex little understood, interaction between hereditary and environmental factors; this interaction continues throughout life. To construct questions about complex behavior in terms of heredity *versus* environment is to oversimplify the essence and nature of human development and behavior.

'In an examination of Jensen's data, we find that observed racial differences in intelligence can be attributed to environmental factors. Thus, identical twins reared in different environments can show differences in intelligence test scores which are fully comparable to the differences found between racial groups.

'We must also recognize the limitations of present-day intelligence tests. Largely developed and standardized on white middle-class children, these tests tend to be biased against black children to an unknown degree. While IQ tests do predict school achievement, we cannot demonstrate that they are accurate as measures of innate endowment. Any generalizations about the ability of black or white children are very much limited by the nature of existing IQ tests.

'We also draw attention to the fact that the concept of race is most frequently defined "socially", by skin color, but that genetic race differences are very difficult to determine. Many of the studies cited by Jensen have employed a social definition of race, rather than the more rigorous genetic definition. Conclusions about the genetic basis for racial differences are obviously dependent on the accuracy of the definition of race employed.

'The Council of the Society for the Psychological Study of Social Issues reaffirms its long-held position of support for open inquiry on all aspects of human behavior. We are concerned with establishing high standards of scientific inquiry and of scientific responsibility. Included in these standards must be careful interpretation of research findings, with rigorous attention to alternative explanations. In no area of science are these principles more important than in the study of human behavior, where a variety of social factors may have large and far-reaching effects. When research has bearing on social issues and public policy, the scientist must examine the competing explanations for his findings and must exercise the greatest care in his interpretation. Only in this way can he minimize the possibility that others will overgeneralize or misunderstand the social implications of his work.'

This statement was signed unanimously by the members of the Council for the Society for the Psychological Study of Social Issues whose names and professional affiliations are listed below.*

My reply follows:

### Criticism or Propaganda?

I wish to report an interesting social-psychological phenomenon. The facts of the matter require little interpretation on my part. They might provide some student of the sociology of science with material for a case study of the relationship between criticism, propaganda, and scientific responsibility.

On May 2, 1969, the Society for the Psychological Study of Social Issues (SPISSI), a division of the American Psychological Association, put out a news release under the heading 'Psychologists Comment on Current IQ Controversy: Heredity *versus* Environment'. The statement was in response to my 123-page article' How Much Can We Boost IQ and Scholastic Achievement?' in the *Harvard Educational Review*. The five-page news release, signed by the 18 members of the SPSSI Council, was sent to the major news services and to all members of SPSSI, along with a cover letter SPSSI's President Martin Deutsch urging all members to arrange for publication of the SPSSI release in their local newspapers, either as an article or as 'Letters to the Editor'. Deutsch wrote: 'Thank you very much for your cooperation in this important effort – I hope very sincerely that most of you will find or make the time to carry out this task.' How many members of SPSSI, I wonder, did so without ever reading my article? One member of the SPSSI Council wrote on May 19, 1969: 'I had previously read enough of Jensen's recent article in the *Harvard Educational Review* (Vol.

---

* One of the signers later wrote to me ' . . . to let you know my continuing chagrin at having let my name appear on the SPSSI statement attacking you. I tried unsuccessfully to influence its content and had I been responsibly attentive to follow through, I'd have withdrawn my name in the end. I come out with different conclusions than you, but I have never doubted your integrity nor the importance of greater attention to the biological-genetic factors which you have kept before us.'

**39,** No. 1, Winter 1969) to help prepare the SPSSI press release concerning it. However, I did not read the whole thing until this week.'

My article was solicited by the Board of Editors of *HER* with the understanding that it would be followed by detailed critiques from a number of highly qualified psychologists and geneticists. Eight such critiques have already been published in the Spring 1969 *HER* and several more are scheduled by *HER* for future issues. (If my article was actually trivial or erroneous, it seems it should take only one competent critic to put it down. Soliciting and publishing 10 or more criticisms of a single article is probably unprecedented.) I have also defended my article in a two-hour videotaped discussion of it by a panel of two geneticists, two sociologists, and a psychologist, following which I responded to 45 minutes of questions and comments from a studio audience composed mostly of professors in relevant fields on the Berkeley faculty. I welcome such criticisms and discussions. The SPSSI release, however, seems to me clearly not in keeping with this kind of intellectually worthy discourse. I would characterize it not as scientifically responsible criticism, but as sheer propaganda.

In accord with *HER*'s letter of solicitation, my article reviewed the evidence relevant to the relative contributions of heredity and environment to intelligence and scholastic performance and evaluations of efforts to raise the IQ and scholastic performance of disadvantaged children. I was also asked by *HER* to state my position regarding social class and racial differences in intelligence: 'The preponderance of the evidence is, in my opinion, less consistent with a strictly environmental hypothesis than with a genetic hypothesis, which of course, does not exclude the influence of environment or its interaction with genetic factors [p. 82].' The article concluded with a summary of my own research on the triple interaction among the variables intelligence, associative learning ability, and socioeconomic status.

The SPSSI release directly misrepresents my article and, I believe, also the current state of our knowledge concerning the importance of genetic factors in intellectual development. For example, we read in the SPSSI statement: 'We believe that statements specifying the hereditary components of intelligence are unwarranted by the present state of scientific knowledge.' Does this mean that a scholar should not publish a summary of the relevant research to date on this topic? Among the other interesting points in the SPSSI statement are the following:

1. 'There is no direct evidence that supports the view that there is an innate difference between members of different racial groups.' I have pointed out that (*a*) such evidence cannot be 'direct' but must

necessarily be inferential, as is most scientific evidence, (*b*) that definitive genetic research on this topic has not yet been done, and (*c*) that appropriate research should be vigorously pursued to answer these questions.

2. 'A more accurate understanding of the contribution of heredity to intelligence will be possible only when social conditions for all races are equal and when this situation has existed for several generations.' This strikes me as an *anti*-research attitude, since the meaning of 'equal' social conditions is totally undefined in any operational terms, and if taken seriously would completely rule out the possibility of research on this important question, not just for several generations but indefinitely. In fact, genetic methods are available for researching this question, methods that do not set up impossible or operationally undefinable criteria such as absolute environmental equality.

3. SPSSI points out that 'a number of Jensen's key assumptions and conclusions are seriously questioned by many psychologists and geneticists'. Examples follow:

(*a*) 'Recent research indicates that environmental factors play a role from the moment of a child's conception.' In fact, my article contains a section reviewing the effects of prenatal factors on mental development (pp. 65-74).

(*b*) 'To construct questions about complex behavior in terms of heredity *versus* environment is to over-simplify the essence and nature of human development and behavior.' In fact, my article contains a section headed 'Common Misconceptions About Heritability' (pp. 42-46) under which one of the sub-headings is 'Heredity *versus* Environment' in which I explicity disabuse readers of this erroneous way of thinking about heredity and environment.

4. 'We are concerned with establishing high standards of scientific inquiry and of scientific responsibility. Included in these standards must be careful interpretation of research findings, with rigorous attention to alternative explanations.' I have maintained such standards in my article and in my response to critics. SPSSI, in its press release, has not. The SPSSI statement amounts to a censure of me for suggesting the reasonableness of an alternative hypothesis to their apparently 100 percent environmentalist position. I maintain SPSSI's censure of my article is not the way of science. I suggest instead that scientific knowledge is gained most efficiently through what John Platt has called 'strong inference', which means pitting against one another alternative hypotheses that lead to different predictions and then putting these predictions to empirical tests. My article proposes that a genetic hypothesis is a reasonable alternative to a strictly

environmental hypothesis, and it is this point essentially that the SPSSI press release is in protest against.

Part of the SPSSI statement directed against my article is word for word the same as a 1961 resolution SPSSI adopted in opposition to an article by Henry E. Garrett [Garrett, H. E. The SPSSI and racial differences. *American Psychologist*, 1962, **17**, 260-263]. This simple pigeon-holing operation on the part of the SPSSI Council might at least partially explain their illfitting and misleading 'criticism' of my *HER* article.

The SPSSI statement provoked a trenchant observation by Professor R. B. Cattell (1971, p. 24):

The difficulties that psychologists have had in their complex subject in developing unassailable concepts *anywhere* has often resulted in a retreat from abstraction and general laws to a safe (but dreary) particularism. In this retreat of pure environmentalism from the scientific field it is now adopting a scorched earth policy of obscurantism or even downright conceptual nihilism. A sad instance of a masquerade of scientific caution occurred in the SPSSI manifesto in response to Jensen's paper which asserts: 'A more accurate understanding of the contribution of heredity to intelligence will be possible only when social conditions for all races are equal and when this situation has existed for several generations.' In brief, the question can be answered only when impossible conditions are met, wherein the answer would be so obvious that methods of scientific analysis and experimental ingenuity would be superfluous. One is reminded of those critics of Copernicus who pointed out that the question of whether the earth or the sun is the center of the solar system would be answerable only when human beings could be transported to make observations from both vantage points! 'Scientific caution' is sometimes the last refuge of an intellectual nihilist. In any case, it is no compliment to psychology to state, as the SPSSI manifesto does, that this science has no methods or techniques potent enough to conclude more than that the man in the street can do without them.

Other social science groups chimed in with SPSSI. The executive board of the American Anthropological Association sent a list of resolutions to its entire membership (March 5, 1970), some directed at my article, with criticisms peculiarly slanted to obfuscate my position and to imply positions to which I have never subscribed. For example, *Resolution* 15:

Whereas in 1961 the American Anthropological Association, meeting in Philadelphia, resolve that:

> The American Anthropological Association repudiates statements now appearing in the United States that Negroes are biologically and in innate mental ability inferior to whites, and reaffirms the fact that there is no scientifically established evidence to justify the exclusion of any race from the rights guaranteed by the Constitution of the United States. The basic principles of equality of opportunity and equality before the law are compatible with all that is known about human biology. All races possess the abilities needed to participate fully in the democratic way of life and in modern technological civilization.

And whereas a recent article in the *Harvard Educational Review*, by Arthur R. Jensen, Professor of Educational Psychology at the University of California (Berkeley) cast doubt on this conclusion;

And whereas, in response, a special session was organized at the annual meeting of the American Anthropological Association in New Orleans to review the issue once again,

And whereas after discussion of papers by five scientists competent in the relevant disciplines, the session concluded that the article reviewed is not consistent with the facts of psychology, biology or anthropology.

Therefore,

Be it resolved that, although any *ad hominem* response to a scholarly paper is regrettable, it must be concluded that the data assembled in Jensen's article are wholly inadequate for the conclusions drawn and we reassert the 1961 conclusion reached that:

> There is no scientifically established evidence to justify the exclusion of any race from the rights guaranteed by the Constitution of the United States. The basic principles of equality of opportunity and equality before the law are compatible with all that is known about human biology. All races possess the abilities needed to participate fully in the democratic way of life and modern technological civilization.

And add that we specifically repudiate any suggestion that the failure of an educational program could be attributed to genetic differences between large populations.

### Resolution 16

Whereas the question of racism continues to represent a clear and present danger to the proper scientific understanding of mankind,

Be it resolved that, the American Anthropological Association at its annual meeting in New Orleans 20-23 November, 1969 requests all members of the profession upon their return home to use all available outlets in the national and local media to inform the general public concerning the correct facts about the nature of human variability. Reports on this activity shall be included in the *Newsletter* in a special section to be established for this purpose.

As proposed in Resolution 16, a special session was devoted to discussion of my article at the AAA's annual convention in New Orleans. I was not invited to attend, so my knowledge of what transpired is based only on a press report, which stated, 'Jensen was not defended by any of the panelists. Only two members of the large audience expressed sympathy with Jensen, and both of them were psychologists, not anthropologists. It soon became obvious that the issue goes deeper than "racism" ', although several speakers attempted to dismiss Jensen with that label. One anthropologist even referred to him as a "chauvinist, biased racist".' A resolution was introduced attacking my article and there were proposals for 'distributing "thousands" of pamphlets to convey the associations's position to the public' (*Times-Picayune*, New Orleans, November 23, 1969).

A group called Minnesota Psychologists for Social Action held a meeting attended by more than 100 persons on the University of Minnesota campus at which it was proposed to select a committee to write an 'anti-Jensen' paper. Forums on the topic were held at Harvard, Wisconsin, Berkeley, and other university campuses. Most of these, according to the reports, were in the nature of an auto-da-fé rather than a scientific discussion.

At the annual convention of the Eastern Psychological Association, in Spring 1969, a group called Psychologists for Social Action circulated a petition which urged that I should be expelled or at least censured by the American Psychological Association.

Even much of the published discussion involved, in Scriven's (1970) words, 'errors so gross that intrinsic criticism is otiose'. How is one to reply, for example, when in an article entitled 'A Sociologist Looks at the Jensen Report' one reads '. . . there is much accumulated evidence to suggest that IQ is not genetically determined'? I have no way of knowing whether such a statement represents the view of the majority of sociologists, but it is sufficiently alarming that it apparently represents the sincere belief of even one. (Needless to say, no relevant evidence was cited to back up the statement.) What is one to say when (in the same article) we read 'Rosenthal's study of *Pygmalion in the Classroom* (1968) supports the notion that increased self-esteem improves performance', when all the major reviews of this work in professional journals have pointed out that this study's data do not in the least support this conclusion, and when several published attempts to replicate the study have failed to show any effects of teacher expectancy in raising pupils' IQs or scholastic achievement? Yet the *Pygmalion* study is still cited repeatedly by some social scientists even after they have been made aware of the gross methodological and statistical deficiencies of that study and of the repeated failure of attempted replications of the purported effect. Can one but conclude that the need to uphold a dogma at all costs is stronger in such persons than the desire to look at the facts?

Some of the activities that are called 'research' by some sociologists may actually yield quite questionable 'facts'. Let's look at a specific case in point to see just how this sort of thing can come about. A professor of sociology sent out the questionnaire (Fig. 1):

The first public appearance of the results of this survey was in a letter to *The Times* of London (July 8, 1971) in which Friedrichs used his results to contradict a statement attributed to Professor H. J. Eysenck, whose book *Race, Intelligence, and Education* had recently been reviewed in *The Times*.* Friedrichs wrote: 'Professor Eysenck has written that "90 percent" of the experts in the field know that the evidence for the innate inferiority of black men is not far short of conclusive.'

Let's see what Eysenck really said. In the introductory chapter of this book, which covers many topics other than the issue of genetic racial differences, Eysenck states:

Denying what has not been asserted; asserting what has not been denied; arguing about what you think should or would follow from your opponent's position (but which he doesn't think should or would follow); introducing irrelevant points which establish that you are a good guy and he is a bad guy (like being in favor of mother love) –

* A report of Friedrich's survey has since appeared in professional education journal, *Phi Delta Kappan*, 1972, **53**, pp. 287 and 333.

Dear A.P.A. Member:

Your listing has been drawn randomly from the **Directory** of the American Psychological Association in order to sample the evaluation which American psychologists have made of Arthur R. Jensen's widely publicized assessment of compensatory education programs and their relation to the inheritance of intellectual ability.

Your **anonymous** evaluation of Jensen's key conclusion may enable professional educators to better appraise the import of his thesis.

Simply check (√) the appropriate response on the opposite side of this card, place it in the envelope provided, and return it by mail. Thank you.

Dr R. W. Friedrichs, Drew University, Madison, N.J.

---

Arthur R. Jensen's article, 'How Much Can We Boost IQ and Scholastic Achievement?' in the Spring, 1969 *HARVARD EDUCATIONAL REVIEW* states that 'it (is) a not unreasonable hypothesis that genetic factors are strongly implicated in the average Negro-white intelligence difference. The preponderance of the evidence is, in my opinion, less consistent with a strictly environmental hypothesis than with a genetic hypothesis.' (p. 82).

---

Check whether you **agree** (   ); **tend to agree** (   ); are **neutral** (   ); **tend to disagree** (   ); **disagree** (   ); or have **no opinion** (   ) with regard to the quotation taken as a whole.

FIGURE 1

one could write a book on these techniques. What I am trying to establish is simply that it is easy to make it appear that there is disagreement when in reality there is very considerable agreement. The layman cannot readily see through this kind of smoke-screen and may give up in disgust, saying with feeling that 'experts always disagree'. This just is not so; it is simply that the vast areas on which there is universal agreement are not 'news' and are not likely to come to the attention of the man in the street. I would be prepared to assert that experts (real experts, that is) *would agree with at least* 90 *percent of what I am going to say* [emphasis added] – probably the true figure would be a good deal higher, but there is no point in exaggerating (p. 15).

Note first how Friedrichs worded his proposition. Obviously it misrepresents what Eysenck had actually written. Thus Friedrichs's data could give the appearance of finding Eysenck wrong. The next point to note is the questionnaire's quotation from the *HER* article. Read it again, and compare it with the statement I actually made on page 82 of my article:

> The preponderance of the evidence is, in my opinion, less consistent with a strictly environmental hypothesis than with a genetic hypothesis, which of course, *does not exclude the influence of environment or its interaction with genetic factors.* [Emphasis added.]

This last phrase in italics, which Friedrichs's questionnaire omitted, is very important, because the environmentalist theory *does* exclude any genetic component, and many psychologists who have not read my article could easily assume that the statement quoted by Friedrichs represented a symmetrically 'opposite' genetic theory which excludes environmental influences. The omission of the final clause in my sentence could only bias the responses toward disagreement; it could not conceivably bias responses toward agreement. How much confidence then, one may ask, are we to place in the sampling and statistical analyses of such a survey which on the very face of it already reveals such transparent shortcomings? And by what rationalizations could any conclusions from such a study ever be redeemed? (Interestingly enough, Friedrichs acknowledged the critical omission from the quoted statement in a personal letter [October 25, 1970] many months before he sent his results to *The Times*.)

Finally, it would be interesting to know how the results of such a survey, even if properly conducted could (in Friedrichs's words) '. . . enable professional educators to better appraise the import of his [i.e., Jensen's] thesis'. Since when can empirical questions be answered by a show of hands? In science the only thing that really counts is a preponderance of the facts and converging lines of evidence.

One psychologist made the following unsupported (and unsupportable) statement in an invited address at a large university, only to find himself having to answer to the Ethics Committee of the American Psychological Association, which declared that such unsupported defamatory statements are a clear violation of the APA's professional code of ethics:

With the assistance of certain of my associates and myself, we spent the last eight weeks going through every single one of Arthur Jensen's [*HER*] references, and we found fifty-three major errors or misinterpretations, all of them unidimensional and all of them anti-black. So we felt from this that there may be another element, not a scientific one, that had entered into the construction of the original article.

Such were the excesses of some of the professional environmentalists who apparently felt it was necessary at any cost and by any means, fair or foul, to discredit my *HER* article. Such conduct was seldom criticized by academicians, and when it was, the criticism at times was met by even greater hostility and opposition than were originally directed against my article. But as one colleague remarked, there is a double standard of ethics in the social sciences – so long as a breach of honesty or ethics or rigor is made in a 'liberal' direction, the conduct will not cause one bit of loss of reputation by the offender.

A complete suspension of critical and scientific standards was often manifested toward even the slightest, most questionable shreds of evidence that could be made to appear to disprove some major point in my article. Probably the most publicized example of this resulted from a newspaper article (*Los Angeles Times*, October 12, 1969), which has since been referred to many times, even in professional journals and in supposedly serious debate on these issues (e.g. 'What would Jensen say?' *Phi Delta Kappan*, January, 1970, p. 292). The article, with banner headlines, described one sixth-grade class in the Windsor Hills Elementary School of Los Angeles, with 90 percent black pupils and a mean IQ of 115. The report has been held up repeatedly as a refutation of the statement in my *HER* article that it is a not unreasonable hypothesis that genetic factors are implicated in the average difference of one standard deviation (about 15 IQ points) that generally shows up in studies comparing Negroes and whites in the United States. Can the educators who cite this newspaper report as evidence refuting my hypothesis really be methodologically so naïve as to believe that it is actually relevant to the question? One wonders. Perhaps they are. But since there is a 12 percent median overlap nationwide between the Negro and white populations in IQ (i.e., 12 percent of Negroes exceed the white median IQ of 100), why should anyone be surprised to find that there are Negro children having IQs of 115 or

higher, or that they should be concentrated in the affluent integrated neighborhood in Los Angeles? These facts themselves are
not remarkable. The remarkable thing is that they were blown-up
into a headline story, and have since been cited as 'evidence against
Jensen' in scholarly contexts. Statistics released by the Los Angeles
City Schools indicate that their schools with 90 percent or more
minority pupils have an average IQ of 88, while schools with less
than 25 percent minority pupils have an average IQ of 104. Given
a mean IQ of 88, and assuming a normal distribution and a standard deviation of 15, we should expect approximately 3·6 percent
of children in the 90 percent or more minority schools to obtain
IQs *above* 115. Should it be so remarkable, then, that one sixth-
grade class in one 90 percent minority school in a city of three
million has a number of these high IQ pupils with a *mean* IQ of 115?
(In the two previous years the IQs in this affluent school average
near 100.) The report is even less remarkable if one considers that
the pupils attending the Windsor Hills School come from homes
valued in the $35,000 to $150,000 bracket. The newspaper account
adds that, 'Most Windsor Hills students come from wealthy homes
with parents who are doctors, lawyers, or professional people'. Is
it not highly likely that the children of these parents have inherited
a better genetic endowment for intellectual development than the
majority of children in the Watts ghetto? If so, you cannot argue
that their higher IQs are purely a result of the good environment
provided by their affluent parents. Finally, a newspaper story is not
a research report and leaves out the kinds of information needed
for a proper evaluation. For example, the account states that in the
two previous years the mean IQ was near 100, and that just prior
to the testing that yielded a mean of 115 in the sixth-grade class, 72
new pupils had transferred into the school from *private* schools.
The article also notes that, 'in reading scores for pupils in the first,
second, and third grades, Windsor Hills was far below the national
norm'. '. . . These primary reading scores – plus the fact that
Windsor Hills' sixth-grade IQ scores during the past two years
were only average – has led some city school officials to regard the
115 mark as only a "fluke".' Yet such 'evidence' is grasped by
some environmentalists as a drowning man grasps at a straw.

On the Berkeley campus various student groups launched
attacks against me. The campus police kept close track of the acti-

vities of dissident student groups and were usually able to warn me well in advance of a demonstration planned for a particular date in one of my classes. On two occasions there was sufficient advance notice so that my graduate seminar could make arrangements to meet secretly in another part of the building and elude the demonstrators. But on several occasions my students and I had to contend with demonstrators. The largest demonstration filled the lecture room to overflowing, the demonstrators outnumbering the enrolled students by at least two to one. Several uniformed campus police officers and two plainclothes men came to prevent disruption of my lecture. At least half the demonstrators left at my request, which was backed up by the presence of the police. But I did not ask the police to forcibly evict any of those who refused to leave. The demonstrators had brought their own photographer and would have liked nothing more than to have taken photos of the police forcibly removing the demonstrators from my class. Needless to say, the lecture I had planned for that hour could not be given, since the demonstrators engaged in heckling in an obvious attempt to provoke me into calling the police to evict them by force, which I never did.

Various handbills passed out on the campus and displayed on numerous bulletin boards urged students to join demonstrations in my classes and to demand that I be fired. Students holding up placards with 'Fire Jensen' picketed a meeting of the University's Board of Regents. Students marched in the courtyard beneath my office window, carrying the same placards and chanting 'Fire Jensen!' A sound-truck circled around the campus with its loudspeaker blaring 'Fight racism! Fire Jensen!' Pamphlets were distributed bearing my picture and headed: 'HILTER IS ALIVE AND WELL AND SPREADING RACIST PROPAGANDA AT BERKELEY! Come and help fight in the struggle against racism at Jensen's class!' And it told the time and place of my lectures.

I experienced similar demonstrations on other university campuses as an invited lecturer. On three occasions I was prevented from speaking. At my lecture to a group of scientists at the Salk Institute of Biological Research, the notorious Students for a Democratic Society (SDS) on the nearby La Jolla campus of the University of California turned out in full force to demonstrate. They invaded the small auditorium of the Salk Institute and prevented my lecturing by continuously clapping their hands in rhythm and doing this in relays so as to be able to keep it going indefinitely. Repeated appeals from the Salk officials in charge of the meeting failed to dissuade the demonstrators, and after about a half an hour of this demonstration the lecture was called off. However, I stayed over till the next day and gave my lecture, privately announced by individual phone calls to members of the Salk staff. The SDS apparently had been ired by this, for when I returned to Berkeley the next day, the Berkeley chapter of the SDS had already held a rally to plan reprisals against me. The campus police immediately informed me of these SDS activities. The SDS threats seemed sufficiently virulent that it was deemed advisable that I be accompanied on the campus, to and from classes and the parking lot, by two plainclothes bodyguards. This arrangement lasted about two weeks, when the SDS suddenly turned its attack on a professor of political science who had been in the news for having served among President Nixon's advisers on Southeast Asia. The two bodyguards who had been accompanying me were then assigned to the political science professor. Threats still occur sporadically even now, three years after the publication of the *HER* article – phone calls at home late at night (despite an unlisted phone number) and slogans scrawled on my office door or in the Education and Psychology Department elevators, like those I saw only last week: 'Jensen Must Perish' and 'Kill Jensen'. Although custodians continually remove these slogans, they keep appearing. Through it all, I am proud to say, the University Administration and the Academic Senate unequivocally defended my right to free speech and unfettered pursuit of my research.

Such events as I have just recounted might be considered as mere personal annoyances, except that they have a larger impact which threatens to silence open expression and discussion of diverse viewpoints on socially important issues. Other members of the university faculty who might otherwise be inclined to enter the discussion publicly may be made hesitant by the threats from the opposition.

Letters I have received from professors at Berkeley and elsewhere lead me to believe that there may have been many voices which might have been heard in the controversy had they not been silenced by fear. My correspondence files are full of supportive letters from persons in the academic world, often prominent scholars, who make it clear they do not wish to express their views publicly. Many more have approved of my *HER* article privately than have done so publicly. One professor, when asked if he would write a letter-to-the-editor of a scientific journal and include some highly cogent points he had made in private correspondence about the issues raised in my *HER* article, declined apologetically but frankly, saying, 'I have to admit to fears, both of what would happen to me professionally if I became identified with you, and plain gut fear of being beaten up, arson, and the like. These things, if they are not here, are coming.'

Some months before the appearance of my *HER* article, another professor had been asked by a well-known journal to write an article on the inheritance of mental ability. Shortly after my *HER* article came out, the professor's article was returned to him along with the payment for it and with a letter from the editor explaining that in view of the Jensen article '. . . we finally decided against entering the controversy altogether'. Since I thought the article made a valuable contribution to the scientific literature on the genetics of intelligence, I urged the author to submit it for consideration by another journal. He wrote back: 'I am sorry to say it, but because of the abuse which you have received, I have no intention of submitting my paper for publication elsewhere'. Unfortunately, I must conclude from these examples, and from numerous others like them in my experience over the last three years, that harassment of an individual scholar has very real suppressive effects which extend far beyond the particular individual under attack. This is a disturbing threat to free inquiry and the open discussion, which are so essential for progress. It had been my impression that this situation had perhaps begun to improve with regard to discussion of the topics of my *HER* article, although, sadly, just this week I read in the newspapers that a professor of psychology at Harvard University, Dr Richard Herrnstein, has had his classes picketed and disturbed by demonstrators throughout this term for having written an article on the genetics of intelligence and its social implications (*Atlantic Monthly*, September, 1971); also this week a militant band of demonstrators at a California State

College invaded an auditorium and succeeded in preventing Professor William Shockley from delivering an invited lecture on intelligence and genetics.

I am frequently asked whether the agitation following my article has had any adverse effect on my own research activities. Although this is difficult to judge from my own standpoint, it seems to me the answer in general is no. I do not feel that my subsequent research has been hindered by the whole controversy. I have knowledge of only one major research project in which my *HER* article and my publicly known position of questioning strictly environmental explanations of individual and population differences in intelligence and scholastic performance clearly figured in the project's sudden demise.

In 1968 I had been asked to act as research director of a large study aimed at assesssing the scholastic effects of the racial desegregation of the Berkeley city schools, to be accomplished by busing. In the Spring of 1968, the schools still had considerable *de facto* segregation because of the high degree of residential segregation of Berkeley's white and Negro populations. The first task of the study, prior to the desegregation of the schools in Fall 1968, was to obtain what we called 'baseline' data (in Spring 1968) against which to measure the effects of desegregation in the subsequent years. Berkeley was the first city of over 100,000 population in the United States to institute complete desegregation and equal proportional representation of all racial and socioeconomic groups in all of its public schools by two-way busing. Both majority and minority children are bused from their own neighborhoods to schools which, prior to desegregation, were predominantly either majority or minority. About half the school population are minority, mostly black. I designed what I thought would be the first real study of the effects of desegregation on the scholastic achievement of minority and majority pupils. (I have described the design of the study elsewhere [Assessment of Racial Desegregation in the Berkeley Schools. *Community Psychology Series*, No. 1, 1972].) The baseline data collection was conducted by a research staff of some 30 persons during Spring 1968. It consisted of administering tests and questionnaires (by a staff of specially trained testers, not by the classroom teachers) to the entire elementary schools population of 9000 pupils. The assessment battery consisted of verbal and nonverbal intelligence tests, tests of attention and memory, motivational assessments, scholastic achievement tests, pupil socio-metric and attitude questionnaires, family background data, paren-tal questionnaires of attitudes toward integration and busing, and ratings (by trained observers) of pupil behavior in the classroom. Also, anthropometric measurements and indices of physical matu-rity were obtained on all children. Probably the most innovative aspect of the research design was to make use of sibling data. The most powerful method for statistically controlling differences in family background variables is by comparing the scholastic achieve-ments of younger siblings with that of their older siblings who had been exposed to segregated schools; the younger siblings would have come up through the grades in integrated schools. Thus, in a sense, one has 'experimental' and 'control' subjects with respect to integrated schooling, and, being siblings, they are 'matched' on family background. All these data were obtained as was planned, in Spring 1968, and were analyzed throughout the following summer and fall. In Spring 1969, shortly after the appearance of the *HER* article, our staff of testers went back into the schools to obtain the follow-up data on the first year of desegregation. At the same time the *HER* was being publicized widely in the local papers, which aroused certain political groups in the community to oppose my conducting a study of the effects of integration in the Berkeley schools. The heat was on. In Berekeley's political climate, the school authorities thought that from a public relations standpoint, I was too controversial to be heading the evaluation of the desegre-gation program. It was recognized that the very qualities I con-sidered a virtue as a researcher and which made me outspoken in my writings about important educational issues even when I was unable to echo the popular views, were the very qualities that made me so unacceptable to the politically oriented critics of my appoint-ment as director of the project. The problem was fully discussed with the school officials and an advisory committee which has been formed by the chancellor of the University (and which was respon-sible for selecting me as director). It was decided, with my full approval (although I probably had no real choice in the matter), that the project would be nominally headed by the Dean of the School of Education and that two other persons would be under him, as Director and Program Coordinator, positions which were assigned to persons not previously identified with the project or even with this field of educational research, thereby creating a kind of anonymity at the top of the project which is most visible to the media and the public. It was intended that I should recede far into the background, as research psychologist on the project, hidden from the public firing line but remaining in charge of all the psychometric testing and data analysis.

Unfortunately this did not rescue the project. Almost before the Spring testing program had gotten under way, the Berkeley Board of Education was petitioned at one of its public meetings to halt the evaluation study; the petitioners urged that it 'be destroyed or disassociated with'. The Board did not act at that time, but at its next meeting it announced that the project was to be discontinued immediately. I learned of it the following day, when a school official informed me that the Board was reluctantly forced to this action because the schools are not a research institute but a political unit and therefore had to be sensitive to the political climate of the community. I was dismayed but not very surprised. A few weeks previously, Berkeley's then new superintendent of schools told me that when he first took office, early in 1969, there were people in the community who urged that his first act as superintendent should be to 'get rid of Jensen'. Since there were demands to destroy all the baseline test data collected the year before, these all had to be packed in boxes, carefully labeled, and removed from the Berkeley campus for safe storage elsewhere. There was literally a truck load of data which had to be moved and during the time it was being prepared for storage we were requested by the campus authorities to keep the lights on in our work rooms all through the night, to discourage would-be vandals and aid police surveillance. There had already been at least one recent instance of a Berkeley professor's files and data being destroyed by a band of militant student radicals, so we took no chances with the Berkeley school data that had been collected at the cost of many tens of thousands of dollars. In quality and comprehensiveness, these predesegregation baseline data are practically unique in American educational research. They undoubtedly comprise the most accurate and comprehensive set of baseline measurements ever undertaken for a study of desegregation. In fact, they are one of the most thorough assessments ever made of an elementary school population for any purpose. It is a pity that the data could not have served its original purpose as a basis for assessing the changes in scholastic performance, attitudes, etc. over the course of several years following the total desegregation of the schools. Thus, a real assessment of the educational effects of complete school desegregation still remains an unaccomplished task for educational research. Perhaps it can be done somewhere at some future time. It could still be done in Berkeley, of course, because all the predesegregation baseline data remain completely intact in safe storage.

Many persons apparently fear that recognition of group differences in scholastic aptitudes and motivations, whatever their causes, is tantamount to supporting racially segregated schools. This is an unfortunate misconception. Although I have questioned purely environmental theories of differences in scholastic performance, I have never been opposed to racial desegregation. I am opposed to segregated schools. But as an educator I am concerned that desegregation should be brought about in such a way as to benefit all children. Achieving racial balance in schools, while viewed by many of us as desirable for moral, ethical, and social reasons, will not by itself solve existing educational problems. It will create new problems, and I am anxious that we provide the means for fully and objectively assessing them and for discovering the means for solving them. I am quite convinced on the basis of massive evidence that the educational aptitudes and needs of the majority of white and Negro children are sufficiently different at the present time in our history that both groups, particularly the more disadvantaged group, can be cheated out of the best education we can provide in our schools if uniformity rather than diversity of instructional aims and approaches becomes the rule. Educational diversity and desegregation need not be incompatible goals. I think both are necessary. But achieving racial balance and at the same time ignoring individual differences in children's educational needs could be most destructive to those who are already the most disadvantaged educationally. The allocation of a school's resources for children with special educational problems cannot be influenced by race; it must be governed by individual needs. Making an association, as some persons do, between the 'nature-nurture' question and the issue of racial desegregation of schools is, in my opinion, a most flagrant *non sequitur*. The pros and cons of school integration have no logical or necessary connection with the question whether there are or are not racial genetic differences in mental ability, and the outcome of research on this scientifically legitimate question should have no bearing, either one way or the other, on the issue of school desegregation.

During the height of the demonstrations directed against me on the Berkeley campus in Spring 1969, I was put in telephone contact with an undercover person whom I never met but whose bona fides I was informed of by those concerned with protecting me from harassment. This man attended the rallies and meetings of the various militant radical groups in Berkeley and kept me well apprised of their discussions concerning the strategy and tactics of their campaign against me. My informer was remarkably reliable, and thus I was usually prepared well in advance for the events that occurred during that spring. One day I was told that in a meeting of the Students for a Democratic Society, a militant student group, it was conceded that their tactics of leading disruptive demonstrations and making blatant demands that I be fired had been a failure. They had succeeded only in antagonizing the university's faculty and alienating many students who viewed the SDS's tactics as reminiscent of Hitler's Brown Shirts. The discussion finally led to the decision that the only tactic that stood a chance in the liberal atmosphere of Berkeley would be to discredit me professionally in the eyes of the academic community. The best way to accomplish this, they decided, was to force me to face a tribunal of academically prestigious persons who would take issue with my *HER* article. The hoped for *auto-da-fé* should be highly publicized to the press and the public and should be held in the largest auditorium on the Berkeley campus. This all struck me at the time as quite fanciful since, as far as I knew, the SDS was in no position to command such facilities or participants. So I dismissed the possibility of this plan's materializing and gave it no further thought.

Hence I was quite taken aback when, just two weeks later, I got a phone call from a professor of sociology, who described to me what amounted to almost exactly the same plan I had heard of two weeks before. Call it coincidence. But the fact is that I was being asked (indeed, it was practically demanded of me as if I had no say in the matter) to take part in an affair that was described in a way that did not differ in any essential details from the plan which was hatched in the meeting of the SDS. Wishing to get this request and my reaction to it 'on the record', I told the sociologist I would have to think about it and reply by letter. I wrote to him the following day and sent copies of the letter to the Chancellor and three other university officials who would inevitably become involved in the arrangements for the proposed symposium. This was to insure that my own position was clearly on record. I wrote:

I have considered your proposal in our telephone conversation of May 2, 1969, that plans be made for a symposium concerning my article 'How Much Can We Boost IQ and Scholastic Achievement?' in which the participants would include members of the Berkeley faculty and invited speakers from other universities.

I welcome the opportunity to discuss the topics of my article with colleagues and researchers in fields germane to the issues, and therefore I like the idea of a symposium. In view of the present political climate on our campus, however, I believe such discussions of complex research problems can prove most worth while provided they take place under arrangements that have a high probability of being conducive to a thoughtful, objective examination of the topics under consideration.

As a result of conversations with persons at U.C. and elsewhere who have had much more experience than I concerning the effectiveness of various arrangements for achieving the desirable objectives of a symposium such as you proposed, I have formed some conclusions about the most probably optimal arrangement. This would consist of conducting the entire symposium in a relatively small room, accommodating an audience of not more than 50 persons, restricted to faculty and students, who would participate in the discussion and questions-and-answers at the discretion of the symposium's chairman. The proceedings would be videotaped and sound-taped, which would make it possible for the discussion to reach the widest audience, both on campus, through future showings of the tapes under University auspices, and for the general public under the auspices of ETV and/or radio. This arrangement has the advantages of coming closest to insuring a suitable atmosphere for thoughtful, undistracted discussion by the symposium participants, of preserving a record of the proceedings for future reference, and of being made available to the largest number of viewers among faculty, students, and the general public.

These are, in general, the only conditions under which I would consider taking part in the proposed symposium. In view of the recent politically instigated campus unrest that we have seen here and on other campuses, I believe that the symposium participants will agree with my attitude that we wish to be a party to a scientific discussion, not a campus demonstration. I believe that the conditions I have recommended are the only ones at present that would help to insure the kind of meeting that could do justice to further discussion of my article.

The sociologists who planned this confrontation strongly opposed the arrangements I had proposed. They insisted on holding the debate in a large hall so that the student body and general public could attend, and if I would not participate under these conditions they were prepared to carry on without me. But the University would not agree to pay for the invited speakers unless I participated; and the University Extension agreed to pay for the audio and video recording of the proceedings if this could be done under studio conditions so as to produce a high quality videotape for commercial distribution to other colleges through the University Extension's audio-visual library.

So the symposium finally was held under the conditions I had proposed. The small studio audience was comprised entirely of faculty and researchers from the departments of anthropology, education, genetics, law, political science, psychology, and sociology. As one could have expected, knowing the participants, it was a dignified meeting. Professor Curt Stern (genetics) was chairman, and papers were given by Professors Aaron Cicourel (sociology), Lee Cronbach (psychology), Joshua Lederberg (genetics), William Libby (genetics), and Arthur Stinchombe (sociology). I responded on the average for about five minutes to each paper; this was followed by interchanges among the panelists and then the discussion was opened to the studio audience for about forty-five minutes of questions and reactions. In all, it lasted nearly three hours. From my standpoint it was a success. The videotape has since been shown numerous times on the Berkeley campus and on other campuses (interestingly enough, never by the persons who were so anxious to have this meeting in the first place). Quite contrary to the expected result, the symposium completely failed to discredit me or my position in the eyes of the panelists or of the audiences who have since viewed the entire proceedings on videotape. I, perhaps more than anyone else, feel grateful that the University sponsored the symposium under conditions which insured freedom from disturbances and also guaranteed the widest possible audience through the making of a permanent record on videotape.

To a psychologist observing all these phenomena, the question naturally arises as to why so many otherwise objective and dispassionate intellectuals display such vehement moral indignation and even zealous combativeness toward any explanation of human behavioral differences, especially social class and racial differences, that propounds genetic factors as playing a part. Some social scientists have felt so strongly about this that they have cancelled their participation in research conferences or symposia when they learned that I was to be among the participants. Why in some circles is the person who is critical of 100 percent environmentalistic attempts to explain human differences viewed as a moral pariah? With the exception of such radical political groups as the Students for a Democratic Society, whose aim seems to be to create dissension and disruption by any means they can possibly exploit, I believe that those who have most strongly opposed me on essentially non-scientific grounds have done so out of noble but mistaken sentiments. Their motives are not entirely discreditable. We all feel some uneasiness and discomfort at the notion of differences among persons in traits that we especially value, such as mental abilities, which have obviously important educational, occupational, and social correlates. There are probably no other traits in which we are more reluctant to notice differences, and if circumstances force us to notice them, our first tendency is to minimize them or explain them away. This is even more true when we are confronted with group differences; it seems to us so intrinsically unjust that some socially defined groups, through no fault of their own, should be disadvantaged with respect to traits which all persons value that we are easily inclined to deny such differences or at least attribute them to relatively superficial and external causes and appearances, such as prejudice, biased tests and observations, discriminatory schooling, racism, and other similar explanations which tend to place blame and guilt on other persons and forces in society. And there is considerable plausibility to such thinking because we all know of real instances of these undesirable factors, and we prefer to going on believing they are sufficient explanation for the apparent human differences we are faced with. There seems to be a strong human proclivity to place *blame* for disadvantage or misfortune; the placement of *personal* blame substitutes for the scientific analysis of causality. In ancient times natural disasters such as volcanos, earthquakes, and floods were blamed on the ill-will of personified gods. The physical sciences now provide other, quite different explanations of these phenomena. In some respects, however, the social sciences still have not moved beyond personified blame, leveled at 'society', 'the establishment', 'Capitalism', or whatever – personified entities at which we can vent our anger much as one can feel angry at an individual who intentionally commits a personal offense.

In my experience of lecturing to a variety of audiences – students, teachers, parents, research scientists – on topics in psychology and education, I have found that any statement or trend of thought that minimizes, explains away, glosses over, or places blame on personified institutions for mental and educational differences between individuals or groups is met by an unmistakable rush of warm approval from the audience. I have experienced it when others were speaking and I was among the audience; and I have experienced it when I was the speaker. Nothing, not even loud and prolonged applause, is more reinforcing to a speaker, reinforcing in the very Skinnerian sense of shaping the speaker's utterances further toward eliciting more waves of warm approval from the audience. The lessening of the audience's anxiety is almost palpable, with bits of laughter and the rustle of relaxing tensions among the listeners. And the speaker's trend in the direction that produces this effect is reinforced, often unconsciously and even against his will. Constant awareness, vigilance, and self-discipline are needed in this field to prevent one's lecturing behavior, and even one's thinking, from being shaped by the audience's emotional reactions. One can be carried away by these reinforcements, eventually to find oneself uttering soft-headed sentimentalities and Pollyannaish nonsense that one could hardly sanction while in a more sober frame of mind.

Colleagues have brought up a variety of more intellectual reasons for denying a genetic basis for behavioral differences. One of the commonest reasons is that such knowledge, if it is established and generally accepted by the scientific and intellectual community, might be used by some persons for evil purposes, to promote racial prejudice, discrimination, and segregation and to justify or rationalize the political supression and economic exploitation of racial minorities and the nation's working class in general. As I point out in my paper on ethical issues in genetic research, these consequences do not logically follow from the recognition of genetic behavioral differences. Nearly all scientifically important knowledge can be used for good or ill. Intellectuals should be concerned with men's purposes and the uses to which knowledge will be put; they should never think in terms of suppressing knowledge or the quest for it. One colleague wrote that in his opinion some intellectuals could not view my *HER* article objectively because they feel that unless human equality in abilities, and especially racial equality, is a fact, a society like ours cannot be made to work and progress is impossible; therefore equality *must* be a fact. He drew a religious analogy: 'If there weren't a Heavenly Father to sustain me in my agonies, I couldn't go on living; therefore God exists'.

Some of the reluctance to study the evidence objectively in this field results from confusion of the concept of genetic inequality, that is to say, differences in gene frequencies for particular characteristics, with the moral ideal of equality expressed in 'all men are created equal', meaning equality before the law, equality of political and civil rights, and equality of opportunity in education and employment. Realization of the moral ideal of equality proclaimed in the Declaration of Independence, of course, does not depend upon either phenotypic or genotypic equality of individuals' psychological characteristics.

Another unfortunate misconception has been the notion that when we speak of genetic differences between populations, whether they be social classes or various racial groups, we are speaking about differences that are somehow *sui generis*, intrinsic, unchangeable, protoplasmic differences. But this notion is completely wrong. It is the kind of ignorant belief promulgated in racist tracts. The genetics of population differences deals with specific gene frequencies or 'gene pools' differing in the frequencies of many genes, effects which come about mainly from varying degrees of geographic and social isolation of breeding groups and natural selection of various characteristics by differing environmental pressures. However unsusceptible the individual genes themselves might be to most environmental influences, there is nothing at all 'intrinsic' or 'immutable' about human *gene pools*.

The scientist who has perhaps given the most thought to the causes of resistance to the study of genetic factors in human differences is Professor William Shockley, who for several years has been urging the U.S. National Academy of Sciences, without success, to sponsor research on the genetics of intelligence including its racial aspects. Shockley's speculations concerning the critics who have opposed his advocacy of the scientific study of genetic differences in mental traits are summarized in a recent article in *The Phi Delta Kappan* (January, 1971):

> I doubt neither the sincerity nor the good intentions of these critics. I diagnose their thought-blockage as caused by a theologico-scientific delusion. I call it the 'apple of God's eye obsession' – God meaning for some the proper socio-biological order of the universe. True believers hold that God has designed nature's laws so that good intentions suffice to ensure humanity's well-being; the belief satisfies a human need for self-esteem. Any evidence counter to man's claim to be the 'apple of God's eye' strikes a central blow at his self-esteem, and thereby provokes retaliation reminiscent of the prompt execution of a Greek messenger bearing tidings of defeat in battle. The parallels become clearer in historic perspectives. Galileo and Darwin brought new knowledge that was incompatible with the then-cherished interpretation of humanity's unique place in the universe. Either the new knowledge had to be rejected or else the 'apple of God's eye obsession' had to be painfully revised. The thought-blockers and unsearch dogmatism that reject the relevance of genetics to social problems arise, I propose, because the theory that intelligence is largely determined by the genes and that races may differ in distribution of mental capacity offends equalitarian-environmentalism – an important feature of the contemporary form of the 'apple of God's eye obsession' (p. 307).

A few words are in order concerning the bibliography of articles about my *HER* article included at the end of this volume. The bibliography attempts to be exhaustive rather than selective. Several items are more substantial than the rest, however, and these should be noted.

Of the largely negative critiques which attracted the most attention is the article in the *Bulletin of Atomic Scientists* by Professor Richard Lewontin, an eminent geneticist. (My reply and his rejoinder appeared in the following issues of the *Bulletin.*) Another major critical effort is a volume containing eight articles, *Race and Intelligence*, recently published by the American Anthropological Association (Brace, Gamble and Bond, 1971). Professor H. J. Eysenck's book, *Race, Intelligence, and Education* (published in the United States with the title *The IQ Argument*) is an admirably lucid and readable discussion of the question of race differences in intelligence and its implications for education. The book is especially suited for students and non-professionals who lack the technical background in statistics, measurement theory, and quantitative genetics which are presupposed to some extent by my own writings in this field. For being accurate while avoiding the technical, Eysenck's book is in the best tradition of popular science writing. Probably the most thoughtful and thought-provoking commentary is that by Professor Carl Bereiter (1970) entitled 'Genetics and Educability: Educational Implications of the Jensen Debate'. It is an exceptionally intelligent and penetrating analysis by one of the leading innovators in the education of the disadvantaged. Bereiter concludes:

> One apparently reasonable stance is that the educator need not concern himself with genetics because, in the first place, he is constrained to working with environmental variables and must therefore do the best he can with them, regardless of their relative potency compared to genetic variables; and because, in the second place, education deals with individual children of unknown genetic potential, so that normative data on genetic differences have no application. These are valid points with respect to the work of the teacher in the classroom, for whom genetic principles are most likely to function only as an after-the-fact excuse for educational failures.
>
> At the level of policy, however, education deals with populations rather than with individuals, and it is at this level that genetics becomes potentially relevant. In this paper I have tried to indicate some ways in which genetic considerations can be relevant to educational policy. The mere fact of individual differences in intelligence should encourage us to look for alternative methods of achieving educational objectives that do not rely so heavily upon the abilities represented by IQ. The apparently high heritability of IQ should influence our

expectations as to what may be accomplished through allocation of existing environmental variants: reallocation may produce substantial gains in mean IQ but should not be expected to produce much alteration in the spread of individual differences. The idea of specific heredity-environment interactions suggests the possibility of producing substantial environmental effects on individual differences in intelligence, but it appears that we are a long way from knowing how to produce such effects.

On the matter of social and racial differences, it is probably safe to say that the educational policy-maker need not concern himself with the question of whether these differences have a genetic basis. It is necessary to avoid both the oversimplification that says if there are genetic group differences nothing can be accomplished through educational improvement and the oversimplification that says if group differences in IQ are environmentally caused they can be eliminated by conventional social amelioration. The possibility that cultural differences are related to heredity, however, adds force to the need for schools to come to grips with the problem of providing for cultural pluralism without separatism or segregation. This may well be the major policy problem facing public education in our time (p. 298).

Has any new research appeared since the original publication of the *HER* article in 1969 that would require substantive revision of any of its main points? None has come to my attention, although I have been closely in touch with research in this field. The question is most often raised about the failure of large-scale compensatory education programs, the claim being made that these were evaluated prematurely in 1969. But nothing that has happened since then would warrant any change in the general conclusions about compensatory education which I summarized at that time. In 1969, the largest and best known of the federally sponsored compensatory programs, Head Start, had not yet been officially evaluated, so I was not able to include it in my summary. In 1968, however, the Office of Economic Opportunity (the government agency which administered Head Start) commissioned the Westinghouse Learning Corporation in collaboration with the Ohio State University to make a large-scale study of the effectiveness of Project Head Start. The study was completed in June 1969. The central question of the study was whether the pre-school Head Start program had any appreciable effect on the subsequent scholastic performance of disadvantaged children as contrasted with 'control' children of similar background who had not been exposed to Head Start. The Summer Head Start program showed no positive effects, but the Full-year Head Start showed some positive effect on assessments of school readiness and verbal abilities in the first and second grades. The effects were statistically significant given the large sample sizes, but in absolute terms they were too small to be of any practical educational importance. None of the positive effects approached the magnitude of half a standard deviation above the control samples and at second grade the Head Start children were, on the average, at the 20th percentile on national norms of scholastic achievement (the 50th percentile, of course, being the national average). The Westinghouse evaluation stirred up public controversy and some technical criticisms about details of statistical methodology, but none of the discussion brought forth any evidence which would support conclusions opposite to the essentially negative findings of the Westinghouse Report. (Good technical and evaluative commentaries on the the Westinghouse study of Head Start are to be found in chapters by Professor Sheldon H. White [pp. 163-184] and Professors Donald T. Campbell and Albert Erlebacher [pp. 185-210] in J. Hellmuth (Ed.) *Compensatory Education: A National Debate*. New York: Brunner/Mazel, 1970.)

A common finding in most compensatory programs that have been evaluated, including Head Start, is the subsequent 'fade-out' or 'leveling off' after children leave the program. After six months to a year in regular classes their scholatic performance is generally indistinguishable from that of comparable children who had not been given the compensatory education. An enormous number and variety of compensatory programs have been tried, and many have claimed success, but unfortunately, closer scrutiny usually disproves such claims; they are too often based on subjective impressions and faulty or inadequate evaluation. The U.S. Office of Education, which has funded, literally, thousands of experimental compensatory programs in all parts of the country, recently commissioned the American Institutes for Research in the Behavioral Sciences (AIR) to survey these compensatory programs to determine how many could be deemed a success by rather rigorous criteria. The AIR reviewed 1200 evaluation reports from various compensatory programs for disadvantaged children (over the entire range from pre-school through high school) which had published evaluation reports since January 1968 'which indicated that the program produced cognitive benefits that were statistically and educationally significant'. The results of the AIR study have been summarized as follows (*Report on Education Research*, Washington, D.C., October 27, 1971, pp. 6-7):

Since disadvantaged children generally lag further and further behind their middle-class peers each year, AIR theorized that a successful program would have to produce achievement gains for disadvantaged children which are greater than those of their more advantaged counterparts. Further, this rate of gain would have to be maintained until the disadvantaged children actually caught up. The successful program also had to include a representative sample of not less than thirty children, and achievement gains had to be measured by some reliable testing instrument. Using these criteria AIR narrowed the search to less than 500 programs, and then to 326 who indicated willingness to cooperate in providing data.

Only 3·1 percent of the 326 programs that on the surface appeared to meet our criteria for success were actually found to be successful when subjected to an in-depth analysis,' AIR reported. 'It is not surprising, then, that the success of compensatory education programs is often questioned. One begins to wonder whether the instructional components associated with compensatory education programs are inadequate or whether the fault lies in the evaluation procedures used to determine their effectiveness. Certainly the above results place some of the onus on the people responsible for evaluating compensatory education programs.'

About 21 percent were rejected because they were 'clearly outside the scope' of the AIR study or because their evaluation reports were unavailable or incomplete. The remaining 79 percent were rejected for inadequacies of methodology (42·1 percent) or evaluation (36·8 percent). Under methodology, about 32 percent were rejected simply because they had an inadequate sample of disadvantaged children or because they failed to select or to correctly use adequate measures of cognitive benefit.

Under evaluation, the two most frequent reasons for rejection were statistical and educational significance, said AIR. But more than 13 percent were rejected because they had 'incomplete, totally unclear, or poorly designed evaluations'.

Survivors in the 'new success' category were all from urban areas, possibly because urban school systems generally have their own evaluation departments, notes AIR. Two were pre-school programs using highly structured curricula and serving relatively small groups of children. Six were remedial reading or language arts programs which encompassed several grade levels and considerably more children than the pre-school programs. The remaining two, 'unique among the identified successes', were a beginning reading program for first graders and a program which focused on remediation of learning disorders of elementary and intermediate students.

Since out of the 326 purportedly successful compensatory education programs (selected as the best prospects from among 1200 evaluation reports) only ten held up under careful scrutiny, we are of course left with the question of the statistical significance of the ten studies which met AIR's statistical criteria of success. We know that sampling errors yield a certain small percentage of what appear to be statistically significant results. The only way to tell which of the ten successful programs is genuinely successful, of course, would be to make repeated assessments and to determine if the program's results can be replicated in other school systems and with other personnel. This kind of follow-up is vital if we are to discover the essential characteristics of approaches that might prove beneficial .

It is quite certain by now that further manipulation of the school variables most easily influenced by increased expenditures and administrative fiat stand little chance of appreciably narrowing the achievement gap between children called disadvantaged and those called advantaged. A recent comprehensive survey of the New York City Schools (*New York City School Fact Book*, Institute for Community Studies, Queen's College, New York, 1971) states the following conclusions:

> The evidence we have accumulated is somewhat surprising. We have recorded traditional variables that supposedly affect the quality of learning: class size, school expenditure, pupil/teacher ratio, condition of building, teacher experience, and the like. Yet there seems to be no direct relationship between these school measurements and performance. Schools that have exceptionally small class registers, staffed with experienced teachers, spend more money per pupil, and possess modern facilities do not reflect exceptional academic competence. Nor has the More Effective Schools Program – a saturation services compensatory education program of high cost – shown any noteworthy

results in the year's tabulations. Of 21 schools measured in the MES program, pupils in only four, mostly middle-class white, read on grade level.

In order to corroborate our findings on the lack of influence of these schools variables, we selected a random sample of 20 schools, 10 predominantly white middle-class and 10 predominantly black schools. In examining the differences and similarities, we noticed the large disparity between [these two groups of schools in] academic achievement and pupil performance. Again, as with all the statistics, variables such as the size of the class, or amount of money spent on a pupil's education, did not affect performance. . . . We are faced with the question that the variables we have been accustomed to measuring are not the ones that should be studied.

A recent development in compensatory education is known as 'performance contracting'. Private business firms specializing in the application of various new instructional programs and technologies intended to produce greater than the usual gains in the scholastic achievements of disadvantaged children are contracted by a public school system to manage all or some part of the school's instructional program. The firm is paid according to pupil performance, for example, receiving compensation only for those children whose achievement gains per year in school, as assessed by objective tests, are equal to at least the average of national norms. Early reports of these efforts in the popular press were extremely optimistic; it appeared that private enterprise and the vigorous application of new technology to instruction had finally succeeded where government-financed compensatory programs had so overwhelmingly failed. A recent study of these programs, conducted by a private research organization, was commissioned by the U.S. Department of Health, Education, and Welfare. Eight different 'performance contracting' programs in various parts of the country, involving some 3400 pupils were assessed. It was found that the underprivileged pupils on the average scored no better on standardized achievement tests than similar children in regular classes. The average monthly gain in reading, for example, was about 80 percent of the national norm, which is typical for children in poverty-area schools. The gains in mathematics averaged about the same. In brief, thus far no new instructional program has been discovered which, when applied on a large scale, has appreciably raised the scholastic achievement of disadvantaged children in relation to the majority of the school population.

Such evidence can mean a counsel of despair only to the extent that we cling to the belief that equality of educational opportunity or equality of environmental advantages should necessarily lead to equality of performance. This, I believe, is proving to be a false hope. It is the responsibility of scientific research in genetics, psychology, and education to determine the basis for realistic solutions to the problems of universal public education. Though it may be premature to prescribe at present, I venture the prediction that future solutions will take the form not so much of attempting to minimize differences in scholastic aptitudes and motivation but of creating a greater diversity of curricula, instructional methods, and educational goals and values that will make it possible for children ranging over a wider spectrum of abilities and proclivities genuinely to benefit from their years in school. The current zeitgeist of environmentalist·egalitarianism has all but completely stifled our thinking along these lines. And I believe the magnitude and urgency of the problem are such as to call for quite radical thinking if the educational system is truly to serve the whole of society. We have invested so much for so long in trying to equalize scholastic performance that we have given little or no thought to finding ways of diversifying schools to make them rewarding to everyone while not attempting to equalize everyone's performance in a common curriculum. Recommendations have almost always taken the form of asking what next we might try to make children who in the present school system do not flourish academically become more like those who do. The emphasis has been more on changing children than on revamping the system. A philosophy of equalization, however laudable its ideals, cannot work if it is based on false premises, and no amount of propaganda can make it appear to work. Its failures will be forced upon everyone. Educational pluralism of some sort, encompassing a variety of very different educational curricula and goals, will I think, be the inevitable outcome of the growing realization that the schools are not going to eliminate human differences. Rather than making over a large segment of the school population so they will not be doomed to failure in a largely antiquated elitist-oriented educational system which originally evolved to serve only a relatively small segment of society, the educational system will have to be revamped in order to benefit everyone who is required by the society to attend schools. It seems incredible that a system can still survive which virtually guarantees frustration and failure for a large proportion of the children it should intend to serve. From all the indications, public education in such a form will not much longer survive.

But we should not fail to recognize that to propose radical diversity in accord with individual differences in abilities and interests, as contrasted with uniformity of educational treatment, puts society between Scylla and Charybdis in terms of insuring for all individuals equality of opportunity for the diversity of educational paths. The surest way to maximize the benefits of schooling to all individuals and at the same time to make the most of a society's human resources is to insure equality of educational opportunity for all its members. Monolithic educational goals and uniformity of approaches guarantees unnecessary frustration and defeat for many. On the other hand, educational pluralism runs the risk that social, economic, ethnic background or geographic origin, rather than each child's own characteristics, might determine the educational paths available to him. The individual characteristics appropriate for any one of a variety of educational paths and goals are to be found everywhere, in every social stratum, ethnic group, and neighborhood. Academic aptitudes and special talents should be cultivated wherever they are found, and a wise society will take all possible measures to insure this to the greatest possible extent. At the same time, those who are poor in the traditional academic aptitudes cannot be left by the wayside. Suitable means and goals must be found for making their years of schooling rewarding to them, if not in the usual academic sense, then in ways that can better their chances for socially useful and self-fulfilling roles as adults.

Two additional books, to be published in the near future, will follow this collection of articles. These other books deal with special aspects of the issues raised in the present volume. The first, *Educability and Group Differences*, is an entirely new work concerned with the issues involved in various population differences in educational aptitudes. It is a book-length treatment of those parts of my *HER* article which were generally regarded as the most controversial and which, in terms of solving our educational problems, are probably the most important to examine in detail. The second, *Educational Differences*, is a collection of my articles written since the *HER* article which deal with various psychological and educational aspects of individual differences. These volumes together with the present one will, I believe, provide important grist for future research and innovation in educational psychology.

*January*, 1972                    Arthur R. Jensen

*Institute of Human Learning*
*University of California*
*Berkeley, California*

# How Much Can We Boost IQ and Scholastic Achievement?

## The Failure of Compensatory Education

Compensatory education has been tried and it apparently has failed.

Compensatory education has been practiced on a massive scale for several years in many cities across the nation. It began with auspicious enthusiasm and high hopes of educators. It had unprecedented support from Federal funds. It had theoretical sanction from social scientists espousing the major underpinning of its rationale: the 'deprivation hypothesis', according to which academic lag is mainly the result of social, economic, and educational deprivation and discrimination – an hypothesis that has met with wide, uncritical acceptance in the atmosphere of society's growing concern about the plight of minority groups and the economically disadvantaged.

The chief goal of compensatory education – to remedy the educational lag of disadvantaged children and thereby narrow the achievement gap between 'minority' and 'majority' pupils – has been utterly unrealized in any of the large compensatory education programs that have been evaluated so far. On the basis of a nationwide survey and evaluation of compensatory education programs, the United States Commission on Civil Rights (1967) came to the following conclusion:

> The Commission's analysis does not suggest that compensatory education is incapable of remedying the effects of poverty on the academic achievement of individual children. There is little question that school programs involving expenditures for cultural enrichment, better teaching, and other needed educational services can be helpful

69

to disadvantaged children. The fact remains, however, that none of the programs appear to have raised significantly the achievement of participating pupils, as a group, within the period evaluated by the Commission (p. 138).

The Commission's review gave special attention to compensatory education in majority-Negro schools whose programs 'were among the most prominent and included some that have served as models for others'. The Commission states: 'A principal objective of each was to raise the academic achievement of disadvantaged children. Judged by this standard the programs did not show evidence of much success' (p. 138).[1]

Why has there been such uniform failure of compensatory programs wherever they have been tried? What has gone wrong? In other fields, when bridges do not stand, when aircraft do not fly, when machines do not work, when treatments do not cure, despite all conscientious efforts on the part of many persons to make them do so, one begins to question the basic assumptions, principles, theories, and hypotheses that guide one's efforts. Is it time to follow suit in education?

The theory that has guided most of these compensatory education programs, sometimes explicitly, sometimes implicitly, has two main complementary facets: one might be called the 'average children concept', the other the 'social deprivation hypothesis'.

The 'average children' concept is essentially the belief that all children, except for a rare few born with severe neurological defects, are basically very much alike in their mental development and

[1] Some of the largest and most highly publicized programs of compensatory education that have been held up as models but which produced absolutely no significant improvement in the scholastic achievement of disadvantaged students are: the *Banneker Project* in St Louis (8 years), *Higher Horizons* in New York (5 years), More Effective Schools in New York (3 years), and large-scale programs in Syracuse, Seattle, Philadelphia, Berkeley, and a score of other cities (for detailed reports see U.S. Commission on Civil Rights, 1967, pp. 115-140).

Reports on Project Head Start indicate that initial gains of 5 to 10 points in IQ on conventional intelligence tests are a common finding, but this gain usually does not hold up through the first year of regular schooling. More positive claims for the efficacy of Head Start involve evidence of the detection of medical disabilities in disadvantaged pre-school children and the reportedly favorable effects of the program on children's self-confidence, motivation, and attitudes toward school.

capabilities, and that their apparent differences in these characteristics as manifested in school are due to rather superficial differences in children's upbringing at home, their pre-school and out-of-school experiences, motivations and interests, and the educational influences of their family background. All children are viewed as basically more or less homogeneous, but are seen to differ in school performance because when they are out of school they learn or fail to learn certain things that may either help them or hinder them in their school work. If all children could be treated more alike early enough, long before they come to school, then they could all learn from the teacher's instruction at about the same pace and would all achieve at much the same level, presumably at the 'average' or above on the usual grade norms.

The 'social deprivation hypothesis' is the allied belief that those children of ethnic minorities and the economically poor who achieve 'below average' in school do so mainly because they begin school lacking certain crucial experiences which are prerequisites for school learning – perceptual, attentional, and verbal skills, as well as the self-confidence, self-direction, and teacher-oriented attitudes conducive to achievement in the classroom. And they lack the parental help and encouragement needed to promote academic achievement throughout their schooling. The chief aim of pre-school and compensatory programs, therefore, is to make up for these environmental lacks as quickly and intensively as possible by providing the assumedly appropriate experiences, cultural enrichment, and training in basic skills of the kind presumably possessed by middle-class 'majority' children of the same age.

The success of the effort is usually assessed in one or both of two ways: by gains in IQ and in scholastic achievement. The common emphasis on gains in IQ is probably attributable to the fact that it can be more efficiently 'measured' than scholastic achievement, especially if there is no specific 'achievement' to begin with. The IQ test can be used at the very beginning of Headstart, kindergarten, or first grade as a 'pre-test' against which to assess 'post-test' gains. IQ gains, if they occur at all, usually occur rapidly, while achievement is a long-term affair. And probably most important, the IQ is commonly interpreted as indicative of a more general kind of intellectual ability than is reflected by the acquisition of specific scholastic knowledge and skills. Since the IQ is known to predict scholastic performance better than any other single measurable attribute of the child, it is believed, whether rightly or wrongly, that if the child's IQ can be appreciably raised, academic achievement by and large will take care of itself, given normal motivation and standard instruction. Children with average or above-average IQs generally do well in school without much special attention. So the remedy deemed logical for children who would do poorly in school is to boost their IQs up to where they can perform like the majority – in short to make them all at least 'average children'. Stated so bluntly, the remedy may sound rather grim, but this is in fact essentially what we are attempting in our special programs of pre-school enrichment and compensatory education. This simple theme, with only slight embellishments, can be found repeated over and over again in the vast recent literature on the psychology and education of children called culturally disadvantaged.

*So here is where our diagnosis should begin – with the concept of the IQ: how it came to be what it is; what it 'really' is; what makes it vary from one individual to another; what can change it, and by what amount.*

## The Nature of Intelligence

The nature of intelligence is one of the vast topics in psychology. It would be quite impossible to attempt to review here the main theoretical issues and currents of thought in this field. Large volumes have been written on the subject (e.g., Stoddard, 1943; Guilford, 1967), to say nothing of the countless articles. An enlightening brief account of the history of the concept of intelligence has been presented by Sir Cyril Burt (1968). The term 'intelligence', as used by psychologists, is itself of fairly recent origin. Having been introduced as a technical term in psychology near the turn of the century, it has since filtered down into common parlance, and therefore some restriction and clarification of the term as it will be used in the following discussion is called for.

Disagreements and arguments can perhaps be forestalled if we take an operational stance. First of all, this means that probably the most important fact about intelligence is that we can measure it. Intelligence, like electricity, is easier to measure than to define. And if the measurements bear some systematic relationships to other

data, it means we can make meaningful statements about the phenomenon we are measuring. There is no point in arguing the question
to which there is no answer, the question of what intelligence *really*
is. The best we can do is to obtain measurements of certain kinds of
behavior and look at their relationships to other phenomena and see
if these relationships make any kind of sense and order. It is from
these orderly relationships that we can gain some understanding of
the phenomena.

But how did the instruments by which we measure intelligence
come about in the first place? The first really useful test of intelligence and the progenitor of nearly all present-day intelligence tests
was the Metrical Scale of Intelligence devised in 1905 by Binet and
Simon. A fact of great but often unrealized implications is that the
Binet-Simon test was commissioned by the Minister of Public
Instruction in Paris for the explicit purpose of identifying children
who were likely to fail in school. It was decided they should be
placed in special schools or classes before losing too much ground
or receiving too much discouragement. To the credit of Binet and
Simon, the test served this purpose quite well, and it is now regarded
as one of the major 'breakthroughs' in the history of psychology.
Numerous earlier attempts to devise intelligence tests were much
less successful from a practical standpoint, mainly because the
kinds of functions tested were decided upon in terms of early
theoretical notions about the basic elements of 'mind' and the 'brass
instrument' laboratory techniques for measuring these elemental
functions of consciousness, which were then thought to consist of
the capacity for making fine sensory discriminations in the various
sensory modalities. Although these measurements were sufficiently
reliable, they bore little relationship to any 'real life' or 'common
sense' criteria of behavior ranging along a 'dull' – 'bright' continuum. The psychological sagacity of Binet and Simon as test
constructors derived largely from their intimate knowledge and
observation of the behavior of young children and of what, precisely,
teachers expected of them in school. Binet and Simon noted the
characteristics distinguishing those children described by their
teachers as 'bright' from those described as 'dull', and, from these
observations and considerable trial-and-error, they were finally
able to make up a graded series of test items that not only agreed with
teachers' judgments of children's scholastic capabilities but could

make the discriminations more finely and more accurately than any single teacher could do without prolonged observation of the child in class. The Binet-Simon scale has since undergone many revisions and improvements, and today, in the form developed by Terman, known as the Stanford-Binet Intelligence Scale, it is generally regarded as the standard for the measurement of intelligence.

But the important point I wish to emphasize here is that these Binet tests, and in effect all their descendants, had their origin in the educational setting of the Paris schools of 1900, and the various modifications and refinements they have undergone since then have been implicitly shaped by the educational traditions of Europe and North America. The content and methods of instruction represented in this tradition, it should be remembered, are a rather narrow and select sample of all the various forms of human learning and of the ways of imparting knowledge and skills. The instructional methods of the traditional classroom were not invented all in one stroke, but evolved within an upper-class segment of the European population, and thus were naturally shaped by the capacities, culture, and needs of those children whom the schools were primarily intended to serve. At least implicit in the system as it originally developed was the expectation that not all children would succeed. These methods of schooling have remained essentially unchanged for many generations. We have accepted traditional instruction so completely that it is extremely difficult even to imagine, much less to put into practice, any radically different forms that the education of children could take. Our thinking almost always takes as granted such features as beginning formal instruction at the same age for all children (universally between ages five and six), instruction of children in groups, keeping the same groups together in lock step fashion through the first several years of schooling, and an active-passive, showing-seeing, telling-listening relationship between teacher and pupils. Satisfactory learning occurs under these conditions only when children come to school with certain prerequisite abilities and skills: an attention span long enough to encompass the teacher's utterances and demonstrations, the ability voluntarily to focus one's attention where it is called for, the ability to comprehend verbal utterances and to grasp relationships between things and their symbolic representations, the ability to inhibit large-muscle activity and engage in covert 'mental' activity, to repeat instruction to one-self, to persist in a task until a self-determined standard is attained – in short, the ability to engage in what might be called self-instructional activities, without which group instruction alone remains ineffectual.

The interesting fact is that, despite all the criticisms that can easily be levelled at the educational system, the traditional forms of instruction have actually worked quite well for the majority of children. And the tests that were specifically devised to distinguish those children least apt to succeed in this system have also proved to do their job quite well. The Stanford-Binet and similar intelligence tests predict various measures of scholastic achievement with an average validity coefficient of about 0·5 to 0·6, and in longitudinal data comprising intelligence test and achievement measures on the same children over a number of years, the multiple correlation between intelligence and scholastic achievement is almost as high as the reliability of the measures will permit.

THE GENERALITY AND LIMITATIONS OF INTELLIGENCE

If the content and instructional techniques of education had been markedly different from what they were in the beginning and, for the most part, continue to be, it is very likely that the instruments we call intelligence tests would also have assumed a quite different character. They might have developed in such a way as to measure a quite different constellation of abilities, and our conception of the nature of intelligence, assuming we still called it by that name, would be correspondingly different. This is why I think it so important to draw attention to the origins of intelligence testing.

But in granting that the measurement and operational definitions of intelligence had their origins in a school setting and were intended primarily for scholastic purposes, one should not assume that intelligence tests measure *only* school learning or cultural advantages making for scholastic success and fail to tap anything of fundamental psychological importance. The notion is sometimes expressed that psychologists have mis-aimed with their intelligence tests. Although the tests may predict scholastic performance, it is said, they do not *really* measure intelligence – as if somehow the 'real thing' has eluded measurement and perhaps always will. But this is a misconception. We *can* measure intelligence. As the late Professor Edwin G. Boring pointed out, intelligence, by definition, is what intelligence tests measure. The trouble comes only when we attribute more to 'intelligence' and to our measurements of it than do the psychologists who use the concept in its proper sense.

The idea of intelligence has justifiably grown considerably beyond its scholastic connotations. Techniques of measurement not at all resembling the tasks of the Binet scale and in no way devised with the idea of predicting scholastic performance can also measure approximately the same intelligence as measured by the Binet scale. The English psychologist, Spearman, devoted most of his distinguished career to studying the important finding that almost any and every test involving any kind of complex mental activity correlates positively and substantially with any and every other test involving complex mental activity, regardless of the specific content or sensory modality of the test. Spearman noted that if the tests called for the operation of 'higher mental processes', as opposed to sheer sensory acuity, reflex behavior, or the execution of established habits, they showed positive intercorrelations, although the tests bore no superficial resemblance to one another. They might consist of abstract figures involving various spatial relationships, or numerical problems, or vocabulary, or verbal analogies. For example, a vocabulary test shows correlations in the range of 0·50 to 0·60 with a test that consists of copying sets of designs with colored blocks; and a test of general information correlates about 0·50 with a test that involves wending through a printed maze with a pencil. Countless examples of such positive correlations between seemingly quite different tests can be found in the literature on psychological tests. Spearman made them the main object of his study. To account for the intercorrelations of 'mental' tests, he hypothesized the existence of a single factor common to all tests involving complex mental processes. All such tests measure this common factor to some degree, which accounts for the intercorrelations among all the tests. Spearman called the common factor 'general intelligence' or simply $g$. And he invented the method known as factor analysis to determine the amount of $g$ in any particular test. He and his students later developed tests, like Raven's Progressive Matrices and Cattell's Culture Fair Tests of $g$, which measure $g$ in nearly pure form. We should not reify $g$ as an entity, of course, since it is only a hypothetical construct intended to explain covariation among tests. It is a hypothetical source of variance (individual differences) in test scores. It can be regarded as the nuclear operational definition of intelligence, and when the term intelligence is used it should refer to *g*, the factor common to all tests of complex problem solving.

In examining those tests most heavily loaded with *g*, Spearman characterized the mental processes which they seemed to involve as 'the ability to educe relations and correlates' – that is, to be able to see the general from the particular and the particular as an instance of the general. A similar definition of intelligence was expressed by Aquinas, as 'the ability to combine and separate' – to see the difference between things which seem similar and to see the similarities between things which seem different. These are essentially the processes of abstraction and conceptualization. Tasks which call for problem solving requiring these processes are usually the best measures of *g*. Despite numerous theoretical attacks on Spearman's basic notion of a general factor, *g* has stood like a rock of Gibraltar in psychometrics, defying any attempt to construct a test of complex problem solving which excludes it.

Standard intelligence scales such as the Binet and the Wechsler are composed of a dozen or so subtests which differ obviously in their superficial appearance: vocabulary, general information, memory span for digits, block designs, figure copying, mazes, form boards, and so on. When the intercorrelations among a dozen or more such tests are subjected to a factor analysis principal or components analysis, some 50 percent or more of the total individual differences variance in all the tests is usually found to be attributable to a general factor common to all the tests. Thus, when we speak of intelligence it is this general factor, rather than any single test, that we should keep in mind.

Attempts to assess age differences in intelligence or mental development which rely on complex techniques that bear little formal resemblance to the usual intelligence tests still manage to measure *g* more than anything else. Piaget's techniques for studying mental growth, for example, are based largely on the child's development of the concepts of invariance and conservation of certain properties – number, area, and volume. When a large variety of Piaget tasks are factor analyzed along with standard psychometric tests, including the Stanford-Binet and Raven's Progressive Matrices, is it found that the Piaget tasks are loaded on the general factor to about the same extent as the psychometric tests (Vernon, 1965). That is to say, children fall into much the same rank order of ability on all these cognitive tests. Tuddenham (1968) has developed a psychometric scale of intelligence based entirely upon Piaget's theory of cognitive development. The test makes use of ten of the techniques developed by Piaget for studying conservation, seriation, reversal of perspective, and so on. Performance on these tasks shows about the same relationship to social class and race differences as is generally found with the Stanford-Binet and Wechsler scales. It seems evident that what we call general intelligence can be manifested in many forms and thus permits measurement by a wide variety of techniques. The common feature of all such intercorrelated tests seems to be their requirement of some form of 'reasoning' on the part of the subject – some active, but usually covert, transformation or manipulation of the 'input' (the problem) in order to arrive at the 'output' (the answer).

The conceptually most pure and simple instance of this key aspect of intelligence is displayed in the phenomenon known as cross-modal transfer. This occurs when a person to whom some particular stimulus is exposed in one sensory modality can then recognize the same stimulus (or its essential features) in a different sensory modality. For example, show a person a number of differently shaped wooden blocks, then point to one, blindfold the person, shuffle the blocks, and let the person find the indicated block by using his sense of touch. Or 'write' in bold strokes any letter of the alphabet between a child's shoulder blades. It will be a completely unique stimulus input for the child, never encountered before and never directly conditioned to any verbal response. Yet, most children, provided they already know the alphabet, will be able to name the letter. There are no direct neural connections between the visual and the tactile impressions of the stimulus, and, although the child's naming of the letter has been conditioned to the visual stimulus, the tactile stimulus has been associated with neither the visual stimulus nor the verbal response. How does the child manage to show the cross-modal transfer? Some central symbolic or 'cognitive' processing mechanism is involved, which can abstract and compare properties of 'new' experiences with 'old' experiences and thereby invest the 'new' with meaning and relevance. Intelligence is essentially characterized by this process.

## IS *g* UNITARY OR DIVISIBLE?

It is only when the concept of *g* is attributed meaning above and beyond that derived from the factor analytic procedures from which it gains its strict technical meaning that we run into the needless argument over whether *g* is a unitary ability or a conglomerate of many subabilities, each of which could be measured independently. We should think of *g* as a 'source' of individual differences in scores which is common to a number of different tests. As the tests change, the nature of *g* will also change, and a test which is loaded, say, 0·50 on *g* when factor analyzed among one set of tests may have a loading of 0·20 or 0·80, or some other value, when factor analyzed among other sets of tests. Also, a test which, in one factor analysis, measures only *g* and nothing else, may show that it measures *g* and one or more other factors when factor analyzed in connection with a new set of tests. In other words, *g* gains its meaning from the tests which have it in common. Furthermore, no matter how simple or 'unitary' a test may appear to be, it is almost always possible to further fractionate the individual differences variance into smaller subfactors. I have been doing this in my laboratory with respect to a very simple and seemingly 'unitary' ability, namely, digit span (Jensen, 1967b). Changing the rate of digit presentation changes the rank order of subjects in their ability to recall the digits. So, too, does interposing a 10-second delay between presentation and recall, and interpolating various distractions ('retroactive inhibition') between presentation and recall, and many other procedural variations of the digit span paradigm. Many – but, significantly, not all – of these kinds of manipulations introduce new dimensions or factors of individual differences. It is likely that when we finally get down to the irreducible 'atoms' of memory span ability, so to speak, if we ever do get there, the elements that make up memory span ability will not themselves even resemble what we think of as abilities in the usual sense of the term. And so probably the same would be true not only for digit span, but for any of the subtests or items that make up intelligence tests.

A simple analogy in the physical realm may help to make this clear. If we are interested in measuring general athletic ability, we can devise a test consisting of running, ball throwing, batting, jumping, weight lifting, and so on. We can obtain a 'score' on each one of these and the total for any individual is his 'general athletic ability' score. This score would correspond to the general intelligence score yielded by tests like the Stanford-Binet and the Wechsler scales.

Or we can go a step further in the refinement of our test procedure and intercorrelate the scores on all these physical tasks, factor analyze the intercorrelations, and examine the general factor, if indeed there is one. Assuming there is, we would call it 'general athletic ability'. It would mean that on all of the tasks, persons who excelled on one also tended to be superior on the others. And we would note that some tasks were more 'loaded' with this general factor than others. We would then weight the subtest scores in proportion to their loading on $g$ and then add them up. The total, in effect, is a 'factor score', and gives us a somewhat more justifiable measure of 'general athletic ability', since it represents the one source of variation that all the athletic skills in our test battery share in common.

To go still further, let us imagine that the running test has the highest loading on $g$ in this analysis. To make the issue clear-cut, let us say that all its variance is attributable to the $g$ factor. Does this mean that running ability is not further analyzable into other components? *No, it simply means that the components into which running can be analyzed are not separately or independently manifested in either the running test or the other tests in the battery.* But we can measure these components of running ability independently, if we wish to: total leg length, the ratio of upper to lower leg length, strength of leg muscles, physical endurance, 'wind' or vital capacity, ratio of body height to weight, degree of mesomorphic body build, specific skills such as starting speed – all are positively correlated with running speed. And it we intercorrelate these measures and factor analyze the correlations, we would probably find a substantial general factor common to all these physical attributes, name it what you will. We would combine the measures on these various physical traits into a weighted composite score which would predict running ability as measured by the time the person takes to cross the finish line. The situation seems very similar to the analysis of the psychological processes that make up 'general intelligence'.

FLUID AND CRYSTALLIZED INTELLIGENCE

Raymond B. Cattell (1963) has made a conceptually valid distinction between two aspects of intelligence, *fluid* and *crystallized*. Standard intelligence tests generally measure both the fluid and crystallized components of *g*, and, since the two are usually highly correlated in a population whose members to a large extent share a common background of experience, culture, and education, the fluid and crystallized components may not always be clearly discernible as distinct factors. Conceptually, however, the distinction is useful and can be supported empirically under certain conditions. *Fluid* intelligence is the capacity for new conceptual learning and problem solving, a general 'brightness' and adaptability, relatively independent of education and experience, which can be invested in the particular opportunities for learning encountered by the individual in accord with his motivations and interests. Tests that measure mostly fluid intelligence are those that minimize cultural and scholastic content. Cattell's Culture Fair Tests and Raven's Progressive Matrices are good examples. *Crystallized* intelligence, in contrast, is a precipitate out of experience, consisting of acquired knowledge and developed intellectual skills. Fluid and crystallized intelligence are naturally correlated in a population sharing a common culture, because the acquisition of knowledge and skills in the first place depends upon fluid intelligence. While fluid intelligence attains its maximum level in the late teens and may even begin to decline gradually shortly thereafter, crystallized intelligence continues to increase gradually with the individual's learning and experience all the way up to old age.

OCCUPATIONAL CORRELATES OF INTELLIGENCE

Intelligence, as we are using the term, has relevance considerably beyond the scholastic setting. This is so partly because there is an intimate relationship between a society's occupational structure and its educational system. Whether we like it or not, the educational system is one of society's most powerful mechanisms for sorting out children to assume different roles in the occupational hierarchy.

The evidence for a hierarchy of occupational prestige and desirability is unambiguous. Let us consider three sets of numbers.[1] First

---

[1] I am indebted to Professor Otis Dudley Duncan (1968, pp. 80-100) for providing this information.

the Barr scale of occupations, devised in the early 1920s, provides one set of data. Lists of 120 representative occupations, each definitely and concretely described, were given to 30 psychological judges who were asked to rate the occupations on a scale from 0 to 100 according to the grade of intelligence each occupation was believed to require for ordinary success. Second, in 1964, the National Opinion Research Center (NORC), by taking a large public opinion poll, obtained ratings of the *prestige* of a great number of occupations; these prestige ratings represent the average standing of each occupation relative to all the others in the eyes of the general public. Third, a rating of socioeconomic status (SES) is provided by the *1960 Census of Population: Classified Index of Occupations and Industries*, which assigns to each of the hundreds of listed occupations a score ranging from 0 to 96 as a composite index of the average income and educational level prevailing in the occupation.

The interesting point is the set of correlations among these three independently derived occupational ratings.

The Barr scale and the NORC ratings are correlated 0·91.

The Barr scale and the SES index are correlated 0·81.

The NORC ratings and the SES index are correlated 0·90.

In other words, psychologists' concept of the 'intelligence demands' of an occupation (Barr scale) is very much like the general public's concept of the prestige or 'social standing' of an occupation (NORC ratings), and both are closely related to an independent measure of the educational and economic status of the persons pursuing an occupation (SES index). As O. D. Duncan (1968, pp. 90-91) concludes, '. . . "intelligence" is a socially defined quality and this social definition is not essentially different from that of achievement or status in the occupational sphere. . . . When psychologists came to propose operational counterparts to the notion of intelligence, or to devise measures thereof, they wittingly or unwittingly looked for indicators of capability to function in the system of key roles in the society.' Duncan goes on to note, 'Our argument tends to imply that a correlation between IQ and occupational achievement was more or less built into IQ tests, by virtue of the psychologists' implicit acceptance of the social standards of the general populace. Had the first IQ tests been devised in a hunting culture, "general intelligence" might well have turned out to involve visual acuity and running speed, rather than vocabulary and symbol manipulation. As it was, the concept of intelligence arose in a society where high status accrued to occupations involving the latter in large measure, so that what we now *mean* by intelligence is something like the probability of acceptable performance (given the opportunity) in occupations varying in social status.'

So we see that the prestige hierarchy of occupations is a reliable objective reality in our society. To this should be added the fact that there is undoubtedly some relationship between the levels of the hierarchy and the occupations' intrinsic interest, desirability, or gratification to the individuals engaged in them. Even if all occupations paid alike and received equal respect and acclaim, some occupations would still be viewed as more desirable than others, which would make for competition, selection, and, again, a kind of prestige hierarchy. Most persons would agree that painting pictures is more satisfying than painting barns, and conducting a symphony orchestra is more exciting than directing traffic. We have to face it: the assortment of persons into occupational roles simply is not 'fair' in any absolute sense. The best we can ever hope for is that true merit, given equality of opportunity, act as the basis for the natural assorting process.

## CORRELATION BETWEEN INTELLIGENCE AND OCCUPATIONAL ACHIEVEMENT

Because intelligence is only one of a number of qualities making for merit in any given occupation, and since most occupations will tolerate a considerable range of abilities and criteria of passable performance, it would be surprising to find a very high correlation between occupational level and IQ. Although the rank order of the *mean* IQs of occupational groups is about as highly correlated with the occupations' standing on the three 'prestige' ratings mentioned above as the ratings are correlated among themselves, there is a considerable dispersion of IQs *within* occupations. The IQ spread increases as one moves down the scale from more to less skilled occupations (Tyler, 1965, pp. 338-339). Thus, the correlation, for example, between scores on the Army General Classification Test, a kind of general intelligence test, and status ratings of the civilian occupations of 18,782 white enlisted men in World War II was only 0·42. Since these were mostly young men, many of whom had not yet completed their education or established their career lines, the correlation of 0·42 is lower than one would expect in the civilian population. Data obtained by the U.S. Employment Service in a civilian population shows a correlation of 0·55 between intelligence and occupational status, a value which, not surprisingly is close to the average correlation between intelligence and scholastic achievement (Duncan, *et al.*, 1968, pp. 98-101). Although these figures are based on the largest samples reported in the literature and are therefore probably the most reliable statistics, they are not as high as the correlations found in some other studies. Two studies found, for example, that IQs of school boys correlated 0·57 and 0·71 with their occupational status 14 and 19 years later, respectively (Tyler, 1965, p. 343). It is noteworthy that the longer interval showed the higher correlation.

Duncan's (1968) detailed analysis of the nature of the relationship between intelligence and occupational status led him to the conclusion that 'the bulk of the influence of intelligence on occupation is indirect, via education'. If the correlation of intelligence with education and of education with occupation is, in effect, 'partialled out', the remaining 'direct' correlation between intelligence and occupation is almost negligible. But Duncan points out that this same type of analysis (technically known as 'path coefficients analysis') also reveals the interesting and significant finding that intelligence plays a relatively important part as a cause of differential *earnings*. Duncan concludes: '. . . men with the same schooling and in the same line of work are differentially rewarded in terms of mental ability' (1968, p. 118).

CORRELATIONS BETWEEN INTELLIGENCE AND
JOB PERFORMANCE WITHIN OCCUPATIONS

Intelligence, via education, has its greatest effect in the assorting of individuals into occupational roles. Once they are in those roles, the importance of intelligence *per se* is less marked. Ghiselli (1955) found that intelligence tests correlate on the average in the range of 0·20 to 0·25 with ratings of actual proficiency on the job. The speed and ease of training for various occupational skills, however, show correlations with intelligence averaging about 0·50, which is four to five times the predictive power that the same tests have in relation to work proficiency *after* training. This means that, once the training hurdle has been surmounted, many factors besides intelligence are largely involved in success on the job. This is an important fact to keep in mind at later points in this article.

## IS INTELLIGENCE 'FIXED'?

Since the publication of J. McV. Hunt's well-known and influential book, *Intelligence and Experience* (1961), the notion of 'fixed intelligence' has assumed the status of a popular cliché among many speakers and writers on intelligence, mental retardation, cultural disadvantage, and the like, who state, often with an evident sense of virtue and relief, that modern psychology has overthrown the 'belief in fixed intelligence'. This particular bugaboo seems to have loomed up largely in the imaginations of those who find such great satisfaction in the idea that 'fixed intelligence' has been demolished once and for all.

Actually, there has been nothing much to demolish. When we look behind the rather misleading term 'fixed intelligence', what we find are principally two real and separate issues, each calling for empirical study rather than moral philosophizing. Both issues lend themselves to empirical investigation and have long been subjects of intensive study. The first issue concerns the genetic basis of individual differences in intelligence; the second concerns the stability or constancy of the IQ throughout the individual's lifetime.

*Genotype and Phenotype.* Geneticists have avoided confusion and polemics about the issue of whether or not a given trait is 'fixed' by asking the right question in the first place: how much of the variation (i.e., individual differences) in a particular trait or characteristic that we observe or measure (i.e., the *phenotype*) in a given population can we account for in terms of variation in the genetic factors (i.e., the *genotype*) affecting the development of the characteristic?

The genetic factors are completely laid down when the parental sperm and ovum unite. Thus the individual's genotype, by definition, is 'fixed' at the moment of conception. Of course, different potentials of the genotype may be expressed at different times in the course of the individual's development. But beyond conception, whatever we observe or measure of the organism is a phenotype, and this, by definition, is *not* 'fixed'. The phenotype is a result of the organism's internal genetic mechanisms established at conception and all the physical and social influences that impinge on the organism throughout the course of its development. Intelligence is a phenotype, not a genotype, so the argument about whether or not intelligence is 'fixed' is seen to be spurious.

The really interesting and important question, which can be empirically answered by the methods of quantitative genetics, is: what is the correlation between genotypes and phenotypes at any given point in development? For continuous or metrical characteristics such as height and intelligence, the correlation, of course, can assume any value between 0 and 1. The square of the correlation between genotype and phenotype is technically known as the *heritability* of the characteristic, a concept which is discussed more fully in a later section.

*The Stability of Intelligence Measures.* The second aspect of the issue of 'fixed intelligence' concerns the stability of intelligence measurements throughout the course of the individual's development. Since intelligence test scores are not points on an absolute scale of measurement like height and weight, but only indicate the individual's relative standing with reference to a normative population, the question we must ask is: To what extent do individuals maintain their standing relative to one another in measured intelligence over the course of time? The answer is to be found in the correlation between intelligence test scores on a group of persons at two points in time. Bloom (1964) has reviewed the major studies of this question and the evidence shows considerable consistency.

In surveying all the correlations reported in the literature between intelligence measured on the same individuals at two points in time, I have worked out a simple formula that gives a 'best fit' to all these data. The formula has the virtue of a simple mnemonic, being much easier to remember than all the tables of correlations reported in the literature and yet being capable of reproducing the correlations with a fair degree of accuracy.

$$\hat{r}_{12} = r_{tt} \sqrt{\frac{CA_1}{CA_2}} \tag{1}$$

where $\hat{r}_{12}$ = the estimated correlation between tests given at times 1 and 2.

$r_{tt}$ = the equivalent-forms or immediate test-retest reliability of the test.

$CA_1$ = the subject's chronological age at the time of the first
test.

$CA_2$ = the subject's chronological age at the time of the
second test.

*Limitation:* The formula holds only up to the point where $CA_2$ is
age 10, at which time the empirical value of $r_{12}$ approaches an
asymptote, showing no appreciable increase thereafter. Beyond age
10, regardless of the interval between tests, the obtained test-retest
correlations fall in the range between the test's reliability and the
square of the reliability (i.e., $r_{tt} > r_{12} > r^2_{tt}$). These simple generalizations are intended simply as a means of summarizing the mass of
empirical findings. They accord with Bloom's conclusion, based on
his thorough survey of the published evidence, that beyond age 8,
correlations between repeated tests of general intelligence, corrected
for unreliability of measurement, are between $+0.90$ and unity
(Bloom, 1964, p. 61).

What these findings mean is that the IQ is not constant, but, like
all other developmental characteristics, is quite variable early in life
and becomes increasingly stable throughout childhood. By age 4
or 5, the IQ correlates about $0.70$ with IQ at age 17, which means
that approximately half (i.e., the square of the correlation) of the
variance in adult intelligence can be predicted as early as age 4 or 5.
This fact that half the variance in adult intelligence can be accounted
for by age 4 has led to the amazing and widespread, but unwarranted
and fallacious, conclusion that persons develop 50 percent of their
mature intelligence by age 4! This conclusion, of course, does not
at all logically follow from just knowing the magnitude of the correlation. The correlation between *height* at age 4 and at age 17 is also
about $0.70$, but who would claim that the square of the correlation
indicated the proportion of adult height attained by age 4? The
absurdity of this *non sequitur* is displayed in the prediction it yields:
the average 4-year-old boy should grow up to be 6 ft 7 ins. tall by
age 17!

Intelligence has about the same degree of stability as other
developmental characteristics. For example, up to age 5 or 6,
height is somewhat more stable than intelligence, and thereafter the

developmental rates of height and intelligence are about equally stable, except for a period of 3 or 4 years immediately after the onset of puberty, during which height is markedly less stable than intelligence. Intelligence is somewhat more stable than total body weight over the age range from 2 to 18 years. Intelligence has a considerably more stable growth rate than measures of physical strength (Bloom, 1964, pp. 46-47). Thus, although the IQ is certainly not 'constant', it seems safe to say that under normal environmental conditions it is at least as stable as developmental characteristics of a strictly physical nature.

INTELLIGENCE AS A COMPONENT OF MENTAL ABILITY

The term 'intelligence' should be reserved for the rather specific meaning I have assigned to it, namely, the general factor common to standard tests of intelligence. Any one verbal definition of this factor is really inadequate, but, if we must define it in so many words, it is probably best thought of as a capacity for abstract reasoning and problem solving.

What I want to emphasize most, however, is that *intelligence* should not be regarded as completely synonymous with what I shall call *mental ability*, a term which refers to the totality of a person's mental capabilities. Psychologists know full well that what they mean by intelligence in the technical sense is only a part of the whole spectrum of human abilities. The notion that a person's intelligence, or some test measurement thereof, reflects the totality of all that he can possibly do with his 'brains' has long caused much misunderstanding and needless dispute. As I have already indicated, the particular constellation of abilities we now call 'intelligence', and which we can measure by means of 'intelligence' tests, has been singled out from the total galaxy of mental abilities as being especially important in our society mainly because of the nature of our traditional system of formal education and the occupational structure with which it is coordinated. Thus, the predominant importance of intelligence is derived, not from any absolute criteria or God-given desiderata, but from societal demands. But neither does this mean, as some persons would like to believe, that intelligence exists only 'by definition' or is merely an insubstantial figment of psychological theory and test construction. Intelligence fully meets the usual scientific criteria for being regarded as an aspect of objective reality, just as much as do atoms, genes, and electromagnetic fields. Intelligence has indeed been singled out as especially important by the educational and occupational demands prevailing in all industrial societies, but it is nevertheless a biological reality and not just a figment of social convention. Where educators and society in general are most apt to go wrong is in failing fully to recognize and fully to utilize a broader spectrum of abilities than just that portion which psychologists have technically designated as 'intelligence'. But keep in mind that it is this technical meaning of 'intelligence' to which the term specifically refers throughout the present article.

## THE DISTRIBUTION OF INTELLIGENCE

Intelligence tests yield numerical scores or IQs (intelligence quotients) which are assumed to be, and in fact nearly are, 'normally' distributed in the population. That is, the distribution of IQs conforms to the normal or so-called Gaussian distribution, the familiar 'bell-shaped curve'. The IQ, which is now the most universal 'unit' in the measurement of intelligence, was originally defined as the ratio of the individual's mental age (MA) to his chronological age (CA): $IQ = (MA/CA) \times 100$. (Beyond about 16 years of age, the formula ceases to make sense.) Mental age was simply defined as the typical or average score obtained on a test by children of a given age, and thus the average child by definition has an IQ of 100. Because of certain difficulties with the mental age concept, which we need not go into here, modern test constructors no longer attempt to measure mental age but instead convert raw scores (i.e., the number of test items gotten 'right') directly into IQs for each chronological age group. The average IQ at each age is arbitrarily set at 100, and the IQ is defined as a normally distributed variable with a mean of 100 and a standard deviation of 15 points. (The standard deviation is an index of the amount of dispersion of scores; in the normal distribution 99·7 percent of the scores fall within $\pm$ 3 standard deviations [i.e., $\pm$ 45 IQ points] of the mean.)

There is really nothing mysterious about the fact that IQs are 'normally' distributed, but it is not quite sufficient, either, to say that the normality of the distribution is just an artifact of test construction. There is a bit more to it than that.

Toss a hundred or so pennies into the air and record the number of heads that come 'up' when they fall. Do this several thousand times and plot a frequency distribution of the number of heads that come up on each of the thousands of throws. You will have a distribution that very closely approximates the normal curve, and the more times you toss the hundred pennies the closer you will approximate the normal distribution.

Now, a psychological test made up of 100 or so items would behave in the same manner as the pennies, and produce a perfectly normal distribution of scores, if (*a*) the items have an average difficulty level of $\frac{1}{2}$ [i.e., exactly half of the number of persons taking the test would get the item 'right'], and (*b*) the items are independent, that is, all the inter-item correlations are zero. Needless to say, no psychological test that has ever been constructed meets these 'ideal' criteria, and this is just as well, for if we succeeded in devising such a test it would 'measure' absolutely nothing but chance variation. If the test is intended to measure some trait, such as general intelligence, it will be impossible for all the test items to be completely uncorrelated. They will necessarily have some degree of positive correlation among them. Then, if the items are correlated, and if we still want the test to spread people out over a considerable range of scores, we can achieve this only if the items vary in level of difficulty; they cannot all have a difficulty level of $\frac{1}{2}$. (Imagine the extreme case in which all item intercorrelations were perfect and the difficulty level of all items was $\frac{1}{2}$. Then the 'distribution' of scores would have only two points: half the testees would obtain a score of zero and half would obtain a perfect score.) So we need to have test items which have an *average* difficulty level of $\frac{1}{2}$ in the test overall, but which cover a considerable range of difficulty levels, say, from 0·1 to 0·9. Thus, test constructors make up their tests of items which have rather low average intercorrelations (usually between 0·1 and 0·2) and a considerable range of difficulty levels. These two sets of conditions working together, then, yield a distribution of test scores in the population which is very close to 'normal'. So far it appears as though we have simply made our tests in such a way as to *force* the scores to assume a normal distribution. And that is exactly true.

But the important question still remains to be answered: is intelligence itself – not just our measurements of it – really normally distributed? In this form the question is operationally meaningless, since, in order to find the form of the distribution of intelligence, we first have to measure it, and we have constructed our measuring instruments in such a way as to yield a normal distribution. The argument about the distribution of intelligence thus appears to be circular. Is there any way out? The only way I know of is to look for evidence that out intelligence scales or IQs behave like an 'interval scale'. On an interval scale, the interval between any two points is equal to the interval between any other two points the same numerical distance apart. Thus, intervals on the scale are equal and additive. If we *assume* that intelligence is 'really' normally distributed in the population, and then measure it in such a way that we obtain a normal distribution of scores, our measurements (IQs) can be regarded as constituting an interval scale. If, then, the scale in fact behaves like an interval scale, there is some justification for saying that intelligence itself (not just IQ) is normally distributed. What evidence is there of the IQs behaving like an interval scale? The most compelling evidence, I believe, comes from studies of the inheritance of intelligence, in which we examine the pattern of intercorrelations among relatives of varying degrees of kinship.

But, first, to understand what is meant by 'behaving' like an interval scale, let us look at two well-known interval scales, the Fahrenheit and Centigrade thermometers. We can prove that these are true interval scales by showing that they 'behave' like interval scales in the following manner: Mix a pint of ice water at 0° C with a pint of boiling water at 100° C. The resultant temperature of the mixture will be 50° C. Mix 3 pints of ice water with 1 pint of boiling water and the temperature of the mix will be 25° C. And we can continue in this way, mixing various proportions of water at different temperatures and predicting the resultant temperatures on the assumption of an interval scale. To the extent that the thermometer readings fit the predictions, they can be considered an interval scale.

Physical stature (height) is measured on an interval scale (more than that, it is also a ratio scale) in units which are independent of height, so the normal distribution of height in the population is clearly a fact of nature and not an artifact of the scale of measurement. A rather simple genetic model 'explains' the distribution of height by hypothesizing that individual variations in height are the result of a large number of independent factors each having a small effect in determining stature. (Recall the penny-tossing analogy.) This model predicts quite precisely the amount of 'regression to the population mean' of the children's average height from the parent's average height, a phenomenon first noted by Sir Francis Galton in 1885. The amount of 'regression to the mean' from grandparent to grandchild is exactly double that from parent to child. These regression lines for various degrees of kinship are perfectly rectilinear throughout the entire range, except at the very lower end of the scale of height, where one finds midgets and dwarfs. The slope of the regression line changes in discrete jumps according to the remoteness of kinship of the groups being compared. All this could happen only if height were measured on an interval scale. The regression lines would not be rectilinear if the trait (height) were not measured in equal intervals.

Now, it is interesting that intelligence measurements show about the same degree of 'filial regression', as Galton called it, that we find for height. The simple polygenic model for the inheritance of height fits the kinship correlations obtained for intelligence almost as precisely as it does for height. And the kinship regression lines are as rectilinear for intelligence as for height, throughout the IQ scale, except at the very lower end, where we find pathological types of mental deficiency analogous to midgets and dwarfs on the scale of physical stature. In brief, IQs behave just about as much like an interval scale as do measurements of height, which we know for sure is an interval scale. Therefore, it is not unreasonable to treat the IQ as an interval scale.

Although standardized tests such as the Stanford-Binet and the Wechsler Scales were each constructed by somewhat different approaches to achieving interval scales, they both agree in revealing certain systematic discrepancies from a perfectly normal distribution of IQs when the tests are administered to a very large and truly random sample of the population. These slight deviations of the distribution of IQs from perfect normality have shown up in many studies using a variety of tests. The most thorough studies and sophisticated discussions of their significance can be found in articles by Sir Cyril Burt (1957, 1963). The evidence, in short, indicates that intelligence is *not* distributed quite normally in the population. The distribution of IQs approximates normality quite closely in the IQ range from about 70 to 130. But outside this range there are slight, although very significant, departures from normality. From a scientific standpoint, these discrepancies are of considerable interest as genuine phenomena needing explanation.

Figure 1 shows an idealized distribution of IQs if they were distributed perfectly normally. Between IQ 70 and IQ 130, the percentage of cases falling between different IQ intervals, as indicated in Figure 1, are very close to the actual percentages estimated from large samples of the population and the departures are hardly enough to matter from any practical standpoint.

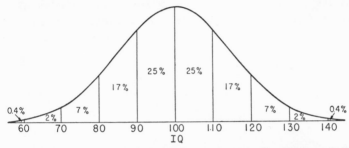

FIGURE 1. *The theoretical normal or Gaussian distribution of IQs, showing the expected percentages of the population in each IQ range. Except at the extremes (below 70 and above 130) these percentages are very close to actual population values. (The percentage figures total slightly more than 100 percent because of rounding.)*

Examination of this normal curve can be instructive if one notes the consequences of shifting the total distribution curve up or down the IQ scale. The consequences of a given shift become more extreme out toward the 'tails' of the distribution. For example, shifting the mean of the distribution from 100 down to 90 would put 50 percent instead of only 25 percent of the population below IQ 90; and it would put 9 percent instead of 2 percent below IQ 70. And in the upper tail of the distribution, of course, the consequences would be the reverse; instead of 25 percent above IQ 110, there would be only 9 percent, and so on. The point is that relatively small shifts in the mean of the IQ distribution can result in very large differences in the proportions of the population that fall into the very low or the very high ranges of intelligence. A 10-point downward shift in the mean, for example, would more than triple the percentage of mentally retarded (IQs below 70) in the population and would reduce the percentage of intellectually 'gifted' (IQs above 130) to less than one-sixth of their present number. It is in these tails of the normal distribution that differences become most conspicuous between various groups in the population that show mean IQ differences, for whatever reason, of only a few IQ points. From a knowledge of relatively slight mean differences between various social class and ethnic groups, for example, one can estimate quite closely the relatively large differences in their proportions in special classes for the educationally retarded and for the 'gifted' and in the percentages of different groups receiving scholastic honors at

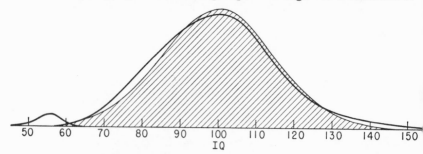

FIGURE 2. *Theoretical 'normal' distribution of IQs (shaded curve) and the actual distribution in the population (heavy line), with the lower hump exaggerated for explanatory purposes. See text for explanation.*

graduation. It is simply a property of the normal distribution that the effects of group differences in the mean are greatly magnified in the different proportions of each group that we find as we move further out toward the upper or lower extremes of the distribution.

I indicated previously that the distribution of intelligence is really not quite 'normal', but shows certain systematic departures from 'normality'. These departures from the normal distribution are shown in Figure 2 in a slightly exaggerated form to make them clear. The shaded area is the normal distribution; the heavy line indicates the actual distribution of IQs in the population. We note that there are more very low IQs than would be expected in a truly normal distribution, and also there is an excess of IQs at the upper end of the scale. Note, too, the slight excess in the IQ range between about 70 and 90.

The very lowest IQs, below 55 or 60, we now know, really represent a different distribution from that of the rest of the intelligence distribution (Roberts, 1952; Zigler, 1967). Whatever factors are responsible for individual differences in the IQ range above 60 are not sufficient to account for IQs below this level, and especially below IQ 50. Practically all IQs below this level represent severe mental deficiency due to pathological conditions, massive brain damage, or rare genetic and chromosomal abnormalities. Only about $\frac{1}{2}$ to $\frac{3}{4}$ of 1 percent of the total population falls into the IQ range below 50; this is fewer than $\frac{1}{3}$ of all individuals classed as mentally retarded (IQs below 70). These severe grades of mental defect are not just the lower extreme of normal variation. Often they are due to a single recessive or mutant gene whose effects completely override all the other genetic factors involved in intelligence; thus they have been called 'major gene' defects. In this respect, the distribution of intelligence is directly analogous to the distribution of stature. Short persons are no more abnormal than are average or tall persons; all are instances of normal variation. But extremely short persons at the very lower end of the distribution are really part of another, abnormal, distribution, generally consisting of midgets and dwarfs. They are clearly not a part of normal variation. One of the commonest types of dwarfism, for example, is known to be caused by a single recessive gene.

Persons with low IQs caused by major gene defects or chromosomal abnormalities, like mongolism, are also usually abnormal in physical appearance. Persons with moderately low IQs that represent a part of normal variation, the so-called 'familial mentally retarded', on the other hand, are physically indistinguishable from persons in the higher ranges of IQ. But probably the strongest evidence we have that IQs below 50 are a group apart from the mildly retarded, who represent the lower end of normal variation, comes from comparisons of the siblings of the severely retarded with siblings of the mildly retarded. In England, where this has been studied intensively, these two retardate groups are called imbecile (IQs below 50) and feebleminded (IQs 50 to 75). Figure 3 shows the IQ distributions of the *siblings* of imbecile and feebleminded children (Roberts, 1952). Note that the siblings of imbeciles have a much higher average level of intelligence than the siblings of the feebleminded. The latter group, furthermore, shows a distribution of IQs that would be predicted from a genetic model intended to account for the normal variation of IQ in the population. This model does not at all predict the IQ distribution for the imbecile sibships. To explain the results shown in Figure 3 one must postulate some additional factors (gene or chromosome defects, pathological conditions, etc.) that cause imbecile and idiot grades of mental deficiency.

Another interesting point of contrast between severe mental deficiency and mild retardation is the fact noted by Kushlick (1966, p. 130), in surveying numerous studies, that 'The parents of severely subnormal children are evenly distributed among all the social strata of industrial society, while those of mildly subnormal

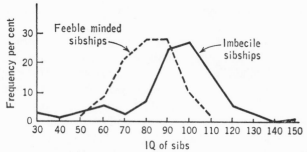

FIGURE 3.　*Frequency distributions of the IQs of sibs of feebleminded and imbeciles of the IQ range 30-68. (Roberts, 1952.)*

subjects come predominantly from the lower social classes. There is now evidence which suggests that mild subnormality in the absence of abnormal neurological signs (epilepsy, electroencephalographic abnormalities, biochemical abnormalities, chromosomal abnormalities or sensory defects) is virtually confined to the lower social classes. Indeed, there is evidence that almost no children of higher social class parents have IQ scores of less than 80, unless they have one of the pathological processes mentioned above.'

In the remainder of this article we shall not be further concerned with these exceptionally low IQs below 50 or 60, which largely constitute a distribution of abnormal conditions superimposed on the factors that make for normal variation in intelligence. We shall be mainly concerned with the factors involved in the normal distribution.

Returning to Figure 2, the best explanation we have for the 'bulge' between 70 and 90 is the combined effects of severe environmental disadvantages and of emotional disturbances that depress test scores. Burt (1963) has found that when, independent of the subjects' test performance there is evidence for the existence of factors that depress performance, and these exceptional subjects' scores are removed from the distribution, this 'bulge' in the 70-90 range is diminished or erased. Also, on retest under more favorable conditions, the IQs of many of these exceptional subjects are redistributed at various higher points on the scale, thereby making the IQ distribution more normal.

The 'excess' of IQs at the high end of the scale is certainly a substantial phenomenon, but it has not yet been adequately accounted for. In his multifactorial theory of the inheritance of intelligence, Burt (1958) has postulated major gene effects that make for exceptional intellectual abilities represented at the upper end of the scale, just as other major gene effects make for the subnormality found at the extreme lower end of the scale. One might also hypothesize that superior genotypes for intellectual development are pushed to still greater superiority in their phenotypic expression through interaction with the environment. Early recognition of superiority leads to its greater cultivation and encouragement by the individual's social environment. This influence is keenly evident in the developmental histories of persons who have achieved exceptional eminence (Goertzel and Goertzel, 1962). Still another possible explanation of the upper-end 'excess' lies in the effects of assortative mating in the population, meaning the tendency for 'like to marry like'. If the degree of resemblance in intelligence between parents in the upper half of the IQ distribution were significantly greater than the degree of resemblance of parents in the below-average range, genetic theory would predict the relative elongation of the upper tail of the distribution. This explanation, however, must remain speculative until we have more definite evidence of whether there is differential assortative mating in different regions of the IQ distribution.

*The Concept of Variance.* Before going on to discuss the factors that account for normal variation in intelligence among individuals in the population, a word of explanation is in order concerning the quantification of variation. The amount of dispersion of scores depicted by the distributions in Figures 1 and 2 is technically expressed as the *variance*, which is the square of the standard deviation of the scores in the distribution. (Since the standard deviation of IQs in the population is 15, the total variance is 225.) *Variance* is a basic concept in all discussions of individual differences and population genetics. If you take the difference between every score and the mean of the total distribution, square each of these differences, sum them up, and divide the sum by the total number of scores, you have a quantity called the *variance*. It is an index of the total amount of variation among scores. Since variance represents variation on an additive scale, the total variance of a distribution of scores can be partitioned into a number of components, each one due to some factor which contributes a certain specifiable proportion of the variance, and all these variance components add up to the total variance. The mathematical technique for doing this, called 'the analysis of variance', was invented by Sir Ronald Fisher, the British geneticist and statistician. It is one of the great achievements in the development of statistical methodology.

## The Inheritance of Intelligence

'In the actual race of life, which is not to get ahead, but to get ahead of somebody, the chief determining factor is heredity.' So said Edward L. Thorndike in 1905. Since then, the preponderance of evidence has proved him right, certainly as concerns those aspects of life in which intelligence plays an important part.

But one would get a quite different impression from reading most of the recent popular textbooks of psychology and education. Genetic factors in individual differences have usually been belittled, obscured, or denigrated, probably for reasons of interest mainly on historical, political, and idealogical grounds which we need not go into here. Some of the following quotations, each from different widely used texts in our field, give some indication of the basis for my complaint. 'We can attribute no particular portion of intelligence to heredity and no particular portion to the environment.' 'The relative influence of heredity and environment upon the intelligence has been the topic of considerable investigations over the last half century. Actually the problem is incapable of solution since studies do not touch upon the problem of heredity and environment but simply upon the susceptibility of the content of a particular test to environmental influences.' 'Among people considered normal, the range of genetic variations is not very great.' 'Although at the present time practically all responsible workers in the field recognize that conclusive proof of the heritability of mental ability (where no organic or metabolic pathology is involved) is still lacking, the assumption that subnormality has a genetic basis continues to crop up in scientific studies.' 'There is no evidence that nature is more important than nurture. These two forces always operate together to determine the course of intellectual development.' The import of such statements apparently filters up to high levels of policy-making, for we find a Commissioner of the U.S. Office of Education stating in a published speech that children '. . . all have similar potential at birth. The differences occur shortly thereafter.' These quotations typify much of the current attitude toward heredity and environment that has prevailed in education in recent years. The belief in the almost infinite plasticity of intellect, the ostrich-like denial of biological factors in individual differences, and the slighting of the role of genetics in the study of intelligence can only hinder investigation and understanding of the conditions, processes, and limits through which the social environment influences human behavior.

But fortunately we are beginning to see some definite signs that this mistreatment of the genetic basis of intelligence by social scientists may be on the wane, and that a biosocial view of intellectual development more in accord with the evidence is gaining greater recognition. As Yale psychologist Edward Zigler (1968) has so well stated:

> Not only do I insist that we take the biological integrity of the organism seriously, but it is also my considered opinion that our nation has more to fear from unbridled environmentalists than they do from those who point to such integrity as one factor in the determination of development. It is the environmentalists who have been writing review after review in which genetics are ignored and the concept of capacity is treated as a dirty word. It is the environmentalists who have placed on the defensive any thinker who, perhaps impressed by the revolution in biological thought stemming from discoveries involving RNA-DNA phenomena, has had the temerity to suggest

that certain behaviors may be in part the product of read-out mechanisms residing within the programmed organism. It is the unbridled environmentalist who emphasizes the plasticity of the intellect, that tells us one can change both the general rate of development and the configuration of intellectual processes which can be referred to as the intellect, if we could only subject human beings to the proper technologies. In the educational realm, this has spelled itself out in the use of panaceas, gadgets, and gimmicks of the most questionable sort. It is the environmentalist who suggests to parents how easy it is to raise the child's IQ and who has prematurely led many to believe that the retarded could be made normal, and the normal made geniuses. It is the environmentalist who has argued for pressure-cooker schools, at what psychological cost, we do not yet know.

Most geneticists and students of human evolution have fully recognized the role of culture in shaping 'human nature', but also they do not minimize the biological basis of diversity in human behavioral characteristics. Geneticist Theodosius Dobzhansky (1968, p. 554) has expressed this viewpoint in the broadest terms: 'The trend of cultural evolution has been not toward making everybody have identical occupations but toward a more and more differentiated occupational structure. What would be the most adaptive response to this trend? Certainly nothing that would encourage genetic uniformity. . . . To argue that only environmental circumstances and training determine a person's behavior makes a travesty of democratic notions of individual choice, responsibility, and freedom.'

EVIDENCE FROM STUDIES OF SELECTIVE BREEDING

The many studies of selective breeding in various species of mammals provide conclusive evidence that many behavioral characteristics, just as most physical characteristics, can be manipulated by genetic selection (see Fuller and Thompson, 1962; Scott and Fuller, 1965). Rats, for example, have been bred for maze learning ability in many different laboratories. It makes little difference whether one refers to this ability as rat 'intelligence', 'learning ability' or some other term – we know that it is possible to breed selectively for whatever the factors are that make for speed of maze learning. To be sure, individual variation in this complex ability may be due to any combination of a number of characteristics involving sensory acuity, drive level, emotional stability, strength of innate turning preferences, brain chemistry, brain size, structure of neural connections, speed of synaptic transmission, or whatever. The point is that the molar behavior of learning to get through a maze efficiently without making errors (i.e., going up blind alleys) can be markedly influenced in later generations by selective breeding of the parent generations of rats who are either fast or slow ('maze bright' or 'maze dull', to use the prevailing terminology in this research) in learning to get through the maze. Figure 4 shows the results of one such genetic selection experiment.* They are quite typical; within only six generations of selection the offspring of the 'dull' strain make 100 percent more errors in learning the maze than do the offspring of the 'bright' strain (Thompson, 1954). In most experiments of this type, of course, the behaviors that respond so dramatically to selection are relatively simple as compared with human intelligence, and the experimental selection pressure is severe, so the implications of such findings for the study of human variation should not be overdrawn. Yet geneticists seem to express little doubt that many behavioral traits in humans would respond similarly to genetic selection. Three eminent geneticists (James F. Crow, James V. Neel, and Curt Stern) of the National Academy of Sciences recently prepared a 'position statement', which was generally hedged by extreme caution and understatement, that asserted: 'Animal experiments have shown that almost any trait can be changed by selection. . . . A selection program to increase human intelligence (or whatever is measured by various kinds of "intelligence" tests) would almost certainly be successful in some measure. The same is probably true for other behavioral traits. The *rate* of increase would be somewhat unpredictable, but there is little doubt that there would be progress' (National Academy of Sciences, 1967, p. 893).

* At a meeting of the Brain Research Association on July 17, 1970, in Cambridge, England, Professor Jerry Hirsch accused me of having faked or altered the graph in Figure 4 to make it more strongly favor an hereditarian interpretation. The figure that appears here was directly reproduced (by photography, not re-drafting) from the source in which I found it (Robinson, R., *Genetics of the Norway Rat*. New York: Pergamon, 1965, page 537). In checking this figure against the original data, it turns out that one data point is in error. I have had the graph re-drafted with the necessary correction, as shown in Figure 4'.

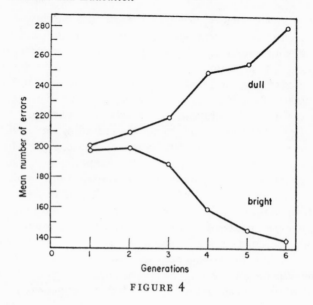

FIGURE 4

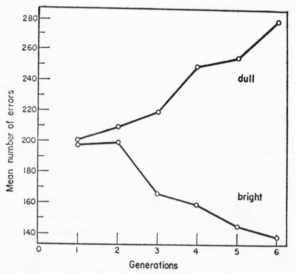

FIGURE 4′. *The mean error scores in maze learning for successive generations of selectively bred 'bright' and 'dull' strains of McGill rats. (After Thompson, 1954.)*

DIRECT EVIDENCE OF GENETIC INFLUENCES ON
HUMAN ABILITIES

One of the most striking pieces of evidence for the genetic control
of mental abilities is a chromosomal anomaly called Turner's
syndrome. Normal persons have 46 chromosomes. Persons with
Turner's syndrome have only 45. When their chromosomes are
stained and viewed under the microscope, it is seen that the sex-
chromatin is missing from one of the two chromosomes that determine the individual's sex. In normal persons this pair of chromosomes is conventionally designated XY for males and XX for
females. The anomaly of Turner's syndrome is characterized as XO.
These persons always have the morphologic appearance of females
but are always sterile, and they show certain physical characteristics
such as diminutive stature, averaging about 5 ft tall as adults. The
interesting point about Turner's cases from our standpoint is that
although their IQs on most verbal tests of intelligence show a
perfectly normal distribution, their performance on tests involving
spatial ability or perceptual organization is abnormally low (Money,
1964). Their peculiar deficiency in spatial-perceptual ability is
sometimes so severe as to be popularly characterized as 'space-form
blindness'. It is also interesting that Turner's cases seem to be more
or less uniformly low on spatial ability regardless of their level of
performance on other tests of mental ability. These rare persons
also report unusual difficulty with arithmetic and mathematics in
school despite otherwise normal or superior intelligence. So here is
a genetic aberration, clearly identifiable under the microscope,
which has quite specific consequences on cognitive processes. Such
specific intellectual deficiencies are thus entirely possible without
there being any specific environmental deprivations needed to
account for them.

There are probably other more subtle cognitive effects associated
with the sex chromosomes in normal persons. It has long been
suspected that males have greater environmental vulnerability than
females, and Nancy Bayley's important longitudinal research on
children's mental development clearly shows both a higher degree
and a greater variety of environmental and personality correlates of
mental abilities in boys than in girls (Bayley, 1965b, 1966,
1968).

POLYGENIC INHERITANCE

Since intelligence is basically dependent on the structural and bio-chemical properties of the brain, it should not be surprising that differences in intellectual capacity are partly the result of genetic factors which conform to the same principles involved in the inheritance of physical characteristics. The general model that geneticists have devised to account for the facts of inheritance of continuous or metrical physical traits, such as stature, cephalic index, and fingerprint ridges, also applies to intelligence. *The mechanism of inheritance for such traits is called polygenic, since normal variation in the characteristic is the result of multiple genes whose effects are small, similar, and cumulative.* The genes can be thought of as the pennies in the coin-tossing analogy described previously. Some genes add a positive increment to the metric value of the characteristic ('heads') and some genes add nothing ('tails') The random segregation of the parental genes in the process of gametogenesis (formation of the sex cells) and their chance combination in the zygote (fertilized egg) may be likened to the tossing of a large number of pennies, with each 'head' adding a positive incre-ment to the trait, thereby producing the normal bell-shaped distri-bution of trait values in a large number of tosses. The actual number of genes involved in intelligence is not known. In fact, the total number of genes in the human chromosomes is unknown. The simplest possible model would require between ten and twenty gene pairs (alleles) to account for the normal distribution of intelligence, but many more genes than this are most likely involved (Gottesman, 1963, pp. 290-291).

THE CONCEPT OF HERITABILITY

The study of the genetic basis of individual differences in intelli-gence in humans has evolved in the traditions and methods of that branch of genetics called quantitative genetics or population genetics, the foundations of which were laid down by British geneti-cists and statisticians such as Galton, Pearson, Fisher, Haldane, and Mather, and, in the United States, by J. L. Lush and Sewall Wright. Probably the most distinguished exponent of the applica-tion of these methods to the study of intelligence is Sir Cyril Burt, whose major writings on this subject are a 'must' for students of individual differences (Burt, 1955, 1958, 1959, 1961, 1966; Burt and Howard, 1956, 1957).

One aim of this approach to the study of individual differences in intelligence is to account for the total variance in the population (excluding pathological cases at the bottom of the distribution) in terms of the proportions of the variance attributable to various genetic and environmental components. It will pay to be quite explicit about just what this actually means.

Individual differences in such measurements of intelligence as the IQ are represented as population variance in a phenotype $V_P$, and are distributed approximately as shown in Figure 1. Conceptually, this total variance of the phenotypes can be partitioned into a number of variance components, each of which represents a source of variance. The components, of course, all add up to the total variance. Thus,

$$V_P = \underbrace{(V_G + V_{AM}) + V_D + V_i}_{V_H} + \underbrace{V_E + 2\,\mathrm{Cov}_{HE} + V_I}_{V_E} + \underbrace{V_e}_{} \qquad (2)$$

$$\qquad\qquad\quad \text{Heredity} \qquad\qquad \text{Environment} \qquad \text{Error}$$

where:

$V_P$ = phenotypic variance in the population

$V_G$ = genic (or additive) variance

$V_{AM}$ = variance due to assortative mating. $V_{AM} = 0$ under random mating (panmixia).

$V_D$ = dominance deviation variance

$V_i$ = epistatis (interaction among genes at 2 or more loci)

$V_E$ = environmental variance

$\mathrm{Cov}_{HE}$ = covariance of heredity and environment

$V_I$ = true statistical interaction of genetic and environmental factors

$V_e$ = error of measurement (unreliability).

Here are a few words of explanation about each of these variance components.

*Phenotypic Variance.* $V_P$ is already clear; it is the total variance of the trait measurements in the population.

*Genic Variance.* $V_G$, the genic (or additive) variance, is attributable to gene effects which are additive; that is, each gene adds an equal increment to the metric value of the trait. Sir Ronald Fisher referred to this component as 'the essential genotypes', since it is the part of the genetic inheritance which 'breeds true' – it accounts for the resemblance between parents and offspring. If trait variance involved nothing but additive genic effects, the average value of all the offspring that could theoretically be born to a pair of parents would be exactly equal to the average value of the parents (called the midparent value). It is thus the genic aspect which is most important to agriculturalists and breeders of livestock, since it is the genic component of the phenotypic variance that responds to selection according to the simple rule of 'like begets like'. The larger the proportion of genic variance involved in a given characteristic, the fewer is the number of generations of selective breeding required to effect a change of some specified magnitude in the characteristic.

*Assortative Mating.* $V_{AM}$, the variance due to assortative mating, is conventionally not separated from $V_G$, since assortative mating actually affects the proportion of $V_G$ directly. I have separated these components here for explanatory reasons, and it is, in fact, possible to obtain independent estimates of the two components. If mating were completely random in the population with respect to a given characteristic – that is, if the correlation between parents were zero (a state of affairs known as *panmixia*) – the $V_{AM}$ component would also be equal to zero and the population variance on the trait in question would therefore be reduced.

Assortative mating has the effect of increasing the desirable but not essential change differences between families in the population. (In the terminology of analysis of variance, assortative mating decreases the proportion of *within* families variance and increases the proportion of *between* families variance.)

For some human characteristics the degree of assortative mating is effectively zero. This is true of fingerprint ridges, for example. Men and women are obviously not attracted to one another on the basis of their fingerprints. Height, however, has an assortative mating coefficient (i.e., the correlation between mates) of about 0·30. The IQ, interestingly enough, shows a higher degree of assortative mating in our society than any other measurable human characteristic. I have surveyed the literature on this point, based on studies in Europe and North America, and find that the correlation between spouses' intelligence test scores averages close to +0·60. Thus, spouses are more alike in intelligence than brothers and sisters, who are correlated about 0·50.

As Eckland (1967) has pointed out, this high correlation between marriage partners does not come about solely because men and women are such excellent judges of one another's intelligence, but because mate selection is greatly aided by the highly visible selective processes of the educational system and the occupational hierarchy. Here is a striking instance of how educational and social factors can have far-reaching genetic consequences in the population. One would predict, for example, that in pre-literate or pre-industrial societies assortative mating with respect to intelligence would be markedly less than it is in modern industrial societies. The educational screening mechanisms and socioeconomic stratification by which intelligence becomes more readily visible would not exist, and other traits of more visible importance to the society would take precedence over intelligence as a basis for assortative mating. Even in our own society, there may well be differential degrees of assortative mating in different segments of the population, probably related to their opportunities for educational and occupational selection. When any large and socially insulated group is not subject to the social and educational circumstances that lead to a high degree of assortative mating for intelligence, there should be important genetic consequences. One possible consequence is some reduction of the group's ability, not as individuals but as a group, to compete intellectually. Thus, probably one of the most cogent arguments for society's promoting full equality of educational, occupational, and economic opportunity lies in the possible genetic consequences of these social institutions.

The reason is simply that assortative mating increases the genetic variance in the population. By itself this will not affect the mean of the trait in the population, but it will have a great effect on the proportion of the population falling in the upper and lower tails of the distribution. Under present conditions, with an assortative mating coefficient of about 0·60, the standard deviation of IQs is 15 points. If assortative mating for intelligence were reduced to zero, the standard deviation of IQs would fall to 12·9. The consequences of this reduction in the standard deviation would be most evident at the extremes of the intelligence distribution. For example, assuming a normal distribution of IQs and the present standard deviation of 15, the frequency (per million) of persons above IQ 130 is 22,750. Without assortative mating the frequency of IQs over 130 would fall to 9900, or only 43·5 percent of the present frequency. For IQs above 145, the frequency (per million) is 1350 and with no assortative mating would fall to 241, or 17·9 percent of the present frequency. And there are now approximately 20 times as many persons above an IQ of 160 as we would find if there were no assortative mating for intelligence.[1] Thus, differences in assortative mating can have a profound effect on a people's intellectual resources, especially at the levels of intelligence required for complex problem solving, invention, and scientific and technological innovation.

But what is the effect of assortative mating on the lower tail of the distribution? On theoretical grounds we should also expect it to increase the proportion of low IQs in the population. It probably does this to some extent, but not as much as it increases the frequency of higher IQs, because there is a longer-term consequence of assortative mating which must also be considered. A number of studies have shown that in populations practising a high degree of assortative mating, persons below IQ 75 are much less successful in finding marriage partners and, as a group, have relatively fewer offspring than do persons of higher intelligence (Higgins, Reed, and Reed, 1962; Bajema, 1963, 1966). Since assortative mating increases variance, it in effect pushes more people into the below IQ 75 group, where they fail to reproduce, thereby resulting in a net selection for genes favoring high intelligence. Thus, in the long run, assortative mating may have a eugenic effect in improving the general level of intelligence in the population.

*Dominance Deviation.* $V_D$, the dominance deviation variance, is apparent when we observe a systematic discrepancy between the average value of the parents and the average value of their offspring on a given characteristic. Genes at some of the loci in the chromo-

---

[1] I am grateful to University of California geneticist Dr Jack Lester King for making these calculations, which are based on the assumption that the heritability of IQ is 0·80, a value which is the average of all the major studies of the heritability of intelligence.

some are recessive (r) and their effects are not manifested in the phenotype unless they are paired with another recessive at the same locus. If paired with a dominant gene (D), their effect is overridden or 'dominated' by the dominant gene. Thus, in terms of increments which genes add to the metric value of the phenotype, if r = 0 and D = 1, then r+r = 0, and D+D = 2, but D+r will equal 2, since D dominates r. Because of the presence of some proportion of recessive genes in the genotypes for a particular trait, not all of the parents' phenotypic characteristics will show up in their offspring, and, of course, vice versa: not all of the offspring's characteristics will be seen in the parents. This makes for a less than perfect correlation between midparent and midchild values on the trait in question. $V_D$, the dominance variance, represents the component of variance in the population which is due to this average discrepancy between parents and offspring. The magnitude of $V_D$ depends upon the proportions of dominant and recessive genes constituting the genotypes for the characteristic in the population.

*Epistasis.* $V_i$ is the variance component attributable to epistasis, which means the interaction of the effects among genes at two or more loci. When genes 'interact', their effects are not strictly additive that is to say, their combined effect may be more or less than the sum of their separate effects. Like dominance, epistasis also accounts for some of the lack of resemblance between parents and their offspring. And it increases the population variance by a component designated as $V_i$.

*Environmental Variance.* 'Environmental' really means all sources of variance not attributable to genetic effects or errors of measurement (i.e., test unreliability). In discussions of intelligence, the environment is often thought of only in terms of the social and cultural influences on the individual. While these are important, they are not the whole of 'environment', which includes other more strictly biological influences, such as the prenatal environment and nutritional factors early in life. In most studies of the heritability of intelligence 'environment' refers to all variance that is not accounted for by genetic factors $[(V_G + V_{AM}) + V_D + V_i]$ and measurement error ($V_e$).

*Covariance of Heredity and Environment.* This term can also be expressed as $2r_{HE} \sqrt{V_H \times V_E}$, where $r_{HE}$ is the correlation between heredity and environment, $V_H$ is the variance due to all genetic factors, and $V_E$ is variance due to all environmental factors. In other words, if there is a positive correlation between genetic and environmental factors, the population variance is increased by a theoretically specifiable amount indicated by the covariance term in Equation 2.

Such covariance undoubtedly exists for intelligence in our society. Children with better than average genetic endowment for intelligence have a greater than chance likelihood of having parents of better than average intelligence who are capable of providing environmental advantages that foster intellectual development. Even among children within the same family, parents and teachers will often give special attention and opportunities to the child who displays exceptional abilities. A genotype for superior ability may cause the social environment to foster the ability, as when parents perceive unusual responsiveness to music in one of their children and therefore provide more opportunities for listening, music lessons, encouragement to practice, and so on. A bright child may also create a more intellectually stimulating environment for himself in terms of the kinds of activities that engage his interest and energy. And the social rewards that come to the individual who excels in some activity reinforce its further development. Thus the covariance term for any given trait will be affected to a significant degree by the kinds of behavioral propensities the culture rewards or punishes, encourages or discourages. For traits viewed as desirable in our culture, such as intelligence, hereditary and environmental factors will be positively correlated. But for some other traits which are generally viewed as socially undesirable, hereditary and environmental influences may be negatively correlated. This means that the social environment tends to discourage certain behavioral propensities when they are out of line with the values of the culture. Then, instead of heredity and environment acting in the same direction, they work in opposite directions, with a consequent reduction in the population variance in the trait. Overt aggressive tendencies may be a good example of behavior involving a negative correlation between genotypic propensities and environmental counter-pressures. An example of negative heredity-environment correlation in the scholastic realm would be found in the case where a child with a poor genetic endowment for learning some skill which is demanded by societal norms, such as being able to read, causes the child's parents to lavish special tutorial attention on their child in an effort to bring his performance up to par.

In making overall estimates of the proportions of variance attributable to hereditary and environmental factors, there is some question as to whether the covariance component should be included on the side of heredity or environment. But there can be no 'correct' answer to this question. To the degree that the individual's genetic propensities cause him to fashion his own environment, given the opportunity, the covariance (or some part of it) can be justifiably regarded as part of the total heritability of the trait. But if one wishes to estimate what the heritability of the trait would be under artificial conditions in which there is absolutely no freedom for variation in individuals' utilization of their environment, then the covariance term should be included on the side of environment. Since most estimates of the heritability of intelligence are intended to reflect the existing state of affairs, they usually include the covariance in the proportion of variance due to heredity.

*Interaction of Heredity and Environment.* The *interaction* of genetic and environmental factors ($V_1$) must be clearly distinguished from the *covariance* of heredity and environment. There is considerable confusion concerning the meaning of interaction in much of the literature on heredity and intelligence. It is claimed, for example, that nothing can be said about the relative importance of heredity and environment because intelligence is the result of the 'interaction' of these influences and therefore their independent effects cannot be estimated. This is simply false. The proportion of the population variance due to genetic × environment interaction is conceptually and empirically separable from other variance components, and its independent contribution to the total variance can be known. Those who call themselves 'interactionists', with the conviction that they have thereby either solved or risen above the whole issue of the relative contributions of heredity and environment to individual differences in intelligence, are apparently unaware that the preponderance of evidence indicates that the interaction variance, $V_I$, is the smallest component of the total phenotypic variance of intelligence.

What *interaction* really means is that different genotypes respond in different ways to the same environmental factors. For example, genetically different individuals having the same initial weight and

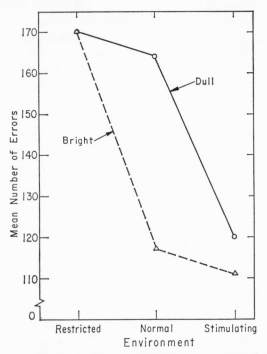

FIGURE 5.   *Illustration of a true genotype × environment interaction for error scores in maze learning by 'bright' and 'dull' strains of rats raised in 'restricted', 'normal', and 'stimulating' environments. (After Cooper and Zubek, 1958.)*

the same activity level may gain weight at quite different rates all under exactly the same increase in caloric intake. Their genetically different constitutions cause them to metabolize exactly the same intake quite differently. An example of genotype × environmental interaction in the behavioral realm is illustrated in Figure 5. Strains of rats selectively bred for 'brightness' or 'dullness' in maze learning show marked differences in maze performance according to the degree of sensory stimulation in the conditions under which they are reared. For the 'bright' strain, the difference between being reared in a 'restricted' or in a 'normal' environment makes a great difference in maze performance. But for the 'dull' strain the big difference is between a 'normal' and a 'stimulating' environment. While the strains differ greatly when reared under 'normal' conditions (presumably the conditions under which they were selectively bred for 'dullness' and 'brightness'), they do not differ in the least when reared in a 'restricted' environment and only slightly in a 'stimulating' environment. This is the meaning of the genetic × environment interaction. Criticisms of the analysis of variance model for the components of phenotypic variance (e.g., Equation 2), put forth first by Loevinger (1943) and then by Hunt (1961, p. 329), are based on the misconception that the model implies that all effects of heredity and environment are strictly additive and there is no 'non-additive' or interaction term. The presence of $V_I$ in Equation 2 explicitly shows that the heredity × environment interaction is included in the analysis of variance model, and the contribution of $V_I$ to the total variance may be estimated independently of the purely additive effects of heredity and environment. The magnitude of $V_I$ for any given characteristic in any specified population is a matter for empirical study, not philosophic debate. If $V_I$ turns out to constitute a relatively small proportion of the total variance, as the evidence shows is the case for human intelligence, this is not a fault of the analysis of variance model. It is simply a fact. If the interaction variance actually exists in any significant amount, the model will reveal it.

Several studies, reviewed by Wiseman (1964, p. 55; 1966, p. 66), provide most of the information we have concerning what may be presumed to be an heredity × environment interaction with respect to human intelligence. The general finding is that children who are more than one standard deviation (*SD*) above the mean IQ show greater correlations with environmental factors than do children who are more than one *SD* below the mean. In other words, if the heritability of IQ were determined in these two groups separately, it would be higher in the low IQ groups. Also, when siblings within the same family are grouped into above and below IQ 100, the scholastic achievement of the above 100 group shows a markedly higher correlation with environmental factors than in the below 100 group. This indicates a true interaction between intelligence and environment in determining educational attainments.

*Error Variance.* The variance due to errors of measurement ($V_e$) is, of course, unwanted but unavoidable, since all measurements fall short of perfect reliability. The proportion of test score variance due to error is equal to $1-r_{tt}$ (where $r_{tt}$ is the reliability of the test, that is, its correlation with itself). For most intelligence tests, error accounts for between 5 and 10 percent of the variance.

DEFINITION OF HERITABILITY

Heritability is a technical term in genetics meaning specifically the proportion of phenotypic variance due to variance in genotypes. When psychologists speak of heritability they almost invariably define it as:

$$h^2 = \frac{(V_G + V_{AM}) + V_D + V_i}{V_P - V_e} \tag{3}$$

Although this formula is technically the definition of $h^2$, heritability estimates in psychological studies may also include the covariance term in Equation 2 in the numerator of Equation 3.*

COMMON MISCONCEPTIONS ABOUT HERITABILITY

Certain misconceptions about heritability have become so widespread and strongly ingrained that it is always necessary to counteract them before presenting the empirical findings on the subject, lest these findings only add to the confusion or provoke the dogmatic acceptance or rejection of notions that are not at all implied by the meaning of heritability.

*Heredity* versus *Environment.* Genetic and environmental factors are not properly viewed as being in opposition to each other. Nor

---

* The covariance of G and E can be independently estimated and may or may not be included in the estimate of $h^2$, depending upon the interpretation one wishes to give to $h^2$. Roberts (1967, pp. 217-218) has suggested that the environment should be defined as affecting the phenotype independently of the genotype. Thus, if individuals' genotypes influence their choice of environments, the environmental variation resulting therefrom would be considered a part of the total genetic variance.

are they an 'all or none' affair. Any observable characteristic, physical or behavioral, is a phenotype, the very existence of which depends upon both genetic and environmental conditions. The legitimate question is not whether the characteristic is due to heredity *or* environment, but what proportion of the population variation in the characteristic is attributable to genotypic variation (which is $h^2$, the heritability) and what proportion is attributable to non-genetic or environmental variation in the population (which is $1-h^2$). For metric characteristics like stature and intelligence, $h^2$ can have values between 0 and 1.

*Individual* versus *Population*. Heritability is a population statistic, describing the relative magnitude of the genetic component (or set of genetic components) in the population variance of the characteristic in question. It has no sensible meaning with reference to a measurement or characteristic in an individual. A single measurement, by definition, has no variance. There is no way of partitioning a given individual's IQ into hereditary and environmental components, as if the person inherited, say, 80 points of IQ and acquired 20 additional points from his environment. This is, of course, nonsense. *The square root of the heritability ($\sqrt{h^2}$), however, tells us the correlation between genotypes and phenotypes in the population, and this permits a probabilistic inference concerning the average amount of difference between individuals' obtained IQs and the 'genotypic value' of their intelligence.*\* (The average correlation between phenotypes and genotypes for IQ is about 0·90 in European and North American

---

\* Just as the square root of a test's reliability coefficient tells us the correlation between obtained scores and true scores, so the square root of a test's heritability tells us the correlation between obtained scores (i.e., the phenotypes) and 'genetic values' (i.e., genotypes) on the trait being measured. ('Value' refers here to a scaled quantity; it implies no 'value judgment'.) Without an absolute scale (as in the case for practically all psychological measurements), these values must be expressed merely as deviation scores, i.e., as deviations from a population mean. For the 'genetic value' to have any valid meaning, it must be expressed (and interpreted) as a deviation from the mean of the population in which the heritability was estimated and also in which the individual in question is a member. Given these conditions, we can determine the standard error of a test score's 'genetic value', analogous to the standard error of measurement. (The analogy is not perfect, however, since true scores and measurement errors are by definition uncorrelated, while genetic (G)

Caucasian populations, as determined from summary data presented later in this paper [Table 2]. The square of this value is known as the heritability – the proportion of phenotypic variance due to genetic variation.) The principle is the same as estimating the 'true' scores from obtained scores in test theory. Statements about individuals can be made only on a probabilistic basis and not with absolute certainty. Only if heritability were unity (i.e., $h^2 = 1$) would there be a perfect correlation between obtained scores and genotypic values, in which case we could say with assurance that an individual's measured IQ perfectly represented his genotype for intelligence. This still would not mean that the phenotype could have developed without an environment, for without either heredity or environment there simply is no organism and no phenotype. Thus the statement we so often hear in discussions of individual differences – that the individual's intelligence is the product of the interaction of his heredity and his environment –

---

and environmental (E) components may be correlated. But this is a soluble problem. The covariance of G and E can be independently estimated and may or may not be included in the estimate of $h^2$, depending upon the interpretation one wishes to give to $h^2$. Roberts (1967) has suggested that the environment should be defined as affecting the phenotype independently of the genotype. Thus, if individuals' genotypes influence their choice of environments, the environmental variation resulting therefrom would be considered a part of the total genetic variance.) It is simply $SE_G = SD\sqrt{1-h^2}$, where $SE_G$ is the standard error of the genetic value, $SD$ is the standard deviation of the test scores, and $h^2$ is the heritability (not corrected for attenuation due to test unreliability). For IQ, assuming $SD = 15$ and $h^2 = 0.75$, the standard error of the genetic value is 7·5 IQ points. This can be interpreted the same as the standard error of measurement. It means that 68 percent of our estimates of individual's genetic values will differ less than 7·5 points from this phenotypic IQ, 95 percent will differ less than 15 (i.e., 2 $SE_G$s), and 99·7 percent will differ less than 22·5 points (3 $SE_G$s). In other words, the probability is very small that two individuals whose IQs differ by, say, 20 or more points have the same genotypes for intelligence or that the one with the lower IQ has the higher genetic value. The individual's estimated genetic value, $\hat{G}_i$, expressed as a deviation score, is $\hat{G}_i = h^2(P_i - \bar{P}_p) + \bar{P}_p$ where $P_i$ is the individual's phenotypic measurement (e.g., IQ), and $\bar{P}_p$ is the population mean. The statement that an individual's test score is within, say $\pm x$ points of his 'true score' is no less probabilistic than saying his score is within $\pm x$ points of his 'genetic value'.

is rather fatuous. It really states nothing more than the fact that the individual exists.

*Constancy*. From what has already been said about heritability, it must be clear that it is not a constant like $\pi$ and the speed of light. $h^2$ is an empirically determined population statistic, and like any statistic, its value is affected by the characteristics of the population. $h^2$ will be higher in a population in which environmental variation relevant to the trait in question is small, than in a population in which there is great environmental variation. Similarly, when a population is relatively homogeneous in genetic factors but not in the environmental factors relevant to the development of the characteristic, the heritability of the characteristic in question will be lower. In short, the value of $h^2$ is jointly a function of genetic and environmental variability in the population. Also, like any other statistic, it is an estimate based on a sample of the population and is therefore subject to sampling error – the smaller the sample, the greater the margin of probable error. Values of $h^2$ reported in the literature do not represent what the heritability might be under any environmental conditions or in all populations or even in the same population at different times. Estimates of $h^2$ are specific to the population sampled, the point in time, how the measurements were made, and the particular test used to obtain the measurements.

*Measurements* versus *Reality*. It is frequently argued that since we cannot really measure intelligence we cannot possibly determine its heritability. Whether we can or cannot measure intelligence, which is a separate issue I have already discussed, let it be emphasized that it makes no difference to the question of heritability. We do not estimate the heritability of some trait that lies hidden behind our measurements. We estimate the heritability of the phenotypes and these are the measurements themselves. Regardless of what it is that our tests measure, the heritability tells us how much of the variance in these measurements is due to genetic factors. If the tests scores get at nothing genetic, the result will simply be that estimates of their heritability will not differ significantly from zero. The fact that heritability estimates based on IQs differ very significantly from zero is proof that genetic factors play a part in individual differences in IQ. To the extent that a test is not 'culture-free' or 'culture-fair', it will result in a lower heritability measurement. It makes no more sense to say that intelligence tests do not really measure intelligence but only *developed* intelligence than to say that scales do not really measure a person's weight but only the weight he has acquired by eating. An 'environment-free' test of intelligence makes as much sense as a 'nutrition-free' scale for weight.

*Know All* versus *Know Nothing*. This expression describes another confused notion: the idea that unless we can know absolutely *everything* about the genetics of intelligence we can know nothing! Proponents of this view demand that we be able to spell out in detail every single link in the chain of causality from genes (or DNA molecules) to test scores if we are to say anything about the heritability of intelligence. Determining the heritability of a characteristic does not at all depend upon a knowledge of its physical, biochemical, or physiological basis or of the precise mechanisms through which the characteristic is modified by the environment. Knowledge of these factors is, of course, important in its own right, but we need not have such knowledge to establish the genetic basis of the characteristic. Selective breeding was practiced fruitfully for centuries before anything at all was known of chromosomes and genes, and the science of quantitative genetics upon which the estimation of heritability depends has proven its value independently of advances in biochemical and physiological genetics.

*Acquired* versus *Inherited*. How can a socially defined attribute such as intelligence be said to be inherited? Or something that is so obviously acquired from the social environment as vocabulary? Strictly speaking, of course, only genes are inherited. But the brain mechanisms which are involved in learning are genetically conditioned just as are other structures and functions of the organism. What the organism is capable of learning from the environment and its rate of learning thus have a biological basis. Individuals differ markedly in the amount, rate, and kinds of learning they evince even given equal opportunities. Consider the differences that show up when a Mozart and the average run of children are given music lessons! If a test of vocabulary shows high heritability, it only means that persons in the population have had fairly equal opportunity for learning all the words in the test, and the differences in their scores are due mostly to differences in capacity for learning. If members of the population had had very unequal exposures to the words in the vocabulary test, the heritability of the scores would be very low.

*Immutability.* High heritability by itself does not necessarily imply that the characteristic is immutable.* Under greatly changed environmental conditions, the heritability may have some other value,

---

* It is also mistaken to argue that heritability has no implications whatever for the probable effects of environmental intervention. Since $1 - h_C^2$ ($h_C^2$ is $h^2$ corrected for attenuation) is the proportion of trait variance attributable to environmental factors, the square root of this value times the standard deviation of the true score trait measurement gives the standard deviation (*SD*) of the effect of existing environmental variations on the particular trait. For IQ this is about 6 points; that is to say, a shift of one *SD* in the sum total of whatever non-genetic influences contribute to environmental variance (i.e., $1 - h_C^2$), will shift the IQ about 6 points. (There is good evidence that environmental effects on IQ are normally distributed, at least in Caucasian populations [Jensen, 1970, 1971].) Thus the magnitude of change in a trait effected by changing the allocation of the existing environmental sources of variance in that trait is logically related to its heritability. This applies, of course, only to existing sources of environmental variance in the population, which is all that can be estimated by $1 - h_C^2$. It can have no relevance to speculations about as yet non-existent environmental influences or entirely new combinations of already existing environmental factors. With respect to IQ, I believe Bereiter (1970) states the situation quite correctly: 'What a high heritability ratio implies, therefore, is that changes within the existing range of environmental conditions can have substantial effects on the mean level of IQ in the population but they are unlikely to have much effect on the spread of individual differences in IQ within that population. If one is concerned with relative standing of individuals within the population, the prospects for doing anything about this through existing educational means are thus not good. Even with a massive redistribution of environmental conditions, one would expect to find the lower quarter of the IQ distribution to be about as far removed from the upper quarter as before' (p. 288). Bereiter goes on to say: 'A high heritability ratio for IQ should not discourage people from pursuing environmental improvement in education or any other area. The potential effects on IQ are great, although it still remains to discover the environmental variables capable of producing these effects.' Whether such specific environmental variables having major effects on IQ are or are not discovered in the immediate future, humane persons will surely agree that environmental conditions for the nation's poor should in any case be improved by all possible means.

or it may remain the same while the mean of the population changes. At one time tuberculosis had a very high heritability, the reason being that the tuberculosis bacilli were extremely widespread throughout the population, so that the main factor determining whether an individual contracted tuberculosis was not the probability of exposure but the individual's inherited physical constitution. Now that tuberculosis bacilli are relatively rare, difference in exposure rather than in physical predisposition is a more important determinant of who contracts tuberculosis. In the absence of exposure, individual differences in predisposition are of no consequence.

Heritability also tells us something about the locus of control of a characteristic. The control of highly heritable characteristics is usually in the organism's internal biochemical mechanism. Traits of low heritability are usually controlled by external environmental factors. No amount of psychotherapy, tutoring, or other psychological intervention will elicit normal performance from a child who is mentally retarded because of phenylketonuria (PKU), a recessive genetic defect of metabolism which results in brain damage. Yet a child who has inherited the genes for PKU can grow up normally if his diet is controlled to eliminate certain proteins which contain phenylalanine. Knowledge of the genetic and metabolic basis of this condition in recent years has saved many children from mental retardation.

*Parent-Child Resemblance.* The old maxim that 'like begets like' is held up as an instance of the workings of heredity. The lack of parent-child resemblance, on the other hand, is often mistakenly interpreted as evidence that a characteristic is not highly heritable. But the principles of genetics also explain the fact that often 'like begets unlike'. A high degree of parent-offspring resemblance, in fact, is to be expected only in highly inbred (or homozygous) strains, as in certain highly selected breeds of dogs and laboratory strains of mice. The random segregation of the parental genes in the formation of the sex cells means that the child receives a random selection of only half of each parent's genes. This fact that parent and child have only 50 percent of their genes in common, along with the effects of dominance and epistasis, insures considerable genetic dissimilarity between parent and child as well as among siblings, who also have only 50 percent of their genes in common. The fact that one parent and a child have only 50 percent of their genes in common is reflected in the average parent-offspring correlation ($r_{po}$) of between 0·50 and 0·60 (depending on the degree of assortative mating for a given characteristic) which obtains for height, head circumference, fingerprint ridges, intelligence, and other highly heritable characteristics. (The correlation is also between 0·50 and 0·60 for siblings on these characteristics; sibling resemblance is generally much *higher* than this for traits of *low* heritability.) The genetic correlation between the average of both parents (called the 'midparent') and a single offspring ($r_{\bar{p}o}$) is the square root of the correlation for a single parent (i.e., $r_{\bar{p}o} = \sqrt{r_{po}}$). The correlation between the average of *both* parents and the average of *all* the offspring ('midchild') that they could theoretically produce ($r_{\bar{p}\bar{o}}$) is the same value as $h^2_N$, i.e., heritability in the narrow sense.[1] It is noteworthy that empirical determinations of the midparent-midchild correlation ($r_{\bar{p}\bar{o}}$) in fact closely approximate the values of $h^2$ as estimated by various methods, such as comparisons of twins, siblings and unrelated children reared together.

EMPIRICAL FINDINGS ON THE HERITABILITY
OF INTELLIGENCE

It is always preferable, of course, to have estimates of the proportions of variance contributed by each of the components in Equation 2 than to have merely an overall estimate of $h^2$. But to obtain reliable estimates of the separate components requires large samples of persons of different kinships, such as identical twins reared together and reared apart, fraternal twins, siblings, half-siblings, parents-children, cousins, and so on. The methods of quantitative genetics by which these variance components, as well as the heritability, can be calculated from such kinship data are technical matters beyond the scope of this article, and the reader must be referred elsewhere for expositions of the methodology of quantitative genetics

---

[1] Heritability in the narrow sense is an estimate of the proportion of genic variance without consideration of dominance and epistasis. This contrasts with Equation 3, the definition of $h^2$, which includes estimates for these two factors. Signified as $h^2_N$, heritability in the narrow sense is conceptually defined as:

$$h^2_N = \frac{(V_G + V_{AM})}{V_p - V_e}$$

(Kempthorne, 1957; Cattell, 1960; Falconer, 1960; Huntley, 1966; Loehlin, in press).

The most satisfactory attempt to estimate the separate variance components is the work of Sir Cyril Burt (1955, 1958), based on large samples of many kinships drawn mostly from the school population of London. The IQ test used by Burt was an English adaptation of the Stanford-Binet. Burt's results may be regarded as representative of variance components of intelligence in populations that are similar to the population of London in their degree of genetic heterogeneity and in their range of environmental variation. Table 1 shows the percentage of variance due to the various components, grouped under 'genetic' and 'environmental', in Burt's analysis.

TABLE 1  **Analysis of Variance of Intelligence Test Scores** (*Burt, 1958*)

| Source of Variance | Percent* | |
|---|---|---|
| *Genetic:* | | |
| Genic (additive) | 40·5 | (47·9) |
| Assortative Mating | 19·9 | (17·9) |
| Dominance & Epistasis | 16·7 | (21·7) |
| *Environmental:* | | |
| Covariance of Heredity & Environment | 10·6 | (1·4) |
| Random Environmental Effects, including $H \times E$ interaction ($V_I$) | 5·9 | (5·8) |
| *Unreliability* (test error) | 6·4 | (5·3) |
| Total | 100·0 | (100·0) |

\* Figures in parentheses are percentages for adjusted assessments. See text for explanation.

When Burt submitted the test scores to the children's teachers for criticism on the basis of their impressions of the child's 'brightness', a number of children were identified for whom the IQ was not a fair estimate of the child's ability in the teacher's judgment. These children were retested, often on a number of tests on several occasions, and the result was an 'adjusted' assessment of the child's IQ. The results of the analysis of variance after these adjusted assessments were made are shown in parentheses in Table 1. Note that the component most affected by the adjustments is the co-variance of heredity and environment, which is what we should expect if the test is not perfectly 'culture-fair'. It means that the adjusted scores reduced systematic environmental sources of variance and thereby came closer to representing the children's innate ability, or, stated more technically, the adjusted scores increased the correlation between genotype and phenotype from 0·88 for unadjusted scores to 0·93 for adjusted scores. (Corrected for test unreliability these correlations become 0·90 and 0·96, respectively. And the heritabilities ($h^2{}_B$) for the two sets of scores are therefore $(0·90)^2 = 0·81$ and $(0·96)^2 = 0·93$, respectively.)

*Kinship Correlations.* The basic data from which variance components and heritability coefficients are estimated are correlations among individuals of different degrees of kinship. Nearly all such kinship correlations reported in the literature are summarized in Table 2. The median values of the correlations obtained in the various studies are given here. These represent the most reliable values we have for the correlations among relatives. Most of the values are taken from the survey by Erlenmeyer-Kimling and Jarvik (1963), and I have supplemented these with certain kinship correlations not included in their survey and reported in the literature since their review (e.g., Burt, 1966, p. 150). The Erlenmeyer-Kimling and Jarvik (1963) review was based on 52 independent studies of the correlations of relatives for tested intellectual abilities, involving over 30,000 correlational pairings from 8 countries in 4 continents, obtained over a period of more than two generations. The correlations were based on a wide variety of mental tests, administered under a variety of conditions by numerous investigators with contrasting views regarding the importance of heredity. The authors conclude: 'Against this pronounced heterogeneity, which should have clouded the picture, and is reflected by the wide range of correlations, a clearly definite consistency emerges from the data. The composite data are compatible with the polygenic hypothesis which is generally favored in accounting for inherited differences in mental ability' (Erlenmeyer-Kimling and Jarvik, 1963, p. 1479).

The compatibility with the polygenic hypothesis to which the authors (as outlined earlier on p. 53) refer can be appreciated in

TABLE 2   **Correlations for Intellectual Ability:
Obtained and Theoretical Values**

| Correlations Between | Number of Studies | Obtained Median r* | Theoretical Value[1] | Theoretical Value[2] |
|---|---|---|---|---|
| *Unrelated Persons* | | | | |
| Children reared apart | 4 | −0·01 | 0·00 | 0·00 |
| Foster parent and child | 3 | +0·20 | 0·00 | 0·00 |
| Children reared together | 5 | +0·24 | 0·00 | 0·00 |
| *Collaterals* | | | | |
| Second Cousins | 1 | +0·16 | +0·14 | +0·063 |
| First Cousins | 3 | +0·26 | +0·18 | +0·125 |
| Uncle (or aunt) and nephew (or niece) | 1 | +0·34 | +0·31 | +0·25 |
| Siblings, reared apart | 3 | +0·47 | +0·52 | +0·50 |
| Siblings, reared together | 36 | +0·55 | +0·52 | +0·50 |
| Dizygotic twins, different sex | 9 | +0·49 | +0·50 | +0·50 |
| Dizygotic twins, same sex | 11 | +0·56 | +0·54 | +0·50 |
| Monozygotic twins, reared apart | 4 | +0·75 | +1·00 | +1·00 |
| Monozygotic twins, reared together | 14 | +0·87 | +1·00 | +1·00 |
| *Direct Line* | | | | |
| Grandparent and grandchild | 3 | +0·27 | +0·31 | +0·25 |
| Parent (as adult) and child | 13 | +0·50 | +0·49 | +0·50 |
| Parent (as child) and child | 1 | +0·56 | +0·49 | +0·50 |

\* Correlations not corrected for attentuation (unreliability).

[1] Assuming assortative mating and partial dominance.

[2] Assuming random mating and only additive genes, i.e., the simplest possible polygenic model.

Table 2 by comparing the median values of the obtained correlations with the sets of theoretical values shown in the last two columns. The first set (Theoretical Value[1]) is based on calculations by Burt (1966), using the methods devised by Fisher for estimating kinship correlations for physical characteristics involving assortative mating and some degree of dominance. The second set (Theoretical Value[2]) of theoretical values is based on the simplest possible polygenic model, assuming random mating and nothing but additive gene effects. So these are the values one would expect if genetic factors alone were operating and the trait variance reflected no environmental influences whatsoever.

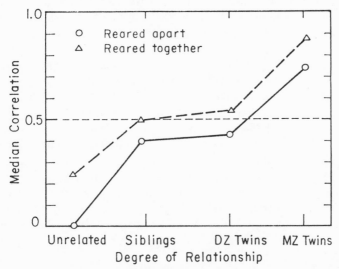

FIGURE 6. *Median values of all correlations reported in the literature up to 1963 for the indicated kinships. (After Erlenmeyer-Kimling and Jarvik, 1963.) Note consistency of difference in correlations for relatives reared together and reared apart.*

First of all, one can note certain systematic departures of the obtained correlations from the theoretical values. These departures are presumably due to non-genetic or environmental influences. The orderly nature of these environmental effects, as reflected in the Erlenmeyer-Kimling and Jarvik median correlations, can be highlighted by graphical presentation, as shown in Figure 6. Note that the condition of being reared together or reared apart has the same effect on the difference in magnitudes of the correlations for the various kinships. (The slightly greater difference for unrelated children is probably due to the fact of selective placement by adoption agencies, that is, the attempt to match the child's intelligence with that of the adopting parents.)

*Heritability Estimates.* By making certain comparisons among the correlations shown in Table 2 and Figure 6, one can get some insight into how heritability is estimated. For example, we see that the correlation between identical or monozygotic (MZ) twins reared apart is 0·75. Since MZ twins develop from a single fertilized ovum and thus have exactly the same genes, any difference between the twins must be due to nongenetic factors. And if they are reared apart in uncorrelated environments, the difference between a perfect correlation (1·00) and the obtained correlation (0·75) gives an estimate of the proportion of the variance in IQs attributable to environmental differences: $1·00 - 0·75 = 0·25$. Thus 75 percent of the variance can be said to be due to genetic variation (this is the heritability) and 25 percent to environmental variation. Now let us go to the other extreme and look at unrelated children reared together. They have no genetic inheritance in common, but they are reared in a common environment. Therefore the correlation between such children will reflect the environment. As seen in Table 2, this correlation is 0·24. Thus, the proportion of IQ variance due to environment is 0·24; and the remainder, $1·00 - 0·24 = 0·76$ is due to heredity. There is quite good agreement between the two estimates of heritability.

Another interesting comparison is between MZ twins reared together ($r = 0·87$) and reared apart ($r = 0·75$). If $1·00 - 0·75 = 0·25$ (from MZ twins reared apart) estimates the total environmental variance, then $1·00 - 0·87 = 0·13$ (from MZ twins reared together) is an estimate of the environmental variance *within families* in which children are reared together. Thus the difference between $0·25 - 0·13 = 0·12$ is an estimate of the environmental variance *between families*.

The situation is relatively simple when we deal only with MZ twins, who are genetically identical, or with unrelated children, who have nothing in common genetically. But in order to estimate heritability from any of the other kinship correlations, much more complex formulas are needed which would require much more explanation than is possible in this article. I have presented elsewhere a generalized formula for estimating heritability from any two kinship correlations where one kinship is of a higher degree than the other (Jensen, 1967a). I applied this heritability formula to all the correlations for monozygotic and dizygotic (half their genes in common) twins reported in the literature and found an average heritability of 0·80 for intelligence tests scores. (The correlations from which this heritability estimate was derived were corrected for unreliability.) Environmental differences *between* families account for 0·12 of the total variance and differences *within* families account for 0·08. It is possible to derive an overall heritability coefficient from all the kinship correlations given in Table 2. This composite value of $h^2$ is 0·77, which becomes 0·81 after correction for unreliability (assuming an average test reliability of 0·95). This represents probably the best single overall estimate of the heritability of measured intelligence that we can make. But, as pointed out previously, this is an average value of $h^2$ about which there is some disperson of values, depending on such variables as the particular tests used, the population sampled, and sampling error.

*Identical Twins Reared Apart.* The conceptually simplest estimate of heritability is, of course, the correlation between identical twins reared apart, since, if their environments are uncorrelated, all they have in common are their genes. The correlation (corrected for unreliability) in this case is the same as the heritability as defined in Equation 3. There have been only three major studies of MZ twins separated early in life and reared apart. All three used individually administered intelligence tests. The correlation between Stanford-Binet IQs of 19 pairs of MZ twins reared apart in a study by Newman, Freeman, and Holzinger (1937) was 0·67 (0·71 corrected for unreliability). The correlation between 38 pairs of MZ twins reared apart on a composite score based on a vocabulary test and the Domino D-48 test (a non-verbal test of *g*) was 0·77 (0·81 corrected) in a study by Shields (1962). The correlation between 53 pairs on the Stanford-Binet was 0·86 (0·91 corrected) in a study by Burt (1966). Twin correlations in the same group for height and for weight were 0·94 and 0·88, respectively.

The Burt study is perhaps the most interesting, for four reasons: (*a*) it is based on the largest sample; (*b*) the IQ distribution of the sample had a mean of 97·8 and a standard deviation of 15·3 – values very close to those of the general population; (*c*) all the twin pairs were separated at birth or within their first 6 months of life; and (*d*) most important, the separated twins were spread over the entire range of socioeconomic levels (based on classification in terms of the six socioeconomic categories of the English census), and there was a slight, though nonsignificant, negative correlation between the environmental ratings of the separated twin pairs. When the twin pairs were rated for differences in the cultural conditions of their rearing, these differences correlated 0·26 with the differences in their IQs. Differences between the material conditions of their homes correlated 0·16 with IQ differences. (The corresponding correlations for a measure of scholastic attainments were 0·74 and 0·37, respectively. The correlation between the twins in scholastic attainments was only 0·62, indicating a much lower heritability than for IQ.)

*Foster Parents* versus *Natural Parents*. Children separated from their true parents shortly after birth and reared in adoptive homes show almost the same degree of correlation with the intelligence of their biological parents as do children who are reared by their own parents. The correlations of children with their foster parents' intelligence range between 0 and 0·20 and are seldom higher than this even when the adoption agency attempts selective placement (e.g., Honzik, 1957). Parent-child correlations gradually increase from zero at 18 months of age to an asymptotic value close to 0·50 between ages 5 and 6 (Jones, 1954), and this is true whether the child is reared by his parents or not.

*Direct Measurement of the Environment*. Another method for getting at the relative contribution of environmental factors to IQ variance is simply by correlating children's IQs with ratings of their environment. This can be legitimately done only in the case of adopted children and where there is evidence that selective placement by the adoption agencies is negligible. Without these conditions, of course, some of the correlation between the children and their environmental ratings will be due to genetic factors. There are two large-scale studies in the literature which meet these criteria. Also, both studies involved adopting parents who were representative of a broad cross-section of the U.S. Caucasian population with respect to education, occupation, and socioeconomic level. It is probably safe to say that not more than 5 percent of the U.S. Caucasian population falls outside the range of environmental variation represented in the samples in these two studies. The study by Leahy (1935) found an average correlation of 0·20 between the IQs of adopted children and a number of indices of the 'goodness' of their environment, including the IQs and education of both adopting parents, their socioeconomic status, and the cultural amenities in the home. Leahy concluded from this that the environmental ratings accounted for 4 percent (i.e., the square of $r = 0.20$) of the variance in the adopted children's Stanford-Binet IQs, and that 96 percent of the variance remained to be accounted for by other factors. The main criticisms we can make of this study are, first, that the environmental indices were not sufficiently 'fine-grained' to register the subtleties of environmental variation and of the qualities of parent-child relationship that influence intellectual development, and, second, that the study did not make use of the technique of multiple correlation, which would show the total contribution to the variance of all the separate environmental indices simultaneously. A multiple correlation is usually considerably greater than merely the average of all the correlations for the single variables.

A study by Burks (1928) meets both these objections. To the best of my knowledge no study before or since has rated environments in any more detailed and fine-grained manner than did Burks'. Each adoptive home was given 4 to 8 hours of individual investigation. As in Leahy's study, Burks included intelligence measures on the adopting parents as part of the children's environments, an environment which also included such factors as the amount of time the parents spent helping the children with their school work, the amount of time spent reading to the children, and so on. The multiple correlation (corrected for unreliability) between Burks' various environmental ratings and the adopted children's Stanford-Binet IQs was 0·42. The square of this correlation is 0·18, which represents the proportion of IQ variance accounted for by Burks' environmental measurements. This value comes very close to the environmental variance estimated in direct heritability analyses based on kinship correlations.

Burks translated her findings into the conclusion that the total effect of environmental factors one standard deviation up or down the environmental scale is only about 6 IQ points. This is an interesting figure, since it is exactly half the 12 point IQ difference found on the average between normal siblings reared together by their own parents. Siblings differ genetically, of course, having only about half their genes in common. If all the siblings in every family were divided into two groups – those above and those below the family average – the IQ distributions of the two groups would appear as shown in Figure 7. Though the average difference is only 12 IQ

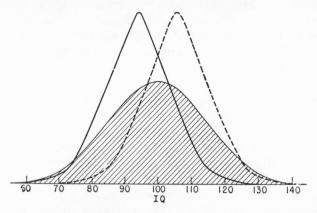

FIGURE 7.    *IQ distributions of siblings who are below (solid curve) or above (dashed curve) their family average. The shaded curve is the IQ distribution of randomly selected children.*

points, note the implications in the proportions of each group falling into the upper and lower ranges of the IQ scale. It would be most instructive to study the educational and occupational attainments of these two groups, since presumably they should have about the same environmental advantages.

Another part of Burk's study consisted of a perfectly matched control group of parents rearing their own children, for whom parent-child correlations were obtained. Sewall Wright (1931) performed a heritability analysis on these parent-child and IQ-environment correlations and obtained a heritability coefficient of 0·81.

## EFFECTS OF INBREEDING ON INTELLIGENCE

One of the most impressive lines of evidence for the involvement of genetic factors in intelligence comes from study of the effects of inbreeding, that is, the mating of relatives. In the case of polygenic characteristics the direction of the effect of inbreeding is predictable from purely genetic considerations. All individuals carry in their chromosomes a number of mutant or defective genes. These genes are almost always recessive, so they have no effect on the phenotype unless by rare chance they match up with another mutant gene at the same locus on a homologous chromosome; in other words, the recessive mutant gene at a given locus must be inherited from both the father and mother in order to affect the phenotype. Since such mutants are usually defective, they do not enhance the phenotypic expression of the characteristic but usually degrade it. And for polygenic characteristics we would expect such mutants to lower the metric value of the characteristics by graded amounts, depending upon the number of paired mutant recessives. If the parents are genetically related, there is a greatly increased probability that the mutant recessives at given loci will be paired in the offspring. The situation is illustrated in Figure 8, which depicts in a simplified way a pair of homologous chromosomes inherited by an individual from a mother (M) and father (F) who are related (Pair A) and a pair of chromosomes inherited from unrelated parents (Pair B). The blackened spaces represent recessive genes. Although both pairs contain equal numbers of recessives, more of them are at the same loci in Pair A than in Pair B. Only their paired genes degrade the characteristics' phenotypic value.

A most valuable study of this genetic phenomenon with respect to intelligence was carried out in Japan after World War II by Schull and Neel (1965). The study illustrates how strictly sociological factors, such as mate selection, can have extremely important genetic consequences. In Japan approximately 5 percent of all marriages are between cousins. Schull and Neel studied the offspring of marriages of first cousins, first cousins once removed, and second cousins. The parents were statistically matched with a control group of unrelated parents for age and socioeconomic factors. Children from the cousin marriages and the control children from unrelated parents (total $N = 2111$) were given the Japanese version of the Wechsler Intelligence Scale for Children (WISC). The degree of consanguinity represented by the cousin marriages in this study had the effect of depressing WISC IQs by an average of 7·4 percent. making the mean of the inbred group nearly 8 IQ points lower than the mean of the control group. Assuming normal distributions of IQ, the effect is shown in Figure 9, and illustrates the point that the most drastic consequences of group mean differences are to be seen in the tails of the distributions. In the same study a similar depressing effect was found for other polygenic characteristics such as several anthropometric and dental variables.

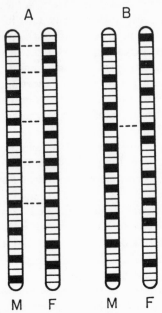

FIGURE 8.   *Simplified schema of chromosomes, illustrating the pairing of recessive (mutant) genes (black spaces) in homologous chromosomes from mother (M) and father (F). Pair A has five pairs of recessives in the same loci on the chromosome, Pair B has only one such pair.*

The mating of relatives closer than cousins can produce a markedly greater reduction in offspring's IQs. Lindzey (1967) has reported that almost half of a group of children born to so-called nuclear incest matings (brother-sister or father-daughter) could not be placed for adoption because of mental retardation and other severe defects which had a relatively low incidence among the offspring of unrelated parents who were matched with the incestuous parents in intelligence, socioeconomic status, age, weight, and stature. In any geographically confined population where social or legal regulations on mating are lax, where individuals' paternity is often dubious, and where the proportion of half-siblings within the same age-groups is high, we would expect more inadvertent inbreeding, with its unfavorable genetic consequences, than in a population in which these conditions exist to a lesser degree.

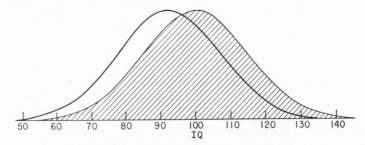

FIGURE 9.   *The average effect of inbreeding to the degree of 1st, 1½, and 2nd cousin matings on the IQ distribution of offspring (heavy line). Shaded curve is the IQ distribution of the offspring of nonconsanguinous matings. (After Schull and Neel, 1965.)*

*Heritability of Special Mental Abilities.* When the general factor, or *g*, is removed from a variety of mental tests, the remaining variance is attributable to a number of so-called 'group factors' or 'special abilities'. The tests of special abilities that have been studied most thoroughly with respect to their heritability are Thurstone's Primary Mental Abilities: Verbal, Space, Number, Word Fluency, Memory, and Perceptual Speed. Vandenberg (1967) has reviewed the heritability studies of these tests and reports that the $h^2$ values range from near zero to about 0·75, with most values of $h^2$ between 0·50 and 0·70. Vandenberg devised a method for estimating the genetic components of these special abilities which are completely independent of *g*. He concluded that at least four of the Primary Mental Abilities (Number, Verbal, Space, and Word Fluency) independently have significant hereditary components.

There have been few studies of the heritability of noncognitive skills, but a study by McNemar (see Bilodeau, 1966, Ch. 3) of motor skill learning indicates that heritabilities in this sphere may be even higher than for intelligence. The motor skill learning was measured with a pursuit-rotor, a tracking task in which the subject must learn to keep a stylus on a metal disc about the size of nickel rotating through a circumference of about 36 inches at 60 rpm. The percentage of time 'on target' during the course of practice yields a learning measure of high reliability, showing marked individual differences both in rate of acquisition and final asymptote of this perceptual-motor skill. Identical twins correlated 0·95 and fraternal twins 0·51 on pursuit-rotor learning, yielding a heritability coefficient of 0·88, which is very close to the heritability of physical stature.

*Heritability of Scholastic Achievement.* The heritability of measures of scholastic achievement is much less, on the average, than the heritability of intelligence. In reviewing all the twin studies in the literature containing relevant data, I concluded that individual differences in scholastic performance are determined less than half as much by heredity as are differences in intelligence (Jensen, 1967a).[1] The analysis of all the twin studies on a variety of scholastic

[1] After this article went to press I received a personal communication from Professor Lloyd G. Humphreys who pointed out some arguments that indicate I may have underestimated the heritability of scholastic achievement and that its heritability may actually be considerably closer to the heritability of intelligence. The argument involves two main points: (1) the fact that some of the achievement tests that entered into the average estimate of heritability are tests of specific achievements, rather than omnibus achievement tests, and therefore would correspond more to the separate subscales of the usual intelligence tests, which are known to have somewhat lower heritabilities than the composite scores; and (2) scores on some of the achievement tests are age-related, so that fraternal twin correlations, in relation to other kinship correlations, are unduly inflated by common factor of age. When age is partialled out of the MZ and DZ twin correlations, the estimate of heritability based on MZ and DZ twin comparisons is increased. However, an omnibus achievement test (Stanford Achievement) yielding an overall Educational Age score had a heritability of only 0·46 (as compared with 0·63 for Stanford-Binet IQ and 0·70 for Otis IQ based on the same set of MZ and DZ twins), with age partialled out of the twin correlations (Newman, Freeman, and Holzinger, 1937, p. 97). Rank in high school graduating class, which is an overall index of scholastic performance and is little affected by age yields heritability coefficients below 0·40 in a nationwide sample (Nichols and Bilbro, 1966). The issue clearly needs further study, but the best conclusion that can be drawn from the existing evidence, I believe, still is that the heritability of scholastic achievement is less than for intelligence, but the amount of the difference cannot be precisely estimated.

measures gives an average $h^2$ of 0·40. The environmental variance of 60 percent can be partitioned into variance due to environmental differences *between* families, which is 54 percent, and differences *within* families of 6 percent. But it should also be noted that the heritability estimates for scholastic achievement vary over a much wider range than to $h^2$ values for intelligence. In general, $h^2$ for scholastic achievement increases as we go from the primary grades up to high school and it is somewhat lower for relatively simple forms of learning (e.g., spelling and arithmetic computation) than for more complex learning (e.g., reading comprehension and arithmetic problem solving). Yet large-sample twin data from the National Merit Scholarship Corporation show that the *between families* environmental component accounts for about 60 percent of the variance in students' rank in their high school graduating class. This must mean that there are strong family influences which cause children to conform to some academic standard set by the family and which reduce variance in scholastic performance among siblings reared in the same family. Unrelated children reared together are also much more alike in school performance than in intelligence. The common finding of a negative correlation between children's IQ and the amount of time parents report spending in helping their children with school work is further evidence that considerable family pressures are exerted to equalize the scholastic performance of siblings. This pressure to conform to a family standard shows up most conspicuously in the small *within families* environmental variance component on those school subjects which are most susceptible to improvement by extra coaching, such as spelling and arithmetic computation.

The fact that scholastic achievement is considerably less heritable than intelligence also means that many other traits, habits, attitudes, and values enter into a child's performance in school besides just his intelligence, and these non-cognitive factors are largely environmentally determined, mainly through influences within the child's family. This means there is potentially much more we can do to improve school performance through environmental means than we can do to change intelligence *per se*. Thus it seems likely that if compensatory education programs are to have a beneficial effect on achievement, it will be through their influence on motivation, values, and other environmentally conditioned habits that play an important part in scholastic performance, rather than through any marked direct influence on intelligence *per se*. The proper evaluation of such programs should therefore be sought in their effects on actual scholastic performance rather than in how much they raise the child's IQ.

## How the Environment Works

### ENVIRONMENT AS A THRESHOLD

All the reports I have found of especially large upward shifts in IQ which are explicitly associated with environmental factors have involved young children, usually under 6 years of age, whose initial social environment was deplorable to a greater extreme than can be found among any children who are free to interact with other persons or to run about out-of-doors. There can be no doubt that moving children from an extremely deprived environment to good average environmental circumstances can boost the IQ some 20 to 30 points and in certain extreme rare cases as much as 60 or 70 points. On the other hand, children reared in rather average circumstances do not show an appreciable IQ gain as a result of being placed in a more culturally enriched environment. While there are reports of groups of children going from below average up to average IQs as a result of environmental enrichment, I have found no report of a group of children being given permanently superior IQs by means of environmental manipulations. In brief, it is doubtful that psychologists have found consistent evidence for any social environmental influences short of extreme environmental isolation which have a marked systematic effect on intelligence. This suggests that the influence of the quality of the environment on intellectual development is not a linear function. Below a certain threshold of environmental adequacy, deprivation can have a markedly depressing effect on intelligence. But above this threshold, environmental variations cause relatively small differences in intelligence. The fact that the vast majority of the populations sampled in studies of the heritability of intelligence are above this threshold level of environmental adequacy accounts for the high values of the heritability estimates and the relatively small proportion of IQ variance attributable to environmental influences.

The environment with respect to intelligence is thus analogous to nutrition with respect to stature. If there are great nutritional lacks, growth is stunted, but above a certain level of nutritional adequacy, including minimal daily requirements of minerals, vitamins, and proteins, even great variations in eating habits will have negligible effects on persons' stature, and under such conditions most of the differences in stature among individuals will be due to heredity.

When I speak of subthreshold environmental deprivation, I do not refer to a mere lack of middle-class amenities. I refer to the extreme sensory and motor restrictions in environments such as those described by Skeels and Dye (1939) and Davis (1947), in which the subjects had little sensory stimulation of any kind and little contact with adults. These cases of extreme social isolation early in life showed great deficiencies in IQ. But removal from social deprivation to a good, average social environment resulted in large gains in IQ. The Skeels and Dye orphanage children gained in IQ from an average of 64 at 19 months of age to 96 at age 6 as a result of being given social stimulation and placement in good homes between 2 and 3 years of age. When these children were followed up as adults, they were found to be average citizens in their communities, and their own children had an average IQ of 105 and were doing satisfactorily in school. A far more extreme case was that of Isabel, a child who was confined and reared in an attic up to the age of 6 by a deaf-mute mother, and who had an IQ of about 30 at age 6. When Isabel was put into a good environment at that age, her IQ became normal by age 8 and she was able to perform as an average student throughout school (Davis, 1947). Extreme environmental deprivation thus need not permanently result in below average intelligence.

These observations are consistent with studies of the effects of extreme sensory deprivation on primates. Monkeys raised from birth under conditions of total social isolation, for example, show no indication when compared with normally raised controls, of any permanent impairment of ability for complex discrimination learning, delayed response learning, or learning set formation, although the isolated monkeys show severe social impairment in their relationships to normally reared monkeys (Harlow and Griffin, 1965).

Thoughtful scrutiny of all these studies of extreme environmental deprivation leads to two observations which are rarely made by psychologists who cite the studies as illustrative explanations of the low IQs and poor scholastic performance of the many children called culturally disadvantaged. In the first place, typical culturally disadvantaged children are not reared in anything like the degree of sensory and motor deprivation that characterizes, say, the children of the Skeels' study. Secondly, the IQs of severely deprived children are markedly depressed even at a very early age, and when they are later exposed to normal environmental stimulation, their IQs rise rapidly, markedly, and permanently. Children called culturally disadvantaged, on the other hand, generally show no early deficit and are usually average and sometimes precocious on perceptual-motor tests administered before 2 years of age. The orphanage children described in Skeels' study are in striking contrast to typical culturally disadvantaged children of the same age. Also, culturally disadvantaged children usually show a slight initial gain in IQ after their first few months of exposure to the environmental enrichment afforded by school attendance, but, unlike Skeels' orphans, they soon lose this gain, and in a sizeable proportion of children the initial IQ gain is followed by a gradual decline in IQ throughout the subsequent years of schooling. We do not know how much of this decline is related to environmental or hereditary factors. We do know that with increasing age children's IQs increasingly resemble their parents' rank order in intelligence whether they are reared by them or not, and therefore with increasing age we should expect greater and more reliable differentiation among children's IQs as they gravitate toward their genotypic values (Honzik, 1957). Of course, the gravitating effect is compounded by the fact that less intelligent parents are also less apt to provide the environmental conditions conducive to intellectual development in the important period between ages 3 and 7, during which children normally gain increasing verbal control over their environment and their own behavior. (I have described some of these environmental factors in detail elsewhere [Jensen, 1968e].)

Heber, Dever and Conry (1968) have obtained data which illustrate this phenomenon of children's gravitation toward the parental IQ with increasing age. They studied the families of 88 low economic class Negro mothers residing in Milwaukee in a set of contiguous slum census tracts, an area which yields the highest known prevalence of identified retardation in the city's schools. Although these tracts contribute about 5 percent of the schools' population, they account for about one-third of the school children classed as mentally retarded (IQ below 75). The sample of 88 mothers was selected by taking 88 consecutive births in these tracts where the mother already had at least one child of age 6. The 88 mothers had a total of 586 children, excluding their newborns. The percentage of mothers with IQs of 80 or above was 54·6; 45·4 percent were below

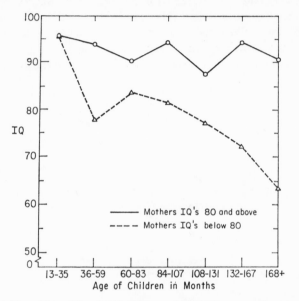

FIGURE 10. *Mean IQs of 586 children of 88 mothers as a function of age of children. Heber, Dever, and Conry, 1968.*)

IQ 80. The IQs of the children of these two groups of mothers were plotted as a function of the children's age. The results are shown in Figure 10. Note that only the children whose mothers' IQs are below 80 show a systematic decline in IQ as well as a short-lived spurt of several points at the age of entrance into school. At 6 years of age and older, 80·8 percent of the children with IQs below 80 were those whose mothers had IQs below 80.

It is far from certain or even likely that all such decline in IQ is due to environmental influences rather than to genetic factors involved in the growth rate of intelligence. Consistent with this interpretation is the fact that the heritability of intelligence measures increases with age. We should expect just the opposite if environmental factors alone were responsible for the increasing IQ deficit of markedly below-average groups. A study by Wheeler (1942) suggests that although IQ may be raised at all age levels by improving the environment, such improvements do not counteract the decline in the IQ of certain below-average groups. In 1940 Wheeler tested over 3000 Tennessee mountain children between the ages of and 6 and 16 compared their IQs with children in the same age range who had been given the same tests in 1930, when the average IQ and standard of living in this area would characterize the majority of the inhabitants as 'culturally deprived'. During the intervening

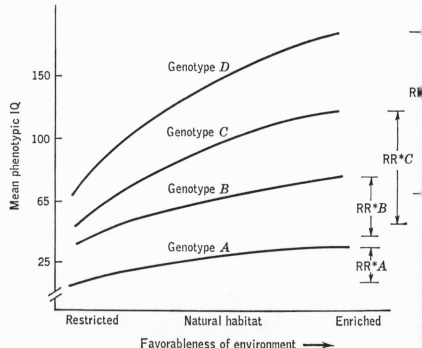

FIGURE 11.    *Scheme of the reaction range concept for four hypothetical genotypes. RR denotes the presumed reaction range for phenotypic IQ. Note: Large deviations from the 'natural habitat' have a low probability of occurrence.* (*From Gottesman, 1963.*)

10 years, state and federal intervention in this area brought about great improvements in economic conditions, standards of health care, and educational and cultural opportunities, and during the same period the average IQ of the region increased 10 points, from 82 to 92. But the decline in IQ from age 6 to age 16 was about the same in 1940 (from 103 to 80) as in 1930 (from 95 to 74).

*Reaction Range.* Geneticists refer to the concept of reaction range (RR) in discussing the fact that similar genotypes may result in quite different phenotypes depending on the favorableness of the environment for the development of the characteristic in question. Of further interest to geneticists is the fact that different genotypes may have quite different reaction ranges; some genotypes may be much more buffered against environmental influences than others. Different genetic strains can be unequal in their susceptibility to the same range of environmental variation, and when this is the case, the strains will show dissimilar heritabilities on the trait in question, the dissimilarity being accentuated by increasing environmental variation. Both of these aspects of the reaction range concept are illustrated hypothetically with respect to IQ in Figure 11.*

The above discussion should serve to counter a common misunderstanding about quantitative estimates of heritability. It is sometimes forgotten that such estimates actually represent *average* values in the population that has been sampled and they do not necessarily apply either to differences *within* various subpopulations or to differences *between* subpopulations. In a population in which an overall $h^2$ estimate is, say, 0·80, we may find a certain group for which $h^2$ is only 0·70 and another group for which $h^2$ is 0·90. All the major heritability studies reported in the literature are based on samples of white European and North American populations, and our knowledge of the heritability of intelligence in different racial

* This hypothetical graph from Gottesman (1963) unfortunately has certain misleading features. Note that the IQ scale on the ordinate is peculiar, with visually equal but numerically unequal intervals. The graph suggests only a theoretical possibility. Actually, there has been no evidence that supports the hypothesis that different genotypes for IQ are affected differentially by the environment. In short, no evidence has been adduced in support of the hypothesis depicted in Figure 11, which remains only a theoretical possibility outside the range of naturally occurring environments.

and cultural groups within these populations is nil. For example, no adequate heritability studies have been based on samples of the Negro population of the United States. Since some genetic strains may be more buffered from environmental influences than others, it is not sufficient merely to equate the environments of various subgroups in the population to infer equal heritability of some characteristic in all of them. The question of whether heritability estimates can contribute anything to our understanding of the relative importance of genetic and environmental factors in accounting for average phenotypic differences between racial groups (or any other socially identifiable groups) is too complex to be considered here. I have discussed this problem in detail elsewhere and concluded that heritability estimates could be of value in testing certain specific hypotheses in this area of inquiry, provided certain conditions were met and certain other crucial items of information were also available (Jensen, 1968c).

Before continuing discussion of environmental factors we must guard against one other misunderstanding about heritability that sometimes creeps in at this point. This is the notion that because so many different environmental factors and all their interactions influence the development of intelligence, by the time the child is old enough to be tested, these influences must totally bury or obscure all traces of genetic factors – the genotype must lie hidden and inaccessible under the heavy overlay of environmental influences. If this were so, of course, the obtained values of $h^2$ would be very close to zero. But the fact that values of $h^2$ for intelligence are usually quite high (in the region of 0·70 to 0·90) means that current intelligence tests can, so to speak, 'read through' the environmental 'overlay'.

PHYSICAL *versus* SOCIAL ENVIRONMENT

The value $1 - h^2$, which for IQ generally amounts to about 0·20, can be called $E$, the proportion of variance due to nongenetic factors. There has been a pronounced tendency to think of $E$ as being wholly associated with individuals' social and interpersonal environment, child rearing practices, and differences in educational and cultural opportunities afforded by socioeconomic status. It is certain, however, that these sociological factors are not responsible for the whole of $E$ and it is not improbable that they contribute only a minor portion of the $E$ variance in the bulk of our population. Certain physical and biological environmental factors may be at least as important as the social factors in determining individual differences in intelligence. If this is true, advances in medicine, nutrition, prenatal care, and obstetrics may contribute as much or more to improving intelligence as will manipulation of the social environment.

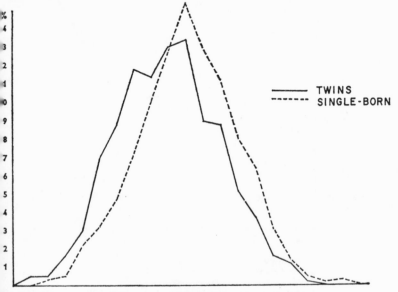

FIGURE 12.   *Distribution of reading scores of twins and single children (all girls). (Husén, 1960.)*

*Prenatal Environment of Twins.* A little known fact about twins is that they average some 4 to 7 points lower in IQ than singletons (Vandenberg, 1968). The difference also shows up in scholastic achievement, as shown in the distribution of reading scores of twin and singleton girls in Sweden (Figure 12).

If this phenomenon were due entirely to differences between twins and singletons in the amount of individual attention they receive from their parents, one might expect the twin-singleton difference to be related to the family's socioeconomic status. But there seems to be no systematic relationship of this kind. The largest study of the question, summarized in Figure 13, shows about the same average amount of twin-singleton IQ disparity over a wide range of socioeconomic groups.

Three other lines of evidence place the locus of this effect in the prenatal environment. Monozygotic twins are slightly lower in IQ than dizygotic twins (Stott, 1960, p. 98), a fact which is consistent

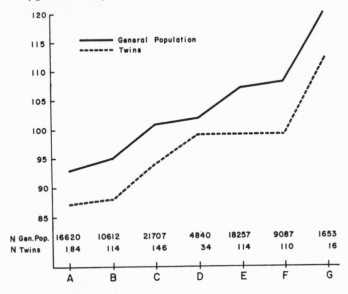

A. Farm workers
B. Workers in towns of less than 2000
C. Workers in larger towns and cities
D. Salaried employees in towns of less than 2000
E. Salaried employees in larger towns and cities
F. Managers and merchants
G. Professional men

FIGURE 13.   *Distribution of IQs by occupation of father, for twins and singletons.* (*Zazzo, 1960.*)

with the finding that MZ twins have a higher mortality rate and greater disparity in birth weights than DZ twins, suggesting that MZ twins enjoy less equal and less optimal intrauterine conditions than DZ twins of singletons. Inequalities in both intrauterine space and fetal nutrition probably account for this. Also, boy twins are significantly lower in IQ than girl twins, which conforms to the well-known greater vulnerability of male infants to prenatal impairment (Stott, 1960). Finally, the birth weight of infants, when matched for gestational age, is slightly but significantly correlated with later IQ, and the effect is independent of sociocultural factors (Churchill, Neff and Caldwell, 1966). In pairs of identical twins, the twin with the lower birth-weight usually has the lower IQ (by 5 to 7 points on the average) at school age. This is true both in white and in Negro twins. The birth-weight differences are reflected in all 11 subtests of the Wechsler Intelligence Scale for Children and are slightly greater on the Performance than on the Verbal tests (Willerman and Churchill, 1967). The investigators interpret these findings as suggesting that nutrient supplies may be inadequate for proper body and brain development in twin pregnancies, and that the unequal sharing of nutrients and space stunts one twin more than its mate.

Thus, much of the average difference between MZ twins, whether reared together or reared apart, seems to be due to prenatal environmental factors. The real importance of these findings, of course, lies in their implications for the possible role of prenatal environment in the development of all children. It is not unlikely that there are individual maternal differences in the adequacy of the prenatal environment. If intrauterine conditions can cause several points of IQ difference between twins, it is not hard to imagine that individual differences in prenatal environments could also cause IQ differences in single-born children and might therefore account for a substantial proportion of the total environmental variance in IQ.

*Abdominal Decompression.* There is now evidence that certain manipulations of the intrauterine environment can affect the infant's behavioral development for many months after birth. A technique known as abdominal decompression was invented by a professor of obstetrics (Heyns, 1963), originally for the purpose of making women experience less discomfort in the latter months of their pregnancy and also to facilitate labor and delivery. For about an hour a day during the last 3 or 4 months of pregnancy, the woman is placed in a device that creates a partial vacuum around her abdomen, which greatly reduces the intrauterine pressure. The device is used during labor up to the moment of delivery. Heyns has applied this device to more than 400 women. Their infants, as compared with control groups who have not received this treatment, show more rapid development in their first 2 years and manifest an overall superiority in tests of perceptual-motor development. They sit up

earlier, walk earlier, talk earlier, and appear generally more precocious than their own siblings or other children whose mothers
were not so treated. At 2 years of age the children in Heyns' experiment had DQs (developmental quotients) some 30 points higher
than the control children (in the general population the mean DQ
is 100, with a standard deviation of 15). Heyns explains the effects
of maternal abdominal decompression on the child's early development in terms of the reduction of intrauterine pressure, which
results in a more optimal blood supply to the fetus and also lessens
the chances of brain damage during labor. (The intrauterine
pressure on the infant's head is reduced from about 22 lb to 8 lb.)
Results on children's later IQs have not been published, but correspondence with Professor Heyns and verbal reports from visitors to
his laboratory inform me that there is no evidence that the IQ of
these children is appreciably higher beyond age 6 than that of
control groups.* If this observation is confirmed by the proper
methods, it should not be too surprising in view of the negligible
correlations normally found between DQs and later IQs. But since
abdominal decompression results in infant precocity, one may

* Heyns' experiment has been repeated, with adequate sample size
and proper experimental controls, by Liddicoat in collaboration with
Heyns (Liddicoat, R. The effects of maternal antenatal decompression
treatment on infant mental development. *Psychologia Africana*, 1968, **12**,
103-121). The results were entirely negative. Liddicoat summarizes the
study as follows:
'A sample of 329 patients from the Queen Victoria Maternity Hospital,
Johannesburg, was tested on the South African version of the Wechsler-
Bellevue adult intelligence test. Each patient was then randomly assigned
to one of two groups; the experimental group received antenatal decompression treatment, and the control group was entitled to receive antenatal
physiotherapy treatment. Their infants were tested on the South African
child development scale at the age of 1, 4 and 9 months, and on the Merrill-
Palmer scale of mental tests at the age of 3 years. Results of the tests
showed no significant difference between the mean scores of the two
groups at any of these age levels. Factors possibly influencing this finding
are discussed' (p. 103). As to the reasons for the earlier promising findings
of Heyns, Liddicoat writes: 'It is possible that the experimental design
of the early surveys did not take full cognizance of some factors which
could influence obtained results, such as socioeconomic status and intellectual level of the mothers, volunteer bias, the provision of strictly comparable controls and the use of a reliable measuring device' (p. 116).
Liddicoat's careful full report is well worth reading.

wonder to what extent differences in intrauterine pressure are responsible for normal individual and group differences in infant precocity. Negro infants, for example, are more precocious in development (as measured on the Bayley Scales) in their first year or two than Caucasian infants (Bayley, 1965a). Infant precocity would seem to be associated with more optimal intrauterine and perinatal conditions. This conjecture is consistent with the finding that infants whose prenatal and perinatal histories would make them suspect of some degree of brain damage show lower DQs on the Bayley Scales than normal infants (Honzik, 1962). Writers who place great emphasis on the hypothesis of inadequate prenatal care and complications of pregnancy to account for the lower average IQ of Negroes (e.g., Bronfenbrenner, 1967) are also obliged to explain why these unfavorable factors do not also depress the DQ below average in Negro infants, as do such factors as brain damage and prenatal and infant malnutrition (Cravioto, 1966). Since all such environmental factors should lower the heritability of intelligence in any segment of the population in which they are hypothesized to play an especially significant role, one way to test the hypothesis would be to compare the heritability of intelligence in that segment of the population for which extra environmental factors are hypothesized with the heritability in other groups for whom environmental factors are supposedly less accountable for IQ variance.

*A Continuum of Reproductive Casualty.* A host of conditions associated with reproduction which are known to differ greatly across socioeconomic levels have been hypothesized as causal factors in average intellectual differences. There is no doubt about the fact of the greater prevalence in poverty areas of conditions unfavorable to optimal pregnancy and safe delivery. The question that remains unanswered is the amount of IQ variance associated with these conditions predisposing to reproductive casualty. The disadvantageous factors most highly associated with social conditions are: pregnancies at early ages, teenage deliveries, pregnancies in close succession, a large number of pregnancies, and pregnancies that occur late in the woman's reproductive life (Graves, Freeman and Thompson, 1968). These conditions are related to low birth-weight, prematurity, increased infant mortality, prolonged labor, toxemia, anemia, malformations, and mental deficiency in the offspring.

Since all of these factors have a higher incidence in low socioeconomic groups and in certain ethnic groups (Negroes, American Indians, and Mexican-Americans) in the United States, they probably account for some proportion of the group differences in IQ and scholastic performance, but just how much of the true differences they may account for no one really knows at present. It is interesting that Jewish immigrants, whose offspring are usually found to have a higher mean IQ than the general population, show fewer disadvantageous reproductive conditions and have the lowest infant mortality rates of all ethnic groups, even when matched with other immigrant and native-born groups on general environmental conditions (Graves *et al.*, 1968).

Although disadvantageous reproductive factors occur differentially in different segments of the population, it is not at all certain ; how much they are responsible for the IQ differences between social classes and races. It is reported by the National Institute of Neurological Diseases and Blindness, for example, that when all cases of mental retardation that can be reasonably explained in terms of known complications of pregnancy and delivery, brain damage, or major gene and chromosomal defects are accounted for, there still remain 75 to 80 percent of the cases who show no such specific causes and presumably represent just the lower end of the normal polygenic distribution of intelligence (Research Profile No. 11, 1965). Buck (1968) has argued that it still remains to be proven that a degree of neurological damage is bound to occur among the survivors of all situations which carry a high risk of perinatal mortality and that a high or even a known proportion of mental retardation can be ascribed to the non-lethal grades of reproductive difficulty. A large study reported by Buck (1968) indicates that the most common reproductive difficulties when occurring singly have no significant effect on children's intellectual status after ages 5, with the one exception of pre-eclamptic toxemia of pregnancy, which caused some cognitive impairment. Most of the complications of pregnancy, it seems, must occur multiply to impair intellectual ability. It is as if the nervous system is sufficiently homeostatic to withstand certain unfavorable conditions if they occur singly.

*Prematurity.* The literature on the relationship of premature birth to the child's IQ is confusing and conflicting. Guilford (1967), in his recent book on *The Nature of Intelligence*, for example, concluded, as did Stoddard (1943), that prematurity has no effect on intelligence. Stott (1966), on the other hand, presents impressive evidence of very significant IQ decrements associated with prematurity. Probably the most thorough review of the subject I have found, by Kushlick (1966), helps to resolve these conflicting opinions. There is little question that prematurity has the strongest known relation to brain dysfunction of any reproductive factor, and many of the complications of pregnancy are strongly associated with the production of premature children. The crucial factor in prematurity, however, is not prematurity *per se*, but low birth-weight. Birth-weight apparently acts as a threshold variable with respect to intellectual impairment. All studies of birth-weight agree in showing that the incidence of babies weighing less than $5\frac{1}{2}$ lb increases from higher to lower social classes. But only about 1 percent of the total variance of birth-weight is accounted for by socioeconomic variables. Race (Negro *versus* white) has an effect on birth-weight independently of socioeconomic variables. Negro babies mature at a lower birth-weight than white babies (Naylor and Myrianthopoulos, 1967). If prematurity is defined as a condition in which birth-weight is under $5\frac{1}{2}$ lb the observed relationship between prematurity and depression of the IQ is due to the common factor of low social class. Kushlick (1966, p. 143) concludes that it is only among children having birth-weights under 3 lb that the mean IQ is lowered, independently of social class, and more in boys than in girls. The incidence of extreme subnormality is higher for children with birth-weights under 3 or 4 lb. But when one does not count these extreme cases (IQs below 50), the effects of prematurity or low birth-weight – even as low as 3 lb – have a very weak relationship to children's IQs by the time they are of school age. The association between very low birth-weight and extreme mental subnormality raises the question of whether the low birth-weight causes the abnormality or whether the abnormality arises independently and causes the low birth-weight.

Prematurity and low birth-weight have a markedly higher incidence among Negroes than among whites. That birth-weight differences *per se* are not a predominant factor in Negro-white IQ differences, however, is suggested by the findings of a study which compared Negro and white premature children matched for birth-weight. The Negro children in all weight groups performed significantly less well on mental tests at 3 and 5 years of age than the white children of comparable birth-weight (Hardy, 1965, p. 51).

*Genetic Predisposition to Prenatal Impairment.* Dennis Stott (1960, 1966), a British psychologist, has adduced considerable evidence for the theory that impairments of the central nervous system occurring prenatally as a result of various stresses in pregnancy may not be the *direct* result of adverse intrauterine factors but may result *indirectly* from genetically determined mechanisms which are triggered by prenatal stress of one form or another.

Why should there exist a genetic mechanism predisposing to congenital impairments? Would not such genes, if they had ever existed, have been eliminated long ago through natural selection? It can be argued from considerable evidence in lower species of mammals observable by zoologists today that such a genetic mechanism may have had survival value for primitive man, but that the conditions of our present industrial society and advances in medical care have diminished the biological advantage of this mechanism for survival of the human species. The argument is that, because of the need to control population, there is a genetic provision within all species for multiple impairments, which are normally only potentialities, that can be triggered off by prenatal stress associated with high population density, such as malnutrition, fatigue from overexertion, emotional distress, infections, and the like. The resulting congenital impairment would tend to cut down the infant population, thereby relieving the pressure of population without appreciably reducing the functioning and efficiency of the young adults in the population. Stott (1966) has presented direct evidence of an association between stresses in the mother during pregnancy and later behavioral abnormalities and learning problems of the child in school. The imperfect correlation between such pre-natal stress factors and signs of congenital impairment suggests that there are individual differences in genetic predisposition to prenatal impairment. The hypothesis warrants further investigation. The prenatal environment could be a much more important source of later IQ variance for some children than for others.

*Mother-Child Rh Incompatibility.* The *Rh* blood factor can involve possible brain-damaging effects in a small proportion of pregnancies where the fetus is *Rh*-positive and the mother is *Rh*-negative. (*Rh*-negative has a frequency of 15 percent in the white and 7 percent in the Negro population.) The mother-child *Rh* incompatibility produces significant physical ill-effects in only a fraction of cases and increases in importance in pregnancies beyond the first. The general finding of slightly lower IQs in second and later born children could be related to *Rh* incompatibility or to similar, but as yet undiscovered, mother-child biological incompatibilities. This is clearly an area greatly in need of pioneering research.

*Nutrition.* Since the human brain attains 70 percent of its maximum adult weight in the first year after birth, it should not be surprising that prenatal and infant nutrition can have significant effects on brain development. Brain growth is largely a process of protein synthesis. During the prenatal period and the first postnatal year the brain normally absorbs large amounts of protein nutrients and grows at the average rate of 1 to 2 milligrams per minute (Stoch and Smythe, 1963; Cravioto, 1966).

Severe undernutrition before 2 or 3 years of age, especially a lack of proteins and the vitamins and minerals essential for their anabolism, results in lowered intelligence, Stoch and Smythe (1963) found, for example, that extremely malnourished South African colored children were some 20 points lower in IQ than children of similar parents who had not suffered from malnutrition. The difference between the undernourished group and the control group in DQ and IQ over the age range from 1 year to 8 years was practically constant. If undernutrition takes a toll, it takes it early, as shown by lower DQs at 1 year and the absence of any increase in the decrement at later ages. Undernutrition occurring for the first time in older children seems to have no permanent effect. Severely malnourished war prisoners, for example, function intellectually at their expected level when they are returned to normal living conditions. The study by Stoch and Smythe, like several others (Cravioto, 1966; Scrimshaw, 1968), also revealed that the undernourished children had smaller stature and head circumference than the control children. Although there is no correlation between intelligence and head circumference in normally nourished children, there is a positive correlation between these factors in groups whose numbers suffer varying degrees of undernutrition early in life. Undernutrition also increases the correlation between intelligence and physical stature. These correlations provide us with an index which could aid the study of IQ deficits due to undernutrition in selected populations.

One of the most interesting and pronounced psychological effects of undernutrition is retardation in the development of cross-modal transfer or intersensory integration, which was earlier described as characterizing the essence of *g* (Scrimshaw, 1968).

The earlier the age at which nutritional therapy is instituted, of course, the more beneficial are its effects. But even as late as 2 years of age, a gain of as much as 18 IQ points was produced by nutritional improvements in a group of extremely undernourished children. After 4 years of age, however, nutritional therapy effected no significant change in IQ (Cravioto, 1966, p. 82).

These studies were done in countries where extreme undernutrition is not uncommon. Such gross nutritional deprivation is rare in the United States. But there is at least one study which shows that some undetermined proportion of the urban population in the United States might benefit substantially with respect to intellectual development by improved nutrition. In Norfolk, Virginia, women of low socioeconomic status were given vitamin and mineral supplements during pregnancy. These women gave birth to children who, at 4 years of age, averaged 8 points higher in IQ than a control group of children whose mothers had been given placebos during pregnancy (Harrell, Woodyard and Gates, 1955). Vitamin and mineral supplements are, of course, beneficial in this way only when they remedy an existing deficiency.

*Birth Order.* Order of birth contributes a significant proportion of the variance in mental ability. On the average, first-born children are superior in almost every way, mentally and physically. This is the consistent finding of many studies (Altus, 1966), but as yet the phenomenon remains unexplained. (Rimland [1964, pp. 140-143] has put forth some interesting hypotheses to explain the superiority of the first-born.) Since the first-born effect is found throughout all social classes in many countries and has shown up in studies over the past 80 years (it was first noted by Galton), it is probably a biological rather than a social-psychological phenomenon. It is almost certainly not a genetic effect. (It would tend to make for slightly lower estimates of heritability based on sibling comparisons.) It is one of the sources of environmental variance in ability without any significant postnatal environmental correlates. No way is known for giving later-born children the same advantage. The disadvantage of being later-born, however, is very slight and shows up conspicuously only in the extreme upper tail of the distribution of achievements. For example, there is a disproportionate number of first-born individuals whose biographies appear in *Who's Who* and in the *Encyclopædia Britannica*.

SOCIAL CLASS DIFFERENCES IN INTELLIGENCE

Social class (or socioeconomic status [SES]) should be considered as a factor separate from race. I have tried to avoid using the terms *social class* and *race* synonymously or interchangeably in my writings, and I observe this distinction here. Social classes completely cut across all racial groups. But different racial groups are disproportionately represented in different SES categories. Social class differences refer to a socioeconomic continuum *within* racial groups.

It is well known that children's IQs, by school age, are correlated with the socioeconomic status of their parents. This is a world-wide phenomenon and has an extensive research literature going back 70 years. Half of all the correlations between SES and children's IQs reported in the literature fall between 0·25 and 0·50, with most falling in the region of 0·35 to 0·40. When school children are grouped by SES, the mean IQs of the groups vary over a range of one of two standard deviations (15 to 30 IQ points), depending on the method of status classification (Eells, *et al.*, 1951). This relationship between SES and IQ constitutes one of the most substantial and least disputed facts in psychology and education.

The fact that intelligence is correlated with occupational status can hardly be surprising in any society that supports universal public education. The educational system and occupational hierarchy act as an intellectual 'screening' process, far from perfect, to be sure, but discriminating enough to create correlations of the magnitude just reported. If each generation is roughly sorted out by these 'screening' processes along an intelligence continuum, and if, as has already been pointed out, the phenotype-genotype correlation for IQ is of the order of 0·80 to 0·90, it is almost inevitable that this sorting process will make for genotypic as well as phenotypic differences among social classes. It is therefore most unlikely that groups differing in SES would not also differ, on the average, in their genetic endowment of intelligence. In reviewing the relevant evidence, the British geneticist, C. O. Carter (1966, p. 192) remarked, 'Sociologists who doubt this show more ingenuity than judgment'. Sociologist, Bruce Eckland (1967), has elaborately spelled out the importance of genetic factors for understanding social class differences.

Few if any students of this field today would regard socioeconomic status *per se* as an environmental variable that primarily *causes* IQ differences. Intellectual differences between SES groups have hereditary, environmental, and interaction components. Environmental factors associated with SES differences apparently are not a major *independent* source of variance in intelligence. Identical twins separated in the first months of life and reared in widely differing social classes, for example, still show greater similarity in IQ than unrelated children reared together or than even siblings reared together (Burt, 1966). The IQs of children adopted in infancy show a much lower correlation with the SES of the adopting parents than do the IQs of children reared by their own parents (Leahy, 1935). The IQs of children who were reared in an orphanage from infancy and who had never known their biological parents show approximately the same correlation with their biological father's occupational status as found for children reared by their biological parents (0·23 *vs.* 0·24) (Lawrence, 1931). The correlation between the IQs of children adopted in infancy and the educational level of their biological mothers is close to that of children reared by their own mothers (0·44), while the correlation between children's IQs and their adopting parents' educational level is close to zero (Honzik, 1957). Children of low and high SES show, on the average, an amount of regression from the parental IQ toward the mean of the general population that conforms to expectations from a simple polygenic model of the inheritance of intelligence (Burt, 1961). When siblings reared within the same family differ significantly in intelligence, those who are above the family average tend to move up the SES scale, and those who are below the family average tend to move down (Young and Gibson, 1965). It should also be noted that despite intensive efforts by psychologists, educators, and sociologists to devise tests intended to eliminate SES differences in measured intelligence, none of these efforts has succeeded (Jensen, 1968c), Theodosius Dobzhansky (1968a, p. 33), a geneticist, states

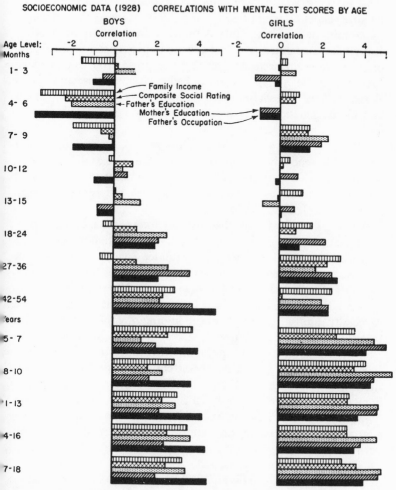

FIGURE 14.   *Correlations between children's mental test scores, at 1 month to 18 years, and five indicators of parents' socioeconomic status at the time the children were born. (Bayley, 1966.)*

that 'There exist some occupations or functions for which only extreme genotypes are suitable'. But surely this is not an all-or-nothing affair, and we would expect by the same reasoning that many different occupational skills, and not just those that are the most extreme, would favor some genotypes more than others. To be sure, genetic factors become more important at the extremes. Some minimal level of ability is required for learning most skills. But while you can teach almost anyone to play chess, or the piano, or to conduct an orchestra, or to write prose, you cannot teach everyone to be a Capablanca, a Paderewski, a Toscanini, or a Bernard Shaw. In a society that values and rewards individual talent and merit, genetic factors inevitably take on considerable importance.

SES differences, and race differences as well, are manifested not only as differences between group means, but also as differences in variance and in patterns of correlations among various mental abilities, even on tests which show no *mean* differences between SES groups (Jensen, 1968b).

Another line of evidence that SES IQ differences are not a superficial phenomenon is the fact of a negative correlation between SES and Developmental Quotient (DQ) (under 2 years of age) and an increasing positive correlation between SES and IQ (beyond 2 years of age), as shown in Figure 14 from a study by Nancy Bayley (1966). (All subjects in this study are Caucasian.) This relationship is especially interesting in view of the finding of a number of studies that there is a negative correlation between DQ and later IQ, an effect which is much more pronounced in boys than in girls and involves the motor more than the attentional-cognitive aspects of the DQ (Bayley, 1965b). Figure 14 shows that on infant developmental scales, lower SES children actually have a 'head start' over higher SES children. But this trend is increasingly reversed at later ages as the tests become less motoric and are increasingly loaded with a cognitive or *g* factor.*

* A recent study by Wilson (1972) compared Bayley scale DQs of MZ and DZ twins at 3-month intervals from 3 to 24 months. Although all SES levels were represented in this sample, only negligible correlations were found between DQ and SES ($r = 0.11$ for age 12 months and $r = 0.20$ for age 24 months). MZ twins showed markedly higher concordance than DZ twins for spurts and lags in DQ during this early

RACE DIFFERENCES

The important distinction between the *individual* and the *population* must always be kept clearly in mind in any discussion of racial differences in mental abilities or any behavioral characteristics. Whenever we select a person for some special educational purpose, whether for special instruction in a grade-school class for children with learning problems, or for a 'gifted' class with an advanced curriculum, or for college attendance, or for admission to graduate training or a professional school, we are selecting an *individual*, and we are selecting him and dealing with him as an individual for reasons of his individuality. Similarly, when we employ someone, or promote someone in his occupation, or give some special award or honor to someone for his accomplishments, we are doing this to an individual. The variables of social class, race, and national origin are correlated so imperfectly with any of the valid criteria on which the above decisions should depend, or, for that matter, with any behavioral characteristic, that these background factors are irrelevant as a basis for dealing with individuals – as students, as employees, as neighbors. Furthermore, since, as far as we know, the full range of human talents is represented in all the major races of man and in all socioeconomic levels, it is unjust to allow the mere fact of an individual's racial or social background to affect the treatment accorded to him. All persons rightfully must be regarded on the basis of their individual qualities and merits, and all social, educational, and economic institutions must have built into them the mechanisms for insuring and maximizing the treatment of persons according to their individual behavior.

If a society completely believed and practiced the ideal of treating every person as an individual, it would be hard to see why there should be any problems about 'race' *per se*. There might still be problems concerning poverty, unemployment, crime, and other social ills, and, given the will, they could be tackled just as any other problems that require rational methods for solution. But if this

---

developmental period. Wilson concluded: 'From these results it was inferred that infant mental development was primarily determined by the twins' genetic blueprint and that, except in unusual cases, other factors served mainly a supportive function' (p. 914).

philosophy prevailed in practice, there would not need to be a 'race problem'.

The question of *race* differences in intelligence comes up not when we deal with individuals as individuals, but when certain identifiable *groups* or subcultures within the society are brought into comparison with one another *as groups or populations*. It is only when the groups are disproportionately represented in what are commonly perceived as the most desirable and the least desirable social and occupational roles in a society that the question arises concerning average differences among groups. Since much of the current thinking behind civil rights, fair employment, and equality of educational opportunity appeals to the fact that there is a disproportionate representation of different racial groups in the various levels of the educational, occupational, and socioeconomic hierarchy, we are forced to examine all the possible reasons for this inequality among racial groups in the attainments and rewards generally valued by all groups within our society. To what extent can such inequalities be attributed to unfairness in society's multiple selection processes? ('Unfair' meaning that selection is influenced by intrinsically irrelevant criteria, such as skin color, racial or national origin, etc.) And to what extent are these inequalities attributable to really relevant selection criteria which apply equally to all individuals but at the same time select disproportionately between some racial groups because there exist, in fact, real average differences among the groups – differences in the population distributions of those characteristics which are indisputably relevant to educational and occupational performance? This is certainly one of the most important questions confronting our nation today. The answer, which can be found only through unfettered research, has enormous consequences for the welfare of all, particularly of minorities whose plight is now in the foreground of public attention. A preordained, doctrinaire stance with regard to this issue hinders the achievement of a scientific understanding of the problem. To rule out of court, so to speak, any reasonable hypotheses on purely ideological grounds is to argue that static ignorance is preferable to increasing our knowledge of reality. I strongly disagree with those who believe in searching for the truth by scientific means only under certain circumstances and eschew this course in favor of ignorance under other circumstances, or who believe that the results of inquiry on some subjects cannot be entrusted to the public but should be kept the guarded possession of a scientific elite. Such attitudes, in my opinion, represent a danger to free inquiry and, consequently, in the long run, work to the disadvantage of society's general welfare. 'No holds barred' is the best formula for scientific inquiry. One does not decree beforehand which phenomena cannot be studied or which questions cannot be answered.

*Genetic Aspects of Racial Differences.* No one, to my knowledge questions the role of environmental factors, including influences from past history, in determining at least some of the variance between racial groups in standard measures of intelligence, school performance, and occupational status. The current literature on the culturally disadvantaged abounds with discussion – some of it factual, some of it fanciful – of how a host of environmental factors depresses cognitive development and performance. I recently co-edited a book which is largely concerned with the environmental aspects of disadvantaged minorities (Deutsch, Katz and Jensen, 1968). But the possible importance of genetic factors in racial behavioral differences has been greatly ignored, almost to the point of being a tabooed subject, just as were the topics of venereal disease and birth control a generation or so ago.

My discussions with a number of geneticists concerning the question of a genetic basis of differences among races in mental abilities have revealed to me a number of rather consistently agreed-upon points which can be summarized in general terms as follows: Any groups which have been geographically or socially isolated from one another for many generations are practically certain to differ in their gene pools, and consequently are likely to show differences in any phenotypic characteristics having high heritability. This is practically axiomatic, according to the geneticists with whom I have spoken. Races are said to be 'breeding populations', which is to say that matings within the group have a much higher probability than matings outside the group. Races are more technically viewed by geneticists as populations having different distributions of gene frequencies. These genetic differences are manifested in virtually every anatomical, physiological, and biochemical comparison one can make between representative samples of identifiable racial groups (Kuttner, 1967). There is no reason to suppose that the brain should be exempt from this generalization. (Racial differences in the relative frequencies of various blood constituents have probably been the most thoroughly studied so far.)

But what about behavior? If it can be measured and shown to have a genetic component, it would be regarded, from a genetic standpoint, as no different from other human characteristics.There seems to be little question that racial differences in genetically conditioned behavioral characteristics, such as mental abilities, should exist, just as physical differences. The real questions, geneticists tell me, are not whether there are or are not genetic racial differences that affect behavior, because there undoubtedly are. The proper questions to ask, from a scientific standpoint are: What is the direction of the difference? What is the magnitude of the difference? And what is the significance of the difference – medically, socially, educationally, or from whatever standpoint that may be relevant to the characteristic in question? A difference is important only within a specific context. For example, one's blood type in the ABO system is unimportant until one needs a transfusion. And some genetic differences are apparently of no importance with respect to any context as far as anyone has been able to discover – for example, differences in the size and shape of ear lobes. The idea that all genetic differences have arisen or persisted only as a result of natural selection, by conferring some survival or adaptive benefit on their possessors, is no longer generally held. There appear to be many genetic differences, or polymorphisms, which confer no discernible advantages to survival.[1]

*Negro Intelligence and Scholastic Performance.* Negroes in the United States are disproportionately represented among groups identified as culturally or educationally disadvantaged. This, plus that fact that Negroes constitute by far the largest racial minority in the United States, has for many years focused attention on Negro intelligence. It is a subject with a now vast literature which has been quite recently reviewed by Dreger and Miller (1960, 1968) and by Shuey (1966), whose 578-page review is the most comprehensive,

---

[1] The most comprehensive and sophisticated discussion of the genic-behavior analysis of race differences that I have found is by Spuhler and Lindzey (1967).

covering 382 studies. The basic data are well known: on the average, Negroes test about 1 standard deviation (15 IQ points) below the average of the white population in IQ, and this finding is fairly uniform across the 81 different tests of intellectual ability used in the studies reviewed by Shuey. This magnitude of difference gives a median overlap of 15 percent, meaning that 15 percent of the Negro population exceeds the white average. In terms of proportions of variance, if the numbers of Negroes and whites were equal, the differences *between* racial groups would account for 23 percent of the total variance, but – an important point – the differences *within* groups would account for 77 percent of the total variance. When gross socioeconomic level is controlled, the average difference reduces to about 11 IQ points (Shuey, 1966, p. 519), which, it should be recalled, is about the same spread as the average difference between siblings in the same family. So-called 'culture-free' of 'culture-fair' tests tend to give Negroes slightly lower scores, on the average, than more conventional IQ tests such as the Stanford-Binet and Wechsler scales. Also, as a group, Negroes perform somewhat more poorly on those subtests which tap abstract abilities. The majority of studies show that Negroes perform relatively better on verbal than on nonverbal intelligence tests.

In tests of scholastic achievement, also, judging from the massive data of the Coleman study (Coleman *et al.*, 1966), Negroes score about 1 standard deviation (SD) below the average for whites and Orientals and considerably less than 1 SD below other disadvantaged minorities tested in the Coleman study – Puerto Rican, Mexican-American, and American Indian. The 1 SD decrement in Negro performance is fairly constant throughout the period from grades 1 through 12.

Another aspect of the distribution of IQs in the Negro population is their lesser variance in comparison to the white distribution. This shows up in most of the studies reviewed by Shuey. The best single estimate is probably the estimate based on a large normative study of Stanford-Binet IQs of Negro school children in five Southeastern states, by Kennedy, Van De Riet and White (1963). They found the SD of Negro children's IQs to be 12·4, as compared with 16·4 in the white normative sample. The Negro distribution thus has only about 60 percent as much variance (i.e., $SD^2$) as the white distribution.

There is an increasing realization among students of the psychology of the disadvantaged that the discrepancy in their average performance cannot be completely or directly attributed to discrimination or inequalities in education. It seems not unreasonable, in view of the fact that intelligence variation has a large genetic component, to hypothesize that genetic factors may play a part in this picture.* But such an hypothesis is anathema to many social scientists. The idea that the lower average intelligence and scholastic performance of Negroes could involve, not only environmental, but also genetic, factors has indeed been strongly denounced (e.g., Pettigrew, 1964). But it has been neither contradicted nor discredited by evidence.

* While it is true that heritability *within* groups cannot *prove* heritability *between* group means, high *within* group heritability does increase the *a priori* likelihood that the *between* groups heritability is greater than zero. In nature, characteristics that vary genetically *among* individuals within a population also generally vary genetically *between* different breeding populations of the same species. Among the genetically conditioned traits known to vary between major racial groups are body size and proportions, cranial size and cephalic index, pigmentation of the hair, skin, and eyes, hair form and distribution on the body, number of vertebrae, fingerprints, bone density, basic metabolic rate, sweating, fissural patterns on the chewing surfaces of the teeth, numerous blood groups, various chronic diseases, frequency of dizygotic (but not monozygotic) twinning, male/female birth ratio, ability to taste phenylthiocarbomide, length of gestation period, and degree of physical maturity at birth (as indicated by degree of ossification of cartilage). In light of all these differences, Spuhler and Lindzey (1967) remark '. . . it seems to us surprising that one would accept present findings in regard to the existence of genetic anatomical, physiological, and epidemiological differences between the races . . . and still expect to find *no* meaningful differences in behavior between races' (p. 413). The high *within* groups heritability of certain behavioral traits, such as intelligence, adds weight to this statement by Spuhler and Lindzey. Recently, Dr John C. DeFries, Professor of Genetics at the University of Colorado, has worked out the mathematical relationship between heritability *within* groups and *between* groups (personal communication). His formulation has been concurred in by other quantitative and behavioral geneticists. Though it would take too much space to explicate here, what it shows essentially is that unless there is absolutely *no* genetic difference whatever between two populations on the trait in question, there is a definite increasing monotonic relationship between the magnitude of *within* groups heritability and *between* groups heritability. Therefore, strictly speaking it is incorrect to claim that there is no relationship whatever between *within* groups and *between* groups heritability.

The fact that a reasonable hypothesis has not been rigorously proved does not mean that it should be summarily dismissed. It only means that we need more appropriate research for putting it to the test. I believe such definitive research is entirely possible but has not yet been done. So all we are left with are various lines of evidence, no one of which is definitive alone, but which, viewed all together, make it a not unreasonable hypothesis that genetic factors are strongly implicated in the average Negro-white intelligence difference. The preponderance of the evidence is, in my opinion, less consistent with a strictly environmental hypothesis than with a genetic hypothesis, which, of course, does not exclude the influence of environment or its interaction with genetic factors.

We can be accused of superficiality in our thinking about this issue, I believe, if we simply dismiss a genetic hypothesis without having seriously thought about the relevance of typical findings such as the following:

*Failure to Equate Negroes and Whites in IQ and Scholastic Ability.* No one has yet produced any evidence based on a properly controlled study to show that representative samples of Negro and white children can be equalized in intellectual ability through statistical control of environment and education.

*Socioeconomic Level and Incidence of Mental Retardation.* Since in no category of socioeconomic status (SES) are a majority of children found to be retarded in the technical sense of having an IQ below 75, it would be hard to claim that the degree of environmental deprivation typically associated with lower-class status could be

TABLE 3  **Estimated Prevalence of Children With IQs Below 75, by Socioeconomic Status (SES) and Race given as Percentages (Heber, 1968)**

| SES | White | Negro |
|---|---|---|
| High 1 | 0·5 | 3·1 |
| 2 | 0·8 | 14·5 |
| 3 | 2·1 | 22·8 |
| 4 | 3·1 | 37·8 |
| Low 5 | 7·8 | 42·9 |

responsible for this degree of mental retardation. An IQ less than 75 reflects more than a lack of cultural amenities. Heber (1968) has estimated on the basis of existing evidence that IQs below 75 have a much higher incidence among Negro than among white children at every level of socioeconomic status, as shown in Table 3. In the two highest SES categories the estimated proportions of Negro and white children with IQs below 75, are in the ratio of 13·6 to 1. If environmental factors were mainly responsible for producing such differences, one should expect a lesser Negro-white discrepancy at the upper SES levels.* Other lines of evidence also show this not to be the case. A genetic hypothesis, on the other hand, would predict this effect, since the higher SES Negro offspring would be regressing to a lower population mean than their white counterparts in SES, and consequently a larger proportion of the lower tail of the distribution of genotypes for Negroes would fall below the value that generally results in phenotypic IQs below 75.

A finding reported by Wilson (1967) is also in line with this prediction. He obtained the mean IQs of a large representative sample

---

* One of my critics has objected to my interpretation of these data (Deutsch, M. 'Happenings on the way back to the forum: Social science, IQ, and race differences revisited.' *Harvard Educational Review*, 1969, **39**, 523-557). Deutsch claims that Negro-white differences in mental retardation increase going from higher to lower SES, and in support of this claim he points to the fact that the difference between 0·5 percent and 3·1 percent is much less than the difference between 7·8 percent and 42·9 percent. But what we are concerned with is a comparison of the *rates* of mental retardation in the Negro and white populations in different socioeconomic strata, and the proper method for showing this is the *per capita ratio* of Negro retardates to white retardates in each SES level. The question is, how many Negro retardates per 100 Negroes are there for every white retardate per 100 whites? On this basis, the Negro-white discrepancy in retardation rate *decreases* going from the highest to the lowest SES group. To appreciate the distinction between *absolute* difference and *rate* difference, consider consumers' reactions to a tax increase on commodity A going from 50 percent up to 55 percent as compared with a tax increase on commodity B going from 5 percent up to 10 percent. Did commodity A or commodity B have the greater gain in tax rate? The absolute difference is the same in both cases, but the *rate* doubled for commodity B while it increased by only a factor of 1·1 for commodity A. Other things being equal, the 5 percent tax increase should have a more depressing effect on the sales of commodity B than of commodity A.

of Negro and white children in a California school district and compared the two groups within each of four social class categories: (1) professional and managerial, (2) white collar, (3) skilled and semiskilled manual, and (4) lower class (unskilled, unemployed, or welfare recipients). The mean IQ of Negro children in the first category was 15·5 points below that of the corresponding white children in SES category 1. But the Negro mean for SES 1 was also 3·9 points below the mean of white children in SES category 4. (The IQs of white children in SES 4 presumably have 'regressed' upward toward the mean of the white population.)

Wilson's data are not atypical, for they agree with Shuey's (1966, p. 520) summarization of the total literature up to 1965 on this point. She reports that in all the studies which grouped subjects by SES, upper-status Negro children average 2·6 IQ points *below* the low-status whites. Shuey comments: 'It seems improbable that upper and middle-class colored children would have no more culture opportunities provided them than white children of the lower and lowest class'.

Duncan (1968, p. 69) also has presented striking evidence for a much greater 'regression-to-the-mean' (from parents to their children) for high status occupations in the case of Negroes than in the case of whites. None of these findings is at all surprising from the standpoint of a genetic hypothesis, of which an intrinsic feature is Galton's 'law of filial regression'. While the data are not necessarily inconsistent with a possible environmental interpretation, they do seem more puzzling in terms of strictly environmental causation. Such explanations often seem intemperately strained.

*Inadequacies of Purely Environmental Explanations.* Strictly environmental explanations of group differences tend to have an *ad hoc* quality. They are usually plausible for the situation they are devised to explain, but often they have little generality across situations, and new *ad hoc* hypotheses have to be continually devised. Pointing to environmental differences between groups is never sufficient in itself to infer a causal relationship to group differences in intelligence. To take just one example of this tendency of social scientists to attribute lower intelligence and scholastic ability to almost any environmental difference that seems handy, we can look at the evidence regarding the effects of 'father absence'. Since the father is absent in a significantly larger proportion of Negro than of white families, the factor of 'father absence' has been frequently pointed to in the literature on the disadvantaged as one of the causes of Negroes' lower performance on IQ tests and in scholastic achievement. Yet the two largest studies directed at obtaining evidence on this very point – the only studies I have seen that are methodologically adequate – both conclude that the factor of 'father absence' *versus* 'father presence' makes no independent contribution to variance in intelligence or scholastic achievement. The sample sizes were so large in both of these studies that even a very slight degree of correlation between father absence and the measures of cognitive performance would have shown up as statistically significant. Coleman (1966, p. 506) concluded: 'Absence of a father in the home did not have the anticipated effect on ability scores. Overall, pupils without fathers performed at approximately the same level as those with fathers – although there was some variation between groups' (groups referring to geographical regions of the U.S.). And Wilson (1957, p. 177) concluded from his survey of a California school district: 'Neither our own data nor the preponderance of evidence from other research studies indicate that father presence or absence, *per se*, is related to school achievement. While broken homes reflect the existence of social and personal problems, and have some consequence for the development of personality, broken homes do not have any systematic effect on the overall level of school success.'

The nationwide Coleman study (1966) included assessments of a dozen environmental variables and socioeconomic indices which are generally thought to be major sources of environmental influence in determining individual and group differences in scholastic performance – such factors as: reading material in the home, cultural amenities in the home, structural integrity of the home, foreign language in the home, pre-school attendance, parents' education, parents' educational desires for child, parents' interest in child's school work, time spent on homework, child's self-concept (self-esteem), and so on. These factors are all correlated – in the expected direction – with scholastic performance within each of the racial or ethnic groups studied by Coleman. Yet, interestingly enough, they are not systematically correlated with differences *between* groups.

For example, by far the most environmentally disadvantaged groups in the Coleman study are the American Indians. On every environmental index they average *lower* than the Negro samples, and overall their environmental rating is about as far below the Negro average as the Negro rating is below the white average. (As pointed out by Kuttner [1968, p. 707], American Indians are much more disadvantaged than Negroes, or any other minority groups in the United States, on a host of other factors not assessed by Coleman, such as income, unemployment, standards of health care, life expectancy, and infant mortality.) Yet the American Indian ability and achievement test scores average about half a standard deviation higher than the scores of Negroes. The differences were in favor of the Indian children on each of the four tests used by Coleman: nonverbal intelligence, verbal intelligence, reading comprehension, and math achievement. If the environmental factors assessed by Coleman are the major determinants of Negro-white differences that many social scientists have claimed they are, it is hard to see why such factors should act in reverse fashion in determining differences between Negroes and Indians, especially in view of the fact that *within* each group the factors are significantly correlated in the expected direction with achievement.

*Early Developmental Differences.* A number of students of child development have noted the developmental precocity of Negro infants, particularly in motoric behavior. Geber (1958) and Geber and Dean (1957) have reported this precocity also in African infants. It hardly appears to be environmental, since it is evident in 9-hour-old infants. Cravioto (1966, p. 78) has noted that the Gesell tests of infant behavioral development, which are usually considered suitable only for children over 4 weeks of age, 'can be used with younger African, Mexican, and Guatemalan infants, since their development at two or three weeks is similar to that of Western European infants two or three times as old'. Bayley's (1965a) study of a representative sample of 600 American Negro infants up to 15 months of age, using the Bayley Infant Scales of Mental and Motor Development, also found Negro infants to have significantly higher scores than white infants in their first year. The difference is largely attributable to the motor items in the Bayley test. For example, about 30 percent of white infants as compared with about 60 percent of Negro infants between 9 and 12 months were able to 'pass' such tests as 'pat-a-cake' muscular coordination, and ability to walk with help, to stand alone, and to walk alone. The highest scores for any group on the Bayley scales that I have found in my search of the literature were obtained by Negro infants in the poorest sections of Durham, North Carolina. The older siblings of these infants have an average IQ of about 80. The infants up to 6 months of age, however, have a Developmental Motor Quotient (DMQ) nearly one standard deviation above white norms and a Developmental IQ (i.e., the non-motor items of the Bayley scale) of about half a standard deviation above white norms (Durham Education Improvement Program, 1966-67, a, b).

The DMQ, as pointed out previously, correlates negatively in the white population with socioeconomic status and with later IQ. Since lower SES Negro and white school children are more alike in IQ than are upper SES children of the two groups (Wilson, 1967), one might expect greater DMQ differences in favor of Negro infants in high socioeconomic Negro and white samples than in low socio-economic samples. This is just what Walters (1967) found. High SES Negro infants significantly exceeded whites in total score on the Gesell developmental schedules at 12 weeks of age, while low SES Negro and white infants did not differ significantly overall. (The only difference, on a single subscale, favored the white infants.)

It should also be noted that developmental quotients are usually depressed by adverse prenatal, perinatal, and postnatal complications such as lack of oxygen, prematurity, and nutritional deficiency.

Another relationship of interest is the finding that the negative correlation between DMQ and later IQ is higher in boys than in girls (Bayley, 1966, p. 127). Bronfenbrenner (1967, p. 912) cites evidence which shows that Negro boys perform relatively less well in school than Negro girls; the sex difference is much greater than is found in the white population. Bronfenbrenner (1967, p. 913) says, 'It is noteworthy that these sex differences in achievement are observed among Southern as well as Northern Negroes, are present at every socioeconomic level, and tend to increase with age'.

*Physiological Indices.* The behavioral precocity of Negro infants is also paralleled by certain physiological indices of development. For example, X-rays show that bone development, as indicated by the rate of ossification of cartilage, is more advanced in Negro as compared with white babies of about the same socioeconomic background, and Negro babies mature at a lower birth-weight than white babies (Naylor and Myrianthopoulos, 1967, p. 81).

It has also been noted that brain wave patterns in African newborn infants show greater maturity than is usually found in the European newborn child (Nelson and Dean, 1959). This finding especially merits further study, since there is evidence that brain waves have some relationship to IQ (Medical World News, 1968), and since at least one aspect of brain waves – the visually evoked potential – has a very significant genetic component, showing a heritability of about 0·80 (uncorrected for attenuation) (Dustman and Beck, 1965).

*Magnitude of Adult Negro-White Differences.* The largest sampling of Negro and white intelligence test scores resulted from the administration of the Armed Forces Qualification Test (AFQT) to a national sample of over 10 million men between the ages of 18 and 26. As of 1966, the overall failure rate for Negroes was 68 percent as compared with 19 percent for whites (*U.S. News and World Report*, 1966). (The failure cut-off score that yields these percentages is roughly equivalent to a Stanford-Binet IQ of 86.) Moynihan (1965) has estimated that during the same period in which the AFQT was adminstered to these large representative samples of Negro and white male youths, approximately one-half of Negro families could be considered as middle-class or above by the usual socioeconomic criteria. So even if we assumed that all of the lower 50 percent of Negroes on the SES scale failed the AFQT, it would still mean that at least 36 percent of the middle SES Negroes failed the test, a failure rate almost twice as high as that of the white population for all levels of SES.

Do such findings raise any question as to the plausibility of theories that postulate exclusively environmental factors as sufficient causes for the observed differences?

## Why Raise Intelligence?

If the intelligence of the whole population increased and our IQ tests were standardized anew, the mean IQ would again be made equal to 100, which, by definition, is the average for the population. Thus, in order to speak sensibly of raising intelligence we need an absolute frame of reference, and for simplicity's sake we will use the *present* distribution of IQ as our reference scale. Then it will not be meaningless to speak of the average IQ of the population shifting to values other than 100.

Would there be any real advantage to shifting the entire distribution of intelligence upward? One way to answer this question is to compare the educational attainments of children in different schools whose IQ distributions center around means, of say, 85, 100, and 115. As pointed out earlier, there is a relationship between educational attainments and the occupations that are open to individuals on leaving school. Perusal of the want-ads in any metropolitan newpaper reveals that there are extremely few jobs advertised which are suitable to the level of education and skills typically found below IQs of 85 or 90, while we see day after day in the want-ads hundreds of jobs which call for a level of education and skills typically found among school graduates with IQs above 110. These jobs go begging to be filled. The fact is, there are not nearly enough minimally qualified persons to fill them.

One may sensibly ask the question whether our collective national intelligence is adequate to meet the growing needs of our increasingly complex industrial society. In a bygone era, when the entire population's work consisted almost completely of gathering or producing food by primitive means, there was little need for a large number of persons with IQs much above 100. Few of the jobs that had to be done at that time required the kinds of abstract intelligence and academic training which are now in such seemingly short supply in relation to the demand in our modern society. For many years the criterion for mental retardation was an IQ below 70. In recent years the National Association for Mental Retardation has raised the criterion to an IQ of 85, since an increasing proportion of persons of more than 1 standard deviation below the average in IQ are unable to get along occupationally in today's world. Persons with IQs of 85 or less are finding it increasingly difficult to get jobs, any jobs, because they are unprepared, for whatever reason, to do the jobs that need doing in this industrialized, technological economy. Unless drastic changes occur – in the population, in educational outcomes, or in the whole system of occupational training and selection – it is hard to see how we can avoid an increase in the rate of the so-called 'hard-core' unemployed. It takes more knowledge and cleverness to operate, maintain, or repair a tractor than to till a field by hand, and it takes more skill to write computer programs than to operate an adding machine, and apparently the trend will continue.

It has been argued by Harry and Margaret Harlow that 'human beings in our world today have no more, or little more, than the absolute minimal intellectual endowment necessary for achieving the civilization we know today' (Harlow and Harlow, 1962, p. 34). They depict where we would probably be if man's average genetic endowment for intelligence had never risen above the level corresponding to IQ 75: '. . . the geniuses would barely exceed our normal or average level; comparatively few would be equivalent in ability to our average high school graduates. There would be no individuals with the normal intellectual capacities essential for making major discoveries, and there could be no civilization as we know it.'

It may well be true that the kind of ability we now call intelligence was needed in a certain percentage of the human population for our civilization to have arisen. But while a small minority – perhaps only 1 or 2 percent – of highly gifted individuals were needed to advance civilization, the vast majority were able to assimilate the consequences of these advances. It may take a Leibnitz or a Newton to invent the calculus, but almost any college student can learn it and use it.

Since intelligence (meaning *g*) is not the whole of human abilities, there may be some fallacy and some danger in making it the *sine qua non* of fitness to play a productive role in modern society. We should not assume certain ability requirements for a job without establishing these requirements as a fact. How often do employment tests, Civil Service examinations, the requirement of a high school diploma, and the like, constitute hurdles that are irrelevant to actual performance on the job for which they are intended as a screening device? Before going overboard in deploring that fact that disadvantaged minority groups fail to clear many of the hurdles that are set up for certain jobs, we should determine whether the educational and mental test barriers that stand at the entrance to many of these employment opportunities are actually relevant. They may be relevant only in the correlational sense that the test predicts success on the job, in which case we should also know whether the test measures the ability actually required on the job or measures only characteristics that happen to be correlated with some third factor which is really essential for job performance. Changing people in terms of the really essential requirements of a given job may be much more feasible than trying to increase their abstract intelligence or level of performance in academic subjects so that they can pass irrelevant tests.

## IQ GAINS FROM ENVIRONMENTAL IMPROVEMENT

As was pointed out earlier, since the environment acts as a threshold variable with respect to IQ, an overall increase in IQ in a population in which a great majority are above the threshold, such that most of the IQ variance is due to heredity, could not be expected to be very large if it had to depend solely upon improving the environment of the economically disadvantaged. This is not to say that such improvement is not to be desired for its own sake or that it would not boost the educational potential of many disadvantaged children. An unrealistically high upper limit of what one could expect can be estimated from figures given by Schwebel (1968, p. 210). He estimates that 26 percent of the children in the population can be called environmentally deprived. He estimates the frequencies of their IQs in each portion of the IQ scale; their distribution is skewed, with higher frequencies in the lower IQ categories and an overall mean IQ of 90. Next, he assumes we could add 20 points to each deprived child's IQ by giving him an abundant environment. (The figure of 20 IQ points comes from Bloom's [1964, p. 89] estimate that the effect of extreme environments on intelligence is about 20 IQ points.) The net effect of this 20-point boost in the IQ of every deprived child would be an increase in the population's IQ from 100 to 105. But this seems to be an unrealistic fantasy. For if it were true that the IQs of the deprived group could be raised 20 points by a good environment, and if Schwebel's estimate of 26 percent correctly represents the incidence of deprivation, then the deprived children would be boosted to an average IQ of 110, which is 7 points higher than the mean of 103 for the non-deprived population! There is no reason to believe that the IQs of deprived children, given an environment of abundance, would rise to a higher level than the already privileged children's IQs. The overall boost in the population IQ would probably be more like 1 or 2 IQ points rather than 5. (Another anomaly of Schwebel's 'analysis' is that after a 20-point IQ boost is granted to the deprived segment of the population, the only persons left in the mentally retarded range are the non-deprived, with 7 percent of them below IQ 80 as compared with zero percent of the deprived!)

Fewer persons, however, are seriously concerned about whether or not we could appreciably boost the IQ of the population as a whole. A more feasible and urgent goal is to foster the educational and occupational potential of the disadvantaged segment of the population. The pursuit of this aim, of course, must involve advances not only in education, but in public health, in social services, and in welfare and employment practices. In considering all feasible measures, one must also take inventory of forces that may be working against the accomplishment of amelioration. We should not overlook the fact that social and economic conditions not only have direct environmental effects, but indirectly can have biological consequences as well, consequences that could oppose attempts to improve the chances of the disadvantaged to assume productive roles in society.

POSSIBLE DYSGENIC TRENDS

In one large midwestern city it was found that one-third of all the children in classes for the mentally retarded (IQ less than 75) came from one small area of the city comprising only 5 percent of the city's population (Heber, 1968). A representative sample of 88 mothers having at least one school-age child in the neighborhood showed an average of 7·6 children per mother. In families of 8 or more, nearly half the children over 12 years of age had IQs below 75 (Heber, Dever and Conry, 1968). The authors note that not all low SES families contributed equally to the rate of mental retardation in this area; certain specifiable families had a greatly disproportionate number of retarded children. Mothers with IQs below 80, for example, accounted for over 80 percent of the children with IQs under 80. Completely aside from the hereditary implications, what does this mean in view of studies of foster children which show that the single most important factor in the child's *environment* with respect to his intellectual development is his foster mother's IQ?

This variable has been shown to make the largest *independent* contribution to variance in children's IQs of any environmental factor (Burks, 1928). If the children in the neighborhoods studied by Heber, which are typical of the situation in many of our large cities, have the great disadvantage of deprived environments, is it inappropriate to ask the same question that Florence Goodenough (1940, p. 329) posed regarding causal factors in retarded Tennessee mountain children: '*Why* are they so deprived?' When a substantial proportion of the children in a community suffer a deplorable environment, one of the questions we need to answer is who creates their environment? Does not the genetic × environment interaction work both ways, the genotype to some extent making its own environment and that of its progeny?

In reviewing evidence from foster home studies on environmental amelioration of IQs below 75 (the range often designated as indicating cultural-familial retardation) Heber, Dever and Conry (1968, p. 17) state: 'The conclusion that changes in the living environment can cause very large increments in IQ *for the cultural-familial retardate* is not warranted by these data.'

What is probably the largest study ever made of familial influences in mental retardation (defined in this study as IQ less than 70) involved investigation of more than 80,000 relatives of a group of mentally retarded persons by the Dight Institute of Genetics, University of Minnesota (Reed and Reed, 1965). From this large-scale study, Sheldon and Elizabeth Reed estimated that about 80 percent of mentally retarded (IQ less than 70) persons in the United States have a retarded parent or a normal parent who has a retarded sibling. The Reeds state: 'One inescapable conclusion is that the transmission of mental retardation from parent to child is by far the most important *single* factor in the persistence of this social misfortune' (p. 48). 'The transmission of mental retardation from one generation to the next, should, therefore, receive much more critical attention than it has in the past. It seems fair to state that this problem has been largely ignored on the assumption that if our social agencies function better, that if everyone's environment were improved sufficiently, then mental retardation would cease to be a major problem' (p. 77).

An interesting sidelight of the Reeds' study is the finding that in a number of families in which one or both parents had IQs below 70 and in which the environment they provided their children was deplorably deprived, there were a few children of average and superior IQ (as high as 130 or above) and superior scholastic performance. From a genetic standpoint the occurrence of such children would be expected. It is surprising from a strictly environmental standpoint. But, even though some proportion of the children of retarded parents are obviously intellectually well endowed, who would wish upon them the kind of environment typically provided by retarded parents? An investigation conducted in Denmark concluded that '. . . it is a very severe psychical trauma for a normally gifted child to grow up in a home where the mother is mentally deficient' (Jepsen and Bredmose, 1956, p. 209). Have we thought sufficiently of the rights of children – of their right to be born with fair odds against being mentally retarded, not to have a retarded parent, and with fair odds in favor of having the genetic endowment needed to compete on equal terms with the majority of persons in society? Can we reasonably and humanely oppose such rights of millions of children as yet not born?

*Is Our National IQ Declining?* It has long been known that there is a substantial negative correlation (averaging about 0·30 in various studies) between intelligence and family size and between social class and family size (Anastasi, 1956). Children with many siblings, on the average, have lower IQs than children in small families, and the trend is especially marked for families of more than five (Gottesman, 1968). This fact once caused concern in the United States, and even more so in Britain, because of its apparent implication of a declining IQ in the population. If more children are born to persons in the lower half of the intelligence distribution, one would correctly predict a decline in the average IQ of the population. In a number of large-scale studies addressed to the issue in Britain and the United States some 20 years ago, no evidence was found for a general decline in IQ (Duncan, 1952). The paradox of the apparent failure of the genetic prediction to be manifested was resolved to the satisfaction of most geneticists by three now famous studies, one by Higgins, Reed and Reed (1962), the others by Bajema (1963, 1966). All previous analyses had been based on IQ comparisons of children having different numbers of siblings, and this was their weakness. The data needed to answer the question properly consist of the average number of children born to *all* individuals at every level of IQ. It was found in the three studies that if persons with very low IQs married and had children, they typically had a large number of children. *But* – it was also found that relatively few persons in the lower tail of the IQ distribution ever married or produced children, and so their reproduction rate is more than counterbalanced by persons at the upper end of the IQ scale, nearly all of whom marry and have children. The data of these studies are shown in Figure 15.

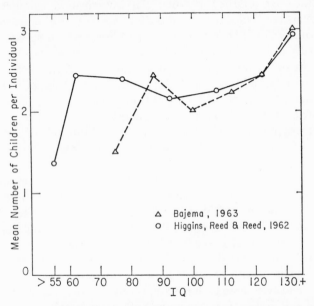

FIGURE 15.   *Mean number of children per adult individual (including those who are childless) at each level of IQ, in two samples of white American populations. Note in each sample the bimodal relationship between fertility and IQ.*

In my opinion these studies are far from adequate to settle this issue and thus do not justify complacency. They cannot be generalized much beyond the particular generation which the data represent or to other than the white population on which these studies were based. The population sampled by Bajema (1963, 1966), for example, consisted of native-born American whites, predominantly Protestant, with above-average educational attainments, living all or most of their lives in an urban environment, and having most of their children before World War II. Results from a study of this population cannot be confidently generalized to other, quite dissimilar segments of our national population. The relationship between reproductive rate and IQ found by Bajema and by Higgins *et al.*, may very well not prevail in every population group. Thus the evidence to date has not nullified the question of whether dysgenic trends are operating in some sectors.

If this conclusion is not unwarranted, then our lack of highly relevant information on this issue with respect to our Negro population is deplorable, and no one should be more concerned about it than the Negro community itself. Certain census statistics suggest that there might be forces at work which could create and widen the genetic aspect of the average difference in ability between the Negro and white populations in the United States, with the possible consequence that the improvement of educational facilities and increasing equality of opportunity will have a *decreasing* probability of producing equal achievement or continuing gains in the Negro population's ability to complete on equal terms. The relevant statistics have been presented by Moynihan (1966). The differential birthrate, as a function of socioeconomic status, is greater in the Negro than in the white population. The data showing this relationship for one representative age-group from the U.S. Census of 1960 are presented in Figure 16.

Negro middle- and upper-class families have fewer children than their white counterparts, while Negro lower-class families have more. In 1960, Negro women of ages 35 to 44 married to unskilled laborers had 4·7 children as compared with 3·8 for non-Negro women in the same situation. Negro women married to professional or technical workers had only 1·9 children as compared with 2·4 for white women in the same circumstances. Negro women with annual incomes below $2000 averaged 5·3 children. The poverty rate for families with 5 or 6 children is $3\frac{1}{2}$ times as high as that for families with one or two children (Hill and Jaffe, 1960). That these figures have some relationship to intellectual ability is seen in the fact that 3 out of 4 Negroes failing the Armed Forces Qualification Test come from families of four or more children.

Another factor to be considered is average generation time, defined as the number of years it takes for the parent generation to reproduce its own number. This period is significantly less in the Negro than in the white population. Also, as noted in the study of Bajema (1966), generation length is inversely related to educational attainment and occupational status; therefore a group with shorter generation length is more likely subject to a possible dysgenic effect.

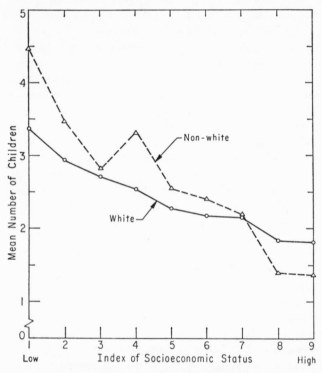

FIGURE 16.    *Average number of children per woman 25 and 29 years of age, married once, with husband present, by race and socio-economic status. From 1960 U.S. Census. (After Mitra, 1966.)*

Much more thought and research should be given to the educational and social implications of these trends for the future. Is there a danger that current welfare policies, unaided by eugenic foresight, could lead to the genetic enslavement of a substantial segment of our population? The possible consequences of our failure seriously to study these questions may well be viewed by future generations as our society's greatest injustice to Negro Americans.

## Intensive Educational Intervention

We began with mention of several of the major compensatory education programs and their general lack of success in boosting the scholastic performance of disadvantaged children. It has been claimed that such mammoth programs have not been adequately pinpointed to meeting specific, fine-grained cultural and cognitive needs of these children and therefore should not be expected to produce the gains that could result from more intensive and more carefully focused programs in which maximum cultural enrichment and instructional ingenuity are lavished on a small group of children by a team of experts.

The scanty evidence available seems to bear this out. While massive compensatory programs have produced no appreciable gains in intelligence or achievement (as noted on pp. 2-3), the majority of small-scale experiments in boosting the IQ and educational performance of disadvantaged children have produced significant gains. It is interesting that the magnitude of claimed gains generally decreases as one proceeds from reports in the popular press, to informal verbal reports heard on visits at research sites and in private correspondence, to papers read at meetings, to published papers without presentation of supporting data, and to published papers with supporting data. I will confine my review to some of the major studies in the last category.

First, some general observations.

*Magnitude of Gains.* The magnitude of IQ and scholastic achievement gains resulting from enrichment and cognitive stimulation programs authentically range between about 5 and 20 points for IQs, and between about one-half to two standard deviations for specific achievement measures (reading, arithmetic, spelling, etc.). Heber (1968) reviewed 29 intensive pre-school programs for disadvantaged children and found they resulted in an average gain in IQ (at the time of children's leaving the pre-school program) of between 5 and 10 points; the average gain was about the same for children whose initial IQs were below 90 as for those of 90 and above.

The amount of gain is related to several factors. The intensity and specificity of the instructional aspects of the program seem to make a difference. Ordinary nursery school attendance, with a rather diffuse enrichment program but with little effort directed at development of specific cognitive skills, generally results in a gain of 5 or 6 IQ points in typical disadvantaged pre-schoolers. If special cognitive training, especially in verbal skills, is added to the program, the average gain is about 10 points – slightly more or less depending on the amount of verbal content in the tests. Average gains rarely go above this, but when the program is extended beyond the classroom into the child's home, and there is intensive instruction in specific skills under short but highly attention-demanding daily sessions, as in the Bereiter-Engelmann program (1966), about a third of the children have shown gains of as much as 20 points.

Average gains of more than 10 or 15 points have not been obtained on any sizeable groups or been shown to persist or to be replicable in similar groups, although there have been claims that average gains of 20 or more points can be achieved by removing certain cultural and attitudinal barriers to learning. The actual evidence, however, warrants the caution expressed by Bereiter and Engelmann (1966, p. 7): '"Miracle cures" of this kind are sometimes claimed to work with disadvantaged children, as when a child is found to gain 20 points or so in IQ after a few months of pre-school experience. Such enormous gains, however, are highly suspect to anyone who is familiar with mental measurements. It is a fair guess that the child could have done as well on the first test except that he misinterpreted the situation, was frightened or agitated, or was not used to responding to instructions. Where genuine learning is concerned, enormous leaps simply do not occur, and leaps of any kind do not occur without sufficient cause.'

The initial IQ on entering also has some effect, and this fact may be obscured if various studies are coarsely grouped. Bereiter and Engelmann (1966, p. 16), in analyzing results from eight different pre-schools for culturally disadvantaged children that followed traditional nursery school methods, concluded that the children's average gain in IQ is *half* the way from their initial IQ level to the normal level of 100. This rule was never more than 2 points in error for the studies reviewed. This same amount of IQ gain is generally noted in disadvantaged children during their first year in regular kindergarten (Brison, 1967, p. 8).

I have found no evidence of comparable gains in non-disadvantaged children. Probably the exceedingly meager gains in some apparently excellent pre-school programs for the 'disadvantaged' are attributable to the fact that the children in them did not come from a sufficiently deprived home background. Such can be the case when the children are admitted to the program on the basis of 'self-selection' by their parents. Parents who seek out a nursery school or volunteer their children for an experimental pre-school are more apt to have provided their children with a somewhat better environment than would be typical for a randomly selected group of disadvantaged children. This seems to have been the case in Martin Deutsch's intensive pre-school enrichment program at the Institute of Developmental Studies in New York (Powledge, 1967). Both the experimental group (E) and the self-selected control groups ($C_{ss}$) were made up of Negro children from a poor neighborhood in New York City whose parents applied for their admission to the program. The E group received intensive educational attention in what is overall the most comprehensive and elaborate enrichment program I know of. The $C_{ss}$ group, of course, received no enriched education. The initial average Stanford-Binet IQs of the E and $C_{ss}$ groups were 93·32 and 94·69, respectively. After two years in the enrichment program, the E group had a mean IQ of 95·53 and the $C_{ss}$ group had 96·52. Both pre- and post-test differences are non-significant. The enrichment program continued for a third year through the first grade. For the children in the E group who had had 3 years of enrichment, there was a significant gain over the C group of 8 months in reading achievement by the end of first grade, a score above national norms. This result is in keeping with the general finding that enrichment shows a greater effect on scholastic achievement than on IQ *per se*.

Many studies have employed no control group selected on exactly the same basis as the experimental group. This makes it virtually impossible to evaluate the effect of the treatment on pre-test – post-test gain, and the problem is made more acute by the fact that enrichment studies often pick their subjects on the basis of their being below the average IQ of the population of disadvantaged children from which they are selected. This makes statistical regression a certainty – the group's mean will increase by an appreciable amount because of the imperfect correlation between test-retest scores over, say, a one-year interval. Since this correlation is known to be considerably lower in younger than in older children, there will be considerably greater 'gain' due to regression for younger groups of children. The net results of selecting especially backward children on the basis of IQ is that a gain in IQ can be predicted which is not at all attributable to the educational treatment given to the children. Studies using control groups nearly always show this gain in the control group, and only by subtracting the control group's gain from the experimental group's gain can we evaluate the magnitude of the treatment effect. Only the gain over and above that attributable to regression really counts.

Still another factor is involved in the inverse relationship generally found between children's age and the size of IQ gains in an enrichment program. Each single item gotten right in a test like the Stanford-Binet adds increasingly smaller increments to the IQ as children get older. Each Stanford-Binet test item, for example, is worth 2 months of mental age. At 4 years of age getting just two additional items right will boost an IQ of 85 up to 93. The same absolute amount of improvement in test performance at 10 years of age would boost an IQ of 85 up to only 88. The typical range of gains found in pre-school enrichment programs, in the age range of 4 to 6, are about what would be expected from passing an additional two to four items in the Stanford-Binet. This amount of gain should not be surprising on a test which, for this age range, consists of items rather similar to the materials and activities traditionally found in nursery schools – blocks, animal pictures, puzzles, bead stringing, copying drawings, and the like. I once visited an experimental pre-school using the Stanford-Binet to assess pre-test – post-test gains, in which some of the Stanford-Binet test materials were openly accessible to the children throughout their time in the school as part of the enrichment paraphernalia. Years ago Reymert and Hinton (1940) noted this 'easy gain' in the IQs of culturally disadvantaged pre-schoolers on tests depending on specific information such as being able to name parts of the body and knowing names of familiar objects. Children who have not picked up this information at home get it quickly in nursery school and kindergarten.

In addition to these factors, something else operates to boost scores

5 to 10 points from first to second test, provided the first test is really the first. When I worked in a psychological clinic, I had to give individual intelligence tests to a variety of children, a good many of whom came from an impoverished background. Usually I felt these children were really brighter than their IQ would indicate. They often appeared inhibited in their responsiveness in the testing situation on their first visit to my office, and when this was the case I usually had them come in on two or four different days for half-hour sessions with me in a 'play therapy' room, in which we did nothing more than get better acquainted by playing ball, using finger paints, drawing on the blackboard, making things out of clay, and so forth. As soon as the child seemed to be completely at home in this setting, I would retest him on a parallel form of the Stanford-Binet. A boost in IQ of 8 or 10 points or so was the rule; it rarely failed, but neither was the gain very often much above this. So I am inclined to doubt that IQ gains up to this amount in young disadvantaged children have much of anything to do with changes in ability. They are largely a result simply of getting a more accurate IQ by testing under more optimal conditions. Part of creating more optimal conditions in the case of disadvantaged children consists of giving at least two tests, the first only for practice and for letting the child get to know the examiner. I would put very little confidence in a single test score, especially if it is the child's first test and more especially if the child is from a poor background and of a different race from the examiner. But I also believe it is possible to obtain accurate assessments of a child's ability, and I would urge that attempts to evaluate pre-school enrichment programs measure the gains against initially valid scores. If there is not evidence that this precaution has been taken, and if there is no control group, one might as well subtract at least 5 points from the gain scores as having little or nothing to do with real intellectual growth.

It is interesting that the IQ gains typically found in enrichment programs are of about the same magnitude and durability as those found in studies of the effects of direct coaching and practice on intelligence tests. The average IQ gain in such studies is about 9 or 10 points (Vernon, 1954).

*What Is Really Changed When We Boost IQ?* Test scores may increase after special educational treatment, but one must then ask which components of test variance account for the gain. Is it *g* that gains, or is it something less central to our concept of intelligence? We will not know for sure until someone does a factor analysis of pre- and post-test scores, including a number of 'reference' tests that were not a part of the pre-test battery. We should also factor analyze the tests at the item level, to see which types of test items reflect the most gain. Are they the items with the highest cultural loadings? It is worth noting that the studies showing authentic gains used tests which are relatively high in cultural loading. I have found no studies that demonstrated gains in relatively noncultural or nonverbal tests like Cattell's Culture Fair Tests and Raven's Progressive Matrices.

Furthermore, if gain consists of actual improvement in cognitive skills rather than of acquisition of simple information, it must be asked whether the gain in skill represents the intellectual skill that the test normally measures, and which, because of the test's high heritability, presumably reflects some important, biologically based aspect of mental development. Let me cite one example. In a well-known experiment Gates and Taylor (1925) gave young children daily practice over several months in repeating auditory digit series, just like the digit span subtests in the Wechsler and Stanford-Binet. The practice resulted in a marked gain in the children's digit span, equivalent to an IQ gain of about 20 points. But when the children were retested after an interval of 6 months without practicing digit recall, their digit performance was precisely at the level expected for their mental age as determined by other tests. The gains had been lost, and the digit test once again accurately reflected the children's overall level of mental development, as it did before the practice period. The well-known later 'fading' of IQ gains acquired early in enrichment programs may be a similar phenomenon.

But there is another phenomenon that probably is even more important as one of the factors working against the persistence of initial gains. This is the so-called 'cumulative deficit' phenomenon, the fact that many children called disadvantaged show a decline in IQ from pre-school age through at least elementary school. The term 'cumulative deficit' may not be inappropriate in its connotations with respect to scholastic attainment, but it is probably a misleading misnomer when applied to the normal negatively accelerated growth rate of developmental characteristics such as intelligence. The same phenomenon can be seen in growth curves of stature, but no one would refer to the fact that some children gain height at a slower rate and level off at a lower asymptote as a 'cumulative deficit'. In short, it seems likely that some of the loss in initial gains is due to the more negatively accelerated growth curve for intelligence in disadvantaged children and is not necessarily due to waning or discontinuance of the instructional effort. The effort required to boost IQ from 80 to 90 at 4 or 5 years of age is miniscule compared to the effort that would be required by age 9 or 10. 'Gains' for experimental children in this range, in fact, take the form of superiority over a control group which has declined in IQ; the 'enriched' group is simply prevented from falling behind, so there is no absolute gain in IQ, but only an advantage relative to a declining control group. Because of the apparently ephemeral nature of the initial gains seen in pre-school programs, judgments of these programs' effectiveness in making a significant impact on intellectual development should be based on long-range results.

A further step in proving the effectiveness of a particular program is to demonstrate that it can be applied with comparable success by other individuals in other schools, and, if it is to be practicable on a large scale, to determine if it works in the hands of somewhat less inspired and less dedicated practitioners than the few who originated it or first put it into practice on a small scale. As an example of what can happen when a small-scale project gets translated to a large-scale one, we can note Kenneth B. Clark's (1963, p. 160) enthusiastic and optimistic description of a 'total push' intensive compensatory program which originated in one school serving disadvantaged children in New York City, with initially encouraging results. Clark said, 'These positive results can be duplicated in every school of this type'. In fact, it was tried in 40 other New York schools, and became known as the Higher Horizons program. After three years of the program the children in it showed no gains whatever and even averaged slightly lower in achievement and IQ than similar children in ordinary schools (U.S. Commission on Civil Rights, 1967, p. 125).

Finally, little is known about the range of IQ most likely to show genuine gains under enrichment. None of the data I have seen in this area permits any clear judgment on this matter. It would be unwarranted to assume at this time that special educational programs push the whole IQ distribution up the scale, so that, for example, they would yield a higher percentage of children with IQs higher than two standard deviations above the mean. After a 'total push' program, IQs, if they change at all, may no longer be normally distributed, so that the gains would not much affect the frequencies at the tails of the distribution. We simply do not know the answer to this at present, since the relevant data are lacking.

*Hothouse or Fertilizer?* There seems to be little doubt that a deprived environment can stunt intellectual development and that immersion in a good environment in early childhood can largely overcome the effects of deprivation, permitting the individual's genetic potential to be reflected in his performance. But can special enrichment and instructional procedures go beyond the prevention or amelioration of stunting? As Vandenberg (1968, p. 49) has asked, does enrichment act in a manner similar to a *hothouse*, forcing an early bloom which is nevertheless no different from a normal bloom, or does it act more like a *fertilizer*, producing bigger and better yields? There can be little question about the hothouse aspect of early stimulation and instruction. Within limits, children can learn many things at an earlier age than that at which they are normally taught in school. This is especially true of forms of associative learning which are mainly a function of time spent in the learning activity rather than of the development of more complex cognitive structures. While most children, for example, do not learn the alphabet until 5 or 6 years of age, they are fully capable of doing so at about 3, but it simply requires more time spent in learning. The cognitive structures involved are relatively simple as compared with, say, learning to copy a triangle or a diamond. Teaching a 3-year-old to copy a diamond is practically impossible; at 5 it is extremely difficult; at 7 the child apparently needs no 'teaching' – he copies the diamond easily. And the child of 5 who has been *taught* to copy the diamond seems to have learned something different from what the 7-year-old 'knows' who can do it without being 'taught'. Though the final performance of the 5-year-old and the 7-year-old may *look* alike, we know that the cognitive structures underlying their performance are different. Certain basic skills can be acquired either associatively by rote learning or cognitively by conceptual learning, and what superficially may appear to be the same performance may be acquired in pre-schoolers at an associative level, while at a conceptual level in older children. Both the 4-year-old and the 6-year-old may know that $2+2 = 4$, but this knowledge can be associative or cognitive. Insufficient attention has been given in pre-school programs so far to the shift from associative to cognitive learning. The pre-schooler's capacity for associative learning is already quite well developed, but his cognitive or conceptual capacities are as yet rudimentary and will undergo their period of most rapid change between about 5 and 7 years of age (White, 1965). We need to know more about what children can learn before age 5 that will transfer positively to later learning. Does learning something on an associative level facilitate or hinder learning the same content on a conceptual level?

While some pre-school and compensatory programs have demonstrated earlier than normal learning of certain skills, the evidence for accelerating cognitive development or the speed of learning is practically nil. But usually this distinction is not made between sheer performance and the nature of the cognitive structures which support the gains in performance, and so the research leaves the issue in doubt. The answer to such questions is to be found in the study of the kinds and amount of transfer that result from some specific learning. The capacity for transfer of training is one of the essential aspects of what we mean by intelligence. The IQ gains reported in enrichment studies appear to be gains more in what Cattell calls 'crystallized', in contrast to 'fluid', intelligence. This is not to say that gains of this type are not highly worth while. But having a clearer conception of just what the gains consist of will give us a better idea of how they can be most effectively followed up and of what can be expected of their effects on later learning and achievement.

*Specific Programs.* Hodges and Spicker (1967) have summarized a number of the more substantial pre-school intervention studies designed to improve the intellectual capabilities and scholastic success of disadvantaged children. Here are some typical examples.

The *Indiana Project* focused on deprived Appalachian white children 5 years of age, with IQs in the range of 50 to 85. The children spent 1 year in a special kindergarten with a structured program designed to remedy specific diagnosed deficiencies of individual children in the areas of language development, fine motor coordination, concept formation, and socialization. Evaluation extended over 2 years, and gains were measured against three control groups: regular kindergarten, children who stayed at home during the kindergarten year, and children at home in another similar community. The average gain (measured against all three controls) after 2 years was 10·8 IQ points on the Stanford-Binet (final IQ 97·4) and 4·0 IQ points on the Peabody Picture Vocabulary Test (final IQ 90·4).

The *Perry Pre-school Project* at Ypsilanti, Michigan, also was directed at disadvantaged pre-school children with IQs between 50 and 85. The program was aimed at remedying lacks largely in the verbal prerequisites for first-grade learning and involved the parents as well as the children. There was a significant gain of 8·9 IQ points in the Stanford-Binet after 1 year of the pre-school, but by the end of second grade the experimental group exceeded the controls, who had had no pre-school attendance, by only 1·6 IQ points, a nonsignificant gain.

The *Early Training Project* under the direction of Gray and Klaus at Peabody College is described as a multiple intervention program, meaning that in included not only pre-school enrichment but work with the disadvantaged children's mothers to increase their ability to stimulate their child's cognitive development at home. Two experimental groups, with two and three summers of pre-school enrichment experience in a special school plus home visits by the training staff, experienced an average gain, 4 years after the start of the program, of 7·2 IQ points over a control group on the Stanford-Binet (final IQ of *E* group was 93·6).

The *Durham Education Improvement Program* (1966-1967b) has focused on pre-school children from impoverished homes. The basic assumption of the program is stated as follows: 'First, Durham's disadvantaged youngsters are considered normal at birth and potentially normal academic achievers, though they are frequently subjected to conditions jeopardizing their physical and emotional health. It is further assumed that they adapt to their environment according to the same laws of learning which apply to all children.' The program is one of the most comprehensive and intensive efforts yet made to improve the educability of children from backgrounds of poverty. The IQ gains over about an 8 to 9 months' interval for various groups of pre-schoolers in the program are raw pre-post test gains, not gains over a control group. The average IQ gains on three different tests were 5·32 (Peabody Picture Vocabulary), 2·62 (Stanford-Binet), and 9·27 (Wechsler Intelligence Scale for children). In most cases, IQs changed from the 80s to the 90s.

The well-known Bereiter-Engelmann (1966) program at the University of Illinois is probably the most sharply focused of all. It aims not at all-round enrichment of the child's experience but at teaching specific cognitive skills, particularly of a logical, semantic nature (as contrasted with more diffuse 'verbal stimulation'). The emphasis is on information processing skills considered essential for school learning. The Bereiter-Engelmann pre-school is said to be academically oriented, since each day throughout the school year the children receive 20-minute periods of intensive instruction in three major content areas – language, reading, and arithmetic. The instruction, in small groups, explicitly involves maintaining a high level of attention, motivation, and participation from every child. Overt and emphatic repetition by the children are important ingredients of the instructional process. The pre-post gains (not measured against a control group) in Stanford-Binet IQ over an 18 months' period are about 8 to 10 points. Larger gains are shown in tests that have clearly identifiable content which can reflect the areas receiving specific instruction, such as the Illinois Test of Psycholinguistic Abilities and tests of reading and arithmetic (Bereiter and Engelmann, 1968). The authors note that the gains are shared about equally by all children.

Bereiter and Engelmann, correctly, I believe, put less stock in the IQ gains than in the gains in scholastic performance achieved by the children in their program. They comment that the children's IQs were still remarkably low for children who performed at the academic level actually attained in the program. Their scholastic performance was commensurate with that of children 10 or 20 points higher in IQ. Such is the advantage of highly focused training – it can significantly boost the basic skills that count most. Bereiter and Engelmann (1966, p. 54) comment, '. . . to have taught children in a two-hour period per day enough over a broad area to bring the average IQ up to 110 or 120 would have been an impossibility'. An important point of the Bereiter-Engelmann program is that it shows that scholastic performance – the acquisition of the basic skills – can be boosted much more, at least in the early years, than can the IQ, and that highly concentrated, direct instruction is more effective than more diffuse cultural enrichment.

The largest IQ gains I have seen and for which I was also able to examine the data and statistical analyses were reported by Karnes (1968), whose pre-school program at the University of Illinois is based on an intensive attempt to ameliorate specific learning deficits in disadvantaged 3-year-old children. Between the average age of 3 years 3 months and 4 years 1 month, children in the program showed a gain of 16·9 points in the Stanford-Binet IQ, while a control group showed a loss of 2·8 over the same period, making for a net gain of 19·7 IQ points for the experimental group. Despite rather small samples (E = 15, C = 14), this gain is highly significant statistically (a probability of less than 1 in 1000 or occurring by chance). Even so, I believe such findings need to be replicated for proper evaluation, and the durability of the gains needs to be assessed by follow-up studies over several years. There remains the question of the extent to which specific learning at age 3 affects cognitive structures which normally do not emerge until 6 or 7 years of age and whether induced gains at an early level of mental development show appreciable 'transfer' to later stages. It is hoped that investigators can keep sufficient track of children in pre-school programs to permit a later follow-up which could answer these questions. An initial small sample size mitigates against this possibility, and so proper research programs should be planned accordingly.

'*Expectancy Gain*'. Do disadvantaged children perform relatively poorly on intelligence tests because their teachers have low expectations for their ability? This belief has gained popular currency through an experiment by Rosenthal and Jacobson (1968). Their notion is that the teacher's expectations for the child's performance act as a self-fulfilling prophecy. Consequently, according to this hypothesis, one way to boost these children's intelligence, and presumably their general scholastic performance as well, is to cause teachers to hold out higher expectations of these children's ability. To test this idea, Rosenthal and Jacobson picked about five children at random from each of the classes in an elementary school and then informed the classroom teachers that, according to test results, the selected children were expected to show unusual intellectual gains in the coming year. Since the 'high expectancy' children in each class were actually selected at random, the only way they differed from their classmates was presumably in the minds of their teachers. Group IQ tests administered by the teachers on three occasions during the school year showed a significantly larger gain in the 'high expectancy' children than in their classmates. Both groups gained in IQ by amounts that are typically found as a result of direct coaching or of 'total push' educational programs. Yet the authors note that 'Nothing was done directly for the disadvantaged child at Oak School. There was no crash program to improve his reading ability, no special lesson plans, no extra time for tutoring, no trips to museums or art galleries. There was only the belief that the children bore watching, that they had intellectual competencies that would in due course be revealed' (p. 181). The net total IQ gain (i.e., Expectancy group minus Control group) for all grades was 3·8 points. Net gain in verbal IQ was 2·1; for Reasoning (nonverbal) IQ the gain was 7·2. Differences were largest in grades 1 and 2 and became negligible in higher grades. The statistical significance of the gains is open to question and permits no clear-cut conclusion. (The estimation of the error variance is at issue: the investigators emphasized the individual pupil's scores as the unit of analysis rather than the means of the E and C groups for each classroom as the unit. The latter procedure, which is regarded as more rigorous by many statisticians, yields statistically negligible results.)

Because of the questionable statistical significance of the results of this study, there may actually be no phenomenon that needs to be explained. Other questionable aspects of the conduct of the experiment make it mandatory that its results be replicated under better conditions before any conclusions from the study be taken seriously or used as a basis for educational policy.* For example,

* The Rosenthal and Jacobson study has since come under devastating critical bombardment. Robert L. Thorndike (1968) in a major review wrote: 'Alas, it is so defective technically that one can only regret it ever got beyond the eyes of the original investigators!' A comprehensive book-length critique, which includes a re-analysis of the original data of the study (which fails to support the original conclusions of Rosenthal and Jacobson) has been prepared by Elashoff and Snow (1971). This volume also contains a review (by Baker and Crist) of all the studies up to 1971

the same form of the group-administered IQ test was used for each testing, so that specific practice gains were maximized. The teachers themselves administered the tests, which is a faux pas par excellence in research of this type. The dependability of teacher-administered group tests leaves much to be desired. Would any gains beyond those normally expected from general test familiarity have been found if the children's IQs had been accurately measured in the first place by individual tests administered by qualified psychometrists without knowledge of the purpose of the experiment? These are some of the conditions under which such an experiment must be conducted if it is to inspire any confidence in its results.

*Conclusions About IQ Gains.* The evidence so far suggests the tentative conclusion that the pay-off of pre-school and compensatory programs in terms of IQ gains is small. Greater gains are possible in scholastic performance when instructional techniques are intensive and highly focused, as in the Bereiter-Engelmann program. Educators would probably do better to concern themselves with teaching skills directly than with attempting to boost overall cognitive development. By the same token, they should deemphasize IQ tests as a means of assessing gains, and use mainly direct tests of the skills the instructional program is intended to inculcate. The techniques for raising intelligence *per se*, in the sense

which have attempted to replicate the Rosenthal and Jacobson '*Pygmalion* Effect'. Elashoff and Snow conclude: '. . . it can be seen that of nine studies (other than Rosenthal and Jacobson) attempting to demonstrate teacher expectancy effects on IQ, none has succeeded. Of twelve expectancy studies including pupils achievement measures as criteria, six have succeeded. Of seven studies including measures of observable pupil behavior, three have succeeded. And of seventeen studies including measures of observable teacher behavior, fourteen have succeeded. Thus it seems that teacher expectancy effects are most likely to influence proximal variables (those "closest" in a psychological sense to the source of the effect, e.g., teacher behavior) and progressively less likely to influence distal variables (or variables psychologically remote from the source of expectations). IQ, the most remote of pupil variables, is unlikely to be affected. These results are consistent with a Brunswikian view of teacher-learner interaction (Snow, 1968). They suggest that expectancies may be important and are certainly deserving of study, but they fail utterly to support *Pygmalion's* celebrated effect on IQ' (p. 159).

of *g*, probably lie more in the province of the biological sciences than in psychology and education.

Gordon and Wilkerson (1966, pp. 158-159) have made what seems to me perhaps the wisest statement I have encountered regarding the proper aims of intervention programs:

> . . . the unexpressed purpose of most compensatory programs is to make disadvantaged children as much as possible like the kinds of children with whom the school has been successful, and our standard of educational success is how well they approximate middle-class children in school performance. It is not at all clear that the concept of compensatory education is the one which will most appropriately meet the problems of the disadvantaged. These children are *not* middle-class children, many of them never *will* be, and they can never be anything but second-rate as long as they are thought of as potentially middle-class children. . . . At best they are different, and an approach which views this difference merely as something to be overcome is probably doomed to failure.

### 'Learning Quotient' *versus* Intelligence Quotient

If many of the children called culturally disadvantaged are indeed 'different' in ways that have educational implications, we must learn as much as possible about the real nature of these differences. To what extent do the differences consist of more than just the well-known differences in IQ and scholastic achievement, and, of course, the obvious differences in cultural advantages in the home?

Evidence is now emerging that there are stable ethnic differences in *patterns* of ability and that these patterns are invariant across wide socioeconomic differences (Lesser, Fifer and Clark, 1965; Stodolsky and Lesser, 1967). Middle-class and lower-class groups differed about one standard deviation on all four abilities (Verbal, Reasoning, Number, Space) measured by Lesser and his co-workers, but the profile or pattern of scores was distinctively different for Chinese, Jewish, Negro, and Puerto Rican children, regardless of their social class. Such differences in patterns of ability are bound to interact with school instruction. The important question is how many other abilities there are that are not tapped by conventional tests for which there exist individual and group differences that interact with methods of instruction.

Through our research in Berkeley we are beginning to perceive what seems to be a very significant set of relationships with respect

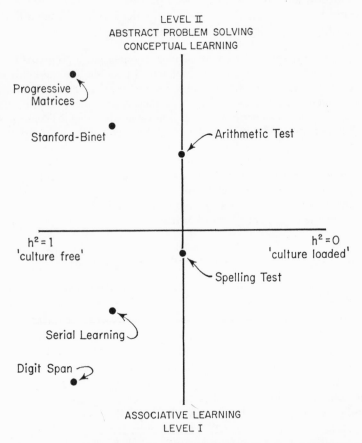

FIGURE 17.   *The two-dimensional space required for comprehending social class differences in performance on tests of intelligence, learning ability, and scholastic achievement. The locations of the various 'tests' are hypothetical.*

to patterns of ability which, unlike those of Lesser *et al.*, seem to interact more with social class than with ethnic background.

In brief, we are finding that a unidimensional concept of intelligence is quite inadequate as a basis for understanding social class differences in ability. For example, the magnitude of test score differences between lower- and middle-class children does not always correspond to the apparent 'cultural loading' of the test. Some of the least culturally loaded tests show the largest differences between lower- and middle-class children. At least two dimensions must be postulated to comprehend the SES differences reported in the literature and found in our laboratory (see Jensen, 1968c, 1969d). These two dimensions and the hypothetical location of various test loadings on each dimension are shown in Figure 17. The horizontal axis represents the degree of cultural loading of the test. It is defined by the test's heritability. I have argued elsewhere (Jensen, 1968c) that the heritability index for a test is probably our best objective criterion of its culture-fairness. Just because tests do not stand at one or the other extreme of this continuum does not mean that the concept of culture-fairness is not useful in discussing psychological tests. The vertical axis in Figure 17 represents a continuum ranging from 'simple' associative learning to complex cognitive or conceptual learning. I have hypothesized two genotypically distinct basic processes underlying this continuum, labeled Level I (associative ability) and Level II (conceptual ability). Level I involves the neural registration and consolidation of stimulus inputs and the formation of associations. There is relatively little transformation of the input, so there is a high correspondence between the forms of the stimulus input and the form of the response output. Level I ability is tapped mostly by tests such as digit memory, serial rote learning, selective trial-and-error learning with reinforcement (feedback) for correct responses, and in slightly less 'pure' form by free recall of visually or verbally presented materials, and paired-associate learning. Level II abilities, on the other hand, involve self-initiated elaboration and transformation of the stimulus input before it eventuates in an overt response. Concept learning and problem solving are good examples. The subject must actively manipulate the input to arrive at the output. This ability is best measured by intelligence tests with a low cultural loading and a high loading on $g$ – for example, Raven's Progressive Matrices.

Social class differences in test performance are more strongly associated with the vertical dimension in Figure 17 than with the horizontal.

## ASSOCIATIVE LEARNING ABILITY

Teachers of the disadvantaged have often remarked that many of these children seem much brighter than their IQs would lead one to expect, and that, even though their scholastic performance is usually as poor as that of middle-class children of similar IQ, the disadvantaged children usually appear much brighter in non-scholastic ways than do their middle-class counterparts in IQ. A lower-class child coming into a new class, for example, will learn the names of 20 or 30 children in a few days, will quickly pick up the rules and the know-how of various games on the playground, and so on – a kind of performance that would seem to belie his IQ, which may even be as low as 60. This gives the impression that the test is 'unfair' to the disadvantaged child, since middle-class children in this range of IQ will spend a year in a classroom without learning the names of more than a few classmates, and they seem almost as inept on the playground and in social interaction as they are in their academic work.

We have objectified this observation by devising tests which can reveal these differences. The tests measure associative learning ability and show how fast a child can learn something relatively new and unfamiliar, right in the test situation. The child's performance does not depend primarily, as it would in conventional IQ tests, upon what he has already learned at home or elsewhere before he comes to take the test. We simply give him something to learn, under conditions which permit us to measure the rate and thoroughness of the learning. The tasks most frequently used are various forms of auditory digit memory, learning the serial order of a number of familiar objects or pictures of objects, learning to associate pairs of pictures of familiar objects, and free recall of names or objects presented from one to five times in a random order.

Our findings with these tests, which have been presented in greater detail elsewhere (Jensen, 1968a, 1968b, 1968d, 1968e; Jensen, 1968f; Jensen and Rohwer, 1968), seem to me to be of great potential importance to the education of many of the children called disadvantaged. What we are finding, briefly, is this: lower-class children, whether white, Negro, or Mexican-American, perform as well on these direct learning tests as do middle-class children. Lower-class children in the IQ range of about 60 to 80 do markedly *better* than middle-class children who are in this range of IQ. Above about IQ 100, on the other hand, there is little or no difference between social class groups on the learning tests.

At first we thought we had finally discovered a measure of 'culture-fair' testing, since we found no significant SES differences on these learning tests. But we can no longer reconcile this interpretation with all the facts now available. Some of the low SES children with low IQs on culturally loaded tests, like the Peabody Picture Vocabulary Tests, do very well on our learning tests, but do not have higher IQs on less culturally loaded tests of $g$, like the Progressive Matrices. It appears that we are dealing here with two kinds of abilities – associative learning ability (Level I) and cognitive or conceptual learning and problem-solving ability (Level II).

One particular test – free recall – shows the distinction quite well, since a slight variation in the test procedure makes the difference between whether it measures Level I or Level II. This is important, because it is sometimes claimed that low SES children do better on our learning tests than on IQ tests because the former are more interesting or more 'relevant' to them, and thus make them more highly motivated to perform at their best. This is not a valid interpretation, since when essentially the same task is made either 'associative' or 'cognitive', we get differences of about one standard deviation in the mean scores of lower- and middle-class children. For example, 20 unrelated familiar objects (doll, toy car, comb, cup, etc.) are shown to children who are then asked to recall as many objects as they can in any order that may come to mind. The random presentation and recall are repeated five times to obtain a more reliable score. Lower- and middle-class elementary school children perform about the same on this task, although they differ some 15 to 20 points in IQ. This free recall test has a low correlation with IQ and the correlation is lower for the low SES children. But then we can change the recall test so that it gives quite different results.

This is shown in an experiment from our laboratory by Glasman (1968). (In this study SES and race are confounded, since the low SES group were Negro children and the middle SES group were white.) Again, 20 familiar objects are presented, but this time the objects are selected so that they can be classified into one of four categories, *animals, furniture, clothing,* or *foods.* There are five items in each of the four categories, but all 20 items are presented in a random order on each trial. Under this condition a large social class difference shows up: the low SES children perform only slightly better on the average than they did on the uncategorized objects; while the middle SES children show a great improvement in performance which puts their scores about one standard deviation above the low SES children. Furthermore, there is much greater evidence of 'clustering' the items in free recall for the middle SES than for the low SES children. That is, the middle-class children rearrange the input in such a way that the order of output in recall corresponds to the categories to which the objects may be assigned. The low SES children show less clustering in this fashion, although many show rather idiosyncratic pair-wise 'clusters' that persist from trial to trial. There is a high correlation between the strength of the clustering tendency and the amount of recall. Also, clustering tendency is strongly related to age. Kindergartens, for example, show little difference between recall of categorized and uncategorized lists, and at this age SES differences in performance are nil. By fourth or fifth grade, however, the SES differences in clustering tendency are great, with a correspondingly large difference in ability to recall categorized lists.

It is interesting, also, that the recall of categorized lists correlates highly with IQ. In fact, when mental age or IQ is partialled out of the results, there are no significant remaining SES differences in recall. Post-test interviews showed that the recall differences for the two social class groups cannot be attributed to the low SES group's not knowing the category names. The children know the categories but tend not to use them spontaneously in recalling the list.

In general, we find that Level I associative learning tasks correlate very substantially with IQ among middle-class children but have very low correlations with IQ among lower-class children (Jensen, 1968b). The reason for this difference in correlations can be traced back to the form of the scatter diagrams for the middle and low SES groups, which is shown schematically in Figure 18. Since large representative samples of the entire school population have not been studied so far, the exact form of the correlation scatter diagram has not yet been well established, but the schematic portrayal of Figure 18 is what could be most reasonably hypothesized on the basis of several lines of evidence now available. (Data on a representative sample of 5000 children given Level I and Level II tests are now being analyzed to establish the forms of the correlation plots for low and middle SES groups.) The form of the correlation as it now appears suggests a hierarchical arrangement of mental abilities, such that Level I ability is necessary but not sufficient for Level II. That is, high performance on Level II

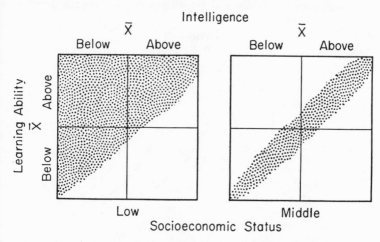

FIGURE 18. *Schematic illustration of the essential form of the correlation scatter-diagram for the relationship between associative learning ability and IQ in Low SES and Upper-Middle SES groups.*

tasks depends upon better than average ability on Level I, but the reverse does not hold. If this is true, the data can be understood in terms of one additional hypothesis, namely, that Level I ability is distributed about the same in all social class groups, while Level II ability is distributed differently in lower and middle SES groups. The hypothesis is expressed graphically in Figure 19. Heritability studies of Level II tests cause me to believe that Level II processes are not just the result of interaction between Level I learning ability and experientially acquired strategies or learning sets. That learning is necessary for Level II no one doubts, but certain neural structures must also be available for Level II abilities to develop, and these are conceived of as being different from the neural structures underlying Level I. The genetic factors involved in each of these types of ability are presumed to have become differentially distributed in the population as a function of social class, since Level II has been most important for scholastic performance under the traditional methods of instruction.

From evidence on age differences in different tasks on the Level I – Level II continuum (e.g., Jensen and Rohwer, 1965), I have suggested one additional hypothesis concerning the develop-

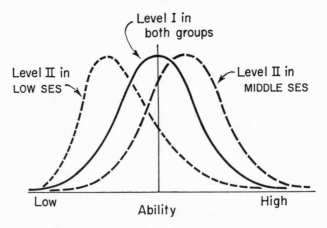

FIGURE 19.   *Hypothetical distributions of Level I (solid line) and Level II (dashed line) abilities in middle-class and culturally disadvantaged populations.*

mental rates of Level I and Level II abilities in lower and middle SES groups, as depicted in Figure 20. Level I abilities are seen as developing rapidly and as having about the same course of development and final level in both lower and middle SES groups. Level II abilities, by contrast, develop slowly at first, attain prominence between 4 and 6 years of age, and show an increasing difference between the SES groups with increasing age. This formulation is consistent with the increasing SES differences in mental age on standard IQ tests, which tap mostly Level II ability.

Thus, ordinary IQ tests are not seen as being 'unfair' in the sense of yielding inaccurate or invalid measures for the many disadvantaged children who obtain low scores. If they are unfair, it is because they tap only one part of the total spectrum of mental abilities and do not reveal that aspect of mental ability which may be the disadvantaged child's strongest point – the ability for associative learning.

Since traditional methods of classroom instruction were evolved in populations having a predominantly middle-class pattern of abilities, they put great emphasis on cognitive learning rather than associative learning. And in the post-Sputnik era, education has

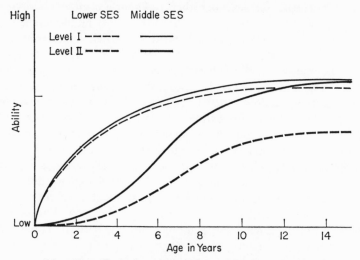

FIGURE 20. *Hypothetical growth curves for Level I and Level II abilities in middle SES and low SES populations.*

seen an increased emphasis on cognitive and conceptual learning, much to the disadvantage of many children whose mode of learning is predominantly associative. Many of the basic skills can be learned by various means, and an educational system that puts inordinate emphasis on only one mode or style of learning will obtain meager results from the children who do not fit this pattern. At present, I believe that the educational system – even as it falteringly attempts to help the disadvantaged – operates in such a way as to maximize the importance of Level II (i.e., intelligence or $g$) as a source of variance in scholastic performance. Too often, if a child does not learn the school subject-matter when taught in a way that depends largely on being average or above average on $g$, he does not learn at all, so that we find high school students who have failed to learn basic skills which they could easily have learned many years earlier by means that do not depend much on $g$. It may well be true that many children today are confronted in our schools with an educational philosophy and methodology which were mainly shaped in the past, entirely without any roots in these children's genetic and cultural heritage. The educational system was never allowed to evolve in such a way as to maximize the actual potential for learning that is latent in these children's patterns of abilities. If a child cannot show that he 'understands' the meaning of $1+1 = 2$ in some abstract, verbal, cognitive sense, he is, in effect, not allowed to go on to learn $2+2 = 4$. I am reasonably convinced that all the basic scholastic skills can be learned by children with normal Level I learning ability, provided the instructional techniques do not make $g$ (i.e., Level II) the *sine qua non* of being able to learn. Educational researchers must discover and devise teaching methods that capitalize on existing abilities for the acquisition of those basic skills which students will need in order to get good jobs when they leave school. I believe there will be greater rewards for all concerned if we further explore different types of abilities and modes of learning, and seek to discover how these various abilities can serve the aims of education. This seems more promising than acting as though only one pattern of abilities, emphasizing $g$, can succeed educationally, and therefore trying to inculcate this one ability pattern in all children.

If the theories I have briefly outlined here become fully substantiated, the next step will be to develop the techniques by which school learning can be most effectively achieved in accordance with different patterns of ability. By all means, schools must discover $g$ wherever it exists and see to it that its educational correlates are fully encouraged and cultivated. There can be little doubt that certain educational and occupational attainments depend more upon $g$ than upon any other single ability. But schools must also be able to find ways of utilizing other strengths in children whose major strength is not of the cognitive variety. One of the great and relatively untapped reservoirs of mental ability in the disadvantaged, it appears from our research, is the basic ability to learn. We can do more to marshal this strength for educational purposes.

If diversity of mental abilities, as of most other human characteristics, is a basic fact of nature, as the evidence indicates, and if
the ideal of universal education is to be successfully pursued, it
seems a reasonable conclusion that schools and society must
provide a range and diversity of educational methods, programs,
and goals, and of occupational opportunities, just as wide as the
range of human abilities. Accordingly, the ideal of equality of
educational opportunity should not be interpreted as uniformity
of facilities, instructional techniques, and educational aims for all
children. Diversity rather than uniformity of approaches and aims
would seem to be the key to making education rewarding for
children of different patterns of ability. The reality of individual
differences thus need not mean educational rewards for some
children and frustration and defeat for others.

# A Theory of Primary and Secondary Familial Mental Retardation

## Diagnosis and Taxonomy of Mental Retardation

Recent evidence derived from experimental studies of learning in mentally retarded children and adults leads to a hypothesis of a hierarchy of mental abilities. The hypothesis has important implications for the taxonomy and diagnosis of mental retardation. This paper explicates the hypothesis and reviews some of the relevant experimental evidence. The implications of the hypothesis for the education of the retarded are also indicated.

### ESTABLISHED DIAGNOSTIC CATEGORIES

Two broad categories of mental retardation are now generally recognized. The first category is diagnostically the most obvious; it is the variety of severe mental defects resulting in IQs for the most part below 50 and accompanied by physical abnormalities or clear signs of neurological damage. This category of mental deficiency forms a distribution of ability which, in a sense, stands apart from the normal distribution of mental abilities in the general population. Most of these severe defects appear to be due to (a) single mutant genes, often labeled 'major gene' defects, (b) chromosomal defects, and (c) brain damage. Examples of (a) are recessive genetic defects such as phenylketonuria, galactosemia, amaurotic family idiocy, microcephaly, and hypertelorism, to name but a few. Examples of (b) are Down's syndrome (mongolism), due to triplication of chromosome 21, giving the child 47 rather than the normal 46 chromosomes; Kleinfelter's syndrome, due to an extra female sex chromosome in the male (XXY); and Turner's syndrome, a marked deficiency in spatial ability due to a missing sex chromosome in the female (XO instead of the normal XX). Examples of (*c*) are birth trauma, kernicterus due to prematurity or to rhesus incompatibility, and brain damaging diseases such as maternal rubella (German measles), neonatal septicemia, meningitis, and encephalitis.

The majority of persons with IQs below 50 are included in these diagnostic categories. Studies in England have found that among individuals in this severely subnormal range of IQ no specific causal factor was identifiable in about 30 percent of the cases (Kushlick, 1966, p. 130).

In the IQ range from 50 to 70, on the other hand, at least 75 percent of the individuals included therein appear clinically normal, evincing no signs of neurological damage, sensory defects, or physical stigmata. In fact, a report of the National Institute of Neurological Diseases and Blindness states that in 75 to 80 percent of *all* cases of mental retardation there is no specific identifiable cause such as those found in the categories outlined above (Research Profile No. 11, 1965).

These cases of retardation with no clinically identifiable cause are now commonly labeled cultural-familial retardation. The vast majority bearing this designation fall in the IQ range from 50 to 70. The evidence seems quite clear that these clinically normal persons are a part of the normal distribution of intelligence in the population, a distribution which is determined mainly by polygenic inheritance – that is, the influence of a large number of genes each of which contributes a small increment to mental ability (Gottesman, 1963). Familial retardation represents the bottom 2 to 3 percent of the lower tail of this normal distribution. Some 70 to 80 percent of all persons identified as retarded at some point in their lives are in the familial category (Heber, Dever and Conry, 1968).

The well-known excess or bulge at the lower end of the IQ distribution is attributable to major gene defects and brain damage which override normal polygenic determinants of intelligence. A study in England based on a complete sample of 3361 children showed actual frequencies not in excess of the frequencies expected from the normal or Gaussian distribution *above* IQs of 45. But the frequency of IQs *below* 45 was almost 18 times greater than would be expected (Roberts, 1952).

The most convincing evidence that the severely subnormal and the mildly subnormal familial retardates are different distributions and not different parts of a single underlying continuum of causal factors is the differences in amount of regression toward the mean IQ of the general population seen in the siblings of two types of retarded children. The siblings of familial retardates, on the average, have an IQ about half-way between the IQ of their retarded sib and the mean of the general population, an amount of regression that is rather precisely predictable from a polygenic model of the inheritance of intelligence. The very same amount of regression toward the mean is found in siblings of gifted children. On the other hand, the siblings of retardates with extremely low intelligence (IQs below 45 or 50) have an average IQ which is the same as the mean for the general population. In other words, the mental defect of the retarded sibling is superimposed upon and overrides the normal polygenic basis for intellectual development. Presumably the majority of the severely retarded would have been of normal or superior intelligence were it not for the devastating effect of a mutant gene, an abnormal chromosome, or brain damage (Shields and Slater, 1961).

It is still uncertain whether the normal distribution of polygenically determined intelligence extends below IQ 50 or thereabouts. The determination of this is made extremely difficult by the very small proportion of all retardates below IQ 50 that would be expected at this extreme of the normal curve. It is entirely possible, however, that some proportion of the 30 percent of the severely subnormal for whom no clinically identifiable etiology can be found are actually the lowest extreme of the normal distribution.

## CULTURAL-FAMILIAL RETARDATION

Having now made this basic distinction between subnormality due to major genetic defects and neurologic damage, on the one hand, and cultural-familial retardation, on the other, the remainder of this paper is concerned with taking a diagnostically more analytic look at the cultural-familial category of mental retardation. This is not a sharply defined category. Traditionally, the criteria for the diagnosis of cultural-familial includes IQs in the range from 50 to 70 or 75 and to this criterion is generally added some assessment of social competence. Persons not deficient in social competence are seldom regarded as retarded, despite a low IQ, except within the traditional school setting. From an educational standpoint and in terms of the scholastic requirements for entry into an ever-increasing proportion of today's occupations, IQs below 85 are usually associated with educational retardation within the context of ordinary schooling, and consequently also with limited occupational opportunities. In pre-literate and pre-industrial societies most persons in the IQ range from 70 to 85 would not be perceived as retarded or occupationally disadvantaged, but in today's technological society they are at a marked disadvantage. More occupations today call for a higher level of developed skills than was true for past generations. Largely for this reason the American Association on Mental Deficiency has changed the intelligence test part of the criterion for retardation from two standard deviations (IQ 70) below the population mean to only one standard deviation (IQ 85) below the mean.

Edgerton (1968), an anthropologist who has studied mental retardation in primitive tribes, has expressed the doubt that the persons he has observed in industrial societies with the diagnosis of retardation in the IQ range 50 to 70 would be competent even in simpler, pre-literate societies. Edgerton claims that the demands of life in African tribal society, for example, involve an amount of learning of customs, knowledge, and skills that is more than could be coped with by most persons regarded as mildly retarded by the usual IQ criterion. This is an important observation in the light of the major hypothesis put forth in this paper, for it falls in line with the observations that initially led to the studies which form the basis for our hypothesis, namely, the observation that some, perhaps many, of the children found to be retarded in school performance and on IQ tests appear to be normal and even bright in terms of a variety of criteria that clearly lie outside the scholastic realm.

The most likely reason that students of mental retardation have in the past failed to note or to emphasize this observation is that the criterion of social incompetence, as well as low IQ and poor scholastic performance, has determined the diagnosis of retardation and, even more than the intelligence test or scholastic criteria, has been the chief basis for admission to institutions for the retarded. A much broader spectrum of mental retardation is to be found in the public schools than in special residential institutions, and it would be difficult, if not impossible, to observe in institutions one type of retardation we have seen frequently in public schools – a 'bright' child with a presumably valid low IQ (i.e., 50-75) which, in addition to his low scholastic performance, often results in his being placed in a special class for the retarded or for 'slow learners'.

A reformulation of the classification of cultural-familial retardation would therefore seem to be in order. A monolithic conception of this category, for example, has led to disputes over the claim that many persons are retarded only during their school years and once they leave school they become non-retarded. Mental retardation is thus viewed as a condition that results largely from the imposition of middle class standards and values by the schools. However, Heber *et al.* (1968) have noted that this interpretation fails to consider that the opportunities and criteria for evaluating mental retardation are very different for the pre-school and post-school populations. Assessment based on clinical psychological tests have shown approximately the same incidence of retardation in the pre- and post-school population as are found in school, which only means that the criteria used in the psychological clinic are much the same as those used in schools. In the pre- and post-school years the IQ is less important and behavioral maturity and social competence are more important criteria in the assessment of retardation. Despite the general stability of the IQ throughout and beyond the school years, there are marked differences among children classed by the school as retarded. They differ in their social and occupational competence after leaving school, and these differences are only slightly correlated with IQ and scholastic performance. Some other important dimensions of ability, not assessed by the usual IQ tests nor highly correlated with scholastic performance, would seem to be involved in this phenomenon. We are concerned to find the nature of these non-IQ abilities and their educational and social implications.

## Mental Retardation and Social Class

Kushlick (1966, p. 130) has pointed out the fact that parents of severely subnormal children are evenly distributed among all the social strata of industrial society, Cultural-familial retardation, on the other hand, is predominantly concentrated in the lower social classes. On the basis of a number of surveys made largely in England, Kushlick concludes that 'mild subnormality in the absence of abnormal neurological signs (epilepsy, electroencephalographic abnormalities, biochemical abnormalities, chromosomal abnormalities, or sensory defects) is virtually confined to the lower social classes'. He goes on to say 'there is evidence that almost no children of higher social class parents have IQ scores of less than 80, unless they have one of the pathological processes mentioned above'. The same conclusion has been drawn by other investigators (e.g., Hardy, 1965) and is entirely consistent with the writer's experience gained in conducting studies in schools in lower-class and middle-class neighborhoods. The incidence of mild retardation is undoubtedly strongly associated with socioeconomic status (SES). Anyone who has attempted to do research on the relationship between retardation and SES knows the extreme difficulty in finding subjects in the IQ range from about 50 or 60 up to about 80 or 85 in the middle and especially upper-middle class segment of the population. Conversely, it has been our experience that it is not nearly as difficult to find gifted children (IQs above 130) in the lower classes as it is to find mildly retarded children in the upper classes. The Scottish National Survey established on a large scale that *high* intellectual ability is more widely distributed over different social environments than is low intellectual ability (Maxwell, 1953). This finding, of course, reflects the increasing *range* of mental test scores that we find as we move from the upper to the lower levels of occupational status. The upper bound of the IQ range changes relatively little going down the occupational scale, while the lower bound of the IQ range decreases markedly in going downward from the professions to unskilled labor (Tyler, 1965, pp. 338-339).

The association of the incidence of retardation with SES is also entirely consistent with the results of research on the relationship of SES to intelligence over the entire range of IQs. Correlations between the occupational status of adults and their IQs range between 0·50 and 0·70 (Tyler, 1965, p. 343) and between parents' occupation and children's IQ the correlations are, of course, lower than this – half of all such correlations reported in the literature are between 0·25 and 0·50 (Jensen, 1968c).

## GENETIC AND ENVIRONMENTAL FACTORS

The correlation between IQ and SES has led some writers to attribute the cause of this association strictly to environmental factors associated with SES. Neff (1938), for example, concluded from his extensive review of the evidence that environmental factors alone were sufficient to account for the observed relationship between SES and IQ. This conclusion, however, is decisively contradicted by evidence found in Neff's own review. If Neff accepts as valid the correlations he cites between the IQs of pairs of identical and fraternal twins, he must acknowledge the conclusions derived from these correlations, namely, that individual differences in intelligence have a genetic component. Once this is accepted, Neff's argument collapses unless it could be shown that there is no correlation whatsoever between the genetic component of intelligence variance and persons' occupational and educational status, which are the chief indices of SES. Similarly, a recent textbook states: 'Inborn or biological differences in intelligence exist, but between individuals, not between large social or racial groups [Havighurst and Neugarten, 1967, p. 159]'. For this statement to be true it would have to mean that all the factors involved in social mobility, educational attainments, and the selection of persons into various occupations have managed scrupulously to screen out all variance associated with genetic factors among individuals in various occupational strata. The possibility that the selection processes lead to there being only environmental variance among various socioeconomic groups and occupations – a result that could probably not be accomplished even by making an explicit effort toward this goal – is so unlikely that the argument amounts to a *reductio ad absurdum*. If individual differences in intelligence are due largely to genetic factors, then it is virtually impossible that average intelligence differences between social classes (based on educational and occupational criteria) do not include a genetic component.

This argument goes as follows. Twin studies and other methods for estimating the heritability of intelligence have yielded heritability values for the most part in the range from 0·70 to 0·90, with a mean value of about 0·80 (Jensen, 1967). Heritability ($h^2$) is a technical concept in quantitative genetics, referring to the proportion of variance in a metric characteristic, such as height and intelligence, that is attributable to genetic factors. $1 - h^2 = E$, the proportion of variance due to non-genetic or environmental factors, which of course includes prenatal as well as postnatal influences. The correlation between phenotypes (the measureable characteristic) and genotypes (the genetic basis of the phenotypes) is the square root of the heritability, i.e., $\sqrt{h^2}$. An average estimate of $\sqrt{h^2}$ for intelligence is 0·90, which is the correlation between phenotype and genotype. An average estimate of the correlation between occupational status and IQ (i.e., phenotypic intelligence) is 0·50. What Neff (1938) and Havighurst and Neugarten (1967) are saying, essentially, is that the correlation between IQ and occupation (or SES) is due entirely to the environmental component of IQ variance. In other words, their hypothesis requires that the correlation between the genotypes and SES be zero. So we have three correlations between three sets of variables: (*a*) between phenotype and genotype, $r_{pg} = 0·90$; (*b*) between phenotype and status, $r_{ps} = 0·50$; and (*c*) the hypothesized correlation between genotype and status, $r_{gs} = 0$. The first two correlations ($r_{pg}$ and $r_{ps}$) are determined empirically, and are represented here by average values reported in the research literature. The third correlation ($r_{gs}$) is hypothesized to be zero by those who, like Neff and Havighurst and Neugarten, believe genetic factors play a part in individual differences but not in group differences. The question then becomes: is this set of correlations possible? The first two correlations we know are possible, because they are empirically obtained values. The correlation seriously in question is the hypothesized $r_{gs} = 0$. We know that mathematically the true correlations among a set of variables, 1, 2, 3, must meet the following general requirement: $r^2_{12} + r^2_{13} + r^2_{23} - 2r_{12}r_{13}r_{23}$ cannot have a value greater than 1·00. The fact is that when the values of $r_{ps} = 0·50$ and $r_{gs} = 0$ are inserted in the above formula, they yield a value greater than 1. This means that $r_{gs}$ must in fact be greater than zero.

Perhaps an even simpler way of regarding this problem is as follows: if only the $E$ (environmental) component determined IQ differences between status groups, then the $h^2$ component of IQs would be regarded as random variation with respect to status. Thus, in correlating IQ with status, the IQ test in effect is like a test with a reliability of $1 - h^2 = 1 - 0 \cdot 80 = 0 \cdot 20$. That is to say, only the $E$ component of variance is not random with respect to indices of SES. Therefore the theoretical maximum correlation that IQ could have with SES would be $\sqrt{0 \cdot 20} = 0 \cdot 45$. This value is very close to the obtained correlations between IQ and SES. So if we admit no genetic component in SES differences, we are forced to conclude that persons have been fitted to their socio-economic status (meaning largely educational attainments and occupational status) almost *perfectly* in terms of their environmental advantages or disadvantages. In other words, it must be concluded that persons' innate abilities, talents, and proclivities play no part in their educational and occupational placement. This seems a preposterous conclusion. The only way one can reject the conclusion that there are genetic intelligence differences between SES groups is to reject the evidence on the heritability of individual differences in intelligence. But the evidence for a substantial genetic component in intellectual differences is among the most consistent and firmly established research findings known in the fields of psychology and behavioral genetics. Much of the relevant evidence has been reviewed in detail elsewhere (Jones, 1954; Burt, 1955, 1958, 1959, 1961a, 1966; Fuller and Thompson, 1960; Erlenmeyer-Kimling and Jarvik, 1963; Gottesman, 1963, 1968; Huntley, 1966; Eckland, 1967; Jensen, 1967, 1968a, 1969).

More direct lines of evidence for SES genetic intelligence differences are also available. For example, the weak effect of SES as a causal factor in intellectual differences is seen in studies of identical twins separated shortly after birth and reared in different homes. The most valuable of these studies is by Sir Cyril Burt (1966), since the 53 pairs of identical twins in his study were separated at birth or within the first 6 months after birth and were reared apart in families that ranged across all the SES categories of the British census. Furthermore, there was a slightly negative but nonsignificant correlation between co-twins with respect to the SES of the homes in which they were reared. Yet the correlation between the Stanford-Binet IQs of co-twins at about 10 years of age was $0 \cdot 87$, which corresponds to an average difference of about 6 points on the IQ scale. (Corrected for attenuation, i.e., test unreliability, the difference is about 4 points.) Not all of even this small difference is due to social environmental factors; some of the difference, perhaps as much as half, is probably attributable to prenatal factors. Co-twins are not equally advantaged with respect to intrauterine space and prenatal nutrition; this is reflected in inequalities in their birth weights, inequalities which are correlated (positively) with their later IQs (Willerman and Churchill, 1967).

Another line of evidence is from studies of adopted children. The correlation between their IQs and the educational level of their biological parents is about the same as for children reared by

TABLE 1 **IQs of Adopted and Control (own) Children in Homes of Different Occupational Categories[1]**

| | *Adopted Children* | | | *Control (own) Children* | | |
|---|---|---|---|---|---|---|
| *Occupation of Father* | *N* | *Mean IQ* | *SD* | *N* | *Mean IQ* | *SD* |
| Professional | 43 | 112·6 | 11·8 | 40 | 118·6 | 12·6 |
| Business manager | 38 | 111·6 | 10·9 | 42 | 117·6 | 15·6 |
| Skilled trades | 44 | 110·6 | 14·2 | 43 | 106·9 | 14·3 |
| Farmers | — | — | — | — | — | — |
| Semi-skilled | 45 | 109·4 | 11·8 | 46 | 101·1 | 12·5 |
| Slightly skilled ⎫<br>Day labor ⎭ | 24 | 107·8 | 13·6 | 23 | 102·1 | 11·0 |
| General mean | 194 | 110·6 | | 194 | 109·7 | |

[1] Taken from Leahy (1935).

their biological parents, while the correlation between the adopted children and the education of the adopting parents is close to zero (Honzik, 1957). Children reared from infancy in an orphanage, and with no knowledge of their biological parents, show nearly the same correlation (about 0·25) between IQ and father's occupational status (graded into five categories) as is found for children reared by their parents (Lawrence, 1931). Also, adopted children show a smaller dispersion of mean IQ level as a function of SES of the adopting parents than do children reared by their own parents. Leahy (1935) matched two sets of parents on a number of SES indices – parents rearing their own children and foster parents of adopted children. Table 1 shows the mean IQs of the adopted and control children as a function of the father's or foster father's occupation. The variance among the occupational means for the control children's IQs is 15 times greater than among the mean IQs for adopted children (56·24 *vs.* 3·72).

Siblings have on the average only half of their genes in common, and show an average correlation of 0·5 for intelligence and other highly heritable traits. The average absolute intelligence difference between sibs reared together is about 12 IQ points on the Stanford-Binet. Most of the intelligence difference between siblings reared together is attributable to their genetic differences. There is evidence that when siblings reared in the same family move into different social strata, the sibs with IQs above the family average are more likely to move to a SES above that of their family and sibs with IQs below the family average are more likely to move down in SES (Young and Gibson, 1965). This condition would, of course, cause the gene pools for intelligence to differ among SES levels.

Since the mean IQ differences between SES categories reflect some combination of genetic and environmental determinants of intelligence, and since there is a broad spread of IQs about each category mean, as shown by the standard deviations of 10 to 12 points *within* SES categories, there should be increasing proportions of children falling below IQ 75, the borderline of mental retardation, in the IQ distribution of each SES category from the highest to the lowest. If genetic factors are predominant, the increasing proportion of IQs below 75 as we move down the scale of SES, should be in evidence throughout the scale, even between the higher SES categories in which there is no environmental disadvantage or deprivation in the usual sense of the term. Even the most disadvantaged environments found in industrial society, short of rare cases of almost total social isolation, do not produce IQs below 75 in the majority of children reared in such deprived environments. Thus genetic factors are almost certainly implicated in this degree of retardation, even when it occurs at the lowest end of the SES continuum. On the basis of large normative studies of the Stanford-Binet, Heber *et al.* (1968) have estimated the prevalence of IQs below 75 as a function of SES and race, as shown in Table 2. It should be kept in mind that the estimates in Table 2 are based on Stanford-Binet IQs. We now have good reason to believe that on some other tests of mental ability, to be described shortly, the percentages for whites and Negroes would be much more similar than those in Table 2, and SES differences would be very much smaller.

All this is quite consistent with what is known about polygenic inheritance. It we accept the polygenic theory of the inheritance of intelligence, which is strongly supported by the evidence, it follows that a certain proportion of the population will have relatively low

TABLE 2 **Estimated Prevalence of Children with IQs Below 75, by Socioeconomic Status (SES) and Race Given as Percentages[1]**

| SES | White | Negro |
|---|---|---|
| High 1 | 0·5 | 3·1 |
| 2 | 0·8 | 14·5 |
| 3 | 2·1 | 22·8 |
| 4 | 3·1 | 37·8 |
| Low 5 | 7·8 | 42·9 |

[1] Taken from Heber *et al.* (1968).

intelligence. Furthermore, if we recognize the fact of what geneticists call assortative mating – the tendency for like to marry like – we should expect that the frequency of genes for intelligence would become unequally assorted in different families and groups in the population. If persons were mated on a purely random basis, the average absolute difference in IQ between husbands and wives would be about 18 IQ points.[1] The degree of assortative mating in our society, however, is such that the average absolute difference between husbands and wives is actually between 10 to 13 IQ points, according to various studies. Thus, in terms of the polygenic theory the binomial expansion of $(\frac{1}{2}A + \frac{1}{2}a)^{2n}$ (where $A$ and $a$ represent intelligence enhancing and non-enhancing genes, respectively, and $n$ is the number of gene loci) must be regarded as

[1] The mean absolute difference between all possible pairs of scores in a normal distribution is equal to $2\sigma/\sqrt{\pi}$. For the Stanford-Binet test $\sigma = 16\cdot4$.

representing only the relative frequencies of these genes in the population. On the average, the frequencies of $A$ and $a$ genes in the population are assumed to be equal. Within a group selected for intelligence, however, the relative frequencies of $A$ and $a$ genes may be quite different, say, 20 percent $A$ and 80 percent $a$, so that the binomial expansion of $(0 \cdot 2A + 0 \cdot 8a)^{2n}$ will yield a skewed distribution of values, in this case having a preponderance of low values. The normal distribution of phenotypes in the total population should be thought of as the average of many differently skewed distributions for various 'breeding groups'. A variety of social, ethnic, educational, and economic factors in our society insures a high degree of assortative mating with respect to intelligence.

Given this polygenic model, plus the fact of assortative mating, we should predict that mental retardation would not occur in all families with equal probability. From this model it would be estimated that at least 25 percent of retarded persons would have one or both parents retarded. A corollary of this is that if none of the retarded reproduced, there would be a substantial reduction in the frequency of retardation in the next generation.

The most monumental study of this matter has been carried out by two geneticists, Elizabeth and Sheldon Reed, and their colleagues, at the University of Minnesota (Reed and Reed, 1965). They began with 289 retarded persons (IQ below 70) who were resident in a state institution for the retarded at some time during the years 1911 to 1918. From this nucleus of 289 retardates, the investigation branched out to include the study of 82,217 of their relatives. Practically all the descendants of the grandparents of the probands (i.e., the originally selected retardates) were included. Family pedigrees were traced over as many as seven generations, the primary aim being to determine as accurately as possible the mental status of all persons in the study. This involved searching school records for the subjects' grades and IQ scores and following their occupational histories. Analysis of these massive data lead to some clear conclusions.

First, it should be pointed out that in the following discussion of the Reeds' study the term 'retarded' always means an IQ below 70. Since such individuals constitute about 3 percent of the white population, it means there are close to 6 million retardates in the white population of the United States.

The Reeds found that only 0·5 percent of children of normal parents (i.e. IQs above 70) with normal siblings were retarded.[1] The remaining 2·5 percent of the population who are retarded, therefore, have at least one parent or an aunt or uncle who is retarded. In other words, some 5 million of the 6 million retardates in the United States have a retarded parent or a normal parent who has a retarded sibling. Among 15,000 unselected retardates 48·3 percent had one or both parents retarded. The belief that the retarded of one generation contribute only a negligible proportion of the retarded of the next generation is therefore patently false.

Assortative mating occurred to a very high degree in families with a high incidence of retardation; retardates rarely marry anyone much above their own level. However, it is of some interest that 30 percent of illegitimate children born to the 289 probands were retarded, while only 11 percent of legitimate children were retarded. One might expect just the opposite. The explanation is that a high percentage of illegitimate children in this group were the product of incestuous relationships which would, of course, increase the probability of producing genotypes in the retarded range.

It is certainly true that the children of retarded parents are often subjected to a culturally and intellectually impoverished environment that would tend to depress their mental development. Yet, it is most important to note that of the children of retarded parents fewer than half are retarded. This would be difficult to explain strictly in terms of environmental influence. But it is what we should expect in terms of the polygenic theory. Although nearly all the children born into subnormal homes are presumably subjected to influences unfavorable to intellectual development, the fact that more than half of such children are not mentally retarded

---

[1] It is of interest that this is close to the percentage of retarded found among the offspring of Terman's gifted group. These were 1528 school children selected for IQs over 135 (mean IQ of entire group = 152). Their development has been followed into adulthood (most of them are now in their fifties). Among the 2452 children born to gifted parents, only 13 or 0·53 percent were retarded. Most of these cases were probably due either to major gene defects or brain damage rather than to polygenic inheritance. The average IQ of all the offspring of the gifted group was 132·7 when they were last tested (Terman and Oden, 1959, p. 404).

suggests that the more intelligent children must have received more desirable gene combinations.

Another striking finding is that retardation was extremely rare in some families. For example, in 37 of the families of the 289 cases, the only retardate was the proband. In some large families comprising over 2400 persons there were less than 1 percent retarded.

It is instructive from the standpoint of genetics to note the frequency of retardation among relatives of the probands as the

TABLE 3　**The Percentages of Retardation in the Relatives of the Probands According to Degree of Relationship and Category of Classification[1]**

| Category | First Degree | Second Degree | Third Degree | Average Percentage Retarded |
|---|---|---|---|---|
| Primarily genetic | 33·6 | 9·2 | 3·7 | 8·8 (452 of 5149) |
| Probably genetic | 50·7 | 16·8 | 5·3 | 13·2 (496 of 3759) |
| Environmental | 21·4 | 2·0 | 1·1 | 3·3 (60 of 1831) |
| Unknown | 15·6 | 2·6 | 2·1 | 3·7 (275 of 7327) |
| All categories Percentages | 28·0 | 7·1 | 3·1 | 7·1 |
| Totals | (532 of 1897) | (434 of 6070) | (317 of 10,099) | (1283 of 18,006) |

[1] Taken from Reed and Reed (1965).

distance of relationship increases. The results of such an analysis are shown in Table 3. The probands were classified on the basis of case histories into one of four categories describing the most likely cause of retardation. The percentage of retarded relatives for three degrees of relationship was also determined, as shown in Table 3. First degree relationships are those with whom the proband has one-half of his genes in common: mother, brothers, sisters, and children. Second degree relationships are those with whom the proband has one-fourth of his genes in common: grandparents, uncles, aunts, half-siblings, nephews, nieces, and grandchildren.

Relatives of the third degree are those with whom the proband has one-eighth of his genes in common: half-uncles and aunts, half-nephews and nieces, great-nephews and nieces, and first cousins.

The point of primary interest in Table 3 is the rapid drop in the incidence of retardation as we go from first to second to third degree relatives. (Recall that the incidence of retardation in the general population is about 3 percent.) Note also that the etiological categories differ in the percentage of retarded relatives and in the rate of decline as the degree of relationship becomes more distant. Why should the category 'primarily genetic' have fewer retarded relatives than the 'probably genetic' category? First, because the 'primarily genetic' category included some probands

TABLE 4 **IQ Range of Tested Children of Retardate Unions**[1]

| | IQ Range | | | | | | | |
| Type of Union | 0–49 | 50–69 | 70–89 | 90–110 | 111–130 | 131 + | Total | Average IQ | Percent Retarded |
|---|---|---|---|---|---|---|---|---|---|
| Retardate × retardate | 6 | 29 | 36 | 17 | 1 | 0 | 89 | 74 | 39·4 |
| Male retardate × normal | 0 | 12 | 41 | 75 | 24 | 1 | 153 | 95 | 7·8 |
| Female retardate × normal | 6 | 15 | 32 | 43 | 10 | 1 | 107 | 87 | 19·6 |
| Male retardate × unknown | 3 | 16 | 68 | 80 | 20 | 1 | 188 | 90 | 10·1 |
| Female retardate × unknown | 10 | 29 | 64 | 79 | 22 | 2 | 206 | 87 | 19·0 |
| Total | 25 | 101 | 241 | 294 | 77 | 5 | 743 | 86 | 17·0 |

[1] Taken from Reed and Reed (1965).

with major gene defects about which there was no doubt concerning genetic origin (and, as was pointed out earlier, these defects are very rare); second, because the chief criterion for classification into the category 'probably genetic' was that the proband have retarded relatives in the first degree of relationship.

Table 4 indicates the IQ frequency distributions of children resulting from various matings in which either one or both parents were retarded. It is most interesting that a number of bright (IQs 111-130) and definitely superior (131 +) children resulted from such matings, despite the fact that some of these children came from what the Reeds described as 'extremely impoverished environment'. The largest number (294) of children from retardate unions was found in the average range of IQs from 90 to 110, again despite impoverished environment. Note, however, the skew of the overall distribution (i.e. the bottom 'Total' line).

Another interesting feature of these data is that the mating of male retardate × normal female results in a significantly lower percentage of retarded offspring than the mating of a female retardate × normal male. Two hypotheses are suggested by this: (*a*) When the mother is retarded, the child's early environment may be more severely lacking in the kinds of mother-child interaction that promote mental development; (*b*) the retardate mothers may provide a poor *prenatal* environment for the developing fetus. Adverse intrauterine conditions could also have a genetic basis.

Table 5 shows the results of various retardate matings in more precise terms, made possible by having IQ scores on both parents.

TABLE 5  **IQ Range of Tested Children of Retardate Unions in Which Both Parents Had Been Tested[1]**

| Type of Union | IQ Range | | | | | | Total | Average IQ of Children | Percent Retarded |
|---|---|---|---|---|---|---|---|---|---|
| | 0–49 | 50–69 | 70–89 | 90–110 | 111–130 | 131 + | | | |
| Both parents IQ 60 or below; average IQ 60 (12) | 5 | 23 | 12 | 6 | 0 | 0 | 46 | 67 | 60·9 |
| Father IQ 69 or below, average IQ 62; mother IQ 70 or above, average IQ 92 (26) | 3 | 3 | 20 | 43 | 12 | 1 | 82 | 94 | 7·3 |
| Mother IQ 69 or below, average IQ 63; father IQ 98 (15) | 0 | 9 | 18 | 20 | 2 | 0 | 49 | 86 | 18·4 |
| Total (53) | 8 | 35 | 50 | 69 | 14 | 1 | 177 | 82 | 24·3 |

[1] Taken from Reed and Reed (1965).

Like low IQs, high IQs tend to cluster in particular families, rather than occurring in random distribution among families. In one family where the parents had IQs of 157 and 151, the three children had IQs of 132, 134 and 149. An unusual union in which one parent had an IQ of 135 and the other an IQ of 67 resulted in five children with IQs of 112, 115, 113, 97, 131 (average IQ of parents = 101, average IQ of children = 114).

All these findings taken together would seem to provide a more than adequate answer to the view expressed in a well-known book on mental subnormality by Masland, Sarason, and Gladwin (1958, p. 196): 'We do not propose to *deny* that heredity is a factor, particularly in mental deficiency, but rather that we should leave it out of our accounting until it is supported by more than speculation and bias.' The hereditary aspect of mental retardation is obviously now supported by more than 'speculation and bias'.

Furthermore, there would seem to be some eugenic implication in the Reeds' conclusion that

> ... the 1 to 2 percent of our population composed of fertile retardates produced 36·1 percent of the retardates of the next generation, while the other 98 to 99 percent of the population produced only 63·9 percent of the retarded persons in the next generation [p. 48].

The fact that the majority of the mildly retarded (IQs 50-70) are found in the lowest socioeconomic classes means that the majority of the mildly retarded children are born to parents who have the least to offer their children. The Reeds do not believe that social deprivation is a primary cause of retardation in the IQ range below 70. They state:

> We must assume that some cases of mental retardation are due primarily to social deprivation, but we don't find a large proportion of our probands who are available for this classification after an allocation has been completed for the causes which appear to have been present [p. 75].

They proceed to say: 'One inescapable conclusion is that the transmission of mental retardation from parent to child is by far the most important *single* factor in the persistence of this social misfortune [p. 48]'. The problem is how to prevent the approximately 6 million retarded persons in the United States from transmitting it genetically or environmentally. The Reeds conclude:

> The transmission of mental retardation from one generation to the next, should, therefore, receive much more critical attention than it has in the past. It seems fair to state that this problem has been largely ignored on the assumption that if our social agencies function better, that if everyone's environment were improved sufficiently, then mental retardation would cease to be a major problem. Unfortunately, mental retardation will never disappear, but it can be reduced by manipulating the genetic and environmental factors involved. . . . When voluntary sterilization for the retarded becomes a part of the culture of the United States, we should expect a decrease of about 50 percent per generation in the number of retarded persons, as a result of all methods combined to reduce retardation [p. 77].

An important point, in terms of the theory of primary and secondary retardation proposed in this paper, must be made concerning the interpretation and conclusions of the Reeds' study of familial retardation. It should especially be noted that all the retardates in this study were found by tracing down the more than 82,000 'blood' relationships of the 289 *institutionalized* probands. As will be shown in a later section, there is good reason to believe that institutionalized retardates differ in important ways from many individuals with IQs in the 50 to 70 range who do not become institutionalized. It seems very likely that a high proportion of the institutionalized retarded are the result of different genetic factors than those involved in the majority of non-institutionalized persons with IQs below 70 to 75. Study of the relatives of institutionalized persons is also likely to give a much stronger weight to hereditary than to environmental and educational factors in the causation of retardation. We have found that there are some psychologically fundamental differences in the patterns of mental abilities between (*a*) institutionalized retardates, (*b*) non-institutionalized retardates from socially deprived backgrounds, and (*c*) retardates from non-deprived or middle-class backgrounds.

MOTORIC PRECOCITY AND LATER INTELLIGENCE

Another interesting and important fact in terms of its diagnostic implications in the light of our theory of primary and secondary retardation is the low but significant negative correlation generally found between performance on infant mental tests, such as the Bayley Scales, and later IQ. Infant tests for children under 2 years of age yield a Developmental Quotient (DQ), as distinguished from the IQ, which can be obtained beyond 2 years of age by means of tests such as the Stanford-Binet. Bayley (1965b) has shown that it is the motor subtests rather than the perceptual-attentional subtests that largely account for the slightly negative correlation between DQ and IQ. Furthermore, up to about 1 year of age, the DQ – largely due to the motoric items – has a negative correlation with the SES level of the infants' parents. This inverse relationship between DQ and parental SES is much more marked in boys than in girls, for whom the correlation is close to zero. Bayley believes that genetic factors are involved in these relationships, and the pronounced sex difference at this early age would support this view. Beyond 2 years of age, on the other hand, boys and girls both show an increasingly positive correlation between IQ and SES. Bayley's results are shown in Figure 1. Bayley (1965a) has also found that Negro infants up to 15 months of age perform better

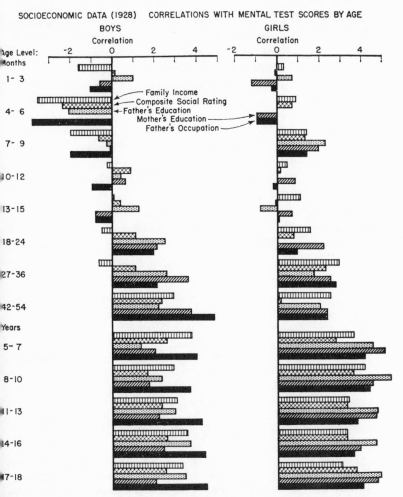

FIGURE 1. *Correlations between children's mental test scores, at 1 month to 18 years, and five indicators of parents' socioeconomic status at the time the children were born (from Bayley, 1966).*

on the Bayley Scales, especially on the motor items, than white infants of comparable age. The highest mean scores on the Bayley Scales for any sizeable group that I have found reported in the literature were obtained on Negro infants of about 6 months of age living in the poorest neighborhoods of Durham, North Carolina (Durham Education Improvement Program, 1966-1967a, 1966-1967b). These infants obtained Developmental Quotients on the motor items of the Bayley Scale averaging about 1 standard deviation above white norms. (On non-motor items they averaged half of a standard deviation above white norms.) The older siblings of these infants, by contrast, had IQs averaging about 1·3 standard deviations below white norms. Thus the negative correlation between DQ and IQ appears very marked in this segment of the Negro population. Similar findings have been reported in at least five other studies (Curti, Marshall, Steggerda and Henderson, 1935; Knoblick and Pasamanick, 1958; Bayley, 1965a; Geber and Dean, 1966; Walters, 1967).

When the test employed involves strictly cognitive rather than motoric aspects of development, negative correlations between performance and SES are found in children even below 12 months of age. For example, Kagan (1966) reports that on certain laboratory tests of cognitive functioning

> lower-class children, as early as 8 to 12 months of age, show slower rates of information processing than middle-class children of the same ordinal position. Lower-class children show less rapid habituation, less clear differentiation among visual stimuli, and, in a play situation, show a high threshold for satiation. The latter measure is obtained by placing the child in a standard playroom with a standard set of toys (quoits on a shaft, blocks, pail, mallet, peg board, toy lawn mower, and toy animals) and by noting the time involved in each activity. Some children play with the blocks for 10 seconds and then skip to the quoits or the lawn mower, playing only 10-20 seconds with each individual activity before shifting to another. A second group of children, called 'high threshold for satiation infants', spends 1 or 2 minutes with an activity without interruption before changing. We do not believe the latter group of infants is taking more from the activity; rather it seems that they are taking longer to satiate on this action. It is important to note that the observation that lower-class infants show high threshold for satiation contrasts sharply with the observation that 4-year-old lower-class children are distractable and

hyperkinetic. We believe both descriptions. The paradox to be explained is why these lower-class children are pokey and lethargic and nondistractible at 12 months of age, yet display polar-opposite behavior at 48 months of age.

## Theory of Primary and Secondary Retardation

The empirical findings on which our hypothesis of primary and secondary retardation is based can be more easily summarized and their relevance more readily indicated if the hypothesis is described first in general terms.

### A HIERARCHY OF ABILITIES

There is much evidence that mental abilities stand in some hierarchical relationship to one another. A number of factor analytic models have yielded results consistent with a hierarchical hypothesis (Vernon, 1950), but, as pointed out by Guilford (1967), the hierarchical factor model is as much a product of the particular method of factor analysis as of the raw data that go into it, and other models than hierarchical ones are possible. However, there are other lines of support for a hierarchical view of abilities which stem from experimental studies of the learning process, such as Gagné's (1962, 1968) work on learning hierarchies, and from studies of the developmental aspects of cognitive processes, such as those reviewed by White (1965). Both lines of evidence indicate that for many abilities there is a natural order of acquisition or emergence, such that when ability B is found, ability A will always be found, but not the reverse. Deficiencies in a lower level ability almost always imply deficiency in some higher level ability, but the reverse need not be the case. Some aspects of the ability hierarchy are attributable to the learning of specific subskills which stand in some hierarchical relationship to one another, these aspects are usually more closely related to the individual's grade in school and to the nature of the instruction he has received up to that point. Learning various operations and concepts in arithmetic is a good example. Other abilities are of a more maturational or developmental nature and are practically impossible to explain in terms of previous learning of specific subskills. The emergence of such abilities is apparently more dependent upon the growth of brain structures than upon learning and experience. Experience may be necessary but it is far from sufficient for certain abilities to become manifest in performance. Abilities that depend upon the maturation of neural structures can also be hierarchical, in the sense that normal maturation of a lower level does not necessarily insure maturation of higher levels in the hierarchy. Failure of maturation at lower levels, on the other hand, will result in some deficiency or impairment of the emergence of higher level functions in behavior, even if their neural substrate is normal.

The essential characteristic that most generally describes the levels of this mental maturation hierarchy is the degree of correspondence between 'input' and 'output'. Lower levels of the hierarchy involve relatively little processing or transformation of the informational input; the stimulus-response correspondence is relatively simple and direct. Higher levels of the mental ability hierarchy depend upon elaborations and transformations of informational input, and upon comparisons of the informational input with previously stored information. Various cognitive tasks can be hypothetically placed along this continuum, from low to high: simple reaction time, Pavlovian conditioning, instrumental conditioning, complex reaction time, pursuit-rotor learning, discrimination learning, immediate memory span for digits (forward), immediate memory span for digits (backward), memory span for digits after a brief delay (i.e., 5-15 seconds) between presentation and recall, serial rote learning, free-recall of uncategorized word lists, paired-associate learning, free-recall of categorized word lists, complex concept learning and problem solving (e.g., verbal analogies, arithmetic 'thought' problems, Raven's *Progressive Matrices*). It should be noted that this continuum is not one of increasing task difficulty *per se*. A digit span test can be made more difficult than a *Progressive Matrices* problem in terms of percentage of the population 'passing' the items. Neither does the continuum necessarily represent one of increasing stimulus (input) complexity. The continuum seems to be best described in terms of the amount of transformation of the input – the amount and complexity of 'mental' activity – called forth in the subject in the process of his responding to the stimulus in order to learn, retain, recall, or produce the correct response to a problem.

*Level I and Level II Abilities.* Although up to now we have regarded these tasks as ranging along a single continuum, our hypothesis, for reasons that will become apparent, holds that the continuum is the resultant of at least two types of ability, which we shall call Level I or 'associative ability' and Level II or 'cognitive' ability.

Levels I and II are viewed as being qualitatively different, as existing in parallel, but as having quite different developmental rates. Individual differences in Levels I and II may in fact be correlated, but not because they are different manifestations of the same underlying structures or processes. That the underlying processes are essentially different and are not inherently correlated could be shown by obtaining groups of persons in whom the correlations are zero or even negative between tests that are highly loaded on Level I and tests loaded on Level II functions, such tests, for example, as digit span (Level I) and the *Progressive Matrices* (Level II). Probably no test on the behavioral level is completely free of both Levels I and II, but different tests can have markedly different loadings on each level.

Correlation between tests of Level I and tests of Level II can occur in a given population mainly for three reasons:

(*a*) The essentially independent genetic factors determining individual differences in Level I and Level II may become associated through assortative mating. That is to say, persons who are below average in, say, scholastic ability, whether because they are below average in Level I or in Level II, or in both, have a greater probability of marrying one another than of marrying someone who is markedly different in ability. This tends to bring together in their offspring poor genetic potential for both Level I and Level II abilities. In the previous section in the review of the research of Reed and Reed (1965) on the genetic transmission of mental retardation, it was shown in Table 4 that more retarded children resulted from matings of a retarded mother with a normal father than from a retarded father and a normal mother. While the explanation in terms of quality of the maternal environment offered by the Reeds is quite possibly sufficient, it is not the only possible explanation. A possible explanation in terms of the theory here proposed is that more of the retarded mothers than of the retarded fathers in the Reeds' sample had genotypes for deficiency in Level I abilities. Because of the demands of earning a living, mentally deficient men are less apt to be able to marry than retarded women, especially if the man's deficiency is in basic Level I processes, which would be a handicap in almost any line of work. Most standard intelligence tests are heavily loaded on Level II ability, and because of the hierarchical dependence of Level II on Level I for its manifestation in performance, a person who is deficient in Level I will also show some deficiency in behavioral indices of Level II. If Level I and Level II are under independent genetic control, and granting the hierarchical relationship between Levels I and II, one would predict that a normal person (i.e., average or above on Levels I and II) mated with a person genetically deficient in Level I would produce a higher proportion of phenotypically retarded children than a normal person mated with a person who is genetically deficient only in Level II abilities.

(*b*) The second basis for correlation between Levels I and II is already evident from the preceding discussion, viz., the functional dependence of the behavioral expression of Level II process on Level I. The degree of this dependence is not yet completely known, but the evidence suggests that the degree of dependence may become increasingly weak above some 'threshold' value of Level I; higher correlations between Level I and Level II tests would therefore be expected in the average to below average range of the distributions than in the above average ranges.

(*c*) Some of the information processing skills involved in Level II tests depend not only on the normal functioning of the neural substrate of Level I but also upon the prior learning of certain skills. The speed and thoroughness of acquisition of these skills depend also upon Level I associative learning ability. Thus there comes about a correlation between measures of Levels I and II.

*Intelligence Tests.* Most standard intelligence tests are made up of items that are a mixture of Level I and Level II functions. Partly for this reason, it has been difficult to infer the two types of processes from total scores on these tests; the scores are too much an amalgam of Level I and Level II functions. Most intelligence tests that are heavily loaded with what Spearman characterized as the *g* factor – a capacity for abstract reasoning – are mainly indices of Level II functioning. Among standardized tests, Raven's *Progressive Matrices* and Cattell's *Culture-Fair Tests* are perhaps the purest measures of Level II ability. The Stanford-Binet and Wechsler tests have slightly lower *g* loadings than the Raven and Cattell tests and also contain subtests which are relatively pure measures of Level I abilities, such as the digit span and digit symbol tests of the Wechsler. Moreover, these conventional IQ tests contain informational items, such as vocabulary and general information, which depend upon previous earning. The low conceptual quality of the definitions required for passing, especially for the easier, more concrete words, and the simple factual content of the general information items, would involve Level I ability as well as Level II. The net effect is that these tests order individuals along a general, crude continuum of intellectual ability, somewhat more heavily weighted with Level II ability, but without making any clear distinction between individuals' relative strength or weakness in Level I and in Level II.

Some children who obtain seemingly valid low IQs in the range 50 to 80 on these tests appear to be socially bright and do not seem in the least retarded in learning the names of classmates, in acquiring playground skills and the practical knowledge of getting along with their neighborhood playmates. For many such children, who usually come from the lower classes, the IQ test is commonly presumed to be invalid because of the cultural loading of its item content. While some of the items in such tests as the Stanford-Binet and Wechsler have an obvious cultural element, as have also many of the group tests used in schools, it has been found that these items are not necessarily those on which lower-class children with low IQs do the most poorly. These children generally do no better, and often they do worse, on the less culturally loaded subtests such as block designs, and on tests like Raven's *Progressive Matrices* and *the Culture-Fair Tests* of Cattell (see Jensen, 1968c). Something besides cultural bias of test items is clearly involved. Eells *et al.* (1951), in their famous study of cultural bias in standard intelligence tests, found that the one characteristic that distinguished most between items showing a large social class difference in the probability of giving the correct answer was the degree of *abstractness* of the test items. This attribute of test items is a more important factor in determining disparity of test scores between upper and lower classes than the factor of cultural content *per se*. Examination of items in standard tests, moreover, supports the conclusion that the more culturally loaded items in tests are also among the least abstract. 'Who wrote *Faust*?' (an item in the Wechsler-Bellevue), for example, is more culturally biased, but also less abstract or conceptual, than some other less cultural items from the same tests, such as 'In what way are an *egg* and a *seed* the same?' and 'If seven pounds of sugar cost twenty-five cents, how many pounds can you get for a dollar?' Probably it was largely because of this inverse relationship between the cultural loading and the abstractness of intelligence test items that it was possible for McGurk (1967) to show that Negro children performed better (relative to whites) on the more culturally loaded items than on the less cultural questions of an intelligence test.

The cultural loading of test items is best regarded as essentially orthogonal to the Level I–Level II dimension along which various tests may range. The writer has argued the point elsewhere that the most objective index of a test's culture-fairness is its heritability coefficient ($h^2$) in the normative population (Jensen, 1968c). The two-dimensional space which must be hypothesized in order to comprehend the facts of SES differences in measured intelligence is shown in Figure 2. The hypothetical positions of various mental tests in this space are indicated.

Although various tests and forms of learning may differ in the extent to which they actually *require* Level II processes, there is little way to prevent Level II processes from entering into a subject's performance on tasks that require no more than Level I. Subjects tend to use whatever abilities they have at their command in approaching a learning or problem-solving situation. Some tasks, however, minimize the usefulness of Level II processes. Mnemonic elaboration, coding, or other mediational processes are more often likely to hinder than to aid digit span memory, for example, and therefore digit span tests tap mostly Level I processes. Paired-associate (PA) learning, on the other hand, can be accomplished with Level I abilities, but Level II can also play a large role in PA learning. Thus, for individuals who are well endowed with Level II ability, such as college students, individual differences in PA learning may be determined largely by Level II, which will largely override individual differences in Level I. In young children, in whom Level II processes are still rudimentary, on the other hand, PA learning would be more a manifestation of

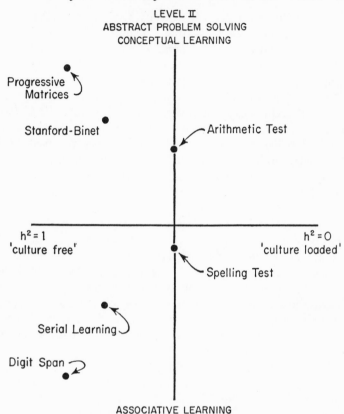

FIGURE 2.   *The two-dimensional space required for comprehending social class differences in performance on tests of intelligence, learning ability, and scholastic achievement. The locations of the various 'tests' are hypothetical.*

Level I ability. Consequently, the correlation among tasks that can potentially involve both Level I and Level II but for which only Level I is essential should decrease with increasing age of the subjects from pre-school to adolescence.

*Relationship of Level I and II to 'Fluid' and 'Crystallized' Intelligence.* Cattell (1963) has proposed a distinction between what he calls *fluid* and *crystallized* general intelligence.

*Fluid* intelligence is a basic capacity for learning and problem solving, a general 'brightness' that is manifested in new learning, novel problem solving, and general intellectual adaptability. It is independent of educational and experience but is invested in the particular opportunities for learning afforded by the circumstances of the individual's life. Tests designed to minimize the importance of cultural and educational advantages, such as Cattel's *Culture-Fair Tests* and Raven's *Progressive Matrices*, are the best measures of fluid intelligence. Fluid intelligence reaches the peak of its growth curve in late adolescence, and thereafter reaches a plateau and begins gradually to decline in middle age, thus paralleling physical structures and functions such as brain weight and vital capacity.

*Crystallized* intelligence consists of learned knowledge and skills. It has been characterized as a 'precipitate out of experience' – the resultant of the interaction of the individual's fluid intelligence and his culture. It increases throughout most of a person's life, depending upon the amount of his fluid intelligence and his opportunities for learning and new experience. From an operational standpoint, the difference between fluid and crystallized intelligence really amounts to the difference between culture-fair and culture-loaded tests.

Levels I and II are seen as being essentially orthogonal to fluid and crystallized intelligence. While many of the tests that characterize Level I processes, such as digit span, are also those that characterize tests of fluid intelligence, not all tests of fluid intelligence are confined to Level I functions. The *Progressive Matrices* and *Culture-Fair Tests*, for instance, are tests of fluid intelligence and are also among the best measures of Level II ability.

*Relationship of Socioeconomic Status to Levels I and II.* As shown in Figure 3, individual differences in Level I and Level II abilities are hypothesized as having different distributions as a function of SES. The distribution of Level I abilities is shown as independent of SES. This may or may not, in fact, be true, but so far we have found little or no evidence that would contradict this simple assumption. When large, truly random samples of the population are tested, however, it should not be surprising to find some difference between SES groups in the distribution of Level I abilities, especially in adults and in children beyond 8 to 10 years of age, for two reasons: (*a*) because of the hierarchical (but not complete) dependence of Level II on Level I ability we should expect assortative mating to affect gene pools for Level I in a manner similar to Level II, though to a much lesser degree, and (*b*) beyond 8 or 10 years of age, when both Level I and Level II processes are already clearly established in children's intellectual performance, it seems doubtful that Level II functions would not

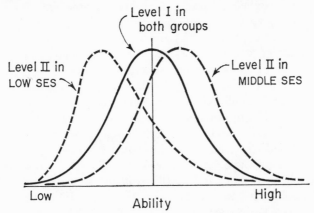

FIGURE 3. *Hypothetical distribution of Level I (solid line) and Level II (dashed line) abilities in middle-class and lower-class populations.*

enter into performance of tasks that are intended as predominantly Level I, especially for children who are well endowed in Level II ability. When performance on a Level I task is further facilitated by bringing Level II processes to bear upon it, upper SES children will show an advantage over lower SES children even in Level I tasks. Provided a sufficient number of different Level I and Level II tasks have been administered, factor analysis can aid in distinguishing the extent of involvement of Level I and Level II processes in the various tests, and factor scores representing Level I and Level II should show greater differences between lower and upper SES groups for the Level II factor and smaller differences for the Level I factor.

Why should Level II ability be different in upper and lower classes, while Level I is hypothesized as having little if any relationship to SES? One of the main factors determining an individual's SES is occupation or the occupation of the spouse. Occupation in turn is related to the individual's ability and educational attainments. Scholastic performance under traditional methods of instruction is heavily dependent upon Level II abilities. This is mainly why IQ tests, which were expressly devised to predict scholastic performance, are largely measures of Level II ability. Since individuals select mates of similar education and occupational status, the genetic component of Level II becomes segregated in the population. The greater the social mobility that is permitted by the society, the greater will be the segregation of genetic factors associated with social mobility, the chief factors in which are educational and occupational attainments in modern industrial society. In the course of generations there will be a gradual elimination of genetic factors making for poor Level II ability in the upper classes. Also, since there is some dependence of Level II upon Level I ability, low grades of Level I ability would also tend to be eliminated from the upper classes. In lower SES groups, on the other hand, education is not the chief means of succeeding, and small demands are made on abstract, conceptual ability, that is, the Level II processes. Level I abilities, however, are required to succeed in many manual occupations, and others' perception of the individual's intelligence or 'wits' is based largely on his Level I ability when indices of scholastic attainments are lacking, are not valued, or are more or less uniformly meager among members of the group. In such cases, assortative mating will take place in terms of practical intelligence, 'wits', cleverness, shrewdness, and the like. The Negro vernacular has its own term for this kind of intelligence: 'mother wit'.

High Level I ability is of value in any society or walk of life, and in primitive cultures it is probably of much more importance to survival than Level II ability. When there is little or no division of labor, except by sex role, every individual needs the ability to learn a large variety of facts and practical skills in order to fulfill his adult role in the society. Therefore there should be positive selection for Level I ability in all strata of all societies. The only condition under which one might expect a diminution of selection against low Level I ability is under circumstances in which no significant economic disadvantage is attached to relative inability to compete and in which vocational ineptitude is no barrier to mating, as might be the case when a society assumes complete support of its least able members and takes no measures to reduce their fecundity.

*Levels I and II and the Focus of Attention.* Rimland (1964), in his book on *Infantile Autism,* proposed a two-factor theory of mental functioning which bears considerable resemblance to the present distinction between Levels I and II. Rimland conceives of this difference as having to do largely with the focus of attention. He postulates that the brain contains a mechanism which focuses attention in a manner analogous to the operation of certain kinds of electronic equipment. His information-theory model of this aspect of brain function states, simply, that there is ordinarily a trade-off between fidelity and bandwidth in human attention. According to Rimland, the bandwidth aspect of mental functioning corresponds to Level II. It permits the individual to view, attend to, and recall specific experiences with respect to a larger context of associations, generalizations, and broad transfer from other experiences, to see differences and similarities between situations, and therefore to be able to deal with abstractions. 'Fidelity', corresponding to Level I, permits an individual to deal in detail with the immediately given physical attributes of stimuli. Rimland believes that persons are capable of trading-off fidelity for bandwidth in their cognitive contact with the world, but each person has his own modal configuration of these capacities which characterizes his cognitive style and his pattern of mental capabilities. Rimland believes that persons whose main strength is Level I, or fidelity-reproductive processes, have a focus of attention that is largely *extracerebral,* that is, focused on real-world events taking place in the here and now of the person's environment. Such persons learn mainly by looking and doing. Unless they are also high in Level II, they are at a disadvantage in the traditional academic realm, which depends heavily upon learning from symbolic or abstract representations in the form of lectures and books. The person whose major strength is Level II, in contrast, directs more of his attention to intracerebral events a good part of the time. In the extreme, such individuals can become 'lost in thought', which can at times put the individual at a disadvantage in dealing with many of the immediate exigencies of practical life. For example, it was said of Ernest O. Lawrence, the Nobel Prize-winning inventor of the cyclotron, that his tendency to become 'lost in thought' while driving his car made him an unsafe driver to such an extent that he found it necessary to employ a chauffeur to drive him to and from work.

An important feature of Rimland's (1964) formulation of a two-process theory of cognitive functioning is that he cites cases in which Level II is almost entirely lacking despite apparently very superior Level I functioning, as found in some autistic children and so-called idiot savants. These observations support the notion that quite distinct brain processes are involved in these two types of ability, and thus they cannot be conceived of as simply different parts of a single underlying continuum of general mental ability. Just the opposite condition is found in Korsakoff's syndrome, in which some but not all Level I functions, such as the consolidation of short-term memory traces, are markedly deficient, although the victim retains the ability for normal performance on Level II tests (Talland, 1965).

CORRELATION BETWEEN LEVEL I AND LEVEL II

At present our hypothesis regards individual differences in Level I and Level II abilities as uncorrelated genotypically (i.e., in terms of their underlying mechanisms) but correlated phenotypically, because Level II functions have some degree of hierarchical dependence on Level I.* [For example, solving an orally presented 'thought problem' in arithmetic involves Level II, but also requires that the subject have sufficient short-term memory (Level I) to retain the elements of the problem in mind long enough to solve it. It is possible to retain the problem in mind without being able to solve it, but the reverse cannot be true.]

Tests of Level I and Level II, should, according to our hypothesis, produce correlation scatter diagrams like those shown in an exaggerated clear-cut form in Figure 4. Level I is represented by tests of associative learning ability and Level II by intelligence tests with a high $g$ loading. Because low Level II ability is not a crucial disadvantage in the lower SES groups, there is not much selection against it, while it tends to be eliminated from the upper

* This aspect of the theory has had to be modified in light of new evidence. See Addendum, pp. 288-291.

SES groups. Thus the scatter diagrams for lower and upper SES groups differ mostly in the proportion of persons falling into the upper left quadrant. Because of the dependence of Level II on Level I in actual test performance, few if any authentic cases should be found in the lower right quadrant of either SES group. But if there is some fairly low threshold value of Level I above which any amount of Level II can be fully manifested, there may be more cases in the lower right quadrant than is depicted in Figure 4. So far we have not found individuals who are superior

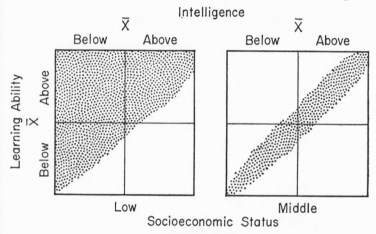

FIGURE 4. *Schematic illustration of the form of the correlation scatter-diagram for the relationship between associative learning ability and IQ in SES and Upper-Middle SES groups.*

in Level II tests and are also authentically deficient in Level I abilities. A few pseudo-deficient Level I cases with high IQs seem to be due to some fluke in the Level I testing, such as failure to understand instructions, excessive anxiety in the laboratory testing situation, etc. However, older brain-damaged and senile subjects could very probably be found in the lower right quadrant of the scatter diagram.

The hypothesized characteristics of the scatter diagram for lower and for upper SES groups implies much higher correlations between tests of Level I and Level II in high than in low SES groups. In fact, it was the finding of this difference in correlations between learning tests and IQ tests for lower and upper SES groups that initially prompted the formulation of this dual-process hypothesis of cognitive functioning.

*Hypothetical Growth Curves of Levels I and II as a Function of SES.* These are shown in Figure 5. Since most of the child's behavioral development up to about 4 years of age is attributable, according to this hypothesis, to the growth of Level I, and since SES groups do not differ appreciably in Level I, there should be little or no differences between SES groups in early childhood.

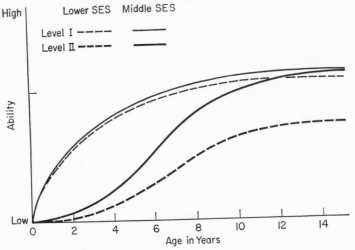

FIGURE 5.   *Hypothetical growth curves for Level I and Level II abilities in middle SES and low SES populations.*

Children who appear retarded during this early stage of development are regarded as very probably retarded in Level I ability. If the degree of retardation is only slight, and if the child possesses normal or superior Level II ability, he will appear to be a 'late bloomer' and during the early school years will come up to par intellectually. Thus, there is a near zero correlation (in fact, a low *negative* correlation for boys) between indices of early development and later IQ.

Figure 5 also illustrates a possible basis for the so-called cumulative deficit' generally found in low SES children, that is, the fact that scholastically they tend to lag further and further behind their middle-class age-mates as they go through school. As the content of the school's curriculum becomes increasingly abstract and conceptual with advancing grades, the child with below-average Level II ability, regardless of his status on Level I, will be at an increasing disadvantage. The cumulative deficit effect will then snowball because of the child's discouraging experience of diminishing returns from his efforts in school. The most important reinforcement in school learning is probably the student's perception of his own success and progress in learning, and when this reinforcement diminishes, the child is, in effect, on an extinction schedule with respect to the behaviors involved in classroom learning. This results in some children's appearing to be unable to learn even the simplest things taught in the classroom, despite the fact that outside the classroom they may learn more difficult things quite readily. Such extinction of school learning behavior could probably be prevented by conducting instruction in the basic school subjects more in accord with Level I processes rather than by means of techniques that maximize the role of Level II abilities in classroom instruction.

*The Heredity-Environment Aspects of Levels I and II.* The previous review of the genetic aspect of mental retardation and of SES differences in intelligence bears directly on the question of the sources of individual differences in Levels I and II. Those who argue from the cultural deprivation hypothesis of SES intelligence differences would claim that Level I tests reflect more nearly the individual's genetic potential, and that tests of Level II reflect the individual's cultural acquisitions. According to this view, the basic source of individual differences in mental ability is seen as consisting of Level I processes, while Level II processes are regarded as the resultant of the interaction of the individual's Level I processes and the opportunities for learning afforded by his environment.

The present theory, on the other hand, postulates separate genetic mechanisms for Level I and Level II abilities. Although the development and manifestation in performance of Level II abilities doubtless depends upon experience and learning (the capability for much of which, in turn, depends upon Level I), experience and learning are regarded as *necessary but not sufficient* for the development of Level II. The idea that individual differences in Level II ability are largely determined by environmental factors, even granted a largely genetic determination of Level I, is contradicted by the evidence on the inheritance of intelligence, most of which is based upon tests that largely measure Level II functions. The purest Level II tests, such as Raven's *Progressive Matrices*, yield heritability estimates as high or higher than are found for omnibus intelligence tests like the Stanford-Binet (e.g., Shields, 1962). There have been no comparable studies of the heritability of Level I *per se*, but there is no reason to believe that Level I abilities are not fully as heritable as Level II. For example, pursuit-rotor learning – a form of perceptual-motor learning in which the subject practices keeping a stylus on a moving metal disc (or 'target') – would seem to be a relatively pure type of Level I ability. Analysis of the correlations between sets of identical and fraternal twins for total time 'on target' in the course of acquiring the pursuit-rotor skill yielded a heritability coefficient of 0·88, which is close to the heritability of physical stature (Bilodeau, 1966, Ch. 3).

RELATIONSHIP OF LEVELS I AND II
TO MENTAL RETARDATION

Severe grades of mental defect due to mutant genes, chromosomal abnormalities, and brain damage probably always involve a marked deficiency in Level I; consequently Level II will also be deficient. Even in the severely retarded, however, the most elemental Level I functions are often prominent, such as high-fidelity transmission of stimulus inputs as commonly seen in the echolalia and echopraxia of imbecile children – in many cases these are their only signs of learned behavior, a high-fidelity 'echoing 'of what they see and hear (O'Connor and Hermelin, 1961). But here we are not primarily concerned with this category of severe mental deficiency. Rather, our present concern is with the milder forms of mental retardation associated with normal polygenic inheritance and due to the fact that polygenic characteristics assume a 'normal' distribution of values in the population and such a distribution has a lower 'tail'. We have postulated two such distributions representing different genetically conditioned aspects of mental development: Level I and Level II. Because there are two underlying distributions, there are theoretically three ways that an individual can be retarded, but phenotypically two of these three 'types' may look much alike from the standpoint of diagnosis. An individual may be diagnosed as retarded because (*a*) he is low on Level I but not on Level II; or because (*b*) he is low on Level II but not on Level I; or because (*c*) he is low on both Level I and Level II. Individuals in the categories (*a*) and (*c*) are probably the least distinguishable in performance and at present we do not know any means for clearly differentiating these groups, since normal Level II ability seems not to be manifested when Level I is very low.

*Primary retardation* here refers to a deficiency in Level I. *Secondary retardation* refers to a deficiency in Level II. This diagnostic distinction, we believe, has important implications for education and for occupational selection and training. While retardation generally refers to individuals who are more than two standard deviations below the general population mean on conventional IQ tests, there is a substantial segment of the population, largely among the groups now called culturally disadvantaged, who fall in the IQ range from 70 to 85 and might be regarded as of 'borderline' intellectual ability in terms of conventional test scores and scholastic performance. The *primary* versus *secondary* distinction would seem especially important with respect to this group. Approximately half the Negro population of the United States, for example, is below IQ 85 on standardized tests, and approximately six times as many Negroes as whites are classified as mentally retarded by traditional criteria (Shuey, 1966). We do not know what proportions are below the average range in the *primary* or in the *secondary* sense, but from the evidence we have gathered so far, it appears that comparatively little of the intellectual retardation found in low SES groups is of the primary type. It is unfortunate that the label 'retarded' is ever used in connection with individuals who are of average ability in Level I processes although they are quite far below average in Level II. Most such individuals are not perceived as retarded once they leave school, and, unless they show emotional instability or other severe behavior problems, they do not become institutionalized. Accurately speaking, they are not 'slow learners'. Neither is their particular pattern of abilities primarily the result of cultural deprivation, in the majority of individuals. Some children with exceptionally high Level II ability come from a culturally deprived background (for some striking examples, see Burt, 1961b). Barnett, a student of mental retardation, has stated that 'Perhaps the major obstacle to analysis and habilitation of retarded behavior is the paucity of measurement methods that amplify rather than homogenize the parameters of individual behavior' [Barnett, undated, p. 16]. The differential assessment of Level I and Level II abilities is a step toward the more refined diagnosis of familial retardation, and it is a diagnostic approach based on a theoretical conception of the development and structure of mental abilities.

## Evidence for the Level I–Level II Hypothesis

GENERAL OBSERVATIONS

The observations that initially gave rise to the studies that led to the dual-process hypothesis proposed here were brought to the writer's attention by school psychologists and teachers in classes for the educable mentally retarded (EMR, with Stanford-Binet IQs between 50 and 75) in schools that contained a large proportion of children called culturally disadvantaged. It was the teacher's impression, confirmed by the writer's own observations made in the classroom, on the playgrounds, and in laboratory testing, that low SES children in the EMR groups appeared in many ways to be much less retarded, and in fact usually appeared quite normal, as compared with middle-class children of the same IQ, even excluding those with sensorimotor disabilities or signs of neurological impairment. The same held true in observations of children not in EMR classes but in the 'slow learner' category of IQs from 75 to 85 or 90. The low SES children, whether white, Negro, or Mexican-American, appeared more mature and capable in social interactions and in activities on the playground than middle SES children, despite very similar scores on a variety of intelligence tests, both verbal and nonverbal, and very similar performance in school subjects such as reading and arithmetic.

We found it possible to devise special tests, which we call 'direct learning tests', that measure how fast the child could learn something new right in the test situation itself. Such tests are much less tests of achievement than the ordinary intelligence tests. Direct learning tests depended relatively little on knowledge or specific skills that have been acquired prior to being tested. The 'direct

learning tests' consist of measures of sh~~o~~
associative learning; they minimized concept~~u~~
it was found that the low SES children in EMR ~~c~~
IQ range from 75 to 85 performed on the average mu~~ch~~
these learning tests than their middle-class counterparts of ~~s~~
IQ. Low SES children of average or above average IQ, howev~~e~~

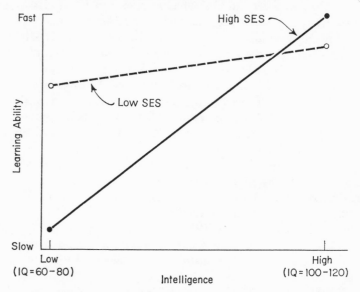

FIGURE 6. *Summary graph of a number of studies showing relationship between learning ability (free recall, serial and paired-associate learning) and IQ as a function of socioeconomic status (SES).*

were found not to perform any differently on the learning tests than middle SES children of the same IQ. This finding suggested that the low SES *versus* middle SES difference was not simply due to the IQ tests being more culturally loaded than our learning tests, such that the IQ underestimated the intelligence of the low SES group. It appeared that two different kinds of ability were being assessed – associative learning abilities, to which we later gave the general label of Level I, and conceptual or cognitive abilities, which we have labeled Level II. The typical results of several of these studies are summarized by Figure 6.

It later became apparent that selecting subjects only from EMR classes actually biased our experimental results *against* the hypothesis. In many schools in low SES neighbourhoods, it was found that the majority of children with IQs in the 50 to 75 range are not found in EMR classes but are in the regular classes, although their scholastic achievement is usually commensurate with their low IQs. The low SES children who are placed in EMR classes are more likely to resemble middle SES children of the same IQ than are low SES children in the regular classes despite IQs in the EMR range. On the other hand, we have found no middle SES children with IQs between 50 and 75 in regular classes. When such children are found, they are in the special EMR classes. The great majority of low SES children in regular classes but with low IQs and with scholastic achievement 2 or 3 years below grade level perform in the same average range as the majority of average IQ middle SES children on our Level I learning tests.

The literature on mental retardation frequently notes that many retardates are regarded as retarded only during their school years and make a normal social and vocational adjustment once they are out of school. From then on most are rarely perceived as retarded (Robinson and Robinson, 1965; Tyler, 1965, pp. 370-377). Only a small minority of individuals diagnosed as retarded while in school are ever placed in institutions or sheltered workshops for the retarded.

We have tested institutionalized familial retardates, as well as those in sheltered workshops, on some of our direct learning tests. We find that almost without exception these individuals are as deficient on our learning tests as on conventional IQ tests, and this is true even when we rule out individuals with any suspicion of organic impairment. (Retardation due to single gene and chromosomal defects has never formally entered into our research, but the several such cases that have been tested showed marked deficiency on the Level I tests.) It seems clear that among groups diagnosed as familial retarded, especially when social incompetence is part of the diagnostic criterion, there is a preponderance of primary retardation.

There is an indication that primary and secondary retardation can exist in different siblings reared together in the same family. Barnett (undated) studied four brothers, 8 to 14 years of age, diagnosed as familial retarded, with both parents also retarded, in an instrumental discrimination learning situation. Instrumental learning clearly qualifies as a Level I process. Two of the brothers (IQs 72 and 55) were grossly superior to the other two (IQs 63 and 48) in instrumental learning. One of the brothers (IQ 72), in fact, performed like a normal adult. All were markedly retarded in school work, although the two showing the better instrumental conditioning were also somewhat better in scholastic performance.

PSYCHOMETRIC EVIDENCE

*MA, IQ, and Cognitive Development and Learning Rate.* As illustrated in Figure 5, different developmental curves are hypothesized for Level I and Level II processes, with Level II becoming increasingly prominent beyond the pre-school years. Mental Age (MA), as derived from tests such as the Stanford-Binet, is an index of the individual's status in this form of cognitive development. But it is also an index of the amount of learning, as represented by the acquisition of knowledge and skills, that has taken place up to the chronological age at which the child is tested. Some part of this knowledge acquisition depends mainly on the child's associative learning ability, which is Level I process. Thus, MA is a composite index representing both cognitive developmental status and amount of learning. The IQ, being a ratio of MA/CA, is an index of the rate of cognitive development and of the rate of learning. Culture-fair tests tap cognitive development more than learning.

*Heterogeneity of Familial Retardation.* If the relationship between Level I and Level II performance is as shown in the correlation scatter diagrams in Figure 4, we should expect to find greater heterogeneity in associative learning abilities among a group of retarded than among average or gifted children, even though all three groups have much the same variance on the IQ (or Level II) measure. Jensen (1963) tested all the children in EMR classes (IQs 50-75) in an urban junior high school on a trial-and-error selective learning task and compared their performance with representative samples of average (IQs 90-110) and gifted children (IQs 135 and above) in the same school. The groups all differed significantly from one another, in the expected direction. But the most striking finding was the extreme heterogeneity of the EMR group on the learning task. Although the standard deviation of their IQs was 7·13 as compared with 8·06 for the average and 4·94 for the gifted, the EMR's variance on various trial and error selective learning tests was from 2 to 5 times greater than the variance of the average group, and from 10 to 25 times greater than the variance of the gifted group. Several of the EMR children performed above the mean level of the gifted group. Interestingly enough, the two fastest learners in the study had IQs of 147 and 65! On the other hand, none of the average or gifted subjects had scores as low as the mean for the retarded. None of the gifted, in fact, was below the mean of the average group. These results are highly consistent with our dual process formulation. Virtually the full range of Level I ability was found among the EMR, though all were deficient in Level II. Also, the lowest part of the range of Level I ability was not found in the average and gifted IQ groups.

If (*a*) there are two underlying ability distributions, Level I and Level II, and if (*b*) omnibus intelligence tests like the Stanford-Binet contain items that measure both Levels to some extent, and if (*c*) one distribution (Level II) but not the other (Level I) is correlated with SES, then we should predict an *increase* in the population variance and an increase in the mean SES difference on tests which are more pure measures of Level II. This is exactly what Cattell (1934) found with a 'culture-fair' measure of $g$, a test which taps Level II almost exclusively. When IQ is derived from Cattell's test in the same fashion that it is derived from the Stanford-Binet, by taking MA/CA, the standard deviation of the Cattell test is 50 percent greater for the Stanford-Binet (i.e., 24 *vs*. 16), and SES IQ differences are greatly magnified by the Cattell test, despite the fact that it contains much less cultural content than the Stanford-Binet. This would be expected from our hypothesis.

A similar finding is that of Higgins and Sivers (1958), who found that large groups of 7- to 9-year-old low SES Negro and white children who did not differ on Stanford-Binet IQ showed a significant difference, with Negroes scoring lower, on Raven's *Colored Progressive Matrices*, a relatively pure test of $g$ or abstract reasoning. Sperrazzo and Wilkins (1958, 1959) (also see Jensen, 1959) found similar Negro-white differences in each of three subgroups on the SES scale.

The Porteus mazes test, often regarded as one of the most culture-free tests and recognized for its sensitivity to brain damage, appears to be more a test of Level I processes than of $g$ or Level II. The test apparently correlates with other intelligence tests because of their partial dependence on Level I functions, not because it measures Level II functions directly. Its lack of loading on Level II makes it particularly suited to distinguishing primary and secondary familial retardation, as shown in a study by Cooper, York, Daston and Adams (1967). They were led to the use of the Porteus test by their impression that the Wechsler and Stanford-Binet tests often result in misleading and erroneous decisions when applied to a population of lower-class Southern Negro adolescents. They state:

> We were first led to question these procedures through observations of Southern Negro adolescents committed to a state institution for the mentally retarded. In the judgment of their teachers, nurses, social workers, and attendants a substantial number of these adolescents were functioning socially and vocationally at levels far above those to be expected of persons mentally retarded.

They point out that 'extended retesting [on Wechsler and Stanford-Binet] failed to produce any reliable discrimination between the adolescents who appeared behaviorally nonretarded and those who were grossly deficient in effective and adaptive social behavior'. Here, then, appears to be a clear-cut example of the failure of IQ tests, which tap mainly Level II, to discriminate between primary and secondary retardation. The Porteus test apparently made this discrimination. Subjects were divided into 2 groups – those for whom judges gave the answer 'yes' to 6 or more of the following questions and those for whom they answered 'no' to 6 or more:

Is he socially alert?
Is he socially effective?
Is his general activity level high?
Is he mentioned more often?
Is his vocational ability high?
Does he have sports ability?
Is his physical appearance good?
Is his social judgment accurate?

Although these 2 groups had mean Wechsler IQs of 56·0 and 63·1, respectively, their mean IQs on the Porteus were 63·6 and 121·7. None of the primary retardates scored above 84 on the Porteus and none of the secondary retardates scored below 102; the highest scored 132.

MEMORY SPAN

Tests of immediate memory span are among the best indices of Level I ability.

Memory span for digits has been underrated as a psychometric test by most clinical psychologists. The main reasons for the depreciation of the digit span tests as it is generally used by clinicians are (*a*) its relatively low reliability as compared with most other subtests, and (*b*) the fact that in some cases it yields results that are highly discrepant from other subtests, as when a person with a very low IQ obtains an average or superior score on digit span. Poor performance on digit span, however, is rarely found in persons of average or superior IQ, unless there is evidence of extreme anxiety, an organic brain condition, or other pathologic disturbance. Wechsler (1958) has stated that 'Except in cases of special defects or organic disease, adults who *cannot* retain 5 digits forward and 3 backward will be found, in 9 cases out of 10, to be feeble-minded or mentally disturbed' [p. 71]. He adds: 'Rote memory more than any other capacity seems to be one of those abilities on which a certain absolute minimum is required, but excesses of which seemingly contribute relatively little to the capacities of the individual as a whole'. This view probably underrates the importance of individual differences in the ability assessed by digit span in the region above the minimum requirement Wechsler speaks of.

The relationship of memory span to general intelligence is actually greater than is generally believed. Memory span for digits formed a part of the original Binet intelligence scale and has been included in all the revisions of the test. It is also among the subtests of the Wechsler Adult Intelligence Scale (WAIS) and the Wechsler Intelligence Scale for Children (WISC). The low reliability of the very brief digit span (DS) test as used in these batteries is probably what misled Wechsler to state that '. . . as a test of general intelligence it [digit span] is among the poorest [Wechsler,

1958, p. 70]'. This statement, however, is belied by the massive normative data presented in Wechsler's own book.

First of all, it must be noted that the reliability of the DS test of the WAIS is between 0·66 and 0·71 for various age-groups. The WISC Manual reports DS reliabilities between 0·50 and 0·60 for various age-groups (Wechsler, 1949). By comparison, the reliability of the Full Scale IQ on both the WAIS and the WISC is between 0·92 and 0·97. Vocabulary has the highest reliability (0·95) of any of the single scales. But low reliability is no real problem with the DS test. Its reliability can be boosted to any desired level simply by increasing the number of series presented. It also helps to standardize the procedure as much as possible, by presenting the digits at a metronomic 1-second rate by means of a tape-recording for auditory digit span or an automatic projector for visual digit span. We obtain reliabilities above 0·90 under these conditions, and a reliability as high as 0·96 has been obtained even among a relatively homogeneous group of university students.

The correlation between DS and Full Scale IQ (minus DS) on the WISC, after correction for attention, ranges between 0·60 and 0·70, and for the WAIS it is 0·75. These correlations compare favorably with those of other individual scales after they are corrected for attenuation. The ability to repeat two digits at age 2½ correlates 0·62 with Stanford-Binet IQ at that age (Terman and Merrill, 1960, p. 342).

Of further interest is Wechsler's claim that DS correlates very little with $g$, the general factor common to all the WAIS subtests. Yet Wechsler (1958, p. 122) presents a factor analysis (Holzinger's bi-factor method) of the WAIS in which a large $g$ factor, accounting for some 50 percent of the total variance, was extracted. The DS test has a loading of 0·63 on $g$ in the age-group 18-19, which is the peak age for DS performance. Corrected for attenuation, this factor loading becomes approximately 0·80, which is a very substantial loading as compared with the $g$ loadings of other subscales. Wechsler's notion that DS ceases to correlate significantly with other measures of intelligence once DS exceeds a certain minimal threshold would seem to be further belied by the correlation of 0·60 (0·73 corrected for attenuation) between the DS and Vocabulary subtests of the WAIS in the normative population. It appears that seemingly small individual differences in immediate memory span, when multiplied over a lifetime of experiences, make for highly significant differences in such acquired indices of intelligence as vocabulary. A person with good short-term memory span plus rapid consolidation of the memory traces would learn more per unit of time from his experience than a person with a shorter span or slower trace consolidation. This seems a reasonable explanation for the substantial correlation between DS and Vocabulary in Wechsler's normative population. Another line of evidence that rote memory abilities do not cease to be important above a minimal threshold was obtained by Jensen (1965b), who derived 12 factor scores from a battery of memory span and serial rote learning tasks administered to university students. The multiple correlation between the 12 factors and students' college grade point average was 0·76 (0·68 after correction for shrinkage).

The reader should not gain the impression that memory span is a unitary ability. There is ample evidence, for example, that the abilities to repeat digits forward and backward are not entirely the same. Korsakoff patients, for instance, show far greater than the normal discrepancy between forward and backward digit span (Wechsler, 1958, p. 71). And factor analyses of the intercorrelations among a variety of tests including forward and backward span have shown that they have different factorial compositions (Jensen, 1965b; Osborne, 1966). From these analyses repeating digits forward can be interpreted as an almost pure measure of Level I ability, while repeating digits backward involves some Level II ability. This is in line with the fact that backward span calls for a transformation of the input, which brings some Level II elements into play. Forward digit span, for example, correlates more with the WISC Information subtest than with Arithmetic 'thought' problems, while backward digit span is just the opposite. Also, backward digit span is more highly correlated with Block Design than is forward digit span, and Block Design is the best measure of *g* among the Performance tests.

Other procedural variations of the digit span task, such as requiring a 10-second delay between presentation and recall of the digit series, introduce further individual differences factors. Subjects do not remain in the same rank-order of ability on immediate and delayed recall (Jensen, 1965b).

The argument that digit span is positively correlated with IQ mainly because more intelligent subjects are capable of more sophisticated strategies for encoding strings of digits is not very convincing. For one thing, digit span correlates at least as highly with IQ at $2\frac{1}{2}$ years of age as at any later ages. Furthermore, digit span reaches a peak at around 19-20 years of age and shows a relatively early gradual decline, following much the same curve as brain weight and vital capacity. This seems hard to account for in terms of conscious strategies for remembering digits. It is more likely that digit span is closely tied to very basic brain functions. Intensive training of digit span ability has been shown not to produce any permanent increase in children's digit span over what would be normal for their mental age (Gates and Taylor, 1925).

*Short-term Memory and Retardation.* Ellis (1963) has proposed the hypothesis that the mentally retarded are essentially characterized by a deficit in short-term memory (STM). He has postulated that the retardate is deficient in both the strength and duration of the stimulus trace. There is considerable support for this theory, most of it based on studies of institutionalized retardates. The position of the present paper is that Ellis' theory applies only to primary retardation as here defined. It is hypothesized that secondary retardation does not involve a STM deficit but depends upon a specific deficiency in Level II, i.e., abstract and conceptual processes. We also believe that the majority of low SES children with IQs in the range from 50 to 85 are intellectually retarded only in the secondary sense and do not evince a STM deficit.

*Interaction of Digit Span, IQ, and SES.* We have found that the substantial correlation between DS and IQ in the normative population of the Wechsler and Stanford-Binet intelligence tests breaks down completely in low SES segments of the population (Jensen, 1968b). The reason for the low or negligible correlation between DS and IQ in low SES groups is attributable, according to our theory, to a deficiency in Level II mechanisms. We hypothesize that there is too little variance in Level II potential in low SES groups for even quite large individual differences in Level I to make any substantial difference in tests of Level II.

If digit span correlated as highly with IQ in the low SES population as it does in the middle-class population, we could claim to
have a culture-free test of general intelligence in the form of digit
span. But we have found that DS and IQ are much less correlated
in low than in middle SES groups. The fact that the low correlation in the low SES group is found even for the most status-fair
tests, such as the *Progressive Matrices*, indicates that the phenomenon we are observing is not a result of DS and IQ differing in
culture-fairness, but rather is a result of their measuring quite
different mental abilities.

In one study (Jensen, 1968b), children from grades 4 to 6 in an
all-Negro school in a low SES neighborhood and children in an
all-white school in an upper-middle-class suburban neighborhood
were given an auditory digit span test and Raven's *Colored Progressive Matrices*. (The mean IQ difference between the two schools is
approximately 2 standard deviations.) The nonparametric correlation (phi coefficient) between digit span and *Progressive Matrices*
was 0·33 for the low SES ($N = 60$) and 0·73 for the upper-middle
SES ($N = 60$). The idea that STM as indexed by DS may be
necessary but is certainly not sufficient for performance on a highly
*g*-loaded test such as the *Progressive Matrices* is supported by a
comparison of the 30 *highest*-scoring children on DS in the Negro
ghetto school (the upper 7·9 percent in DS in grades, 4, 5, 6) with
the 30 *lowest*-scoring children on DS in the white suburban school
(the lower 6·1 percent in DS in grades 4, 5, 6). The mean DS
scores (expressed as percent of the maximum possible score) were
65·3 for the ghetto group and 38·7 for the suburban group. Yet the
corresponding *Progressive Matrices* scores expressed as percent of
possible maximum score) were 64·7 and 72·6, respectively.

A more detailed analysis of auditory digit memory in relation to
IQ in low and high SES groups was performed on groups of pre-
school children between 3 and 5 years of age. The low SES group
($N = 100$) was predominantly Negro children attending day-care
centers; in all cases their parents were receiving public welfare
assistance. The upper-middle SES group ($N = 100$) was composed of white children in private nursery schools. The mean ages
of the high and low SES groups were 50 and 52 months, respectively. All the children were administered a battery of tests composed of auditory digit series of from 2 to 9 digits, the Binet and

Wechsler digit span tests, serial and paired-associate learning of pictures of common objects, and the Peabody Picture Vocabulary Test (PPVT). The various tests yielded 26 variables in all. The intercorrelations among the variables were factor analyzed (i.e., a varimax rotation of the 5 principal components having Eigenvalues greater than 1) separately for the low and high SES groups. The results of the factor analysis were quite different for the two groups. Although the groups differed by 19 points in PPVT IQ (an average mental age difference of 16 months), they showed no appreciable differences in the digit span and serial and paired-associate learning tests. The pattern of intercorrelations among

TABLE 6 **Means, Standard Deviations, and Correlations with Intelligence Factor in Low and High Socioeconomic Groups (N = 100 in each group)[1]**

| Variable | Mean | | Standard Deviation | | Factor Loadings | |
|---|---|---|---|---|---|---|
| | Low SES | High SES | Low SES | High SES | Low SES | High SES |
| Mental age (mo.) | 48·41 | 64·46 | 22·67 | 19·16 | 0·504 | 0·512 |
| Binet digit span | 3·72 | 3·36 | 1·05 | 1·07 | 0·047 | 0·482 |
| WISC digit span | 3·99 | 4·12 | 1·02 | 1·12 | 0·073 | 0·063 |
| | Pos. | Seq. | Pos. | Seq. | Pos. | Seq. | Pos. | Seq. | Pos. | Seq. | Pos. | Seq. |

| Variable | Pos. | Seq. | Pos. | Seq. | Pos. | Seq. | Pos. | Seq. | Pos. | Seq. | Pos. | Seq. |
|---|---|---|---|---|---|---|---|---|---|---|---|---|
| Digit series 2 | 1·99 | 1·99 | 1·99 | 1·99 | 0·05 | 0·05 | 0·09 | 0·05 | 0·032 | 0·032 | 0·023 | 0·023 |
| 3 | 2·82 | 2·85 | 2·88 | 2·91 | 0·40 | 0·31 | 0·38 | 0·29 | 0·138 | 0·181 | 0·214 | 0·210 |
| 4 | 3·06 | 3·20 | 3·02 | 3·13 | 1·13 | 0·88 | 1·15 | 0·95 | 0·023 | 0·010 | **0·877** | **0·870** |
| 5 | 2·00 | 2·46 | 1·83 | 2·42 | 1·32 | 0·98 | 1·58 | 1·21 | 0·157 | 0·156 | **0·563** | **0·511** |
| 6 | 1·02 | 2·01 | 1·05 | 1·95 | 1·03 | 0·83 | 1·03 | 0·90 | 0·340 | 0·478 | 0·372 | 0·273 |
| 7 | 0·54 | 1·53 | 0·56 | 1·63 | 0·65 | 0·63 | 0·84 | 0·88 | 0·325 | **0·534** | 0·072 | 0·017 |
| 8 | 0·41 | 1·66 | 0·38 | 1·46 | 0·49 | 0·71 | 0·60 | 0·65 | 0·138 | **0·698** | 0·057 | 0·020 |
| 9 | 0·26 | 1·71 | 0·28 | 1·71 | 0·37 | 0·83 | 0·49 | 0·91 | 0·148 | **0·760** | 0·133 | 0·194 |

[1] Factor loadings significant beyond 0·001 level are in bold type.

tests differed, however, in the low and high SES groups, and these differences were, of course, reflected in the factor analyses. In the high SES group a single factor accounted for most of the variance on all the tests; the intelligence test and the digit series and learning tests were all substantially intercorrelated, yielding a large general factor common to all. In the low SES group, on the other hand, there was a clear separation of the intelligence factor from the factor representing the digit series and learning tests.

The results are shown in Table 6. It is especially instructive to examine the intelligence factor in detail. The intelligence factor is so defined because it is the only factor with a high loading on PPVT mental age. Digit span on both the Binet and Wechsler is defined as the longest series of digits the subject can recall perfectly (after a single auditory presentation at a rate of 1 second per digit) on 50 percent of the trials. As shown in Figure 6, the low and high SES groups do not differ significantly in means or standard deviations on either the Binet or the Wechsler digit span tests, despite a 16 months difference between the mean mental ages of the groups. Also note that DS has nonsignificant loadings on the intelligence factor in the low SES group and very substantial loadings in the high SES group.

The digit series test, comprised of series of from 2 to 9 digits, were administered in the same manner as the DS test from the Binet and Wechsler, but they are scored differently. Two different scores were obtained. The *position* (Pos.) score is the number of digits recalled in the correct absolute position. The *sequence* (Seq.)

TABLE 7　**Correlation Between Position and Sequence Scoring of Digit Series Test**

| | Series Length | | | | | | | |
|---|---|---|---|---|---|---|---|---|
| *SES* | *2* | *3* | *4* | *5* | *6* | *7* | *8* | *9* |
| High | 1·00 | 0·98 | 0·93 | 0·93 | 0·85 | 0·60 | 0·47 | 0·39 |
| Low | 1·00 | 0·95 | 0·91 | 0·90 | 0·83 | 0·29 | 0·16 | −0·01 |

score is the number of digits correct in forward adjacent sequence, regardless of absolute position. Since the maximum possible sequence score is necessarily 1 less than the maximum possible position score for a given series length, $+1$ is added to the sequence score to make it equivalent to the position score. The reason that the two types of scores were used is that it had been found in a previous study of digit memory in college students that in supraspan series (i.e., series lengths beyond the subject's memory span) the two scores cease to be highly correlated and apparently measure different factors (Jensen, 1965b). In supraspan series the subject seems to retain pair-wise associations between adjacent digits in the series rather than some mental representation of the series as a whole, in which absolute position is retained. Table 7 shows the correlations between position and sequence scores for different series lengths.

Note again in Table 6 that the low and high SES groups do not differ significantly in means or standard deviations on any series by either form of scoring. The loadings on the intelligence factor, however, are entirely different for the low and high SES groups. The low SES group has no appreciable loadings on any series for position scoring. The high SES group has very high loadings for series of 4 and 5 digits, which are the series lengths near the threshold of subjects' memory span at this age. For the high SES group the loadings are approximately the same for position and sequence scores. This is not so for the low SES group, which has its only sizeable digit series of lengths 7, 8, and 9, the clearly supraspan series which more or less force subjects to learn only adjacent associations. This strongly suggests that the intelligence test (PPVT) is measuring different mental processes in the high and low SES groups. It is hard to characterize psychologically the processes of the high SES group, but those of the low SES group appear to be of an associative nature, since their sequence scores are the only ones that correlate with the intelligence factor. These different patterns of correlations within the digit series tests would be most difficult to account for in terms of culture influences, especially in view of the fact that the distributions of scores in the low and high SES groups are indistinguishable. The different correlation patterns more likely reflect fundamental differences in neurological organization.

## ASSOCIATIVE LEARNING AND INTELLIGENCE

Some of the most puzzling research in all of psychology is concerned with the relationship between psychometric intelligence and learning ability. An enormous range of correlations between various learning measures and intelligence test scores has been found, leading to a diversity of conclusions and disputes about the relationship between learning ability and intelligence (Rapier, 1962). Reviews of studies of learning ability in the mentally retarded show that this field is also characterized by similar conflicting findings (Zeaman and House, 1967; Goulet, 1968; Prehm, 1968).

Much of the puzzlement in the research findings is probably due to the failure, first, to distinguish between subjects on the basis of primary and secondary retardation and, second, to pay sufficient attention to the properties of the learning task with respect to its position on the Level I–Level II continuum. If one makes some judgment about whether the subjects of the study were predominantly primary or secondary retardates, and about whether the learning tasks were most heavily dependent on Level I or Level II processes, a considerable degree of order emerges from the various findings. For example, there is no disagreement among various researches that persons called retarded by any criteria are deficient on tests involving abstract and conceptual abilities. This characterizes both primary and secondary retardates. But as we get into the realm of associative learning tasks, the findings appear confusing, because it is in this type of learning that primary and secondary retardates show divergent abilities. The results will depend largely upon the proportions of primary and secondary retardates in the investigator's sample. If the subjects have IQs below 50, they will almost always be primary retardates, and the evidence is quite clear that these subjects are markedly below average in associative learning. If the subjects have IQs in the range 50 to 75 and are institutionalized, the chances are great that most of them are primary retardates, for we know that the vast majority of persons in this IQ range are never institutionalized. Thus, institutionalized subjects usually show a severe deficiency in learning ability. When the subjects are school children with IQs between 50 and 75 and are in special classes for the educable mentally retarded, there will be a considerable mixture of primary and secondary types of retardation, so that great variance will be found on rote learning tasks, and often the group's mean on such tasks will differ little from that of children with average IQs. When the subjects are children of low SES with IQs between 50 and 80, and are in regular classes, there will be little or no evidence of deficiency in associative learning as compared with the performance of middle-class children of average IQ.

Extremely simple forms of learning, which require no discriminations and involve no competition among multiple response alternatives – for example, classical conditioning – do not distinguish even between primary and secondary retardates or between retardates and persons of average or superior IQ. It is only when discriminative features enter the conditioning procedures that some correlation with intelligence is manifested (Zeaman and House, 1967, pp. 195-197).

In general, the evidence leads to the conclusion that there is a moderate correlation between IQ and learning ability for simple discrimination learning, for paired-associate and serial learning, and in learning-set formation (Zeaman and House, 1967). Our theory would predict that these correlations should be higher in groups containing fewer secondary retardates. A test of this hypothesis that does not require the diagnosis of primary and secondary retardation would be to obtain the correlation between IQ and associative learning ability (or any Level I test) in random samples of school children, one group with IQs from 60 to 95, the other group with IQs from 105 to 140. All the instances of secondary retardation could be presumed to be in the 60 to 95 IQ range. The correlation between associative learning and IQ in this range should be lower than in the range 105 to 140. This test of the hypothesis has not yet been made, although some evidence to be reviewed shortly comes very close to it and is consistent with the hypothesis.

Prehm (1968, pp. 37-38), in reviewing the research on rote verbal learning in the retarded has drawn 12 conclusions from the evidence:

[1] The rote verbal learning performance of the retarded is considerably more variable than that of Ss of normal intelligence.

This is what should be expected when the retardate groups are a mixture of primary and secondary types.

[2] The rote learning performance of the retarded is inferior to that of normal Ss. *This is most true when the materials are more abstract than pictures of common objects.*

We should expect that more abstract items would depend more upon Level II processes.

[3] The serial learning performance of the retarded seems to be subject to the same principles (invariance of the serial position curve, isolation effects, etc.) governing the serial performance of Ss of normal intelligence.

In a later section we will mention some important exceptions to this generalization which are predictable from our theory.

[4] When compared to massed practice, disturbed practice enhances the learning performance of the retarded to a greater extent than it does for normal *S*s.

This conclusion supports the hypothesis that primary retardates have a slower rate of consolidation of short-term memory traces, which, prior to consolidation, are easily interfered with or 'erased' by new input; distributed practice allows more time for consolidation and freedom from input and output interference, to the relatively greater advantage of retardates than of normals. It is hypothesized from the present theory that this generalization applies only to primary retardates.

[5] Retardates learn a list of paired associates more readily when the stimulus and response items are the actual objects rather than a picture of that object and when they can pronounce a CVC trigram as a word as opposed to spelling the response.

Paired associate learning tasks can differ in their relative dependence on Level I and Level II processes. Less abstract materials depend less upon Level II processes.

[6] The exposure of stimulus items for longer (4 to 7 seconds) intervals enhances the learning performance of the retarded.

Again, more consolidation time is of relatively greater advantage to the primary retardate.

[7] The retarded use high level mediational strategies in paired-associate learning to a lesser degree than do *S*s of normal intelligence.

This conclusion should hold for both primary and secondary retardates, since mediational strategies are examples of Level II processes.

[8] When non-meaningful and meaningful materials are equated for degree of difficulty, retardates exhibit a learning deficit on both types of material.

[9] The retarded exhibit both a short- and a long-term retention deficit.

This, again, theoretically applies only to primary retardates. There is no question of their STM deficit. Long-term deficit is more difficult to prove, since it depends upon equating groups for degree of original learning, which is rarely accomplished. Zeaman (1965) has concluded on the basis of the present evidence, such as it is, that long-term retention is good even in primary retardates.

[10] The retention deficit of the retarded can be minimized by instituting overlearning procedures. The relationship between amount of overlearning and the amount of retention loss is, however, unclear.

[11] Although associative clustering [in free recall of verbal materials] occurs in the retarded, their performance on tasks of this type is inferior to that of the normal *S*s.

Recent experiments from our laboratory, to be reported in a following section, indicate that free recall *per se* is a Level I ability and that clustering is a Level II process. Our theory thus mediates certain predictions about the relationships among the variables of age, IQ, free recall, and clustering tendency.

[12] The retention performance of the retarded is impaired as a function of both pro-active and retro-active inhibition, with the unlearning of OL [original learning] associations accounting for the effects of retro-active inhibition (RI). Overlearning during OL significantly reduces the effects of RI.

*Conflicting Evidence.* So far in his search of the literature the writer has found only one experimental result which is unequivocally in conflict with the major hypothesis set forth here. Pursuit-rotor learning would seem to be an even purer form of Level I ability than digit span, serial, and paired-associate learning. So we should expect pursuit-rotor learning to show little if any difference between groups of school children who presumably differ in IQ but not in Level I ability. In fact, in one study of the relationship between pursuit rotor learning ability and MA, the correlation was only 0·17 (McNemar, 1933). Wright and Hearn (1964) found a large, significant difference in pursuit-rotor learning between a group of 20 institutionalized mental defectives and a group of 20 high-school and college students, which is consistent with the idea that institutionalized retardates are usually deficient in Level I. The evidence that appears to be in direct conflict with our theory is from a recent experiment by Noble (1968, pp. 230-232), who found highly significant differences among a sample of 500 rural school children of white (W) and Negro (N) ancestry. The groups were matched for age, sex, and conditions of practice (L *vs*. R hand). The outcome was WR > WL > NR > NL. When whites, mulattoes (M), and Negroes, similarly matched on age and sex, were compared, the results were W > M > N. As Noble points out, it is hard to know how to interpret these results. Since we have found no difference between Negro and white children on such Level I measures as digit span and serial learning, though they differ by 15 to 20 points in IQ mostly Level II), it is puzzling why Negro children should perform less well than white children on pursuit-rotor learning, which seems to be a purely Level I task. One likely hypothesis is that pursuit-rotor learning involves a form of work inhibition ('reactive inhibition' in Hullian terminology) which is absent in STM and verbal learning tasks. There could well be racial differences in rates of build-up and dissipation of reactive inhibition, just as there are highly reliable individual differences within races. Pursuit-rotor experiments manipulating distribution of practice, the measure or reminiscence, and other measurements of reactive inhibition such as those described by Jensen (1966), should provide the means for testing this hypothesis.

Goulet (1968) has reviewed the research on serial rote learning in the retarded and concluded that these studies show 'unequivocal findings of superior learning for normal *S*s'. He goes on to state that these studies, however, 'have not provided insight into the specific process of factor responsible for the retardate deficit'.

According to our theory, the serial learning deficit should be found only in primary retardates, since serial learning is a Level I ability closely related to memory span. All the studies of serial learning reviewed by Goulet were based on groups of retardates among whom could be expected a preponderance of primary retardates. The one study which probably had a relatively smaller proportion of primary retardates was one by Cassell (1957). Cassell selected from a population of 152 retardates the 52 subjects who could read; non-readers were excluded. The 52 retarded *S*s who could read showed only a marginal difference from a group of normal children in serial learning ability. Among the retardates, the readers did not differ from the non-readers in IQ. We conjecture that while all were more or less equally deficient in Level II ability, more of the readers were not deficient in Level I ability (i.e., they were secondary retardates) and therefore were of normal ability in serial learning. There can be little doubt that authentic primary familial retardates are markedly deficient in serial learning ability. A study by Jensen (1965a), for example, showed that institutionalized young adult familial retardates were markedly inferior in serial rote learning compared with normal children matched for Stanford-Binet mental age.

Two main types of evidence support the contention that serial learning is essentially a Level I ability. In the first place, normal subjects, when questioned after a serial learning experiment, claim not to resort to the use of strategies, mnemonic devices, mediational techniques, or other 'higher level' mental processes in serial rote learning. Their subjective reports of how they learned the serial list are in marked contrast to their reports on paired-associate learning, in which verbal mediational processes play a prominant role in normal adult subjects. Furthermore, neither normals nor retardates show an improvement in serial learning when given special instructions to use verbal mediators in learning the serial list. The same type of instructions, however, greatly facilitate paired-associate learning, relatively more in retardates than in normals (Jensen and Rohwer, 1963a, 1963b). Paired-associates can be learned by means of Level I associative processes, but they also permit the greater play of Level II elaborative processes for subjects who possess these abilities.

Second, Jensen (1965b) has found that individual differences in serial learning are highly correlated with STM for digit series. When a battery of 14 different memory span tests and 17 serial learning measures were factor analyzed together, the loadings of both the memory span and serial learning measures were of approximately the same magnitude on the general factor common to all tests in the battery. Between 67 and 78 percent of the variance in the various serial tasks and between 67 and 82 percent of the variance on the memory span tasks was accounted for by the communalities (i.e., the common factor variance).

A series of experiments by Jensen and Roden (1963) showed a relationship between memory span and the degree of skewness of the serial position curve in normal subjects. Subjects with longer memory spans made relatively fewer errors in the first half of the serial position surve than did subjects with shorter memory spans.

Since the degree of skewness (i.e., the piling up of errors more toward the end of the serial list during the learning trials prior to mastery) is related to memory span, we should expect from our theory that primary retardates should not only be slower in learning a serial list, but should produce a less skewed serial position curve. Consistent with this prediction, Barnett, Ellis and Pryer (1960) found a tendency for normal high school students to make relatively more errors for middle items and fewer errors for the beginning items than retarded subjects. The writer tested this hypothesis further by administering an 8-item serial list composed of pictures of familiar objects (i.e., comb, spoon, house, dog, shoe, etc.) to a group of 20 familial mentally retarded (Stanford-Binet IQs between 50 and 70 with a mean of 58) young adults in a state institution for the retarded. No subjects with sensorimotor handicaps or a history or signs of neurological abnormality were included in this sample. Subjects learned by the usual anticipation method. Since the absolute speed of learning was not the essential point of the study, in order to maximize the number who would attain the criterion of mastery (one errorless trial), the serial presentation was subject-paced and subjects were encouraged to guess rather than fail to respond in anticipating each item. Four of the 20 $S$s had to be dropped for failure to attain criterion; their repeated failures and mounting frustration after a reasonable length of time made it inadvisable to continue the task. The serial position curve for the remaining 16 $S$s who attained criterion, plotted as the mean percentage of total errors occurring at each position, is shown in Figure 7. This serial position curve is extremely atypical from that of normal subjects. It is quite unlike any the writer has seen in his serial learning experiments with normal subjects or any of the 70 serial position curves he has found in the literature and which closely fit the idealized serial position curve predicted by a theoretical model of serial learning (Jensen, 1962). The serial position curve of the retardates shows none of the skewness of normal serial position curves; the peak of errors comes before the middle of the series rather than just past the middle (i.e., position 4 rather than position 5). It is interesting to note that the best-fitting model of the serial position curve predicts a relative decrease in skewness as the length of the list increases even for normal $S$s (Jensen, 1962). An 8-item list for primary retardates is probably the equivalent of a list of 20 or more items for normal *S*s. For lists of this length the skewness of the serial position curve even for normal subjects would be hardly perceptible.

One serial learning experiment with retardates used the von Restorff effect (also called the isolation effect) to introduce a Level II factor into the serial learning. It is a well-established phenomenon that causing one item in the middle of a serial list to stand out

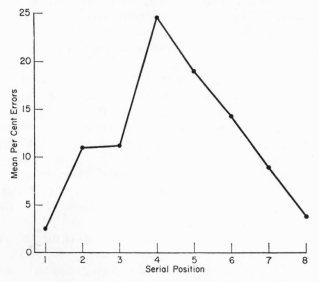

FIGURE 7. *Serial position curve for 16 primary mentally retarded young adults (IQ 50-70). Note the lack of skewness typically found in the serial position curve of normal subjects.*

from the others by making it distinctive in some way results in fewer errors on this distinctive item than if it had not been made distinctive. McManis (1966) made an item distinctive by printing it in red, while the remaining items in the serial list were printed in black. Both retarded and normal subjects showed a reduction of errors on the item isolated by this means. When the item in the same serial position was isolated by making it distinctly different in meaningfulness (inserting a low-meaningful item in a list of high-meaningful items), however, only the normal subjects showed the isolation effect – the retardates did not. The registration of the item's meaningfulness is mainly a Level II process, involving the arousal of the subjects' network of verbal associations. Since these spontaneous associative processes are notably deficient in retardates, this form of item distinctiveness in serial learning did not affect their performance.

## PAIRED-ASSOCIATE LEARNING

Paired-associate (PA) learning apparently differs from serial learning mainly in benefiting to a larger degree from past verbal experience. PA learning can be more influenced by verbal mediational processes than serial learning (Jensen and Rowher, 1963a). Also, the developmental growth curves for serial and PA learning appear to be markedly different. Serial learning ability reaches an asymptote much earlier in life than PA learning. Jensen and Rohwer (1965), in comparing serial and PA learning in children from kindergarten to twelfth grade, found little improvement in serial learning ability beyond 8 or 9 years of age, while PA learning ability showed improvement up to 18 years of age. Beyond 7 or 8 years of age serial learning is more highly correlated with IQ than with mental age, while the reverse is true for PA learning, which suggests that PA learning benefits more from cumulated past verbal experience. Four out of 7 studies of PA learning in which retardates were compared with normals of the *same mental age* showed no significant difference in learning rate; and 4 out of 9 studies in which the retarded and normal groups were of equal chronological age (and therefore differed both in IQ and MA) showed no significant difference in PA learning (Goulet, 1968). Furthermore, all but one of the studies showing retarded subjects to be inferior to normals in PA learning used institutionalized retardates. These findings support the notion that PA learning is largely a Level I function which is facilitated by amount of prior verbal experience largely associated with age, and may also involve Level II processes (mediational strategies, mnemonic elaboration, etc.) when the learning materials are of an abstract nature or are otherwise such as to evoke Level II processes in the learner. The evocation of Level II processes, however, can hinder as well as facilitate PA learning. Wallace and Underwood (1964) found, for example, that retardates do not suffer interference from *conceptual* similarity among items in the PA list, as do subjects of normal intelligence. This type of interference is clearly associated with Level II processes. Other things being equal, however, *abstractness* of the items in PA learning causes greater difficulty in learning for retardates relative to matched MA normals, for example, paired-pictures *versus* paired-objects (Iscoe and Semler, 1964; Semler and Iscoe, 1965).

ROTE LEARNING, IQ, AND SOCIOECONOMIC STATUS

A number of studies by the writer and some of his colleagues and graduate students at Berkeley are explicitly relevant to the theory outlined previously.

The first study in this series (Jensen, 1961) compared groups of Mexican-American and Anglo-American fourth and sixth grade school children of different levels of IQ ranging from 60 to 120 on a number of learning tasks consisting of immediate free recall of a dozen familiar objects, serial learning and paired-associate learning of familiar and abstract objects. On these measures of learning ability, Mexican-American children of low IQ (Mean IQ = 82·89, $SD = 5·82$) were much faster learners than Anglo-Americans of the same IQ (Mean IQ = 81·78, $SD = 3·93$). Bright Mexican-Americans (Mean IQ = 117·33, $SD = 4·27$), on the other hand, showed little difference in learning ability. The relationships for all learning tasks are essentially those summarized in Figure 6. Teachers of the children in this study remarked that the low IQ Mexican-American children seemed much brighter on the playground than the Anglo-American children of similar IQ, although both low IQ groups performed equally poorly in scholastic subjects. Our interpretation is that most of the Mexican-American group in this range of IQs (73 to 89) are somewhat retarded only in Level II functions, while the Anglo-American group in this IQ range is retarded in both Level I and Level II. (The Level II retardation may be either direct or indirect, that is, due to the functional dependence of Level II processes on the more basic Level I processes.)

Rohwer and Lynch (1968) administered a paired-associate test consisting of 24 picture pairs presented 2 times at a rate of 3 seconds per pair to groups of low SES and middle SES children from kindergarten to sixth grade. More than 90 percent of the low SES children were Negro; all of the middle SES children were white. The low and middle SES groups have an average IQ difference at the various grade levels of between 15 and 20 points. The difference in their scholastic achievement is even more striking. Many children of the low SES group are described by their teachers as 'nonlearners' in the classroom, and the majority of these children lag 2 or 3 grade levels behind middle SES children on standard achievement tests. The performances of these groups on PA learning are shown in Figure 8. Analysis of variance showed no

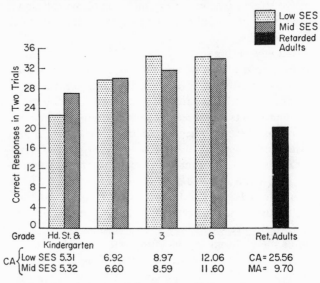

FIGURE 8.   *Comparisons of low and middle socioeconomic groups at various ages with retarded adults on a paired-associate task (24 picture pairs presented two times at a rate of 3 seconds per pair) (from Rohwer, 1967).*

significant differences between the low and middle SES groups. (The difference between grade levels was significant.) The fact that these 2 groups which differ so markedly in IQ and scholastic performance do not differ on this paired-associate learning task leads to the interpretation that the groups differ in Level II but not in Level I abilities. To check this interpretation, Rohwer and Lynch administered the test under the same conditions to a group of retarded young adults in a state institution for the retarded. All were familial retardates without a history or signs of neurological impairment. The fact that they were in an institution is regarded as indicative that most, probably all, are primary retardates. Their average Stanford-Binet MA of 9·70 (IQ of 59) is equivalent to that of normal children in the fifth grade. Yet these retardates showed poorer paired-associate learning ability than the 5-year-old children in Head Start and kindergarten. Also consistent with our hypothesis is the fact that the correlation between PA learning scores and MA (with CA partialed out) is 0·51 for the middle SES group and 0·10 for the low SES group. The correlation scatter diagrams of the 2 SES groups show the characteristics depicted in Figure 4.

In a more recent experiment, Rohwer (1968a) administered four 25-item PA tests (picture-pairs) to groups (total $N = 288$, with 48 in each group) of low SES Negro and upper-middle SES white children in grades K, 1, and 3. These SES groups at all grade levels differed by from about 1·5 to 2 standard deviations (20 to 30 IQ points) on the Peabody Picture Vocabulary IQ and on Raven's *Colored Progressive Matrices*. On the total PA learning score a significant difference between the lower and upper SES groups was found only for the kindergarten children. Rohwer comments

... these results suggest that in the development of the kind of learning ability assessed by the PA test, the discrepancy between upper-strata white children and lower-strata Negro children progressively narrows with succeeding grade levels.

Rohwer goes on to note that this is in marked contrast with the results obtained with the PPVT and the Raven, which show increasing divergence between the SES groups from grades K to 3. This is just what would be predicted from the hypothesized growth curves for Level I and Level II processes (depicted in Figure 5). This is the only study so far that has failed to show a significant SES difference in the correlations between associative learning ability and psychometric intelligence, although the differences are in the predicted direction. The MA correlated with total PA score 0·64 in the high SES and 0·52 in the low SES group; IQ correlated with PA 0·27 and 0·22 in high and low SES groups, and the corresponding correlations for Raven raw scores were 0·44 and 0·41.

A study by Rapier (1968) helps to establish the phenomenon described in Figure 6 as a function mainly of social class rather than of race, as might be incorrectly interpreted from the fact that most of our experiments have confounded race and SES. When school children are retested on the basis of SES, there will be a preponderance of Negro and Mexican-American children, 8 to 12 years of age, in public schools. She compared low and middle SES children in special classes for the educable mentally retarded (mean Stanford-Binet IQs for low SES was 70·20, *SD* = 3·64, range = 63-68, and for middle SES 71·45, *SD* = 4·95, range = 63-78) and low and middle SES children of above-average intelligence in regular classes (IQ for SES 104·5, *SD* = 3·23, range 100-110, and for middle SES 105·1, *SD* = 3·70, range = 100-110). There were 20 *S*s in each of the 4 groups. All children whose records indicated any sensorimotor, neurological, or emotional disabilities were excluded. (It is an interesting point that Rapier was able to obtain the 20 low SES retarded children from three special classes in one school district but had to canvass 10 special classes in 4 school districts to locate 20 middle SES retarded children.) Serial and PA learning tasks (using pictures of familiar objects) were given to all subjects: 1 serial list and 3 different PA lists administered on 3 different days. (Other experimental variables manipulated in this experiment, involving special instructions to prompt verbal mediation of PA learning, are not central to our present hypothesis.) Rapier's overall results reveal the same relationships as shown in Figure 6, but, unlike the other studies in our series, the results were in the predicted direction but not significantly so on the first day's serial and PA learning tests. IQ showed a significant effect, but SES and the interaction of IQ × SES were non-significant. On the second day's tests, however, there was a significant IQ × SES interaction, with the low SES retardates and normals showing no appreciable difference in trials to criterion in PA learning (4·6 *vs.* 4·9) and the middle SES retardates and normals showing a large difference in PA learning trials to criterion 7·7 *vs.* 4·0). SES, IQ, and SES × IQ were all significant beyond the 0·01 level on the third day of testing. The normal subjects of the low and middle SES groups did not differ significantly in trials to criterion in PA learning (5·95 *vs.* 5·10), but the low and middle SES retarded groups differed markedly in learning trials (6·6 *vs.* 10·1).

The learning-to-learn effects of 3 daily sessions on these rote-learning tasks mainly brought about a divergence of the middle and low SES retardates because the middle SES retarded group showed relatively little learning-to-learn (i.e., generalized practice effect).

Also consistent with our hypothesis were Rapier's findings concerning the difference in correlations between IQ and the learning scores for the middle and low SES groups. The average $r$ between intelligence and the learning tests was 0·44 for the middle SES and 0·14 for the low SES group; in terms of variance in PA learning accounted for by the variance in the psychometric tests, this represents 19 percent *vs.* 2 percent.

Rohwer, Lynch, Levin, and Suzuki (1968) compared large groups (total $N = 432$) of first, third, and sixth grade children from greatly contrasting high- and low-strata schools. The high-strata school's population was white; the low-strata school's population was Negro. The modal occupational category of fathers of the students in high-strata schools was professional whereas that of fathers of students of low-strata schools was semi-skilled or unskilled manual. The children in the two schools differed widely in psychometric intelligence and achievement. Yet total scores on a variety of PA learning tasks showed no significant difference ($F < 1$) between school strata. Rohwer *et al.* state '. . . the average performance of children from low-strata schools was virtually the same as that of children from high-strata schools' [p. 19]. This is especially interesting in view of the fact that the relatively low IQs of the low-strata children are commensurate with their generally poor scholastic performance as assessed by standardized tests and the fact that the teachers of these children describe them generally as being 'slow to learn and difficult to teach'. The PA learning task involves largely Level I ability while the schools' instructional methods apparently rely heavily on Level II abilities – those abilities measured by intelligence tests with a high $g$ loading.

In a study by Jensen and Rohwer (1969), 100 low SES Negro pre-school children in day care centers and 100 upper-middle SES white children in private nursery schools, all between 3 and 5 years of age, were given digit span tests, a serial learning test, and four paired-associate learning (both using pictures of familiar objects), along with the Peabody Picture Vocabulary Test as the measure of IQ. The correlation between MA and serial learning was 0·49 for the high SES and 0·27 for the low SES; the correlation between MA and the total of four PA tests was 0·58 for high SES and 0·20 for low SES. The multiple correlation was determined between MA, on the one hand, and CA, serial learning, PA learning, and digit span, on the other. Corrected for shrinkage, the multiple-$R$ was 0·66 for the high SES and 0·42 for the low SES group. This corresponds to 44 percent and 18 percent of the variance, respectively. In other words, the Level I tests – learning and memory span (plus CA) – predict more than twice as much of the variance in MA for high SES as for low SES children.

FREE RECALL AND ASSOCIATIVE CLUSTERING

The technique of free recall as a measure of learning and STM especially lends itself to the investigation of the Level I–Level II distinction. In the free recall of uncategorized lists (abbreviated as $FR_u$), the subject is presented briefly with a number of items (words, pictures, or objects) and then is asked to recall as many of the names as possible within some specified time limit. A number of experimental parameters can be varied – the number of items, the method and rate of presentation. Usually the items are presented in a new randomized order on each trial. Uncategorized lists are composed of items which are relatively unrelated to one another by any supraordinate concept or category labels. The procedures for free recall of categorized lists ($FR_c$) is the same as $FR_u$ except that the list is composed of items which can be grouped into two or more perceptual or conceptual categories, usually categories that can be readily given a supraordinate category label, like furniture, musical instruments, food, etc. Perceptual categories are those based on resemblance among items on the basis of qualities that range along various dimensions of primary stimulus generalization, such as color, size, and shape. Conceptual categories are mediated by semantic associations, usually of a hierarchical type involving indirect associations among items via their supraordinate category labels.

Comparisons of the amounts of free recall of categorized and uncategorized lists are most valuable from the standpoint of our theory. It has been argued that the reason that low SES children perform so much better on our Level I learning tasks than would be predicted from their IQs and scholastic performance is that our Level I learning tasks (e.g., digit span, serial and PA learning) are less academic, more 'interesting', more 'relevant', and therefore more motivating to low SES children than are the usual intelligence tests. To rule out this motivational hypothesis as the explanation for our findings, we need two tasks that are essentially indistinguishable in general appearance and procedure, and thus will not elicit different motivational sets, but also which differ clearly in the extent to which performance on the tasks depends upon Level I and Level II abilities. Free recall of uncategorized and categorized lists meets these requirements. $FR_u$ taps mainly Level I ability, or at least requires nothing more than Level I ability, involving simply the reproduction of the input. $FR_c$ also requires nothing more than Level I ability, but it can also reflect Level II ability, i.e., the transformation of the random order of input into conceptual categories as reflected in the order of the subject's output of the items – the phenomenon known as 'clustering'. Thus, the random input may be *chair, shoe, bed*, and *hat*; and if there is clustering according to the supraordinate categories of furniture and clothing, the output order will be *chair bed, shoe hat*. The rearrangement of the random input order on the basis of hierarchically arranged verbal mediators is clearly an abstract, conceptual process of the type that characterizes Level II. The amount of material recalled is increased when clustering is possible. Thus, more material is recalled from categorized than from uncategorized lists, and persons who are high on Level II ability should presumably have a relatively greater advantage over persons with low Level II ability in $FR_c$ as compared with $FR_u$.

*Associative Clustering in the Mentally Retarded.* Studies of free recall and associative clustering in the retarded have been reviewed by Goulet (1968) and Prehm (1968). Three facts are well established both for normal and for retarded subjects: (*a*) perceptual and conceptual clustering both increase with age; (*b*) there is an increase both in the number of items recalled and in the degree of associative clustering over repeated trials; and (*c*) there is a positive correlation between individual differences in the amount of associative clustering and the number of items recalled.

A number of conclusions can be drawn from studies of the retarded. Retardates show less clustering and poorer recall than normals of the same CA. The results for comparisons of retardates and normals of equal MA are more ambiguous, but most studies indicate that MA is a chief source of variance in clustering; retardates and normals matched on MA show similar degrees of clustering (Goulet, 1968). One study, by Rossi (1963), suggests, however, that the level of MA at which retardate *versus* normal comparisons are made is an important factor, since clustering tendency increases with increasing MA at a faster rate in normals than in retardates. In general, we have claimed that above 5 or 6 years of age, MA, as measured by standard tests such as the Stanford-Binet, is essentially an index of the individual's developmental status in Level II functioning, and these results of equal-MA comparisons reflect just what we should expect according to this formulation.

Compared with normal persons of equal CA, retardates are found to show not only *quantitative* differences in clustering but also *qualitative* differences (Prehm, 1968). Normal subjects cluster items mainly by supraordinate categories; retardates show more pair-wise coordinate groupings, often of an idiosyncratic nature. For example, *bed* and *shoe* may be recalled together consistently on repeated trials. Other items in the list would usually lead to *bed* and *shoe* being separated by normal subjects into the clusters of *furniture* and *wearing apparel*. The retardates' basis for clustering is a coordinate association rather than hierarchical conceptual associations; for example, he will say *bed* and *shoe* go together because 'you put your shoes under your bed'.

*Social Class Differences in Associative Clustering.* How do groups of children differing markedly in Level II ability (e.g., IQ) but not differing appreciably in Level I (e.g., digit span and serial learning) compare in free recall and associative clustering? This question has been investigated in two studies in our laboratory, using subjects drawn from the same subject pool as that used in our other studies comparing low and middle SES groups in Level I and Level II performance. The prediction from our theory was that low and high SES children would differ little in $FR_u$ but would differ markedly in $FR_c$, and that the SES difference between $FR_u$

and $FR_c$ would be greater with increasing age of the subjects. These predictions, of course, follow directly from the theory of the relationship between SES and Levels I and II.

Glasman (1968) used several 20-item lists of 4 categories each, with 5 items per category. The categories were: animals, foods, furniture, musical instruments, jobs, eating utensils, clothing, and vehicles. The items consisted of models, toys, or other three-dimensional representations of real objects. The 20 items were presented singly for 3 seconds each, in a random order, for 5 trials. After every trial subjects were allowed 2 minutes to verbally recall the items in any order; the *S*s output was tape-recorded. There were 32 *S*s in each of the 4 groups formed by the $2 \times 2$ design; Kindergarten *vs.* 5th Grade and low SES *vs.* high SES. The low SES group was composed of Negro children from a school in a low SES neighborhood; the high SES group was drawn from an all white school in an upper-middle-class neighborhood. Thus social class and race are confounded in this experiment. The mean IQs (PPVT) of the groups were 90 for low SES and 120 for high SES. The grade levels were matched on IQ. The main results of the study are shown in Figures 9 and 10. The measure of clustering (Figure 10) is the one most commonly used in studies of clustering, and is described by Bousfield and Bousfield (1966). A cluster is defined as a sequence of two responses from the same category which are immediately adjacent. The Bousfield formula corrects this value by subtracting the expected value for a random sequence of the items recalled. The results shown in Figures 9 and 10 clearly bear out our theoretical predictions. At Grade 5 the low SES and high SES groups differ by approximately 1 standard deviation, both in recall and in clustering. (The Grades $\times$ SES interaction is statistically significant beyond the 0·05 level for recall and beyond the 0·001 level for clustering.)

Since $FR_c$ is essentially a Level II function, it should be correlated with MA about equally in both the low and high SES groups. This was what Glasman found. Correlation between MA and amount of *recall* was 0·62 for low SES and 0·72 for high SES; the correlation between MA and amount of *clustering* was 0·76 for low SES and 0·77 for high SES. The correlations are much higher for fifth graders than for Kindergartners, who show very little clustering and are presumably still operating in this task by a

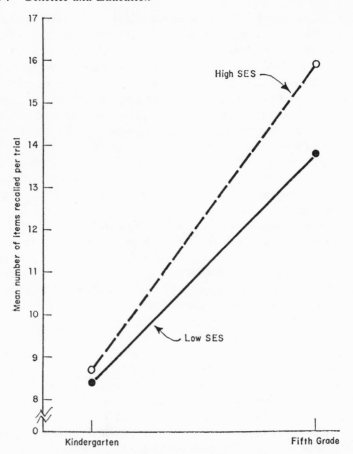

FIGURE 9.   *Mean number of items per trial (over 5 trials) in free recall of a categorized list, as a function of Grade and Socioeconomic Status (SES) (from Glasman, 1968).*

Level I process. (The correlation of MA and recall is 0·06 at Kindergarten and 0·59 at Grade 5; the correlation between MA and clustering is 0·02 at Kindergarten and 0·68 at Grade 5.) These results are highly consistent with predictions based on the hypothetical growth curves for Level I and Level II abilities as a function of SES, shown in Figure 5. $FR_c$ performance is so strongly related to MA that when the data of Figures 9 and 10 were subjected to an analysis of covariance, with MA as the control variable, all the main effects and the interactions were completely wiped out.

Although Glasman's study demonstrated age and social class differences in the free recall of *categorized* lists, it was not designed to study age and SES differences in performance on the free recall of categorized *versus* noncategorized lists. A noncategorized list is made up of unrelated or remotely associated items which cannot

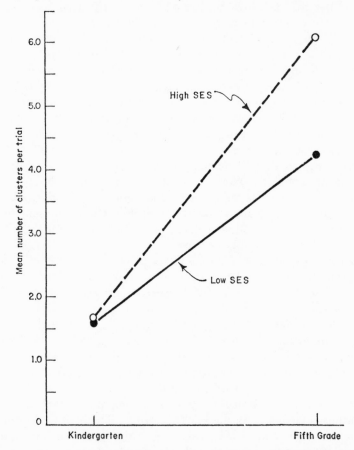

FIGURE 10. *Mean number of associative clusters per trial (over 5 trials) in the free recall of a categorized list, as a function of Grade and Socioeconomic Status (SES) (from Glasman, 1968).*

be readily grouped according to supraordinate categories. Subjective organization of the items in the list is likely to consist of pairs of items related on the basis of primary generalization, clang association, or functional relationship. A noncategorized list therefore lends itself less than a categorized list to evoking Level II processes. Consequently, subjects differing in Level II ability (but not in Level I) should show less difference in $FR_u$ than in $FR_c$.

Jensen and Frederiksen (in press) tested this prediction directly. The low SES and high SES groups were drawn from essentially the same populations as those in the Glasman study, i.e., lower-class Negro and middle- to upper-middle-class white children. The age factor was again investigated by comparing Grades 2 and 4. Sets of 20 objects were used for the noncategorized and categorized lists; the 4 categories of the latter were: clothing, tableware, furniture, and animals. Forty $S$s received the noncategorized list, consisting of 20 common but unrelated objects, including 1 object from each of the 4 categories of the categorized lists. Forty $S$s received the categorized list with the items presented in a random order, and another 40 $S$s had the same categorized lists with the items presented in a 'blocked' fashion, i.e., all items within a given category are presented in immediate sequence – a procedure which prompts clustering and facilitates recall. Five trials of presentation followed by free recall were given in all conditions. For the categorized lists, the results were essentially the same as those of the Glasman experiment: Grade 4 was superior to Grade 2 under all conditions, and the SES differences were greater at Grade 4 than at Grade 2. Whereas at Kindergarten there was no difference between SES groups, a difference in free recall clearly emerges by Grade 2, in favor of the high SES group. At Grade 4 there is a large interaction between SES level and $FR_u$ *vs.* $FR_c$ for both random and blocked lists, although the blocked condition reduces the SES difference by boosting the recall performance of the low SES group. In other words, when the input is already categorized and therefore no transformation of the input is called for, the output is facilitated in the low SES group. The high SES group, on the other hand, spontaneously transforms the random input into clustered (i.e., categorized) output and obtains approximately the same facilitation as when the input is already blocked into categories. Recall of the noncategorized list showed a relatively small difference in favor of the high SES group at both second and fourth grades. Also, for the noncategorized list there is no significant interaction between SES and grades – the SES difference is nearly the same at Grades 2 and 4. This is in marked contrast to the categorized lists, which show a large SES × Grades interaction.

All these findings on free recall are highly consistent with our theory that social class differences in ability involve mainly Level II processes rather than Level I.

## Implications for Education

If the theory of primary and secondary retardation becomes fully substantiated by further research, it should raise important questions for educational practices. The first question concerns whether different approaches to instruction can yield more optimal effects if they take account of the differences between primary and secondary retardation. It would seem that this distinction should imply quite different techniques and goals of instruction.

Why has traditional schooling been so unsuccessful in teaching children with low IQs but with quite normal Level I learning ability? Many such children do not acquire the basic scholastic skills even in 12 years of schooling. How can one account for this in cases where the child has normal learning ability? One hypothesis is that basic skills are generally taught in such a manner as to make their acquisition heavily dependent upon abstract, conceptual abilities. The criterion of learning in the eyes of many teachers, and the types of pupil performance on which reinforcements from the teacher and contingent, often emphasize the signs of Level II competence – evidence of broad transfer, of broad conceptual generalization of specific learning, of the ability to perform verbal transformations and elaborations on what has been learned, such as being able to 'tell it back in your own words' and the ability to say something formally different but conceptually similar. Teachers look for these signs of Level II performance in their pupils. Teachers encourage it, and reward it. The manifestation of Level I ability in its own right is not encouraged or rewarded. It is viewed only as a means to Level II performance. Consequently, the children with the better than average IQs experience a schedule of reinforcements from the teacher and from their perception of their own progress, a schedule of reinforcements which is quite ample for sustaining the behaviors that promote further learning. The low IQ child, on the other hand, even though he may be average or above in Level I learning ability, experiences, in effect, a schedule of non-reinforcement, which results in the experimental extinction of the behaviors that promote learning. One of the major tasks of future research is to determine the full extent to which Level I abilities can be capitalized upon the teaching of scholastic skills. When Level II performance is made (*a*) the criterion of learning, (*b*) the basis for teacher dispensed reinforcement, and (*c*) the demonstration of having learned by passing achievement tests, the child who is deficient in Level II ability will fail to learn much that could easily be learned by means of Level I.

The writer observed one first-grade class of presumably 'slow-learning' children called culturally disadvantaged. The majority of these children could not say the alphabet or name the letters of the alphabet. Many apparently could not even discriminate the letters of the alphabet, despite the fact that their teacher had spent part of every school day for 6 months in trying to impart a knowledge of the letters to these children. In their ability to learn school subjects, these children appeared so extremely retarded that the writer suspected primary retardation. The writer's colleague, Dr William Rohwer, offered to test these children individually on a picture paired-associates learning test which had already been shown to differentiate primary and secondary retardation (see Figure 9). The children in this class learned, on the average, 16 of the 24 paired-associates in 1 presentation of the list, presented at the rate of 3 seconds per pair. Their performance was completely on a par with that of middle-class children of comparable age in another school who were making normal progress scholastically. Why, then, were the disadvantaged children not learning even letters and simple number facts, to say nothing of reading and writing? Some hours spent in systematic observation of this class and similar classes have led to some psychological speculations that might help to explain these phenomena.

First of all, it was quite apparent that the children's exceedingly poor scholastic performance could not be attributed to any lack of good will, dedication, or effort on the part of the teachers. Furthermore, the teachers had learned well the principle of reinforcement, and readily dispensed encouragement and approval. However, what seemed to be getting reinforced more than anything else was the child's *efforts* rather than his successes. Reinforcing the behaviors that are signs of effort, when the effort does not eventuate in success, indeed increases motivation – but it also leads to frustration. Probably the most potent reinforcement for learning is the child's self-perception of his own *success*, that is, of his own increasing mastery of whatever it is he is attempting to do. Much too few of these instances of success were in evidence in the classes I observed, although the children's effortful but failing attempts at teacher-determined tasks were frequently reinforced by the teacher's well-intentioned praise and approval. Why were there so few opportunities for success? Partly because some of the things being taught were too far beyond the children's present capabilities, but mostly because the teachers seemed to be operating under a preconception of what kinds of behavior constitute learning and should be shaped through reinforcement – it is mainly the child's verbal behavior which evinces Level II processes. Since at the beginning of the term the children were good at Level I associative learning, the teachers tend not to want to 'waste their time' on rote activities but instead try to elicit and reinforce almost exclusively those forms of behavior, mostly verbal, which are most characteristic of children with superior IQs. Conceptual brightness, verbally expressed, is the supreme value, even to many devoted teachers who pride themselves on being specialists in teaching the culturally disadvantaged. A child's learning of $2 + 2 = 4$ is perceived as being inferior to learning to solve $2 + ? = 4$. The school places excessive valuation and emphasis on what Sheldon White (1965) has called cognitive learning as contrasted with associative learning. Is this possibly the cause of the seemingly poor scholastic potential of many 'disadvantaged' children with normal Level I abilities?

Is there a failure to capitalize on existing Level I abilities? To reinforce effort but not success? To make success dependent on Level II abilities when these are meager or undeveloped in some children? These are the conditions that could produce behavioral consequences reminiscent of phenomena described by Pavlov: experimental extinction, conditional inhibition, and experimental neurosis. Accordingly, when the behaviors that are necessary for learning are repeatedly unreinforced, the behaviors extinguish. In addition, the stimulus conditions under which such extinction takes place become conditioned inhibitors. Not only are conditioned inhibitors the stimuli for not responding, but conditioned inhibitors also become aversive stimuli, from which the subject turns away, either passively or actively. Unresponsiveness, drowsiness, inattentiveness, as well as aimless hyperactivity are some of the symptoms of conditioned inhibition. Nearly all the stimuli in the classroom and especially the teacher and all those things on which the child must focus his attention – books, papers, pencils, and blackboards – all can become conditioned inhibitors for the kinds of behavior essential for learning. Pavlov found in his attempts to establish differential conditioned responses in dogs that when the discriminative stimuli were so similar as to be beyond the dog's capacity to discriminate them, the dog's behavior deteriorated, a condition that Pavlov called 'experimental neurosis'. It is a condition that can occur without there being any punishment. It occurs simply by withholding reinforcements when the animal fails to make impossibly difficult discriminations. The dog's behavior becomes unstable, hyperactive, and highly resistant to further training. After an experimental neurosis has developed, even the simplest discriminations, which the dog could normally have learned without difficulty, become inordinately difficult or even impossible for the dog to learn. Itard observed manifestations of this condition in Victor, the wild boy of Aveyron, while training him in color and form-matching tasks. When the required discriminations were made too difficult, Victor's once normal responding turned to violent anger (Broadhurst, 1961, p. 728). The writer has observed children's behavior in some elementary school classes that closely resembles the manifestations of extinction, conditioned inhibition, and experimental neurosis as described by Pavlov.

Being importuned simply to 'try harder' also could be expected to hinder the emergence of whatever Level II processes the child might otherwise evince in learning and problem solving. The well-established Yerkes-Dodson principle states that the optimum level of motivation for performance on complex tasks is lower than for performance on simple tasks. Consequently, if relatively complex learning and problem solving require Level II processes, and if the degree of motivation and arousal is beyond the optimum level for these complex processes, performance will be hindered, and the less complex Level I processes, being nearer their optimal level of motivation, will predominate over Level II. Since the relationship of the Yerkes-Dodson principle to Level I and Level II functions remains speculative, it points to an important area for future research, viz., the relationship of drive states to the potentiation of Level I and Level II functions.

Undoubtedly the most urgent research for its implications for education concerns the question of the extent to which Level II processes can be acquired through appropriate instruction by children of normal Level I ability. The fact that siblings and unrelated children reared in the same family can differ markedly on measures of Level II ability strongly suggests that individual differences in Level II are not solely a product of environmental influences but probably have a substantial genetic component. But this should not rule out the possibility that at least some aspects of Level II functioning can be learned through Level I processes, especially when these are average or above. Some of the cognitive strategies that can facilitate learning and can be acquired by all children of normal Level I ability have been described by Rohwer (1968b), who is conducting an extensive program of research on instructional methods for inculcating, stimulating, or simulating Level II processes in children who do not evince them spontaneously. It is most important that the many children of seemingly meager educational potential in terms of the traditional criteria, but who evince normal Level I abilities, should be given every opportunity to use these abilities in acquiring the basic skills and in achieving realistic educational and vocational goals. Among the important tasks for future research is the further investigation of the theory here proposed and the discovery of means for making the most of Level I abilities in the educational process.

## ADDENDUM TO 'A THEORY OF PRIMARY AND SECONDARY FAMILIAL MENTAL RETARDATION'

Since the publication of this paper our research has further elucidated the relationship between Level I and Level II abilities. This addendum briefly summarizes the current state of the evidence and my theoretical interpretations thereof.

## The Basic Observations

There are several interrelated empirical observations which my theoretical formulation attempts to explain.

First, there is the fact that retarded children, in the IQ range between 50 and 80, are a relatively homogeneous group in performance on practically all standard intelligence tests. Most individual tests, such as the Stanford-Binet and the Wechsler scales have their highest reliability and concurrent validity in this range of the IQ distribution.

Second, there is the fact that within this rather homogeneous group with respect to IQ, there is apparently a very much greater range of other abilities, including cognitive abilities, provided they are non-academic in the traditional sense of the word. These abilities have been noted in the casual observations of parents, teachers, school psychologists, and the like, as great differences in the acquisition of skills on the playground, in social skills, and in practical knowledge and shrewdness in coping with the environment.

Third, there is the fact that children of the lowest socioeconomic status (SES), who comprise by far the largest proportion of the aclinical mentally retarded, show the greatest discrepancy, on the average, between their low IQs and these other kinds of abilities I have referred to. This seems especially true of Negro children of low SES. Middle-class white children with low IQs, on the other hand, generally show a more all-round retardation. Their poor performance on IQ tests is more consistent with their general behavior, in and out of school, than seems to be the case with low SES retarded children, whose mental handicap often seems confined almost entirely to the more academic aspects of schooling.

These casual observations by teachers and school psychologists have contributed largely to the popular belief that the standard IQ tests are somehow culturally biased against children of low SES and in favor of middle-class white children. The tests are seen as seriously underestimating the intelligence of low SES children.

The fact that the IQ predicts scholastic performance equally well for low SES as for middle SES children is usually explained away by saying that schooling itself, both the academic curricula and the methods of instruction, is culturally biased in favor of the middle class. Until a few years ago I had subscribed completely to this commonly held viewpoint, and my research in this area actually began with an attempt to formalize these observations in the psychological laboratory and thereby to demonstrate, by more precise and rigorous scientific methods than had yet been applied, that the much higher incidence of retardation among children of low SES, particularly among minority children, was the fault of the IQ tests and also, possibly, of the schools. My own research in this vein has since led me to reject this view. But the theory I have gradually arrived at to replace it is quite different from the simple alternative that existed before I began my research.

In order to analyze the basic observations which I have just described, a series of laboratory studies were conducted in which we compared retarded and average children of lower and middle SES (including Negro, Mexican, and white children) on a number of standard IQ tests and also on a considerable variety of other cognitive tasks. (We were not interested in sensory and motor skills of other abilities outside the cognitive domain.)

What these studies show, aside from any theoretical interpretation, are essentially the following points:

1. On a variety of tests of rote learning and short-term memory, retarded children score much less far below children of average IQ than on tests involving abstraction, reasoning, problem solving, and conceptual learning. Consequently, some considerable proportion of children who are retarded in terms of IQ are able to perform at an average level or above on a certain class of tasks that clearly involve mental ability. These are represented in our laboratory studies by (*a*) Trial-and-error selective learning with visual and auditory reinforcements for correct responses. (These problems have involved the trial-and-error acquisition of anywhere from 2 to 12 S-R associations.) (*b*) Serial rote learning, using lists of familiar objects (e.g., cup, comb, pencil, etc.), pictures of familiar objects, colored geometric forms, nonsense syllables, and common nouns. (*c*) Paired-associates learning, using the same or similar materials as in the serial learning. (*d*) Free recall

learning (e.g., presenting 20 familiar objects and asking the subject to recall, in any order they come to mind, the names of as many of the items as possible when they are put out of sight), using the same materials as above. (*e*) Digit span memory under different conditions of presentation and recall (e.g., recall immediately after presentation of the string of digits; recall 10 seconds after presentation; and recall after three successive presentations of the same string of digits).

What all these tasks have in common, as contrasted with tasks on which all retardates perform much more poorly, is that they call for little or no transformation of the stimulus input in order for the subject to arrive at the response output. Stimulus and response are highly similar. What the tasks call for essentially is accurate registration of sensory experiences, immediately giving already well-learned names or labels to these, and at some later point in time repeating these labels in response to partial stimulus cues. It is a kind of recording and playback on cue, as contrasted with the other class of cognitive tasks, those on which retardates perform most poorly, involving transformation and mental manipulation of the input in order to produce the answer – the relating and comparing of present stimuli with past learning, generalization and transfer of old learning to the new problem, the abstraction of conceptual and semantic similarities and differences, etc. All of these latter processes especially characterize those kinds of intelligence test items which are most highly loaded with *g*, the general factor common to all intelligence tests, which Spearman characterized as an ability for the 'eduction of relations and correlates'. For convenience I have labeled these two broad types of mental ability Level I (for non-transformational learning and retention) and Level II (for intelligence as characterized by *g*).

2. Level I and Level II abilities show an interaction with SES such that retarded low SES children are on the average superior in Level I ability to middle SES children of the same IQ. Those retardates who appear most adequate in non-academic activities are generally average or above average in Level I. It is not uncommon, for example, to find low SES Negro children with IQs below 60 who perform in the average range or above on Level I tests. Yet their counterparts in this respect are exceedingly rare among low IQ middle- and upper-middle-class white children,

who almost always perform well below the average on Level I tests.

Institutionalized retardates (and usually those in 'sheltered workshops'), as contrasted with a representative sample of all retardates in the population, are usually low both in Level I and Level II abilities. It is therefore doubtful if my findings would ever have been made had I tested only institutionalized individuals. There are marked differences between retardates who become more or less self-sufficient out in the world and those who must be cared for. Psychometrically this difference is not much related to IQ but is more markedly related to Level I ability.

In attempting to understand these findings, our first thought was that the Level II tests were more culturally biased against low SES individuals and that therefore, for any given IQ, the low SES person was really more intelligent than the high SES person, and this difference would show up in the presumably less culture-biased Level I tests. In short, I at first thought I had found in my Level I tests a culture-free or a culture-fair means of measuring intelligence. But this idea has proved to be wrong. A variety of Level II tests differing in degree of culture-loading all show highly consistent results. We have found no tests, verbal or nonverbal, with any appreciable complexity or substantial $g$ loading on which properly diagnosed retarded children score in the average range. And surprisingly enough, low SES children, especially if they are Negro, actually score slightly higher on the verbal and the more obviously culture-loaded tests than on nonverbal tests of the type that attempt to minimize middle-class cultural content. Also, the experimental manipulation of task variables in laboratory learning experiments so as to either minimize or maximize the role of Level II processes leads me to the conclusion that the Level I–Level II distinction is not a matter of the culture-loading of the tests that measure each type of ability but of the different kinds of mental processes require in the two classes of tests. Nor is the difficulty of the task the essential basis of distinction. Level I and Level II test items can be made equally difficult in terms of their $p$ values (i.e., the percentage of the population that can perform successfully). The essential distinction between Level I and Level II is in the complexity of the mental transformations or manipulations required for successful performance on the task. Moreover, twin and sibling correlations and estimates of the heritability (i.e., the proportion of the total variance in test scores attributable to genetic factors) of Level I and Level II tests give no indication of significantly lower heritability of Level II than of Level I tests. If Level II tests reflect environmental or cultural influences to a greater extent than Level II tests, one should expect lower heritability values for Level II tests. But this is not the case, and, if anything, slightly the reverse seems to be true.

## Level I and Level II in the General Population

In order to determine just how far below the average of the population retarded children stand on Level I tests, we have given such tests to large, representative samples of the school age population, now totalling 15,000 children in all. And to study the relationship between Level I and Level II abilities, verbal and nonverbal intelligence tests, representative of Level II, have also been administered to the same large samples. These large-scale data obtained from the general population put our findings with the mentally retarded into a proper perspective and show that they are not isolated phenomena peculiar to retardates but are a consequence of certain population characteristics.

The regression of Level I test scores on IQ or Level II scores in all samples appears to be linear throughout the IQ range from about 50 to 150. The slope of the regression line and the correlation between Level I and Level II abilities differs from one sub-population group to another. It is lower in low SES groups and higher in upper SES groups. It is especially lower among Negroes as compared with whites. In various studies the correlation between Levels I and II have ranged from 0·10 to 0·40 in low SES groups, comprised largely of Negro children, and from 0·50 to 0·70 in middle SES groups comprised largely of white children. (However, a sample of Oriental-American children, although of lower SES than the white sample, showed an even higher correlation between Levels I and II than was found in the white sample.) Because the regression of Level I on Level II has a steeper slope (higher correlation) in higher than in lower SES groups, the regression lines of lower and upper SES groups must inevitably cross. Consequently, in the region of low IQ that characterizes mental retardation, the lower SES group obtains higher average scores on Level I tests – which is the phenomenon described earlier. These relationships are shown in Figure 11.

Thus, the phenomenon of higher Level I ability among lower than among upper SES retardates, on the average, is seen to be a consequence of the lower correlation between Levels I and II in the low SES group as compared with the higher SES group. But what we did not expect to find before we finally tested children in adequately large numbers throughout the entire range of IQ is the *reverse* phenomenon at the upper end of the IQ scale, that is,

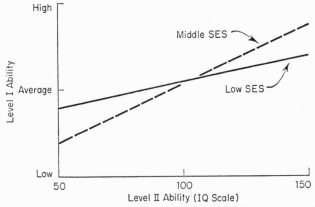

FIGURE 11. *Typical regression lines of Level I upon Level II ability in middle and low socioeconomic groups.*

the finding that low SES children (most of whom are Negro in these studies) with high IQs perform significantly less well than their middle SES counterparts in IQ. This came as something of a surprise, but it is now based on such substantial evidence that its factual status is beyond reasonable doubt. From a scientific, theoretical standpoint it is, of course, a simpler, more regular picture than we would have if the regression were not linear and the consequent reverse symmetry at the low and high ends of the IQ scale did not obtain.

This finding, furthermore, helps to clarify a point about which there was some doubt in the earlier stages of our research. This was the question of whether low SES retardates performed better on Level I tests, relative to those of middle SES, simply because

Level I tests were less culturally biased than the IQ tests. This culture-bias hypothesis seems untenable in view of the fact that in the range of IQ above 100, low SES children perform relatively *less* well on Level I tests. Also, when we have given various Level II tests which differ obviously in culture-loading, such as the Peabody Picture Vocabulary Test and Raven's *Progressive Matrices*, and then have examined the regression of the less culture-loaded on the more culture-loaded test, we find no cross-over of the regression lines of the low and middle SES groups; the lines are quite parallel. In short, comparison of lower and upper SES groups on Level I *vs.* Level II tests gives a quite different picture from that of comparing the two groups on culture-loaded *vs.* culture-fair tests.

## Nature of the Relationship Between Levels I and II

Does the correlation between Level I and Level II abilities represent a functional dependence of Level II upon Level I? For example, is above-average Level I ability a necessary but not sufficient condition for above-average Level II ability in the sense, say, that knowledge of subtraction is a necessary but not sufficient condition for solving problems in long division? Obviously some degree of learning and memory (i.e., Level I ability) are essential for intellectual development. But above some low threshold of Level I ability, is there any functional dependence of individual differences in Level II upon individual differences in Level I? We know, of course, that there is some correlation, often quite substantial, between Levels I and II. But correlation does not necessarily imply functional dependence of one set of processes upon another, in this case Level II upon Level I. This question has puzzled us for some time. It probably cannot be answered definitively on the basis of the evidence now available. A number of lines of evidence, however, suggest a hypothesis that seems most likely to be true.

In the first place, the wide range of correlations between Levels I and II, going from 0·20 to 0·80 (after corrections for attenuation of range) in various subpopulations, seems inconsistent with a high degree of functional dependence between the two types of ability. If the correlation were completely a result of functional dependence, it is difficult to see why the dependency should be so much higher in one population group than in another. Secondly, a high degree of functional dependence would imply an increasing correlation between Levels I and II with increasing age from early childhood to early maturity, since this is the period of marked development of Level II abilities. But we have found no evidence of greater correlation between Levels I and II with increasing age, and, if anything, slightly the opposite is the case. Subjects with high IQs but low Level I ability are somewhat less common among younger children between the ages 4 and 7 than among children beyond 10 years of age. It is as if Level I ability acts as scaffolding for the development of Level II abilities and then falls away in importance as the Level II abilities are consolidated. The child who is below average in Level I and above average in Level II will appear to be a slow developer in Level II in early childhood; he is in a sense a slow learner who, because of good Level II ability, is able thoroughly to understand and consolidate everything he learns and incorporate it into the cognitive structures we call intelligence. Later in development these Level II cognitive structures become relatively more important in educational attainments, and the child who is relatively low in Level I but high in Level II becomes much less handicapped in school than the child who shows the opposite pattern of abilities. The low I–high II child is one who learns with difficulty in school when the learning is more or less rote and affords little opportunity to grasp concepts and relationships; he is slow in acquiring skills that require sheer repetition; but once acquired, he can fully bring them to bear in logical reasoning and problem solving. He *understands* what he learns, though he may have learned it slowly. Such children, who often seem to get off to a slow start in the early grades in school, appear to become brighter and intellectually more capable as they progress in school and as the academic subject-matter makes increasing demands on conceptual and abstract thinking and involves relatively less sheer acquisition of simple skills and factual information. The high I–low II child, on the other hand, presents a very different picture. In early childhood he may appear quite bright and quick in picking up all kinds of simple skills and verbal knowledge; he may appear linguistically precocious; he may do quite well in scholastic subjects and skills that depend upon learning by repetition such as penmanship, spelling, mechanical arithmetic, memorizing the words of songs, etc., but he experiences increasing difficulty and frustration – sometimes to the point of hating school – as the conceptual and abstract demands of the subject-matter increase from earlier to later grades. It becomes increasingly difficult to understand what is learned, and, when ultimately in some academic subjects learning and understanding become one and the same, the pupil with a marked deficiency in Level II is almost totally handicapped. While one can find some small percentage of pupils of below-average Level I ability who are doing very well, say, in algebra or science, there are virtually no below-average Level II pupils who are succeeding in these subjects.

If there is at most only a slight degree of functional dependence of Level II upon Level I, as suggested by the fact that some few older children with very high Level II ability are found to be well below average in Level I, what is the basis for the correlation between Levels I and II and for the fact that it differs so markedly in different populations? The most plausible explanation is in terms of genetic assortment. If Levels I and II are controlled by two different polygenic systems, these can become assorted together to any degree in a given population through selective and assortative mating. I have rejected the idea that only Level I ability is genetically determined and that Level II abilities are learned, acquired, or developed out of Level I abilities entirely as a result of environmental influences. If this were the case, the heritability of intelligence (Level II) should not be as high as we know it to be – about 0·70 to 0·80 in present-day populations. Also, according to this notion, Level I should have much higher heritability than Level II. But the correlations obtained on siblings and twins give no indication that Level I abilities are significantly more heritable than Level II abilities, and if anything, Level I ability appears less heritable than Level II. It seems much more likely that both Level I and Level II are controlled by distinct polygenic systems and are correlated to varying degrees in different population groups because these groups have differed in the kinds of demands that would cause the genetic factor underlying Levels I and II to become assorted together. We know there is a high degree of assortative mating for intelligence in European and North American

Caucasian populations. In fact, in Western society there is probably a higher degree of assortative mating for intelligence than for any other trait.

This should not be too surprising since educational attainments, occupational level, and socioeconomic status, which are the basis for assortative mating, are highly correlated with intelligence. If Level I ability also has some correlation with occupational and socioeconomic status independently of intelligence (Level II), we should expect the genetic factors involved in Levels I and II to become associated through assortative mating. This is consistent with the observation that omnibus-type intelligence tests which involve an admixture of both Level I and Level II (e.g., the Stanford-Binet and Wechsler tests) show a higher correlation with practical criteria such as educational achievement and occupational status than do factorially more pure tests of Level II, such as the Raven Matrices. Populations that have not long been stratified educationally and occupationally would have had less assortative mating for these abilities, and consequently would show a lower correlation between them, as we find, for example, in the American Negro population as contrasted with the white. Also, Level II ability, being more highly related to the academic and intellectual demands of schooling and higher occupational status is more subject to assortative mating and consequently to genetic stratification in terms of socioeconomic status. Good Level I ability, on the other hand, is more or less equally advantageous in all cultures and walks of life and would therefore become less differentiated than Level II among various population groups.

## Physiological Basis of Levels I and II Abilities

This is quite speculative, but from what we know about the organization of the nervous system it is an interesting hypothesis that the basic locus of Level I abilities is in the electrochemical processes involved in short-term memory and the neural consolidation of memory traces. The biochemical basis of these processes is evinced, for example, in the fact that learning and memory, which involve neural consolidation, can be altered by chemical means. Level II abilities, on the other hand, are hypothesized to depend upon the structural aspects of the brain – the number of neural elements and the complexity and organization of their potential interconnections.

The evolution of the nervous system, represented in the hierarchy of phyla, is most evident in the development of Level II processes. The growth of mental ability in the individual similarly reflects largely the gradual emergence of Level II processes from infancy to maturity.

G. Stanley Hall's famous dictum that 'ontogeny recapitulates phylogeny' appears to hold true for mental as well as physical development. The growth curves of Level I and II are quite different, with Level I approaching its developmental asymptote at an earlier age than Level II.

## Theoretical Overview

The picture is that of a very fundamental division of mental abilities into Level I (learning and memory) and Level II (intelligence, i.e., analytical understanding, reasoning, abstraction, conceptual thinking). Individual differences in both Levels I and II are viewed as due mainly to independent polygenic factors. The distributions of Levels I and II abilities in the population are approximately normal. The correlation between Levels I and II is due mainly to the common assortment of the genes involved in the two types of ability. (But there is also some moderate degree of functional dependence of Level II upon Level I.) The genetic correlation differs in various subpopulations, being lower in the low SES segment of the population and higher in the middle and upper-middle-class segment. The correlation is lower in the American Negro than in the white population. Because education makes greater demands on Level II than on Level I and the occupational hierarchy and socioeconomic status are highly related to educational attainments in Western societies, there is a much greater mean difference between social classes in Level II than Level I. While Level I is distributed about very similar means in lower and upper SES groups, the means of the Level II distributions may differ by one standard deviation or more. (One standard deviation is equivalent to about 15 IQ points.)

Mental retardation of the type which is a part of the normal distribution of abilities in the population can be described as *primary* retardation if it involves marked deficiency in both Levels I and II and as *secondary* retardation if there is a deficiency only in Level II ability. Secondary retardates often appear normally bright and capable of learning and achievement in many situations, although they invariably experience great difficulties in school work under the traditional curricula and methods of instruction. Many secondary retardates who are regarded as backward children while in school later become socially and economically adequate persons once they are out of the academic situation. Primary retardates, on the other hand, appear to be much more handicapped in the world of work. A serious shortcoming of ordinary IQ tests is that they measure predominantly Level II and fail to distinguish between primary and secondary retardation. Tests that reliably measure both Levels I and II should be developed for use in schools, in personnel selection, and in the armed forces. This formulation also has important implications for the education of children now popularly called culturally disadvantaged, most of whom have normal Level I ability but are often quite far below average in Level II. Such children might benefit educationally from instructional methods which make the acquisition of scholastic skills less dependent upon Level II abilities and more fully engage Level I abilities as a means of raising their educational attainments.

# Estimation of the Limits of Heritability of Traits by Comparison of Monozygotic and Dizygotic Twins

This paper has three aims: (1) to present a new formula for extracting heritability estimates from twin data; (2) to show the results of the application of the formula to data from past studies of the heritability of intelligence, scholastic achievement, personality traits, and physical characteristics; and (3) to urge that heritability estimates be obtained in all large-scale educational testing programs, in the standardization of intelligence, aptitude, and educational achievement tests, and in the Selective Service and Armed Forces qualification tests.

*Previous Estimates of Heritability.* Although the twin method in itself does not provide sufficient information for testing detailed genetic models, it provides both the most efficient and the least ambiguous basis for an overall estimate of heritability of quantitative traits (Vandenberg, 1966). Heritability $(h^2)$ is defined here as the proportion of phenotypic variance attributable to genotypic variance, i.e., $h^2 = V_G/V_P$. The comparison of monozygotic (MZ) twins reared together and dizygotic (DZ) twins reared together is much more feasible and has been a much more common practice than the study of MZ twins reared apart. MZ twins reared apart are rare and difficult to find (Shields, 1962; Burt, 1966). Estimating heritability from MZ twins reared apart has the one advantage that it presents little theoretical difficulty, provided one can assume zero correlation between the relevant environmental effects acting on the separated twins, in which case $h^2 = r_{MZ}$, the intraclass correlation between MZ twins.

The prevailing method of estimating heritability from MZ and

DZ twins has been by means of the $H$ index devised by Holzinger (1929). That Holzinger's $H$ index is not a satisfactory estimate of $h^2$ is now generally recognized in behavior genetics, but the precise nature of the inadequacy of the $H$ index and the problem of estimating $h^2$ from MZ and DZ twin data have remained conceptually obscure (Neel and Schull, 1954; Fuller and Thompson, 1960; Gottesman, 1963; Vandenberg, 1966). Nichols (1965) proposed an improvement on the $H$ index, called the $HR$ index, but it, too, is unsatisfactory as an index of $h^2$. One serious criticism of $H$ and $HR$ is that one is not a monotonic function of the other, and neither is a monotonic function of $h^2$.* Vandenberg has proposed

* The differences between $h^2$, $H$, and $HR$ can be understood precisely only in terms of the actual components of genetic and environmental variance that enter into each of these indices of heritability. If heritability is defined as $h^2$, the following analysis shows that Holzinger's $H$ and Nichols's $HR$ are not proper indices of $h^2$.

The total phenotypic variance, $V_p$, may be partitioned into genetic and environmental components, $V_G$ and $V_E$. (Actually $V_p = V_G + V_E + V_{Error}$, but for the sake of simplicity we will omit the error variance in the following analysis.) The total genetic variance, $V_G$, may be partitioned into two components: genetic variance *between* families (or between the means of the various sets of twins), $V_{GB}$, and genetic variance *within* families, $V_{GW}$. Thus, $V_G = V_{GB} + V_{GW}$. Similarly, the total environmental variance, $V_E$, may be partitioned into *between* families and *within* families components, $V_{EB}$ and $V_{EW}$. Thus, $V_E = V_{EB} + V_{EW}$.

In terms of these variance components

$$h^2 = \frac{V_{GB} + V_{GW}}{V_{GB} + V_{GW} + V_{EB} + V_{EW}} = \frac{V_G}{V_G + V_E} = \frac{V_G}{V_P}$$

$$H = \frac{k \, V_{GB}}{(1 - k) \, V_{GB} + V_{GW} + V_{EW}}$$

where $k = 1 - \dfrac{V_{GCDZ}}{V_{GB}}$

and $V_{GCDZ}$ is the genetic variance that dizygotic twins have in common. Under random mating $V_{GCDZ}/V_{GB} = \frac{1}{2}$. With positive assortative mating $V_{GCDZ}/V_{GB} > \frac{1}{2}$, and, therefore $k < \frac{1}{2}$. Thus, the greater the degree of assortative mating, the more that $H$ underestimates $h^2$. But even when mating is random (and $k = \frac{1}{2}$), $H$ does not equal $h^2$ for most sets of values of the variance components.

$$HR = \frac{V_{GB}}{V_{GB} + V_{EB}}$$

Only under the unrealistic assumptions that $V_{GB} = V_{GW}$ (i.e., random mating) and $V_{EB} = V_{EW}$ (i.e., environmental differences *within* families using $F$ (the variance ratio) as a test of the significance of $Vw_{DZ}/Vw_{MZ}$ (DZ within-pair variance/MZ within-pair variance), but this is as faulty as an index of heritability as the $H$ index itself, since $F$ is a linear function of $H$.[1] Determining the variance ratio $F$, however, is an essential step prior to computing $h^2$; if $F$ is not statistically significant, $h^2$ cannot be presumed to differ significantly from zero.[2, 3]

*A New Formula for $h^2$.* The rationale of the new formula for $h^2$ based on the comparison of MZ and DZ twins is developed in the following 13 points. (In all cases, the correlations are corrected for unreliability. Also, if $h^2$ is to be generalized to a population, it should be established that the total variances for either halves of the MZ and DZ pairs do not differ significantly from an estimate of the population variance.)

(1)  Total true-score phenotypic variance (i.e., total variance − error variance):

$$V_P = V_G + V_E + V_e, \tag{1}$$

where $V_P$ = phenotypic variance, $V_G$ = hereditary (genotypic) variance, $V_E$ = systematic environmental variance (between families), $V_e$ = unsystematic or random environmental variance (within families).

(2)  Dividing equation (1) by $V_P$:

$$1{\cdot}00 = h^2 + E^2 + e^2,$$

---

are as great as *between* families) does $HR = h^2$. Under these conditions $H < h^2$. It is quite easy to state in words just what $h^2$ and $HR$ consist of (though they differ), but to try to state $H$ in words shows that, although it can be made mathematically explicit, it is conceptually very muddled in terms of expressing the relative contributions of genetic and environmental factors to the total variance.

Since $H$ and $HR$ are not monotonic functions of $h^2$, there is no transformation by which one can convert values derived from one index to the other.

[1]  $F = 1/(1 - H)$.

[2]  The validity of $F$ as a test of statistical significance in this case requires the assumption that the distributions corresponding to $Vw_{DZ}$ and $Vw_{MZ}$ do not differ significantly in kurtosis.

[3]  $h^2$ cannot be computed in those rare cases where $r_{MZ} < r_{DZ}$, since this would yield negative heritability. If $r_{MZ}$ is significantly less than $r_{DZ}$, one reasonable interpretation is that for the particular trait in question MZ twins take on complementary (rather than similar) roles to a greater degree than do DZ twins.

where $h^2 = V_G/V_P$ = heritability (the proportion of total variance due to heredity).

$E^2 = V_E/V_P$ = systematic environmental effects (proportion of total variance due to environmental differences between families (or conversely, environmental variance common to members of the same family).

$e^2 = V_e/V_P$ = unsystematic or random environmental effects (proportion of within family environmental variance).

(3) Holzinger's $H$ index:

$$H = \frac{r_{MZ} - r_{DZ}}{1 - r_{DZ}}.$$

(4) Nichols' $HR$ index:

$$HR = \frac{2(r_{MZ} - r_{DZ})}{r_{MZ}}.$$

(5) $H$, $HR$, and $h^2$ are not monotonic functions of one another. For example:

| $r_{MZ}$ | $r_{DZ}$ | $H$ | $HR$ | $h^2$ |
|------|------|------|------|------|
| 1·00 | 0·50 | 1·00 | 1·00 | 1·00 |
| 0·40 | 0·20 | 0·25 | 1·00 | 0·40 |
| 0·90 | 0·80 | 0·50 | 0·22 | 0·20 |
| 1·00 | 0·99 | 1·00 | 0·02 | 0·02 |

(6) Correlation ($r$) between sets of individuals, $A$ and $B$, on a given trait:

$$r_{AB} = \rho_{G_{AB}} h^2 + \rho_{E_{AB}} E^2,$$

where $\rho_{G_{AB}}$ = genetic correlation between $A$ and $B$.

$\rho_{B_{AB}}$ = correlation between relevant effects of environments of $A$ and $B$ (i.e., degree of environmental similarity).

(7) Generalized formula for $h^2$ based on comparison of two groups of paired individuals ($AB$ and $CD$) such that $\rho_{G_{AB}} > \rho_{G_{CD}}$:

$$h^2 = \frac{r_{AB} - r_{CD} - E^2(\rho_{E_{AB}} - \rho_{E_{CD}})}{\rho_{G_{AB}} - \rho_{G_{CD}}}.$$

(8) Correlations between MZ twins reared together (MZT) and reared apart (MZA), with assumption that for MZT, $\rho_E = 1$ and for MZA, $\rho_E = 0$. For both $\rho_G = 1$. (a) $r_{MZT} = (1)h^2 + (1)E^2$. (b) $r_{MZA} = (1)h^2 + (0)E^2 = h^2$.

(9) Correlation between DZ twins reared together:

$$r_{DZT} = \rho_{oo} h^2 + (1)E^2,$$

where $\rho_{oo}$ = the genetic correlation between offspring (siblings).

(10) Estimation of $h$ from comparison of MZ and DZ twins, with assumption that $\rho_{E_{MZ}} = \rho_{E_{DZ}}$.

$$(a)\ r_{MZ} - r_{DZ} = (h^2 + E^2) - (\rho_{oo}h^2 + E^2). \quad (b)\ h^2 = \frac{r_{MZ} - r_{DZ}}{1 - \rho_{oo}}.$$

(11) Proportion of total variance due to systematic (between families) environmental differences:

$$E^2 = \frac{r_{DZ} - \rho_\infty r_{MZ}}{1 - \rho_{oo}}.$$

(12) Proportion of total variance due to unsystematic (within families) environmental variance:

$$e^2 = 1 - h^2 - E^2 = 1 - r_{MZ}.$$

(13) $\rho_{oo}$ (the genetic correlation between siblings or DZ twins) derived from the genetic correlation between non-inbred parents $(\rho_{PP})$ (Li, 1955):*

$$\rho_{oo} = \frac{1}{1 + \frac{1}{2}\rho_{PP}} \cdot \tfrac{1}{2}(1 + \rho_{PP}) = \frac{1 + \rho_{PP}}{2 + \rho_{PP}}.$$

* This simple formula is a conservative approximation to the genetic correlation between offsprings, $\rho_{oo}$, since it assumes that the assortative mating occurs for the first time in the parental generation, all previous generations having random mating. The larger the number of previous generations with assortative mating, the higher will be the value of $\rho_{oo}$, up to a limit. When assortative mating has been maintained at a more or less constant level for many generations, the population is said to be at equilibrium under assortative mating. Under this condition, for any given equilibrium value of assortative mating (i.e., the phenotypic parental correlation), the genetic correlation between offspring (full siblings or dizygotic twins) is given by the following formula, which has been thoroughly explicated by Crow and Felsenstein (1968); the following is an algebraic equivalent of their formula number 49 (p. 95), which obviates explaining here their different sets of symbols:

$$\rho_{oo} = \frac{h_N^2\, V_t \left( \dfrac{h_N^2\, r_{pp}}{1 - h_N^2\, r_{pp}} + \tfrac{1}{2} \right) + \tfrac{1}{4}(h_B^2 - h_N^2)V_t}{V_t + \left( \dfrac{h_N^2\, r_{pp}}{1 - h_N^2\, r_{pp}} \right) h_N^2\, V_t}$$

where $h_N^2$ = narrow heritability
$h_B^2$ = broad heritability
$V_t$ = total variance
$r_{pp}$ = parental correlation.

In terms of the traditional variance components model, the proposed formula yields a true estimate of $h^2$ within the limits of sampling error, although it should be pointed out that this estimate of $h^2$ also contains any variance attributable to the interaction of genotype and environment. However, the formula apparently yields the maximum amount of information concerning variance components that can be obtained from $r_{MZ}$ and $r_{DZ}$. Furthermore, the new formula for $h^2$ has the advantage of taking account of the genetic effects of assortative mating. The parameter $\rho_{oo}$ (genetic correlation between siblings) may be estimated for a given trait from theoretical or empirical considerations of both.[1] Taking account of $\rho_{oo}$, the genetic correlation between siblings, permits greater precision in estimating $h^2$ when there is some basis for determining the degree of assortative mating for the trait in question. In lieu of a precise estimate of assortative mating, one can obtain the extreme limits of $h^2$ for a given set of data from some consideration of the reasonable bounds of assortative mating. For most traits, especially those in the abilities domain, the extreme limits would be $\rho_{oo} = 0 \cdot 50$ (for siblings resulting from random mating) to $\rho_{oo} = 0 \cdot 66$ (for siblings resulting, theoretically of course, from a self-mated mother). For some traits in which there might be negative assortative mating, $\rho_{oo}$ could take values less than $0 \cdot 50$. Negative assortative mating may occur for traits in the personality domain, where certain traits may be complementary in marital couples and thus negatively correlated, such as dominance-submissiveness.

*Results.* Heritability estimates based on the various formulas are shown in Table 1. The first part of the table shows results from a number of studies (Holzinger, 1929; Newman, Freeman and

---

[1] The parameter $\rho$ includes more than what geneticists generally refer to as the genetic correlation; $\rho$ is actually a weighted average of the proportions of additive, dominance, and epistatic sources of genetic variance. Therefore, $\rho$ is a complex quantity whose value is close to $\frac{1}{2}$ but is not known precisely. Because of dominance and epistasis, $\rho$ may be less than $\frac{1}{2}$ under random mating, and if dominance and epistasis are large relative to the additive genic effect, $\rho$ could be less than $\frac{1}{2}$ even under assortative mating. The total genetic variance, $h^2$, cannot be precisely analyzed into additive, dominance, and interactive effects on the basis of twin data alone. Jinks and Fulker (1970), however, have proposed a method for estimating genotype × environment interaction from twin data. The serious student is urged to study the article by Jinks and Fulker, which is the most thorough and sophisticated treatment of heritability in the recent literature. The Mendelian algebra which forms the very basis of heritability estimation is admirably treated in a recent article by Burt (1971).

TABLE 1  **Summary of Twin Correlations and Heritability Estimates for Intelligence, Scholastic Performance, and Physical Characteristics**

| Test or measures | Correlations[a,b] | | | | | Heritability Estimates[b] | | | | | | | | | | |
| --- | --- | --- | --- | --- | --- | --- | --- | --- | --- | --- | --- | --- | --- | --- | --- | --- |
| | MZ Twins r | MZ Twins N | DZ Twins r | DZ Twins N | $F^c$ | H | HR | $\rho_{00}=0.50$ $h^2$ | $E^2$ | $\rho_{00}=0.55$ $h^2$ | $E^2$ | $\rho_{00}=0.60$ $h^2$ | $E^2$ | $\rho_{00}=0.66$ $h^2$ | $E^2$ | $e^2$ |
| Stanford-Binet IQ 1 | 97 | 83 | 56 | 172 | 14·28 | 93 | 85 | 82 | 15 | 91 | 06 | (102) | (−06) | (120) | (−24) | 03 |
| S-B IQ, adjusted scores 1 | 98 | 83 | 58 | 172 | 20·00 | 95 | 83 | 83 | 15 | 89 | 06 | (100) | (−06) | (118) | (−23) | 05 |
| Binet IQ 2 | 93 | 50 | 66 | 52 | 4·61 | 78 | 57 | 53 | 40 | 59 | 34 | 66 | 27 | 78 | 15 | 07 |
| Binet IQ 3 | 96 | 50 | 67 | 50 | 7·75 | 87 | 59 | 57 | 39 | 63 | 33 | 71 | 25 | 84 | 12 | 04 |
| Otis IQ 3 | 97 | 50 | 65 | 50 | 11·24 | 91 | 65 | 63 | 34 | 70 | 27 | 79 | 18 | 93 | 04 | 03 |
| Various intelligence measures 4 | 92 | 14$^d$ | 56 | 11$^e$ | 5·26 | 81 | 78 | 72 | 20 | 80 | 12 | 90 | 02 | (105) | (−14) | 08 |
| Dominoes Test and Mill Hill Vocabulary 5 | 80 | 36 | 54 | 8 | 2·31 | 57 | 66 | 53 | 27 | 58 | 22 | 66 | 14 | 77 | 03 | 20 |
| Primary Mental Abilities | | | | | | | | | | | | | | | | |
| Composite 6 | 79 | 26 | 44 | 26 | 2·80 | 64 | 96 | 76 | 03 | (84) | (−05) | (95) | (−16) | (111) | (−32) | 21 |
| Swedish Military Induction Test 7 | 95 | 215 | 74 | 42 | 5·05 | 80 | 44 | 42 | 53 | 47 | 48 | 53 | 42 | 62 | 33 | 05 |
| National Merit Scholarship Qualification Test 8 | 92 | 687 | 66 | 482 | 4·02 | 75 | 55 | 51 | 41 | 56 | 35 | 63 | 28 | 74 | 17 | 08 |
| Educational age 3 | 94 | 50 | 73 | 50 | 4·38 | 77 | 44 | 41 | 53 | 46 | 46 | 52 | 42 | 61 | 33 | 0 |
| General scholastic achievement 1 | 95 | 83 | 87 | 172 | 2·42 | 59 | 16 | 15 | 80 | 16 | 78 | 19 | 76 | 22 | 73 | 05 |
| Reading and spelling 1 | 99 | 83 | 97 | 172 | 3·10 | 68 | 04 | 04 | 95 | 05 | 94 | 05 | 94 | 06 | 93 | 01 |
| Reading 9 | 94 | 134 | 65 | 180 | 5·49 | 82 | 61 | 57 | 37 | 63 | 31 | 71 | 23 | 84 | 10 | 06 |
| Arithmetic 1 | 91 | 83 | 79 | 172 | 2·23 | 55 | 26 | 23 | 67 | 25 | 66 | 29 | 62 | 34 | 57 | 09 |
| Arithmetic 9 | 92 | 134 | 55 | 181 | 5·38 | 81 | 80 | 74 | 18 | 82 | 10 | (92) | (−00) | (108) | (−17) | 08 |
| Standing height 1 | 96 | 83 | 47 | 172 | 13·16 | 92 | 102 | (98) | (−02) | (109) | (−13) | (123) | (−27) | (144) | (−48) | 04 |
| Standing height 3 | 93 | 50 | 64 | 50 | 5·21 | 81 | 62 | 57 | 36 | 64 | 30 | 72 | 21 | 84 | 09 | 07 |
| Weight 1 | 93 | 83 | 59 | 172 | 5·85 | 83 | 73 | 68 | 25 | 76 | 18 | 85 | 08 | (100) | (−07) | 07 |
| Weight 3 | 92 | 50 | 63 | 50 | 4·44 | 78 | 62 | 57 | 35 | 64 | 28 | 72 | 20 | 84 | 08 | 08 |
| Head length 1 | 96 | 83 | 50 | 172 | 12·50 | 92 | 96 | 92 | 04 | (102) | (−06) | (115) | (−19) | (135) | (−39) | 04 |
| Head length 3 | 91 | 83 | 58 | 50 | 4·63 | 78 | 72 | 65 | 26 | 73 | 18 | 82 | 09 | (96) | (−05) | 09 |
| Head breadth 1 | 98 | 83 | 54 | 172 | 22·73 | 96 | 90 | 88 | 10 | 98 | 00 | (110) | (−12) | (129) | (−31) | 02 |
| Head breadth 3 | 89 | 50 | 55 | 50 | 4·06 | 75 | 77 | 69 | 20 | 76 | 13 | 86 | 03 | (101) | (−12) | 11 |
| Eye color 1 | 100 | 50 | 52 | 50 | ∞ | 100 | 96 | 96 | 04 | (107) | (−07) | (120) | (−20) | (141) | (−41) | 00 |

[a] Correlations of mental and scholastic tests corrected for attenuation; correlations for physical measurements not corrected. Decimals omitted. [b] Decimals omitted. [c] $F$, the variance ratio of DZ within-pair variance/MZ within-pair variance. [d] Median of 14 independent studies. [e] Median of 11 independent studies.
1, Burt (1958); 2, Holzinger (1929); 3, Newman, Freeman and Holzinger (1937); 4, Erlenmeyer-Kimling and Jarvik (1963); 5, Shields (1962); 6, Blewett (1954); 7, Husén (1965); 8, Nichols (1959); 9, Husén (1960).

Holzinger, 1937; Burt, 1955, 1958; Husen, 1959, 1960; Shields, 1962; Erlenmeyer-Kimling and Jarvik, 1963; Nichols, 1965), using a variety of intelligence tests in different populations. The most extreme limits of $h^2$ to be found in this table summarizing all the major twin studies using intelligence tests range from 0·42 (Swedish Military Induction Test) to 0·93 (Otis IQ test).[1] In considering this wide range of values, it should be kept in mind that heritability estimates are specific both to the population from which the twin samples are drawn and to the particular test used for measuring intelligence.

The most representative estimates are those based on the data summarized by Erlenmeyer-Kimling and Jarvik (1963), which represent the median values of all the twin studies reported in the literature up to 1963. We see that for these data the extreme lower and upper limits of $h^2$ (going from random-mating to self-mating) are 0·72 and 0·90. Since there is known to be assortative mating for intelligence, the best estimates of $h^2$ would be obtained from values of $\rho_{oo}$ (sibling genetic correlation) close to 0·55, resulting from a genetic correlation of 0·25 between parents. This yields $h^2 = 0·80$, $E^2 = 0·12$, and $e^2 = 0·08$. Thus, according to these data – the average of all the major twin studies – four times as much of the variance in measured intelligence is attributable to heredity as to environment.

This statement can be expressed, also, in terms of the average difference in IQ between persons paired at random from the population.[2] Given an intelligence test like the Stanford-Binet, with a standard deviation of 16 IQ points in the white population of the United States, the average difference among such persons would be 18 IQ points. If everyone inherited the same genotype for intelligence (i.e., $h^2 = 0$), but all nongenetic environmental variance (i.e., $E^2 + e^2$) remained as is, people would differ, on the

[1] Note that for some values of $\rho_{oo}$, $h^2$ exceeds 1·00 and $E^2$ becomes a negative value. These 'impossible' values (enclosed in parentheses in Table 1) set the upper limit of the estimate of $\rho_{oo}$.

[2] Assuming a normal distribution in the population, the mean absolute difference between all possible pairs of scores in the distribution is given by Gini's formula: $|\bar{x}| = 2\sigma/\sqrt{\pi}$ (Kendall, M. G., *The Advanced Theory of Statistics* (New York: Hafner, 1960), 3rd ed., vol. 1, pp. 241-242). The mean absolute difference when the proportion of variance attributable to heredity, $h^2$, is removed $= 2\sqrt{\sigma^2(1-h^2)}/\sqrt{\pi}$.

average, by 8 IQ points. On the other hand, if hereditary variance remained as is, but there were no environmental variation between families (i.e., $E^2 = 0$), the average difference among people would be 17 IQ points. If *all* nongenetic sources of individual differences were removed (i.e., $E^2 + e^2 = 0$), the average intellectual difference among people would be 16 IQ points. (Error in measurement has been subtracted from all these figures.) These results decidedly contradict the popular notion that the environment is of predominant importance as a cause of individual differences in measured intelligence in our present society. The results show, furthermore, that current IQ tests certainly do reflect innate intellectual potential (to a degree indicated by $h^2$), and that biological inheritance is far more important than the social-psychological environment in determining differences in IQs. This is not to say, however, that as yet undiscovered biological, chemical, or psychological forms of intervention in the genetic or developmental processes could not diminish the relative importance of heredity as a determinant of intellectual differences.

*Scholastic achievement.* The middle section of Table I summarizes studies based on tests of scholastic achievement. In general, individual differences in scholastic performance are determined less than half as much by heredity than are individual differences in intelligence.[1] The largest source of individual differences in school achievement is the environmental differences *between* families. Variance in achievement due to differential environmental effects *within* families is extremely small.

The fact that school achievement is highly susceptible to environmental influences, while intelligence apparently is not, suggests important implications for education that have not yet been explored.

*Physical characteristics.* The third section of Table 1 is interesting for comparative purposes, showing results for highly heritable physical characteristics. (Since for these there is probably little assortative mating, the most plausible values of $\rho_{oo}$ would lie between 0·05 and 0·55). It can be seen that overall the heritability

[1] Rank in high school graduating class has values of $h^2$ ranging from 0·16 to 0·24 for males (for $\rho_{oo} = 0·50$-0·66) and 0·28 to 0·42 for females; corresponding values of $E^2$ for males are 0·67 to 0·59 and for females 0·62 to 0·48.

of intelligence is closer to that for physical characteristics such as height, weight, and head length than to scholastic achievement.

Figure 1 presents these results graphically. The shaded area is the range of possible values of $h^2$ when $\rho_{oo}$ varies between 0·50 and 0·66. This form of graphic presentation may be useful for comparing various tests given to the same population or for

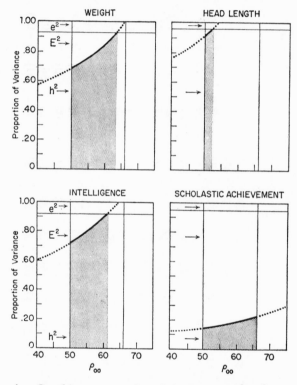

FIGURE 1. *Graphic representation of the limits of $h^2$, $E^2$, and $e^2$. The values are computed between the range of $\rho_{oo} = 0·50$ (sibling genetic correlation under random-mating) and $\rho_{oo} = 0·66$ sibling genetic correlation under self-mating). The shaded area shows the actual possible values for a particular study yielding specific values for $r_{M}z$ and $r_{D}z$. The dotted portion of each curve represents a range of values beyond 'reasonable' limits for the traits in question. (Data: weight, head length, intelligence, scholastic achievement.)*

TABLE 2  **Heritability of Personality Traits**

| Personality scales | Correlations† | | | | Heritability Estimates* | | | | | | | | |
|---|---|---|---|---|---|---|---|---|---|---|---|---|---|
| | | | | | $\rho_{PP} = -1.00$ $\rho_{oo} = 0.00$ | | $\rho_{PP} = -0.66$ $\rho_{oo} = 0.25$ | | $\rho_{PP} = 0.00$ $\rho_{oo} = 0.50$ | | $\rho_{PP} = 1.00$ $\rho_{oo} = 0.66$ | | |
| MMPI‡ | MZ | DZ | H | HR | $h^2$ | $E^2$ | $h^2$ | $E^2$ | $h^2$ | $E^2$ | $h^2$ | $E^2$ | $e^2$ |
| Social introversion | 45 | 12 | 37 | 147 | 33 | 12 | 44 | 01 | (66) | (−21) | (99) | (−54) | 55 |
| Depression | 44 | 14 | 35 | 136 | 30 | 14 | 40 | 04 | (60) | (−16) | (90) | (−46) | 56 |
| Psychaesthenia | 41 | 11 | 34 | 146 | 30 | 11 | 40 | 01 | (60) | (−19) | (90) | (−49) | 59 |
| Psychopathic deviate | 48 | 27 | 28 | 88 | 21 | 27 | 28 | 20 | 42 | 06 | (63) | (−15) | 52 |
| Schizophrenia | 44 | 24 | 27 | 91 | 20 | 24 | 27 | 17 | 40 | 04 | (60) | (−16) | 56 |
| Paranoia | 27 | 08 | 21 | 141 | 19 | 08 | 25 | 02 | (38) | (−11) | (57) | (−30) | 73 |
| Hysteria | 37 | 23 | 19 | 76 | 14 | 23 | 19 | 18 | 28 | 09 | (32) | (−05) | 63 |
| Hypochondriasis | 41 | 28 | 17 | 63 | 13 | 28 | 17 | 24 | 26 | 15 | 39 | 02 | 59 |
| Hypomania | 32 | 18 | 17 | 88 | 14 | 18 | 19 | 13 | 28 | 04 | (42) | (−10) | 68 |
| Masculinity-femininity | 41 | 35 | 09 | 29 | 06 | 35 | 08 | 33 | 12 | 29 | 18 | 23 | 59 |
| CPI§ | | | | | | | | | | | | | |
| Self-control | 56 | 27 | 40 | 105 | 29 | 27 | 38 | 18 | (58) | 02 | (87) | (−13) | 44 |
| Rigidity | 47 | 13 | 39 | 147 | 34 | 13 | 45 | 02 | (68) | (−21) | (102) | (−55) | 53 |
| Dominance | 58 | 13 | 52 | 155 | 45 | 13 | (60) | (−02) | (90) | (−32) | (135) | (−77) | 42 |
| Responsibility | 57 | 29 | 39 | 98 | 28 | 29 | 37 | 20 | 56 | 01 | (84) | (−27) | 43 |
| Intellectual efficiency | 59 | 27 | 43 | 107 | 32 | 27 | 43 | 16 | (64) | (−05) | (96) | (−37) | 41 |

* Decimals omitted.

† Not corrected for attenuation. Decimals omitted.

‡ Minnesota Multiphasic Personality Inventory data ($N = 120$ MZ, 132 DZ pairs) from Vandenberg (1966).

§ California Personality Inventory data (males only, $N = 207$ MZ, 120 DZ pairs) from Nichols (1966).

comparing various subgroups in the population on a particular test. For statistical purposes, confidence bands[1] can be placed around the lines separating $h^2$, $E^2$, and $e^2$.

*Personality traits.* Table 2 summarizes the heritability estimates for a number of personality scales. For most of these personality traits 'impossible' values of $h^2$ and $E^2$ result when $\rho_{PP} > 0$, that is, when there is positive assortative mating. It may well be that this genetic additive model is grossly inappropriate for dealing with heritability of personality traits. The personality measures differ most conspicuously from intelligence, scholastic achievement, and physical traits in yielding large values of $e^2$ (within family environmental variance) as compared with $E^2$ (between family of environmental variance). Also, $h^2$ shows much greater sex differences for personality traits than for abilities. In terms of the present formulation of $h^2$, there are obviously serious difficulties in making sense out of the twin data on personality scales. Precisely where the trouble lies is not understood, but the present formulation at least highlights the problem.

*Further applications of $h^2$.* Finally, because the estimation of heritability provides important information concerning sources of variance in our tests, I would urge that provision for assessing heritability become a routine part of large-scale educational testing programs, test standardization, and ability testing in the Armed Forces. Modern data-processing techniques now make this entirely feasible. The practice would require that testees carefully identify all their blood relations who are likely to be in the tested population: parents, siblings, half siblings, cousins, and especially twins. The zygosity of twins can now be determined with better than 90 percent accuracy by means of a brief questionnaire. We know that tests of ability differ widely in the degree to which they reflect innate factors on the one hand, or social, cultural, and educational

---

[1] The confidence limits for $h^2$ are determined by using the standard errors of $r_{MZ}$ and $r_{DZ}$ $(SE_r = (1 - r^2)\sqrt{N - 1})$. The upper and lower limits of $r_{MZ}$ and $r_{DZ}$ are set by $r \pm (x)SE_r$, where $x$ is the number of $SE$'s for a given level of confidence, $P$. From these upper and lower limiting values of both $r_{MZ}$ and $r_{DZ}$, the upper and lower limits of $h^2$ are calculated. The probability that the true value of $h^2$ lies outside these limits is $P^2$. Essentially the same procedure is used to obtain confidence limits for $E^2$ and $e^2$.

influences on the other. Heritability estimates thus can provide important information concerning major classes of variables determining individual differences on a given test.

One criterion of a 'culture-free' or 'culture-fair' test is the degree to which it yields high estimates of $h^2$ in a population in which there is actually a wide range of environmental variation. Do culturally or economically disadvantaged minority groups within our population show lower heritability than more advantaged groups in test scores used for job placement, for educational selection, and for determining qualification for the Armed Services? Although $h^2$ has no necessary connection with a test's validity for predicting some criterion, such as suitability for the Armed Forces or success in college, $h^2$ should be of great interest to educators, since $1 - h^2$ is an indication of the proportion of variance in abilities we potentially can influence by presently existing educational and social psychological means. Large-scale testing programs should try to account for as many of the major sources of variance in test scores as possible. Three of these sources are defined by $h^2$, $E^2$, and $e^2$.

# IQs of Identical Twins Reared Apart

Comparison of monozygotic (MZ) twins reared apart is conceptually the simplest method of estimating the broad heritability of a characteristic. Theoretically, the characteristic's total phenotypic variance ($V_P$) in the population is analyzable into a genetic component ($V_G$), a nongenetic (or 'environmental') component ($V_E$), a component attributable to the covariance of genotypes and environments ($V_{GE}$), a component due to the interaction (i.e., the non-additive effects) of genetic and environmental factors ($V_I$), and a variance component due to measurement error ($V_e$). Thus:

$$V_P = V_G + V_E + V_{GE} + V_I + V_e.$$

Heritability in the broad sense is defined as $h^2 = V_G/V_P$, or, if corrected for attenuation (errors of measurement), as

$$h_c{}^2 = V_G/(V_P - V_e).$$

The correlation between pairs of individuals can be expressed as the proportion of the variance components that the members of each pair have in common:

$$r = \frac{\text{Sum of Variance Components in Common}}{\text{Total Variance}}$$

In an idealized experiment to estimate $h^2$, therefore, we would assign each member of a pair of genetically identical individuals to different environments entirely at random at the moment of conception, and then determine the correlation between the pairs at some later stage of their development. Since the environmental conditions are randomized there would be no correlation between

307

pairs due to environmental effects and there would be no correlation between genotypes and environments, at least at the outset. (Different genotypes can influence the environment differently, thereby producing some genotype × environment covariance. This component is usually regarded as part of the genetic variance in heritability studies of socially conditioned characteristics.) $V_G$, therefore, is the only component our idealized pair would share in common, and so the correlation between them would be equal to $V_G/V_P = h^2$.

The closest approximation to this idealized experiment in reality is the study of MZ twins separated soon after birth, or in infancy and early childhood, and reared separately. Unfortunately, in such studies there is always some uncertainty about the degree to which the nongenetic variance components are common to the separated twins. There is little, if any, real doubt in the major studies about the genetic component. Errors in the determination of zygosity in these studies are highly improbable. Any such errors, of course, would subtract from $V_G$ and thus would result in a lower value of $h^2$. The nongenetic components are much more questionable. There is never truly random assignment of separated twins to their foster homes. Some separated twins are reared, for example, in different branches of the same family. And twins put out for adoption rarely go into the poorest homes. Furthermore, separated twins have the same mother prenatally, and to whatever extent there are favorable or unfavorable maternal conditions that might affect the twins' intrauterine development, these conditions are presumably more alike for twins than for singletons born to different mothers. On the other hand, twin correlation due to common nongenetic factors is counteracted to some unknown extent by effects occurring immediately after fertilization which create inequalities in the development of the twins. Darlington (1954) points to nuclear, nucleocytoplasmic, and cytoplasmic differences occurring in the first stages of cell division that would cause MZ twins to be less alike than their genotype at the moment of fertilization. Some of these conditions of embryological asymmetry do not affect singletons or dizygotic (DZ) twins. Partly for this reason DZ twins are more alike in birth weight than MZ twins. Although the biologic discordances referred to by Darlington affect only a minority of MZ twins, he concludes that their total effect is sufficient to lead to a gross underestimate in all twin studies of the force of genetic determination.

The correlation between MZ twins reared apart, therefore, cannot be taken at its face value as the most valid estimate of $h^2$. It must be checked against estimates of $h^2$ obtained by other means which involve more complex formulas (and often additional assumptions) for estimating heritability from a variety of kinship correlations, including unrelated children reared together and the comparison of correlations for MZ and DZ twins. Estimates of $h^2$ from MZ twins reared apart are, so to speak, cross-validated when similar values of $h^2$ are found by other methods, assuming that similar biases do not operate in the same direction or that they are statistically controlled. There is, in fact, quite substantial agreement among the various methods and types of data for estimating heritability. Using practically all the appropriate data to be found in the literature, heritability estimates for intelligence are distributed about an average value of close to 0·8 (Jensen, 1969). MZ twins reared apart show a correlation of similar magnitude for intelligence.

The questions posed by the present study are: do the major researches on MZ twins reared apart show consistency with one another in estimates of the heritability of intelligence? Are the main parameters of these samples sufficiently alike to permit the data from the several studies to be analyzed as a total composite that would allow new and stronger inferences than would be possible for any one of the studies viewed by itself?

## Method

The published literature contains only four major studies of the intelligence of MZ twins reared apart (Newman *et al.*, 1937; Shields, 1962; Juel-Nielsen, 1965; Burt, 1966). There are a few single sets of separated MZ twins scattered in the literature, but they are either psychiatric cases or do not present adequate intelligence test data for the purpose of the present analysis. The four major studies, based on twins from the Caucasian populations of England, Denmark, and the United States, comprise a total of 122 sets of MZ twins separated early in life and reared apart. Details concerning the twin's sex, age of separation, environmental circumstances, case histories, and so on, are to be found in the original publications. The present analysis is based on the individual intelligence test scores of the 244 subjects.

## THE DATA

*Burt (1966).* The 53 pairs in Burt's sample were obtained largely from schools in London. All had been separated at birth or during their first 6 months of life. The IQ scores provided by Burt for the present analysis are what he describes as 'final assessments', which are a composite of a group test and one or more individually administered intelligence tests. The tests consisted of '. . . (i) a group test of intelligence containing both nonverbal and verbal items, (ii) an individual test (the London Revision of the Terman-Binet Scale) used primarily for standardization, and for doubtful cases (iii) a set of performance tests, based on the Pintner-Patterson tests and standardized by Miss Gaw (1925)'. The test results, which generally covered other children in the school as well, were submitted to the teachers for comment or criticism; and, wherever any question arose, the child was re-examined. It was not practicable for the same person to test every child. I was helped by three principal assistants, and in a few cases by research students, all of whom had been trained by me personally. The methods and standards therefore remained much the same throughout the inquiry. If any divergence occurred, it would tend to lower rather than to raise the correlations' (Burt, 1966, p. 140). It could be expected that the final assessments would produce higher reliability than is generally found for single tests scores and probably higher validity of the scores as a measure of innate ability. This was Burt's intention in arriving at the final assessments: to obtain the most accurate estimates of each child's intelligence that psychometric techniques would permit. Thus, children whose scores did not accord with their teacher's impressions were retested on other tests and the results averaged, so that specific factors in any given test would tend to average out. Such composite scores, therefore, would be expected to have somewhat lesser variance than single test scores and also to reflect to a lesser degree effects of specific knowledge and cultural factors, that is, they should be more 'culture fair'. Elsewhere, Burt (1958) states: 'Environment appears to influence test results chiefly in three ways: (*a*) the cultural amenities of the home and the educational opportunities provided by the school can undoubtedly affect a child's performance in intelligence tests of the ordinary type, since so often they demand an acquired facility with abstract and verbal modes of expression; (*b*) quite apart from what the child may learn, the constant presence of an intellectual background may stimulate (or seem to stimulate) his latent powers by inculcating a keener motivation, a stronger interest in intellectual things, and a habit of accurate, speedy, and diligent work; (*c*) in a few rare cases illness or malnutrition during the prenatal or early postnatal states may, almost from the very start, permanently impair the development of the child's central nervous system. The adjusted assessments may do much towards eliminating the irrelevant effects of the first two conditions, but it is doubtful whether they can adequately allow for the last.' The correlations for the 53 pairs of monozygotic twins reared apart are reported by Burt (1966, Table 2) as 0·77 for the group test, 0·86 for the individual test (Stanford-Binet), and 0·87 for the final assessment.

*Shields* (*1962*). The 44 pairs in Shields' sample were mostly* adults obtained from all parts of the British Isles. (One twin was found as far away as South America.) Most of Shields' twins were separated before 6 months of age and 21 of the pairs were separated at birth. Complete intelligence test scores were obtained on only 38 of the 44 sets of twins. Two tests were used: Raven's Mill Hill Vocabulary Scale (a synonyms multiple-choice test), and the Dominoes (D48) test (a timed 20-minute nonverbal test of intelligence). The Dominoes Test has a high *g* loading (0·86) and correlates 0·74 with Raven's Progressive Matrices. Since Shields presented the results of these tests in the form of raw scores, it was necessary to convert them to the standard IQ scale. Shields states that a raw score of 19 on the Vocabulary Scale and of 28 on the Dominoes Test correspond to IQ 100 in the general population. The raw score means were transformed in accord with these population IQ values and the sample standard deviation was transformed to accord with the population value of $SD = 15$. The IQs thus obtained on each test were then averaged (unweighted) to yield a single IQ measure for each subject.

*Newman et al.* (*1937*). These 19 twin pairs were obtained in the United States and were tested as adults. In 18 cases the age of

* Two pairs were aged 8 and 14 years.

TABLE 1  **IQs for MZ Twins Reared Apart**

| | | | | | | | | | |
|---|---|---|---|---|---|---|---|---|---|
| |||||||||| *Burt (1966)*, N = 53 Pairs |
| A | B | A | B | A | B | A | B | A | B |
| 68 | 63 | 94 | 86 | 93 | 99 | 115 | 101 | 104 | 114 |
| 71 | 76 | 87 | 93 | 94 | 94 | 102 | 104 | 125 | 114 |
| 77 | 73 | 97 | 87 | 96 | 95 | 106 | 103 | 108 | 115 |
| 72 | 75 | 89 | 102 | 96 | 93 | 105 | 109 | 116 | 116 |
| 78 | 71 | 90 | 80 | 96 | 109 | 107 | 106 | 116 | 118 |
| 75 | 79 | 91 | 82 | 97 | 92 | 106 | 108 | 121 | 118 |
| 86 | 81 | 91 | 88 | 95 | 97 | 108 | 107 | 128 | 125 |
| 82 | 82 | 91 | 92 | 112 | 97 | 101 | 107 | 117 | 129 |
| 82 | 93 | 96 | 92 | 97 | 113 | 108 | 95 | 132 | 131 |
| 86 | 83 | 87 | 93 | 105 | 99 | 98 | 111 | — | — |
| 83 | 85 | 99 | 93 | 88 | 100 | 116 | 112 | — | — |

*Shields (1962)*, N = 38 Pairs*

| A | B | A | B | A | B | A | B | A | B |
|---|---|---|---|---|---|---|---|---|---|
| 95 | 87 | 109 | 102 | 102 | 108 | 76 | 79 | 84 | 68 |
| 96 | 100 | 98 | 110 | 113 | 111 | 91 | 84 | 121 | 121 |
| 95 | 79 | 101 | 87 | 89 | 93 | 103 | 116 | 107 | 111 |
| 71 | 75 | 99 | 108 | 88 | 110 | 98 | 94 | 74 | 69 |
| 86 | 84 | 99 | 97 | 96 | 99 | 94 | 76 | 79 | 84 |
| 105 | 105 | 69 | 71 | 85 | 84 | 95 | 101 | 107 | 106 |
| 93 | 76 | 86 | 85 | 89 | 84 | 96 | 97 | — | — |
| 83 | 89 | 107 | 105 | 90 | 107 | 63 | 73 | — | — |

*Newman* et al. *(1937)* N = 19 Pairs

| A | B | A | B | A | B | A | B | A | B |
|---|---|---|---|---|---|---|---|---|---|
| 85 | 97 | 89 | 93 | 102 | 96 | 94 | 95 | 105 | 115 |
| 78 | 66 | 94 | 102 | 122 | 127 | 84 | 85 | 96 | 77 |
| 99 | 101 | 105 | 106 | 116 | 92 | 90 | 91 | 79 | 88 |
| 106 | 89 | 77 | 92 | 109 | 116 | 88 | 90 | — | — |

*Juel-Nielsen (1965)* N = 12 Pairs

| A | B | A | B | A | B | A | B | A | B |
|---|---|---|---|---|---|---|---|---|---|
| 120 | 128 | 100 | 94 | 99 | 105 | 114 | 124 | — | — |
| 104 | 99 | 111 | 116 | 100 | 94 | 114 | 113 | — | — |
| 99 | 108 | 105 | 97 | 104 | 103 | 112 | 100 | — | — |

* IQs transformed from raw scores on Mill Hill Vocabulary tests and the Domino D48 Test. (See text for explanation.)

separation was less than 25 months, and in 9 it was less than 6 months. About the one pair that was separated at 6 years (and tested at age 41) Newman *et al.*, state: '. . . the twins were separated at 6 years, somewhat late for our purposes; but we had information that the environments of the twins had been so markedly different since separation that we decided to add the case to our collection' (p. 142). (These twins differed by 9 IQ points.)

Stanford-Binet IQs were obtained on all subjects.

*Juel-Nielsen (1965)*. These 12 pairs were obtained in Denmark. The age of separation ranges from 1 day to $5\frac{3}{4}$ years; 9 were separated before 12 months. IQs were obtained by an individual test, a Danish adaptation of the Wechsler-Bellevue Intelligence Scale (Form I), which in the general population has a mean $= 100$ and $SD = 15$.

The IQs of all the twins in the four studies are given in Table 1.

## Results

The main statistical parameters of the separate studies and of the combined data are shown in Table 2. The few instances of slight

TABLE 2 **Statistics on IQs of MZ Twins**

| *Study* | *N (Pairs)* | *Mean IQ* | *SD* | $|\bar{d}|$ | $SD_d$ | $r_i$ | $r_d$ |
|---------|-------------|-----------|------|-------------|--------|-------|-------|
| Burt | 53 | 97·7 | 14·8 | 5·96 | 4·44 | 0·88 | 0·88 |
| Shields | 38 | 93·0 | 13·4 | 6·72 | 5·80 | 0·78 | 0·84 |
| Newman *et al.* | 19 | 95·7 | 13·0 | 8·21 | 6·65 | 0·67 | 0·76 |
| Juel-Nielsen | 12 | 106·8 | 9·0 | 6·46 | 3·22 | 0·68 | 0·86 |
| Combined | 122 | 96·8 | 14·2 | 6·60 | 5·20 | 0·82 | 0·85 |

discrepancies between these statistics and the corresponding figures of the original authors are all within the range of rounding error. All the present analyses were calculated by computer, with figures carried to five decimals and not rounded till the final product.

DISTRIBUTION OF IQS

The mean IQ of the MZ twins is slightly below the population mean. This is a general finding for twins reared together or apart and is probably related to the intrauterine disadvantages of twinning, including lowered birth weight. The small Juel-Nielsen sample is atypical in having a mean IQ above 100. The standard deviation of the twin IQs in only slightly less than the 15 points in the general population. Figure 1 shows the form of the IQ distribution. It extends over a range of 71 IQ points, or 4·7 sigmas, which would include approximately 98 percent of the general population. A chi-square test of the goodness of fit shows that the IQ distribution of Figure 1 does not depart significantly from

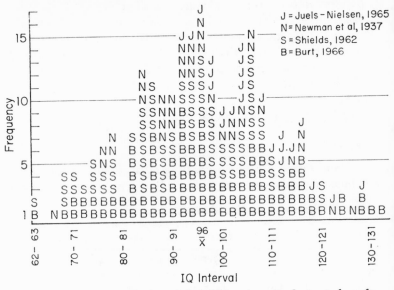

FIGURE 1.   *IQ distribution of 244 MZ twins reared apart, from four studies. The distribution does not deviate significantly from normality.*

normality. The chi-square based on eight subdivisions of the distribution is only 3·08, $p = 0.80$. (Chi-square with 7 degrees of freedom must exceed 14·07 for significance at the 0·05 level.) It can be concluded that the IQs of the total sample of 244 twins are quite typical and representative of the distribution of intelligence in the general population.

## CORRELATION BETWEEN TWINS

The intraclass correlations ($r_i$) between twins are given in Table 2. A correlation scatter diagram for all twins is shown in Figure 2.

Twins were assigned to the *A* and *B* axes in such a way as to equalize the means of the two distributions. The intraclass correlation ($r_i$) represented by the scatter diagram is 0·82. Corrected for attentuation (i.e., test unreliability), assuming the upper-

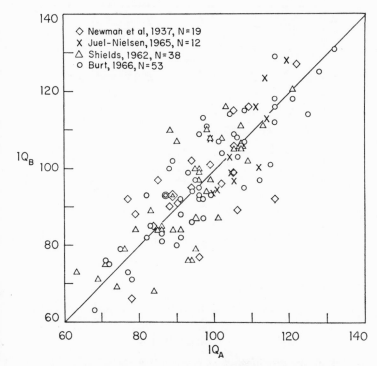

FIGURE 2. *Scatter diagram showing correlation between IQs of 122 sets of co-twins (A and B assigned at random). The obtained intraclass correlation ($r_i$) is 0·82. The diagonal line represents perfect correlation ($r_i = 1·00$).*

bound for Stanford-Binet test reliability of 0·95, the twin correlation would be 0·86.

It is interesting to compare the scatter diagram for IQs shown in Figure 2 with a scatter diagram for the socioeconomic status (SES) of the homes in which the twins were reared. The one study which classified subjects in terms of SES, based on parents' or foster parents' occupation, is Burt's. The six categories were

(1) higher professional, (2) lower professional, (3) clerical, (4) skilled, (5) semi-skilled, (6) unskilled. The seven cases reared in residential institutions are omitted from this analysis, since there

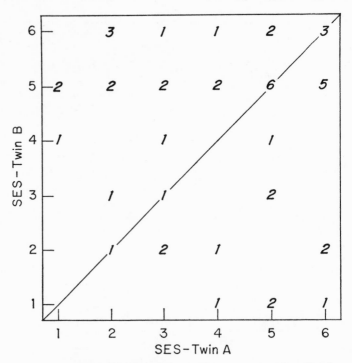

FIGURE 3. *Scatter diagram of socioeconomic status (SES, based on six occupational categories of the parents, from 'professional' (#1) to 'unskilled' (#6)) for 46 co-twins in the Burt (1966) study. The numbers in the scatter diagram represent frequencies of twin-pairs. (Assignment to A and B is the same as in Figure 2.) The intraclass correlation ($r_i$) between co-twins' SES is 0·03.*

is no basis for assignment to one of the six SES categories. The scatter diagram is shown in Figure 3. It represents a correlation of 0·03 between the SES of the homes of the separated twins in Burt's sample. Obviously virtually none of the correlation between twins' IQs is attributable to similarities in their home environments when these are classified by SES in terms of the parents' occupation.

The intraclass correlations for IQ in the four studies differ from one another mainly because of differences in the restriction of range of IQs in the various samples. The magnitude of $r_i$ is, of course, partly a function of the sample variance. The magnitude of $r_i$ by itself, therefore, can be a somewhat deceptive indicator of the actual magnitude of twin differences (or similarities) relative to the population variance. For this reason the most crucial statistic in twin data is the absolute difference between twins.

## TWIN DIFFERENCES IN IQ

The mean absolute difference ($|d|$) between twins and the standard deviation of the differences ($SD_d$) are shown in Table 2. Since the absolute difference between twins also contains measurement error due to imperfect reliability of the tests, the $|d|$ of 6·60 should be compared to the value of 4·68, which is the mean difference between forms $L$ and $M$ of the Stanford-Binet administered to the same persons. The $SD$ of these differences is 4·13 (Terman and Merrill, 1937, p. 46). Some of this difference, of course, reflects gains due to the practice effect of the first test upon the second. But the mean difference of 6·60 can be corrected for attenuation assuming the upper bound reliability for the Stanford-Binet of 0·95, which results in a 'true' absolute difference of 5·36.

It is proposed that the absolute differences between twin's IQs can be used to compute a correlation coefficient which has the same scale as the Pearson and intraclass correlation but indicates the degree of similarity between twins relative to the similarity between persons paired at random from the general population. This can be called a 'difference correlation', signified as $r_d$. This is a useful statistic in studying kinship resemblance because it preserves the actual magnitude of the difference between kinship pairs. For example, even if there were a perfect Pearson $r$ (or intraclass correlation) between relatives, $r_d$ would be less than 1·00 if there was any mean difference between the related persons (as would be the case if one member of each pair of MZ twins were reared in a very unfavorable environment and one member in a very favorable environment). Thus $r_d$ should be reported in twin studies (and other kinship studies) to supplement the usual correlation coefficient (Pearson or intraclass). The value of $r_d$ is not sensitive to the sample variance. Imagine that by some fluke we obtained a sample of twins with no differences between the means of the twin pairs; even if the average difference between members of each pair were small, the intraclass correlation (or Pearson $r$) between twins would be zero, suggesting that the heritability is zero. Especially when twin samples are small, it makes more sense to ask what is the magnitude of the twin differences relative to differences among unrelated persons in the general population. The answer is provided by $r_d$. The formula for $r_d$ is

$$r_d = 1 - \left(\frac{|\bar{d}_k|}{|\bar{d}_P|}\right)^2,$$

where

$|\bar{d}_k|$ = mean absolute difference between kinship members,

$|\bar{d}_P|$ = mean absolute difference between all possible paired comparisons in the general population, and

$$|\bar{d}_P| = \frac{2\sigma}{\sqrt{\pi}} = 1 \cdot 13\sigma.$$

Unless one has an estimate of $\sigma$ in the population from which the kinship groups are a sample or to which one wishes to generalize concerning $r_d$, this statistic cannot be used.

It can be seen in Table 2 that the values of $r_d$ are much more consistent than $r_i$ among the four studies. Corrected for attenuation (reliability = 0·95) the composite $r_d$ of 0·85 becomes 0·88. This value should be interpreted as an estimate of $h^2$ only with caution, since it is uncertain just how much of the nongenetic variance is common to the separated twins. The studies do not differ significantly in $r_d$, because the values of $|d|$ themselves do not show significant differences among the studies. An analysis of variance to test the significance of differences in $|d|$ in the four studies yielded an $F = 0·87$, $df = 3$ and 118, $p < 0·46$. Thus the studies clearly do not differ significantly in the magnitude of twin differences. Bartlett's test was performed on the standard deviations of the absolute differences ($SD_d$) and revealed that on this parameter the differences among the studies are nonsignificant at the 0·01 level.

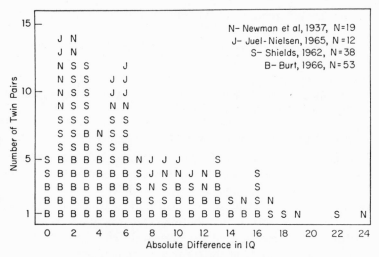

FIGURE 4. *Distribution of absolute differences ($|\bar{d}|$) in IQ between co-twins reared apart. This distribution closely approximates the chi distribution.*

Figure 4 shows the frequency distribution of the absolute differences between twins.* These are, of course, composed of environmental effects plus errors of measurement. Extreme differences are rare; in only 4 cases does $|d|$ exceed the average difference of 17 IQ points between all possible pairs of persons in the population; and in only 19 cases (16 percent) do the differences exceed

* Since Burt's data consist of composite test scores, it is interesting to see if they result in a significantly different distribution of twin differences than those found in the three other studies. The most appropriate test of this is the Kolmogorov-Smirnov two-sample test, a nonparametric test of whether two independent samples can be regarded as drawn from the same population or from populations with the same distribution; it is simultaneously sensitive to any kind of differences in the distributions – central tendency, dispersion, skewness, etc. When the distribution of Burt's twin differences is compared with the distribution of the twin differences in the other three studies combined the Kolmogorov-Smirnov test yields a chi-square value of 1·50 ($df = 2$) which is statistically non-significant. (A chi-square value of 5·99 or more is required for significance at the 0·05 level.) Therefore it may be concluded that the distribution of twin differences in Burt's sample does not differ significantly from the distribution of twin differences in the three other studies.

the average difference of 12 IQ points between full siblings reared together, while 16 percent of the differences exceed the mean difference of about 11 IQ points generally found between DZ twins reared together. Since the differences shown in Figure 4 represent environmental effects (and random errors of measurement), these results should permit some inference about the distribution of environmental effects on IQ.

DISTRIBUTION OF ENVIRONMENTAL EFFECTS

The distribution of absolute differences shown in Figure 4 closely resembles a chi distribution. If one draws pairs of values at random from a normal distribution, the absolute differences between the values in each pair yield the chi distribution, which, in effect, is one-half of the normal distribution. One can think of the chi distribution as consisting of the normal distribution folded over on itself, with the fold at the median. (The corresponding deviations above and below the median, of course, are added together.) Therefore, one can graphically test a distribution for goodness of fit to the chi distribution by plotting the obtained distribution on a normal probability scale after the percentiles of the distribution have been 'unfolded' at the median. This 'unfolding' is simply achieved by the transformation 50 + %ile/2. If these values when plotted on the normal probability scale fall approximately along a straight line, it is evidence that the distribution does not differ significantly from chi. Figure 5 shows this plot. The goodness of fit of the data to a straight line is practically perfect, including an IQ difference of 24 points. This is the frequently cited case of Gladys (IQ 92) and Helen (IQ 116) in the study by Newman *et al.* (p. 245). They were separated at 18 months and tested at the age of 35 years. They had markedly different health histories as children; Gladys suffered a number of severe illnesses, one being nearly fatal, while Helen enjoyed unusually good health. Gladys did not go beyond the third grade in school while Helen obtained a B.A. degree from a good college and became a high school teacher of English and history.

What Figure 5 means is that the nongenetic or environmental effects, which are wholly responsible for the twin differences, are normally distributed. (The absolute differences are due to environmental effects plus measurement error; it is assumed that errors of measurement are distributed normally.) Note that this says nothing about the distribution of environments *per se*. The conclusion refers to the *effects* of environment on IQ. There is no evidence in these data of asymmetry or of threshold conditions for the effects of environment on IQ.

Since the IQs (i.e., phenotypes) are themselves normally distributed (Figure 1), and since the environmental effects on IQ have

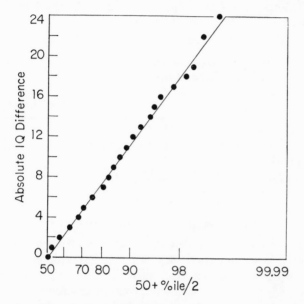

FIGURE 5. *The absolute differences in IQ between co-twins plotted against a normal probability scale. The close fit to the straight line shows that environmental effects on the IQ, as represented by co-twin differences, are normally distributed.*

been shown to be normally distributed in this sample, it follows that the genotypes for IQ also are normally distributed. (The sums of two normal variates also have a normal distribution.) That is to say, if $P = G + E$ (where $P$ is phenotypic value, $G$ is genotypic value, and $E$ is environmental effect), it can be concluded that for these IQ data, $P$, $G$, and $E$ are each normally distributed.

Since $P$, $G$, and $E$ are distributed normally, it is meaningful to estimate the standard deviations of their distributions. (We assume test reliability of 0·95 and normally distributed errors of measure-ment.) Given these conditions and a twin correlation $(r_d)$ of 0·85, the estimates that would obtain in a population with $\sigma = 15$ are shown in Table 3. Since in a normal distribution six sigmas en-compass virtually 100 percent of the population (actually all but 0·27 percent), and since the standard deviation of environmental effects on IQ is $4·74 \pm 0·3$, it can be said that the total range of environmental effects in a population typified by this twin sample is $6 \times 4·74 = 28·4$ IQ points.

TABLE 3 **Components of Variance in IQs Estimated from MZ Twins Reared Apart**

| Source | $\sigma$ | $\sigma^2$ | % Variance |
|---|---|---|---|
| Heredity | 13·83 | 191·25 | 85 |
| Environment | 4·74 | 22·50 | 10 |
| Test Error | 3·35 | 11·25 | 5 |
| Total (Phenotypes) | 15·00 | 225·00 | 100 |

GENOTYPE × ENVIRONMENT INTERACTION

A corollary to the finding that environmental effects are normally distributed is the question of whether a favorable environment raises the IQ more or less than an unfavorable environment de-presses the IQ. If favorable and unfavorable environmental effects were asymmetrical, we should expect to find that the higher and lower IQs from each pair of twins would have different distribu-tions about their respective means. This is in fact not the case. Probably the way to see this most clearly is to plot the IQs of the higher and lower twins in each pair against the absolute difference between the twins. This plot is shown in Figure 6. The mean IQs of the higher and lower twins are 100·12 and 93·52, respectively. The difference is significant beyond the 0·001 level. The corre-sponding *SD*s are 13·68 and 13·86; the difference is nonsignificant. The straight lines through the data points are a least squares best fit. The slopes of these lines (in opposite directions) are not signifi-cantly different. The correlation (Pearson $r$) between IQ and absolute difference is $+0·15$ for the lower twins and $-0·22$ for the higher twins. The difference (disregarding the sign of *r*) is completely nonsignificant.

We can also ask: Is there an interaction between environment and genotype for intelligence? If there is, we should expect a

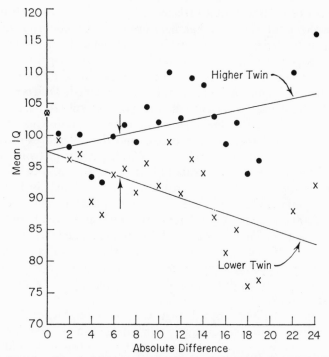

FIGURE 6.   *IQ of the higher twin (H) and the lower twin (L) plotted against their absolute difference in IQ. The straight lines are a least squares best fit to all the data (122 twins). The straight arrows indicate the bivariate means.*

correlation between the mean IQ of each twin pair (reflecting their genotypic value) and the absolute difference between the twins (reflecting environmental differences).[1] This correlation (Pearson *r*), based on the 122 pairs, turns out to be −0·15, which is not

[1] This method of assessing the G × E interaction was originally suggested and explicated by J. L. Jinks and D. W. Fulker in 'Comparison of the biometrical, genetical, MAVA, and classical approaches to the analysis of human behavior'. *Psychological Bulletin*, 1970, **73**, 311-349.

significantly different from zero. These data, then, do not show evidence of a genotype × environment interaction for IQ.

The present data do not permit any strong inferences about the sources of environmental variance, but other twin research indicates that a substantial and perhaps even a major proportion of the nongenetic variance is attributable to prenatal and other biological influences rather than to differences in the social-psychological environment. The cytoplasmic discordances and the like pointed out by Darlington have already been mentioned. Differences in the favorableness of the intrauterine environment are reflected in differences in birth weight between twins (the differences being greater for MZ than for DZ twins), and the differences in birth weight are known to be related to IQ disparities in twins. In a review of this evidence, Scarr (1969) found that MZ twins who were both over 2500 grams in birth weight differed[1] in later IQ by 4·9 points in favor of the heavier twin; when one twin was less than 2500 grams, the IQ difference was 13·3; and when both twins were less than 2500 grams, the IQ difference was 6·4. The mean difference of 6·9 IQ points between the heavier and lighter MZ twins (52 pairs) in the studies summarized by Scarr is not far from the mean IQ difference of 6·6 between all the twins in the present study.

It is sometimes argued that the IQ resemblance between MZ twins reared apart is largely attributable to similarities in their home environments. To the extent that this is true, it should lead to the prediction that characteristics with *lower* heritability (and consequently greater susceptibility to environmental influences), should show an even higher correlation between MZ twins reared apart, as compared with MZ twins reared together, than characteristics of *higher* heritability. In this connection it is instructive to compare the IQ with tests of scholastic achievement for MZ twins reared together and reared apart. A review of studies of the heritability of scholastic achievement has shown much lower values of $h^2$ (the average being about 0·40) than for IQ (Jensen, 1967). The studies by Burt and Newman *et al.* provide the necessary scholastic achievement data for the relevant comparisons. These are shown

---

[1] These are all absolute (unsigned) differences.

in Table 4. Note that when twins are reared together (MZT), they correlate higher in scholastic achievement than when reared apart (MZA). No such large difference is found for IQ between MZT and MZA. If the MZA twin resemblance in IQ were due to environmental similarities, these similarities should be even more strongly reflected by scholastic achievement, and this is clearly not the case. Estimates of *within* and *between* family environmental effects may be obtained from the correlations in Table 4. For IQ

TABLE 4 **Correlation between MZ Twins Reared Together (MZT) and Reared Apart (MZA) for IQ and Scholastic Achievement**

| | IQ | | Sch. Ach. | | Number | |
|---|---|---|---|---|---|---|
| *Study* | *MZT* | *MZA* | *MZT* | *MZA* | *MZT* | *MZA* |
| Burt | ·918 | ·863 | ·983 | ·623 | 95 | 53 |
| Newman *et al.* | ·910 | ·670 | ·955 | ·507 | 50 | 19 |
| Combined | ·915 | ·824 | ·976 | ·595 | 145 | 72 |

the *within* environments effect is 8·5 percent of the variance and the *between* environments effect is 9·1 percent of the variance. For scholastic achievement the *within* environments effect is 2·4 percent and the *between* environments effect is 38·1 percent. These results suggest that the differences between identical twins in IQ arise largely from prenatal factors rather than from influences in the social-psychological environment. Just the opposite conclusion would pertain in the case of scholastic achievement.

## Conclusion

Analysis of the data from the four major studies of the intelligence of MZ twins reared apart, totaling 122 twin pairs, leads to conclusions not found in the original studies or in previous reviews of them. A statistical test of the absolute difference between the separated twins' IQs indicates that there are no significant differences among the twin samples in the four studies. All of them can be viewed as samples from the same population and can therefore be pooled for more detailed and powerful statistical treatment.

The 244 individual twins' IQs are normally distributed, with the mean = 96·82, $SD$ = 14·16. The mean absolute difference between twins is 6·60 ($SD$ = 5·20), the largest difference being 24 IQ points. The frequency of large twin differences is no more than would be expected from the normal probability curve.

The overall intraclass correlation between twins is 0·824, which may be interpreted as an upper-bound estimate of the heritability of IQ in the English, Danish, and North American Caucasian populations sampled in these studies.

The absolute differences between members of twin pairs (attributable to nongenetic effects and measurement error) closely approximate the chi distribution; this fact indicates that environmental effects are normally distributed. If $P = G + E$ (where $P$ is phenotypic value, $G$ is genotypic value, and $E$ is environmental effect) it can be concluded that for this population $P$, $G$, and $E$ are each normally distributed. There is no evidence of asymmetry or of threshold conditions for the effects of environment on IQ. The lack of a significant correlation between twin-pair means (reflecting genotype values) and twin-pair differences (reflecting environmental effects) indicates a lack of genotype × environment interaction; that is to say, the magnitude of differential environmental effects is not systematically related to the intelligence level of twin pairs. Additional evidence from comparison of the difference between MZ twins reared together with the difference between MZ twins reared apart suggests that most of the small twin difference in IQ may be attributable to prenatal intrauterine factors rather than to later effects of the individual's social-psychological environment.

# The Ethical Issues

The range of ethical issues concerning research and research applications in human genetics is so great that I will not even attempt to review it here. It involves diverse questions about raising human embryos in 'test tubes', the use of artificial insemination in human research, the cross-fostering of fetuses, and direct alteration of chromosomes and genes by what is now called genetic surgery, and goes all the way to questions of eugenics and population quantity and quality control.

But the most frequently heard objection to further research into human genetics, particularly research into the genetics of behavioral characteristics, is that the knowledge gained might be misused. I agree. Knowledge also, however, makes possible greater freedom of choice. It is a necessary condition for human freedom in the fullest sense. I therefore completely reject the idea that we should cease to discover, to invent, and to know (in the scientific meaning of that term) merely because what we find could be misunderstood, misused, or put to evil and inhumane ends. This can be done with almost any invention, discovery, or addition to knowledge. Would anyone argue that the first caveman who discovered how to make a fire with flint stones should have been prevented from making fire, or from letting others know of his discovery, on the grounds that it could be misused by arsonists? Of course not. Instead, we make a law against arson and punish those who are caught violating the law. The real ethical issue, I believe, is not concerned with whether we should or should not strive for a greater scientific understanding of our universe and of ourselves. For a scientist, it seems to me, this is axiomatic.

An important distinction, often not made or else overlooked, is that between scientific research and the specific use of the research findings in a technological application with a highly predictable outcome. The classic example is the atomic bomb. Should Einstein have desisted from the research that led to $e = mc^2$? Nuclear physics can, of course, be misused. But it need not be. For it can also be used to cure cancer and to provide electric power. Moral decisions involve the uses of knowledge and must be dealt with when these are considered. Before that, however, my own system of values holds that increasing knowledge and understanding is preferable to upholding dogma and ignorance.

In a society that allows freedom of speech and of the press, both to express and to criticize diverse views, it seems to me the social responsibility of the scientist is clear. He must simply do his research as competently and carefully as he can, and report his methods, results, and conclusions as fully and as accurately as possible. When speaking as a scientist, he should not introduce personal, social, religious, or political ideologies. In the bizarre racist theories of the Nazis and in the disastrous Lysenkoism of the Soviet Union under Stalin, we have seen clear examples of what happens when science is corrupted by servitude to political dogma.

For the past two years, I have been embroiled in debate over my article 'How Much Can We Boost IQ and Scholastic Achievement?' (*Harvard Educational Review*, 1969, **39**, 1-123). Though there are many possible grounds for raising ethical questions concerning research and publication on the genetic aspect of human abilities, in this case I think a block has been raised because of obvious implications for the understanding of racial differences in ability and achievement. Serious consideration of whether genetic as well as environmental factors are involved has been taboo in academic, scientific, and intellectual circles in the United States. But despite taboo, the question persists. My belief is that scientists in the appropriate disciplines must finally face this question squarely and not repeatedly sweep it under the rug. In the long run, the safest and sanest thing we can urge is intensive, no-holds-barred inquiry in the best tradition of science.

We must clearly distinguish between research on racial differences and racism. Racism implies hate or aversion and aims at denying equal rights and opportunities to persons because of their racial origin. It should be attacked by enacting and enforcing laws and arrangements that help to insure equality of civil and political rights and to guard against racial discrimination in educational and occupational opportunities. But to fear research on genetic racial differences, or the possible existence of a biological basis for differences in abilities, is, in a sense, to grant the racist's assumption: that if it should be established beyond reasonable doubt that there are biological or genetically conditioned differences in mental abilities among individuals or groups, then we are justified in oppressing or exploiting those who are most limited in genetic endowment. This is, of course, a complete *non sequitur*. Equality of human rights does not depend upon the proposition that there are no genetically conditioned individual differences or group differences. Equality of rights is a moral axiom: it does not follow from any set of scientific data.

I have always advocated dealing with persons as individuals, and I am opposed to according differential treatment to persons on the basis of their race, color, national origin, or social-class background. But I am also opposed to ignoring or refusing to investigate the causes of the well-established differences among racial groups in the distribution of educationally relevant traits, particularly IQ. Purely environmental explanations of racial differences in intelligence will never gain the status of scientific knowledge unless genetic theories are put to the test and disproved by evidence.

There is a perhaps understandable reluctance to come to grips scientifically with the problem of race differences in intelligence – to come to grips with it, that is to say, in the same way that scientists would approach the investigation of any other phenomenon. This reluctance is manifested in a variety of 'symptoms' found in most writings and discussions of the psychology of race differences. These symptoms include a tendency to remain on the remotest fringes of the subject, to sidestep central questions, and to blur the issues and tolerate a degree of vagueness in definitions, concepts, and inferences that would be unseemly in any other realm of scientific discourse. Many writers express an unwarranted degree of skepticism about reasonably well-established quantitative methods and measurements. They deny or belittle facts already generally accepted – accepted, that is, when brought to bear on inferences outside the realm of race differences – and they demand practically impossible criteria of certainty before even seriously proposing or investigating genetic hypotheses, as contrasted with extremely uncritical attitudes toward purely environmental hypotheses. There is often a failure to distinguish clearly between scientifically answerable aspects of the question and the moral, political, and social-policy issues; there is a tendency to beat dead horses and to set up straw men on what is represented, or misrepresented, I should say, as the genetic side of the argument. We see appeals to the notion that the topic is either too unimportant to be worthy of scientific curiosity, or is too complex, or too difficult, or that it will be forever impossible for any kind of research to be feasible, or that answers to key questions are fundamentally 'unknowable' in any scientifically acceptable sense. Finally, we often see the complete denial of intelligence and race as realities, or as quantifiable attributes, or as variables capable of being related to one another. In short, there is an altogether ostrich-like dismissal of the subject.

I believe these obstructive tendencies will be increasingly overcome the more widely and openly the subject is researched and discussed among scientists and scholars. As some of the taboos against open discussion of the topic fall away, the issues will become clarified on a rational basis. We will come to know better just what we do and do not yet know about the subject, and we will be in a better position to deal with it objectively and constructively through further research.

In recent years, however, we have witnessed more and more the domination of ideologically motivated environmentalist dogma concerning the causes of large and socially important differences in average educational and occupational performance among various subpopulations in the United States, particularly those socially identified as racial groups. For example, the rate of occurrence of mental retardation, with IQs below 70 plus all the social, educational, and occupational handicap that this implies, is six to eight times higher in our Negro population than in the rest of the population. According to research sponsored by the National Institutes of Health, as many as 20 to 30 percent of the black children in some of our largest urban centers suffer severe psychological handicaps. Yet the Government *has* not supported, *does* not, and *will* not, as of this date, support any research proposals that could determine whether or not any genetic factors are involved in this differential rate of mental handicap. To ignore such a question, in terms of our present knowledge, I submit, may not be unethical – but it is, I believe, short-sighted, socially irresponsible, and inhumane.

More important than the issue of racial differences *per se* is the probability of dysgenic trends in our urban slums. The social-class differential in birthrate appears to be much greater in the Negro than in the white population. That is, the educationally and occupationally least able among Negroes have a higher reproductive rate than their white counterparts, and the most able segment, the middle class, of the Negro population have a lower reproductive rate than their white counterparts. If social-class intelligence differences within the Negro population have a genetic component, as in the white population, this condition could both create and widen genetic intelligence differences between Negroes and whites. The social and educational implications of this trend, if it exists and persists, are enormous. The problem obviously deserves thorough investigation by social scientists and geneticists and should not be ignored or superficially dismissed because of well-meaning wishful thinking. I find myself in agreement with Professor Dwight Ingle, who has said, 'If there are important average differences in genetic potential for intelligence between Negroes and non-Negroes, it may be that one necessary means for Negroes to achieve true equality is biological'. The possible consequences of our failure to seriously study these questions may well be viewed by future generations as our society's greatest injustice to Negro Americans.

Carl Jay Bajema, a Harvard geneticist and researcher on population trends who is frequently cited by my critics in support of their notion that there are no dysgenic trends to worry about (based on his earlier, limited research), now has this to say (in *Bio-Science*, 1971, **29**, 71-5):

The overall net affect of current American life-styles in reproduction appears to be slightly dysgenic – to be favoring an increase in harmful genes which will genetically handicap a larger proportion of the next generation of Americans. American life-styles in reproduction are, in part, a function of the population policy of the United States. What will be the long-range genetic implications of controlling or not controlling population size in an industrialized welfare state democracy such as America? . . . [He concludes] . . . Each generation of mankind faces anew the awesome responsibility of making decisions which will affect the quantity and genetic quality of the next generation. A society, if it takes its responsibility to future generations seriously, will take steps to insure that individuals yet unborn will have the best genetic and cultural heritage possible to enable them to meet the challenges of the environment and to take advantage of the opportunities for self-fulfillment present in that society.

Finally, some persons who call themselves environmentalists tend to cast the issues of genetic research on intelligence and race as a battle between the good guys and the bad guys. I resent this. The simple-minded morality play in which I have been wittingly or unwittingly cast in the role of villain has presented the issue of ethics as if ethical behavior were the sole possession of the environmental dogmatists, and as if those of us who would suggest looking into genetic factors were ethical and moral pariahs!

'Knowledge can be misused, but this does not excuse efforts to block inquiry and debate or to deny laymen in a democratic society the right to know. Closed systems of belief can also be misused, and ignorance is a barrier to progress. All possible causes for people's being disadvantaged should be investigated, and hopefully the application of knowledge to their advancement will be guided by moral principle' (Professor Dwight Ingle in *Perspectives in Biology and Medicine*, 10, 1967). In my view, society will benefit most if scientists treat these problems in the spirit of scientific inquiry rather than as a battlefield upon which one or another preordained ideology may seemingly triumph.

# A Note on Why Genetic Correlations are not Squared

Psychologists are often puzzled and confused by the fact that geneticists do not square the correlations between twins (or other kinship correlations) in order to obtain the percentage of variance explained by genetic factors. (Or, in the case of correlation between unrelated children reared together, the percentage of variance due to environmental factors.) Recent prominent examples of this confusion are found in Spuhler and Lindzey (1967, pp. 403-404) and in Guilford (1967, pp. 351-352). These authors incorrectly square kinship correlations and thereby arrive at erroneous conclusions. Most psychologists have learned to treat correlations as the square root of variance explained. But it is incorrect to take the square of twins or other kinship correlations to determine the proportion of variance attributable to genetic or environmental effects. The unsquared correlation itself is correctly interpreted as a proportion. Here is the reason: If the correlation between phenotype (i.e., obtained score) and genotype (i.e., the hypothetical genetic value of the individuals) is $r_{pg}$, and if the correlation between phenotypes of pairs of individuals with the same genotypes but nothing else in common (e.g., identical twins reared apart in random environments) is $r_{pp'}$, then $r_{pp'} = r_{pg}^2$, or

$$\sqrt{r_{pp'}} = r_{pg}.$$

A good analogy is with test reliability. Two equivalent forms of a test have only their true-score variance in common (analogous to genetic variance) and the error variance (analogous to environmental variance) is not in common, that is, is uncorrelated. The correlation between equivalent forms, $r_{tt}$, is the reliability, or the

333

percentage of true score variance ('genetic variance') the tests share in common. The $\sqrt{r_{tt}}$ is the correlation of obtained scores with true scores. Thus, the correlation between identical twins reared in uncorrelated environments is directly analogous to the correlation between equivalent forms of a test. The correlation in each case indicates the percentage of variance in common, or the percentage of genetic (or true score) variance.

Another way of regarding the problem is in terms of the 'common elements' formula for correlation (given in McNemar, 1949, pp. 117-118). This is

$$r_{xy} = \frac{N_c}{\sqrt{N_x + N_c} \sqrt{N_y + N_c}}.$$

where

$N_c$ is number of elements common to variables $X$ and $Y$,

$N_x$ is number of elements unique to $X$,

$N_y$ is number of elements unique to $Y$.

A visually simple example is to consider the correlation of half-siblings, who have 25 percent of their genetic variance in common. The variance can be represented by squares, as in Figure 1.

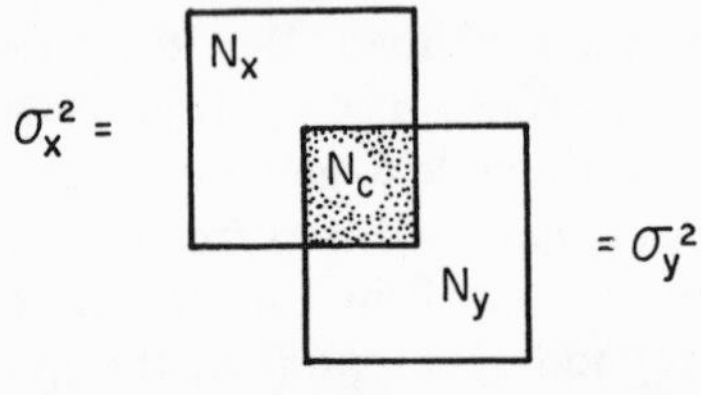

FIGURE 1.   *Correlation of half-siblings who have 25 percent of their genetic variance in common.*

Assume $\sigma_x^2 = \sigma_y^2$, as would be the case for two sets of half-sibs. For simplicity assume $\sigma_x^2$, and $\sigma_y^2$ each equals 100. (Also, for simplicity assume there is no environmental variance.) Then, applying the common elements formula for correlation, we have

$$r_{xy} = \frac{25}{\sqrt{75 + 25} \sqrt{75 + 25}}.$$

$$r_{xy} = 02 \cdot 5.$$

This is the correlation between half-sibs and is also the proportion of the genetic variance they have in common. The correlation between obtained scores and that part of the genetic variance that half-sibs share in common is $\sqrt{0\cdot25} = 0\cdot50$. This can be visualized in Figure 2.

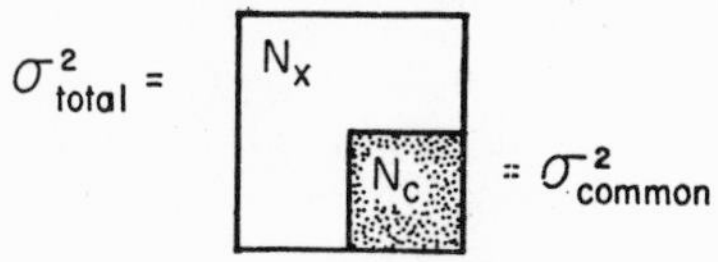

FIGURE 2. *Correlation between obtained scores and shared genetic variance of half-sibs.*

Again, applying the common elements formula:

$$r_{tc} = \frac{25}{\sqrt{75+25}\ \sqrt{0+25}}.$$
$$r_{tc} = 0\cdot50.$$

Now, in this case, if we want to know the percentage of total variance that is explained by the common genetic variance we must square $r_{tc}$, and this gives $0\cdot25$ or 25 per cent, and, as can be seen in the diagram, this is one-fourth of the total area (variance).

# References

ALTUS, W. D. Birth order and its sequelae. *Science*, 1966, **151**, 44-59.

ANASTASI, A. Intelligence and family size. *Psychological Bulletin*, 1956, **53**, 187-209.

BAJEMA, C. J. Estimation of the direction and intensity of natural selection in relation to human intelligence by means of the intrinsic rate of natural increase. *Eugenics Quarterly*, 1963, **10**, 175-187.

BAJEMA, C. J. Relation of fertility to educational attainment in a Kalamazoo public school population: A follow-up study. *Eugenics Quarterly*, 1966, **13**, 306-315.

BAJEMA, C. J. The genetic implications of population control. *Bio-Science*, 1971, **21**, 71-75.

BARNETT, B. H. Behavioral individuality in four cultural-familially retarded brothers. Mimeo, undated.

BARNETT, C. D., ELLIS, N. R., AND PRYER, M. W. Serial position effects in superior and retarded subjects. *Psychological Reports*, 1960, **7**, 111-113.

BAYLEY, N. Comparisons of mental and motor test scores for ages 1-15 months by sex, birth order, race, geographical location, and education of parents. *Child Development*, 1965, **36**, 379-411. (a)

BAYLEY, N. Research in child development: A longitudinal perspective. *Merrill-Palmer Quarterly of Behavior Development*, 1965, **11**, 183-208. (b)

BAYLEY, N. Learning in adulthood: The role of intelligence. In H. J. Klausmeier and C. W. Harris (Eds.), *Analyses of concept learning*. New York: Academic Press, 1966, pp. 117-138.

BAYLEY, N. Behavioral correlates of mental growth: Birth to thirty-six years. *American Psychologist*, 1968, **23**, 1-17.

BEREITER, C., AND ENGELMANN, S. *Teaching disadvantaged children in the pre-school*. Englewood Cliffs, New Jersey: Prentice-Hall, 1966.

BEREITER, C., AND ENGELMANN, S. An academically oriented pre-school for disadvantaged children: Results from the initial experimental group. In D. W. Brison and J. Hill (Eds.), *Psychology and early childhood education*. Ontario Institute for Studies in Education, 1968, No. 4, pp. 17-36.

BILODEAU, E. A. (Ed.), *Acquisition of skill*. New York: Academic Press, 1966.

BLEWETT, D. B. An experimental study of the inheritance of intelligence. *Journal of Mental Science*, 1954, **100**, 922-933.

BLOOM, B. S. *Stability and change in human characteristics*. New York: Wiley, 1964.

BOUSFIELD, A. K., AND BOUSFIELD, W. A. Measurement of clustering and of sequential constancies in repeated free recall. *Psychological Reports*, 1966, **19**, 935-942.

BRISON, D. W. Can and should learning be accelerated? In D. W. Brison (Ed.), *Accelerated learning and fostering creativity*. Toronto, Canada: Ontario Institute for Studies in Education, 1968, pp. 5-9.

BROADHURST, P. L. Abnormal animal behavior. In H. J. Eysenck (Ed.), *Handbook of abnormal psychology*. New York: Basic Books, 1961, pp. 726-763.

BRONFENBRENNER, U. The psychological costs of quality and equality in education. *Child Development*, 1967, **38**, 909-925.

BUCK, C. Discussion of 'Culturally related reproductive factors in mental retardation' by Graves *et al.* Paper read at Conference on Sociocultural Aspects of Mental Retardation, Peabody College, Nashville, Tennessee, June 1968.

BURKS, B. S. The relative influence of nature and nurture upon mental development: A comparative study of foster parent-foster child resemblance and true parent-true child resemblance. *Yearb. Nat. Soc. Stud. Educ.*, 1928, **27**, (I), 219-316.

BURT, C. The evidence for the concept of intelligence. *British Journal of Educational Psychology*, 1955, **25**, 158-177.

BURT, C. The distribution of intelligence. *British Journal of Psychology*, 1957, **48**, 161-175.

BURT, C. The inheritance of mental ability. *American Psychologist*, 1958, **13**, 1-15.

BURT, C. Class Differences in general intelligence: III. *British Journal of Statistical Psychology*, 1959, **12**, 15-33.

BURT, C. Intelligence and social mobility. *British Journal of Statistical Psychology*, 1961, **14**, 3-24. (a)

BURT, C. The gifted child. *British Journal of Statistical Psychology*, 1961, **14**, 123-139. (b)

BURT, C. Is intelligence distributed normally? *British Journal of Statistical Psychology*, 1963, **16**, 175-190.

BURT, C. The genetic determination of differences in intelligence: A study of monozygotic twins reared together and apart. *British Journal of Psychology*, 1966, **57**, 137-153.

BURT, C. Mental capacity and its critics. *Bull. Brit. Psychol. Soc.*, 1968, **21**, 11-18.

BURT, C. Quantitative genetics in psychology. *British Journal of Mathematical and Statistical Psychology*, 1971, **24**, 1-21.

BURT, C., AND HOWARD, M. The multifactorial theory of inheritance and its application to intelligence. *British Journal of Statistical Psychology*, 1956, **9**, 95-131.

BURT, C., AND HOWARD, M. The relative influence of heredity and environment on assessments of intelligence. *British Journal of Statistical Psychology*, 1957, **10**, 99-104.

CARTER, C. O. Differential fertility by intelligence. In J. E. Meade and A. S. Parkes (Eds.), *Genetic and environmental factors in human ability*. New York: Plenum Press, 1966, pp. 185-200.

CASSELL, R. H. Serial verbal learning and retroactive inhibition in aments and children. *Journal of Clinical Psychology*, 1957, **13**, 369-372.

CATTELL, R. B. Occupational norms of intelligence and the standardization of an adult intelligence test. *British Journal of Psychology*, 1934, **25**, 1-28.

CATTELL, R. B. The multiple abstract variance analysis equations and solutions: For nature-nurture research on continuous variables. *Psychological Review*, 1960, **67**, 353-372.

CATTELL, R. B. Theory of fluid and crystallized intelligence: A critical experiment. *Journal of Educational Psychology*, 1963, **54**, 1-22.

CHURCHILL, J. A., NEFF, J. W., AND CALDWELL, D. F. Birth weight and intelligence. *Obstetrics and gynecology*, 1966, **28**, 425-429.

CLARK, K. B. Educational stimulation of racially disadvantaged children. In A. H. Passow (Ed.), *Education in depressed areas.* New York: Teachers College Press, Colombia University, 1963, pp. 142-162.

COLEMAN, J. S., *et al. Equality of educational opportunity.* U.S. Department of Health, Education, and Welfare, 1966.

COOPER, G. D., YORK, M. W., DASTON, P. G., AND ADAMS, H. B. The Porteus Test and various measures of intelligence with Southern Negro adolescents. *American Journal of Mental Deficiency*, 1967, **71**, 787-792.

COOPER, R., AND ZUBEK, J. Effects of enriched and restricted early environments on the learning ability of bright and dull rats. *Canadian Journal of Psychology*, 1958, **12**, 159-164.

CRAVIOTO, J. Malnutrition and behavioral development in the pre-school child. *Pre-school child malnutrition.* National Health Science, Public., 1966, No. 1282.

CRAVIOTO, J., DE LICARDIE, E. R., AND BIRCH, H. G. Nutrition, growth, and neurointegrative development: An experimental and ecologic study. *Pediatrics*, 1966, **38**, 319-372.

CROW, J. F., AND FELSENSTEIN, J. The effect of assortative mating on the genetic composition of a population. *Eugenics Quarterly*, 1968, **15**, 85-97.

CURTI, M., MARSHALL, F. B., STEGGERDA, M., AND HENDERSON, E. M. The Gesell schedules applied to one-, two-, and three-year old Negro children of Jamaica, B.W.I. *Journal of Comparative and Physiological Psychology*, 1935, **20**, 125-156.

DARLINGTON, C. D. Heredity and environment. Proc. IX International Congress of Genetics. *Caryologia*, 1954, **190**, 370-381.

DAVIS, K. Final note on a case of extreme isolation. *American Journal of Sociology*, 1947, **57**, 432-457.

DEUTSCH, M., KATZ, I., AND JENSEN, A. R. (Eds.) *Social class, race, and psychological development*. New York: Holt, Rinehart & Winston, 1968.

DOBZHANSKY, T. Genetic differences between people cannot be ignored. *Scientific Res.*, 1968, **3**, 32-33. (a)

DOBZHANSKY, T. On genetics, sociology, and politics. *Perspectives in Biology and Medicine*, 1968, **11**, 544-554. (b)

DREGER, R. M., AND MILLER, K. S. Comparative psychological studies of Negroes and whites in the United States. *Psychological Bulletin*, 1960, **57**, 361-402.

DUNCAN, O. D. Is the intelligence of the general population declining? *American Sociological Review*, 1952, **17**, 401-407.

DUNCAN, O. D., FEATHERMAN, D. L., AND DUNCAN, B. Socioeconomic background and occupational achievement: Extensions of a basic model. Final Report, Project No. 5-0074 (EO-191) U.S. Department of Health, Education, and Welfare, Office of Education, Bureau of Research, May 1968.

Durham Education Improvement Program, Duke University, 1966-1967. (a)

Durham Education Improvement Program, Research. Durham, North Carolina, 1966-1967. (b)

DUSTMAN, R. E., AND BECK, E. C. The visually evoked potential in twins. *Electroenceph. Clin. Neurophysiol.*, 1965, **19**, 570-575.

ECKLAND, B. K. Genetics and Sociology: A reconsideration. *American Sociological Review*, 1967, **32**, 173-194.

EDGERTON, R. B. Anthropology and mental retardation: A plea for the comparative study of incompetence. In H. J. Prehm, L. A. Hamerlynck, and J. E. Crosson (Eds.), *Behavioral research in mental retardation*. Eugene, Ore: University of Oregon Press, 1968, pp. 75-87.

EELLS, K., DAVIS, A., HAVIGHURST, R. J., HERRICK, V. E., AND TYLER, R. *Intelligence and cultural differences*. Chicago: University of Chicago Press, 1951.

ELASHOFF, JANET D., AND SNOW, R. E. *'Pygmalion' reconsidered: A case study in statistical inference: Reconsideration of the Rosentham-Jacobson data on teacher expectancy*. Worthington, Ohio: Charles A. Jones Publishing Co., 1971.

ELLIS, N. R. The stimulus trace and behavioral inadequacy. In N. R. Ellis (Ed.), *Handbook of mental deficiency*. New York: McGraw-Hill, 1963, pp. 134-158.

ERLENMEYER-KIMLING, L., AND JARVIK, L. F. Genetics and intelligence: A review. *Science*, 1963, **142**, 1477-1479.

FALCONER, D. S. *An introduction to quantitative genetics*. New York: Ronald Press, 1960.

FREEMAN, R. A. Schools and the elusive 'average children' concept. *Wall Street Journal*, July 8, 1968, p. 12.

FULLER, J. L., AND THOMPSON, W. R. *Behavior genetics*. New York: Wiley, 1960.

GAGNÉ, R. M. The acquisition of knowledge. *Psychological Review*, 1962, **69**, 355-365.

GAGNÉ, R. M. Contributions of learning to human development. *Psychological Review*, 1968, **75**, 177-191.

GATES, A. I., AND TAYLOR, G. A. An experimental study of the nature of improvement resulting from practice in mental function. *Journal of Educational Psychology*, 1925, **16**, 583-593.

GEBER, M. The psycho-motor development of African children in the first year, and the influence of maternal behavior. *Journal of Social Psychology*, 1958, **47**, 185-195.

GEBER, M., AND DEAN, R. F. A. The state of development of newborn African children. *Lancet*, 1957, **1**, 1216-1219.

GEBER, M., AND DEAN, R. F. A. Precocious development in new-born African infants. In Y. Brackbill and G. Thompson (Eds.), *Readings in infancy and childhood.* New York: Free Press, 1966.

GHISELLI, E. E. The measurement of occupational aptitude. *University of California Publications in Psychology*, Vol. 8, No. 2, Berkeley, Calif.: University of California Press, 1955.

GLASMAN, L. D. A social-class comparison of conceptual processes in children's free recall. Unpublished doctoral dissertation, University of California, 1968.

GOERTZEL, V., AND GOERTZEL, M. G. *Cradles of eminence.* London: Constable, 1962.

GOODENOUGH, F. L. New evidence on environmental influence on intelligence. *Yearb. Nat. Soc. Stud. Educ.*, 1940, **39**, Part I, 307-365.

GORDON, E. W., AND WILKERSON, D. A. *Compensatory education for the disadvantaged.* New York: College Entrance Examination Board, 1966.

GOTTESMAN, I. I. Genetic aspects of intelligent behavior. In N. R. Ellis (Ed.), *Handbook of mental deficiency.* New York: McGraw-Hill, 1963, pp. 253-296.

GOTTESMAN, I. I. Biogenetics of race and class. In M. Deutsch, I. Katz, and A. R. Jensen (Eds.), *Social class, race, and psychological development.* New York: Holt, Rinehart & Winston, 1968, pp. 11-51.

GOULET, L. R. Verbal learning and memory research with retardates: An attempt to assess developmental trends. In N. R. Ellis (Ed.), *International review of research in mental retardation*, Vol. 3. New York: Academic Press, 1968.

GRAVES, W. L., FREEMAN, M. G., AND THOMPSON, J. D. Culturally related reproductive factors in mental retardation. Paper read at Conference on Sociocultural Aspects of Mental Retardation, Peabody College, Nashville, Tennessee, June 1968.

GUILFORD, J. P. *The nature of human intelligence.* New York: McGraw-Hill, 1967.

HARDY, J. B. Perinatal factors and intelligence. In S. F. Osler and R. E. Cooke (Eds.), *The biosocial basis of mental retardation.*

Baltimore, Maryland: The Johns Hopkins Press, 1965, pp. 35-60.

HARLOW, H. F., AND GRIFFIN, G. Induced mental and social deficits in Rhesus monkeys. In S. F. Osler and R. E. Cooke (Eds.), *The biosocial basis of mental retardation.* Baltimore, Maryland: The Johns Hopkins Press, 1965, pp. 87-106.

HARLOW, H. F., AND HARLOW, M. K. The mind of man. In *Yearbook of science and technology.* New York: McGraw-Hill, 1962.

HARRELL, R. F., WOODYARD, E., AND GATES, A. I. *The effects of mothers' diets on the intelligence of offspring.* New York: Bureau of Publications Teachers College, 1955.

HAVIGHURST, R. J., AND NEUGARTEN, B. L. *Society and education,* 3rd ed. Boston: Allyn & Bacon, 1967.

HEBER, R. Research on education and habilitation of the mentally retarded. Paper read at Conference on Sociocultural Aspects of Mental Retardation, Peabody College, Nashville, Tennessee, June, 1968.

HEBER, R., DEVER, R., AND CONRY, J. The influence of environmental and genetic variables on intellectual development. In H. J. Prehm, L. A. Hamerlynck, and J. E. Crosson (Eds.), *Behavioral Research in mental retardation.* Eugene, Oregon: University of Oregon Press, 1968, pp. 1-23.

HEYNS, O. S. *Abdominal decompression.* Johannesburg: Witwatersrand University Press, 1963.

HIGGINS, C., AND SIVERS, C. A comparison of Stanford-Binet and Colored Raven Progressive Matrices IQ's for children with low socioeconomic status. *Journal of Consulting Psychology,* 1958, **22**, 465-468.

HIGGINS, J., REED, S., AND REED, E. Intelligence and family size: A paradox resolved. *Eugenics Quarterly,* 1962, **9**, 84-90.

HILL, A. C., AND JAFFEE, F. S. Negro fertility and family size preferences. In T. Parsons and K. B. Clark (Eds.), *The Negro American.* Cambridge, Mass.: Houghton-Mifflin, 1966, pp. 134-159.

HODGES, W. L., AND SPICKER, H. H. The effects of pre-school experiences on culturally deprived children. In W. W. Hartup and N. L. Smothergill (Eds.), *The young child: Reviews of research*. Washington, D.C.: National Association for the Education of Young Children, 1967, pp. 262-289.

HOLZINGER, K. J. The relative effect of nature and nurture influences on twin differences. *Journal of Educational Psychology*, 1929, **20**, 241-248.

HONZIK, M. P. Developmental studies of parent-child resemblance in intelligence. *Child Development*, 1957, **28**, 215-228.

HONZIK, M. P. The mental and motor test performances of infants diagnosed or suspected of brain injury. Final Report, Contract SA 43 PH 2426. Washington, D.C.: National Institute of Health, National Institute of Neurological Diseases and Blindness, Collaborative Research, May 1962.

HUNT, J. MCV. *Intelligence and experience*. New York: Ronald Press, 1961.

HUNTLEY, R. M. C. Heritability of intelligence. In J. E. Meade and A. S. Parker (Eds.), *Genetic and environmental factors in human ability*. New York: Plenum Press, 1966, pp. 201-218.

HUSÉN, T. *Psychological twin research*, Vol. 1. Stockholm: Almqvist & Wiksell, 1959.

HUSÉN, T. Abilities of twins. *Scandinavian Journal of Psychology*, 1960, **1**, 125-135.

INGLE, D. J. Editorial: The need to study biological differences among racial groups: Moral issues. *Perspectives in Biology and Medicine*, 1967, **10**, 497-499.

ISCOE, I. AND SEMLER, I. J. Paired-associate learning in normal and mentally retarded children as a function of four experimental conditions. *Journal of Comparative and Physiological Psychology*, 1964, **57**, 387-392.

JENSEN, A. R. A statistical note on racial differences in the Progressive Matrices. *Journal of Consulting Psychology*, 1959, **23**, 272.

JENSEN, A. R. Learning abilities in Mexican-American and Anglo-American children. *California Journal of Educational Research*, 1961, **12**, 147-159.

JENSEN, A. R. An empirical theory of the serial-position effect. *Journal of Psychology*, 1962, **53**, 127-142.

JENSEN, A. R. Learning abilities in retarded, average, and gifted children. *Merrill-Palmer Quarterly*, 1963, **9**, 123-140.

JENSEN, A. R. Rote learning in retarded adults and normal children. *American Journal of Mental Deficiency*, 1965, **69**, 828-834. (a)

JENSEN, A. R. Individual differences in learning: Interference factor. Cooperative Research Project No. 1867, U.S. Office of Education, 1965. (b)

JENSEN, A. R. The measurement of reactive inhibition in humans. *Journal of General Psychology*, 1966, **75**, 85-93.

JENSEN, A. R. Estimation of the limits of heritability of traits by comparison of monozygotic and dizygotic twins. *Proceedings of the National Academy of Sciences, U.S.*, 1967, **58**, 149-156. (a)

JENSEN, A. R. Varieties of individual differences in learning. In R. M. Gagné (Ed.), *Learning and individual differences*. Columbus, Ohio: Merrill, 1967. (b)

JENSEN, A. R. Social class, race, and genetics: Implications for education. *American Educational Research Journal*, 1968, **5**, 1-42. (a)

JENSEN, A. R. Patterns of mental ability and socioeconomic status. *Proceedings of the National Academy of Sciences, U.S.*, 1968, **60**, 1330-1337. (b)

JENSEN, A. R. Another look at culture-fair tests. In *Western Conference on Testing Problems, Proceedings for 1968*, 'Measurement for Eduational Planning'. Berkeley, California: Educational Testing Service, Western Office, 1968, pp. 50-104. (c)

JENSEN, A. R. Intelligence, learning ability, and socioeconomic status. *Journal of Special Education*, 1968. (d)

JENSEN, A. R. Social class and verbal learning. In M. Deutsch, I. Katz, and A. R. Jensen (Eds.), *Social class, race, and psychological development*. New York: Holt, Rinehart & Winston, 1968, pp. 115-174. (e)

JENSEN, A. R. The culturally disadvantaged and the heredity-environment uncertainty. In J. Helmuth (Ed.), *The culturally disadvantaged child*, Vol. 2. Seattle, Washington: Special Child Publications, 1968. (f)

JENSEN, A. R. How much can we boost IQ and scholastic achievement? *Harvard Educational Review*, 1969, **39**, 1-123.

JENSEN, A. R., AND FREDERICKSEN, J. Social-class differences in free recall learning. *Journal of Educational Psychology*, in press.

JENSEN, A. R., AND RODEN, A. Memory span and the skewness of the serial-position curve. *British Journal of Psychology*, 1963, **54**, 337-349.

JENSEN, A. R., AND ROHWER, W. D., JR. Verbal mediation in paired-associate and serial learning. *Journal of Verbal Learning and Verbal Behavior*, 1963, **1**, 346-352. (a)

JENSEN, A. R., AND ROHWER, W. D., JR. The effect of verbal mediation on the learning and retention of paired-associates by retarded adults. *American Journal of Mental Deficiency*, 1963, **68**, 80-84. (b)

JENSEN, A. R., AND ROHWER, W. D., JR. Syntactical mediation of serial and paired-associate learning as a function of age. *Child Development*, 1965, **36**, 611-608.

JENSEN, A. R., AND ROHWER, W. D., JR. Mental retardation, mental age, and learning rate. *Journal of Educational Psychology*, 1968, **59**, 402-403.

JENSEN, A. R., AND ROHWER, W. D., JR. Experimental analysis of learning abilities in culturally disadvantaged children. Final Report on OEO Project No. 2404, U.S. Office of Economic Opportunity, 1969.

JEPSEN, N. P., AND BREDMOSE, G. V. Investigations into the age of mentally deficient women at their first delivery. *Acta Psychiatrica Scandinavica*, 1956 (Monogr. Suppl. 108), pp. 203-210.

JINKS, J. L., AND FULKER, D. W. Comparison of the biometrical genetical, MAVA, and classical approaches to the analysis of human behavior. *Psychological Bulletin*, 1970, **73**, 311-349.

JONES, H. E. The environment and mental development. In L. Carmichael (Ed.), *Manual of child psychology*, 2nd ed. New York: Wiley, 1954, pp. 631-696.

JUEL-NIELSEN, N. Individual and environment: a psychiatric-psychological investigation of monozygous twins reared apart. *Acta psychiatrica et neuroligica Scandinavica*, 1965 (Monogr. Suppl. 183).

KAGAN, J. A developmental approach to conceptual growth. In H. J. Klausmeier and C. W. Harris (Eds.), *Analyses of concept learning*. New York: Academic Press, 1966, pp. 97-115.

KARNES, M. B. A research program to determine the effects of various pre-school intervention programs on the development of disadvantaged children and the strategic age for such intervention. Paper read at American Educational Research Association, Chicago, February 1968.

KEMPTHORNE, O. *An introduction to genetic statistics*. New York: Wiley, 1957.

KENNEDY, W. A., VAN DE RIET, V., AND WHITE, J. C., JR. A normative sample of intelligence and achievement of Negro elementary school children in the Southeastern United States. *Monogr. Soc. Res. Child Development*, 1963, **28**, No. 6.

KNOBLOCH, H., AND PASAMANICK, B. The relationship of race and socioeconomic status to the development of motor behavior patterns in infancy. *Psychiatric Research Reports*, 1958, **10**, 123-133.

KUSHLICK, A. Assessing the size of the problem of subnormality. In J. E. Meade and A. S. Parkes (Eds.), *Genetic and environmental factors in human ability*. New York: Plenum Press, 1966, pp. 121-147.

KUTTNER, R. E. *Biochemical anthropology*. In R. E. Kuttner (Ed.), *Race and modern science*. New York: Social Science Press, 1967, pp. 197-222.

KUTTNER, R. E. Letters to and from the editor. *Perspectives in Biology and Medicine*, 1968, **11**, 707-709.

LAWRENCE, E. M. An investigation into the relation between intelligence and inheritance. *British Journal of Psychology. Monograph Supplement*, 1931, **16**, No. 5.

LEAHY, A. M. Nature-nurture and intelligence. *Genetic Psychology Monographs*, 1935, **17**, 241-305.

LESSER, G. S., FIFER, G., AND CLARK, D. H. Mental abilities of children from different social-class and cultural groups. *Monogr. Soc. Res. Child Development*, 1965, **30**, (4).

LI, C. C. *Population genetics*. Chicago: University of Chicago Press, 1955.

LINDZEY, G. Some remarks concerning incest, the incest taboo, and psychoanalytic theory. *American Psychologist*, 1967, **22**, 1051-1059.

LOEHLIN, J. C. Psychological genetics, from the study of human behavior. In R. B. Cattell (Ed.), *Handbook of modern personality theory*. New York: Aldine, in press.

LOEVINGER, J. On the proportional contributions of differences in nature and nurture to differences in intelligence. *Psychological Bulletin*, 1943, **40**, 725-756.

MCGURK, F. C. J. The culture hypothesis and psychological tests. In R. E. Kuttner (Ed.), *Race and modern science*. New York: Social Science Press, 1967, pp. 367-381.

MCMANIS, D. L. The von Restorff effect in serial learning by normal and retarded subjects. *American Journal of Mental Deficiency*, 1966, **70**, 569-575.

MCNEMAR, Q. Twin resemblances in motor skills, and the effect of practice thereon. *Journal of Genetic Psychology*, 1933, **42**, 70-97.

MCNEMAR, Q. A critical examination of the University of Iowa studies of environmental influences upon the IQ. *Psychological Bulletin*, 1940, **37**, 63-92.

MCNEMAR, Q. *Psychological statistics*. New York: Wiley, 1949.

MASLAND, R. L., SARASON, S. B., AND GLADWIN, T. *Mental subnormality*. New York: Basic Books, 1958.

MAXWELL, J. *Social implications of the 1947 Scottish Mental Survey*. London: University of London Press, 1953.

*Medical World News*. Using speed of brain waves to test IQ. 1968, **9**, 26.

MITRA, S. Income, socioeconomic status, and fertility in the United States. *Eugenics Quarterly*, 1966, **13**, 223-230.

MONEY, J. Two cytogenetic syndromes: Psychologic comparisons. 1. Intelligence and specific-factor quotients. *Journal of Psychiatric Research*, 1964, **2**, 223-231.

MOYNIHAN, D. P. *The Negro family*. Washington, D.C.: Office of Policy Planning and Research, United States Department of Labor, 1965.

MOYNIHAN, D. P. Employment, income, and the ordeal of the Negro family. In T. Parsons and K. B. Clark (Eds.), *The Negro American*. Cambridge, Mass.: Houghton-Mifflin, 1966, pp. 134-159.

NATIONAL ACADEMY OF SCIENCES. Racial Studies: Academy states position on call for new research. *Science*, 1967, **158**, 892-893.

NAYLOR, A. E., AND MYRIANTHOPOULOS, N. C. The relation of ethnic and selected socioeconomic factors to human birthweight. *Ann. Hum. Genet.*, 1967, **31**, 71-83.

NEEL, J. V., AND SCHULL, W. J. *Human heredity*, Chicago: University of Chicago Press, 1954.

NEFF, W. S. Socioeconomic status and intelligence: A critical survey. *Psychological Bulletin*, 1938, **35**, 727-757.

NELSON, G. K., AND DEAN, R. F. A. *Bull. World Health Organ.*, 1959, **21**, 779. Cited by G. Cravioto, Malnutrition and behavioral development in the pre-school child. *Pre-school child malnutrition*. National Health Science, 1966, Public, No. 1282.

NEWMAN, H. H., FREEMAN, F. N., AND HOLZINGER, K. J. *Twins: A study of heredity and environment*. Chicago: University of Chicago Press, 1937.

NICHOLS, R. C. The National Merit twin study. In S. G. Vandenberg (Ed.), *Methods and goals in human behavior genetics*. New York: Academic Press, 1956, pp. 231-244.

NICHOLS, R. C. *National Merit Scholarships Corporation Research Reports*, 1966, **2**, No. 8.

NICHOLS, R. C., AND BILBRO, W. C., JR. The diagnosis of twin zygosity. *Acta Genetica*, 1966, **16**, 265-275.

NOBLE, C. E. The learning of psychomobar skills. *Annual Review Of Psychology*, 1968, **19**, 203-250.

O'CONNOR, N., AND HERMELIN, B. Like and cross modality recognition in subnormal children. *Quarterly Journal of Experimental Psychology*, 1961, **13**, 48-52.

OSBORNE, R. T. Stability of factor structure for the WISC for normal Negro children from pre-school level to first grade. *Psychological Reports*, 1966, **18**, 655-664.

PETTIGREW, T. *A profile of the Negro American*. Princeton, N.J.: Van Nostrand, 1964.

POWLEDGE, F. *To change a child – A report on the Institute for Development Studies*. Chicago: Quadrangle Books, 1967.

PREHM, H. J. Rote verbal learning and memory in the retarded. In H. J. Prehm, L. A. Hamerlynck and J. E. Crosson (Eds.), *Behavioral research in mental retardation*. Eugene, Oregon: University of Oregon, 1968, pp 31-43.

RAPIER, J. L. Measured intelligence and the ability to learn. *Acta Psychologica*, 1962, **20**, 1-17.

RAPIER, J. L. The learning abilities of normal and retarded children as a function of social class. *Journal of Educational Psychology*, 1968, **59**, 102-119.

REED, E. W., AND REED, S. C. *Mental retardation: A family study*. Philadelphia: Saunders, 1965.

RESEARCH PROFILE NO. II. Summary of progress in childhood disorders of the brain and nervous system. U.S. Public Health Service, Washington D.C., 1965.

REYMERT, M. L. AND HINTON, R. T., JR. The effect of a change to a relatively superior environment upon the IQs of one hundred children. *Yearb. Nat. Soc. Stud. Educ.*, 1940, **39** (1), 225-268.

RIMLAND, B. *Infantile autism*. New York: Appleton-Century-Crofts, 1964.

ROBERTS, J. A. F. The genetics of mental deficiency. *Eugenics Review*, 1952, **44**, 71-83.

ROBERTS, R. C. Some concepts and methods in quantative genetics. In J. Hirsch (Ed.), *Behavior-genetic analysis*. New York: McGraw-Hill, 1967, pp 214-257.

ROBINSON, H. B., AND ROBINSON, N. M. *The mentally retarded child. A Psychological approach.* New York: McGraw-Hill, 1965.

ROHWER, W. D., JR. Social class differences in the role of linguistic structures in paired associate learning. Cooperative Research Project No 5-0605, U.S. Office of Education, 1967.

ROHWER, W. D., JR. Socioeconomic status, intelligence and learning proficiency in children. Paper read at the annual meeting of the American Psychological Association, San Francisco, August 1968. (a).

ROHWER, W. D., JR. Mental mnemonics in early learning. *Teachers College Record*, 1968, **70**, pp 213-226. (b).

ROHWER, W. D., JR., AND LYNCH, S. Retardation, school strata, and learning proficiency. *American Journal of Mental Deficiency*, 1968, **73**, pp 91-96.

ROHWER, W. D., JR., LYNCH, S., LEVIN, J. R., AND SUZUKI, N. Grade level, school strata, and learning efficiency. *Journal of Educational Psychology*, 1968, **59**, 26-31.

ROSENTHAL, R., AND JACOBSON, L. *Pygmalion in the classroom.* New York: Holt, Rinehart & Winston, 1968.

ROSSI, E. L. Associative clustering in normal and retarded children. *American Journal of Mental Deficiency*, 1963, **67**, 691-699.

SCARR, SANDRA. Effects of birth weight on later intelligence. *Social Biology*, 1969, **16**, 249-256.

SCHULL, W. J., AND NEEL, J. V. *The effects of inbreeding on Japanese children.* New York: Harper & Row, 1965.

SCHWEBEL, M. *Who can be educated?* New York: Grove, 1968.

SCOTT, J. P., AND FULLER, J. L. *Genetics and the social behavior of the dog.* Chicago: University of Chicago Press, 1965.

SCRIMSHAW, N. S. Infant malnutrition and adult learning. *Saturday Review*, March 16, 1968, p. 64.

SEMLER, I. J., AND ISCOE, I. Concept interference and paired-associates in retarded children. *Journal of Comparative and Physiological Psychology*, 1965, **60**, 465-466.

SHIELDS, J. *Monozygotic twins brought up apart and brought up together.* London: Oxford University Press, 1962.

SHIELDS, J., AND SLATER, E. Heredity and psychological abnormality. In H. J. Eysenck (Ed.), *Handbook of abnormal psychology*. New York: Basic Books, 1961, pp. 298-343.

SHUEY, A. M. *The testing of Negro intelligence*, 2nd ed. New York: Social Science Press, 1966.

SKEELS, H. M. Adult status of children with contrasting early life experiences: A follow-up study. *Child Development Monograph*, 1966, **31**, No. 3, Serial No. 105.

SKEELS, H. M., AND DYE, H. B. A study of the effects of differential stimulation on mentally retarded children. *Proc. Addr. Amer. Ass. Ment. Defic.*, 1939, **44**, 114-136.

SKODAK, MARIE, AND SKEELS, H. M. A final follow-up study of one hundred adopted children. *Journal of Genetic Psychology*, 1949, **75**, 85-125.

SPERRAZZO, G., AND WILKINS, W. L. Further normative data on the Progressive Matrices. *Journal of Consulting Psychology*, 1958, **22**, 35-37.

SPERRAZZO, G., AND WILKINS, W. L. Racial differences on Progressive Matrices. *Journal of Consulting Psychology*, 1959, **23**, 273-274.

SPUHLER, J. N., AND LINDZEY, G. Racial differences in behavior. In J. Hirsch (Ed.), *Behavior-genetic analysis*. New York: McGraw-Hill, 1967, pp. 366-414.

STOCH, M. B., AND SMYTHE, P. M. Does undernutrition during infancy inhibit brain growth and subsequent intellectual development? *Arch. Dis. Childh.*, 1963, **38**, 546-552.

STODDARD, G. D. *The meaning of intelligence*. New York: Macmillan, 1943.

STODOLSKY, S. S., AND LESSER, G. Learning patterns in the disadvantaged. *Harvard Educational Review*, 1967, **37**, 546-593.

STOTT, D. H. Interaction of heredity and environment in regard to 'measured intelligence'. *British Journal of Educational Psychology*, 1960, **30**, 95-102.

STOTT, D. H. *Studies of troublesome children*. New York: Humanities Press, 1966.

TALLAND, G. A. *Deranged memory: A psychonomic study of the amnesic syndrome.* New York: Academic Press, 1965.

TERMAN, L. M. Personal reactions of the Yearbook Committee. In G. M. Whipple (Ed.), *Intelligence: Its nature and nurture,* 39th Yearbook of the National Society for the Study of Education, Part I, 1940, pp. 460-467.

TERMAN, L. M., AND MERRILL, MAUD A. *Measuring intelligence.* Boston: Houghton-Mifflin, 1937.

TERMAN, L. M., AND MERRILL, MAUD A. *Stanford-Binet Intelligence Scale: Manual for the third revision, Form L-M.* Boston: Houghton-Mifflin, 1960.

TERMAN, L. M., AND ODEN, M. *The gifted group at mid-life.* Stanford: Stanford University Press, 1959.

THOMPSON, W. R. The inheritance and development of intelligence. *Res. Pub. Ass. Nerv. Ment. Dis.,* 1954, **33**, 209-331.

THORNDIKE, E. L. Measurement of twins. *Journal of Philos., Psychol., Sci. Meth.,* 1905, **2**, 547-553.

THORNDIKE, R. L. Review of *Pygmalion in the Classroom, American Educational Research Journal,* 1968, **5**, 708-711.

TUDDENHAM, R. D. Psychometricizing Piaget's méthode clinique. Paper read at American Educational Research Association, Chicago, February 1968.

TYLER, L. E. *The psychology of human differences,* 3rd ed. New York: Appleton-Century-Crofts, 1965.

U.S. COMMISSION ON CIVIL RIGHTS. *Racial isolation in the public schools,* Vol. 1. Washington, D.C.: U.S. Government Printing Office, 1967.

*U.S. New and World Report,* Mental tests for 10 million Americans – what they show. October 17, 1966, pp. 78-80.

VANDENBERG, S. G. Contributions of twin research to psychology. *Psychological Bulletin,* 1966, **66**, 327-352. (a)

VANDENBERG, S. G. *Louisiville, Twin Study,* Research Report No. 19. Louisville, Kentucky: University of Louisville School of Medicine, 1966. (b)

VANDENBERG, S. G. Hereditary factors in psychological variables in man, with a special emphasis on cognition. In J. S. Spuhler (Ed.), *Genetic diversity and human behavior*. Chicago: Aldine, 1967, pp. 99-133.

VANDENBERG, S. G. The nature and nurture of intelligence. In D. C. Glass (Ed.), *Genetics*. New York: The Rockefeller University Press and Russell Sage Foundation, 1968.

VERNON, P. E. *The structure of human abilities*. New York: Wiley, 1950.

VERNON, P. E. Symposium on the effects of coaching and practice in intelligence tests. *British Journal of Educational Psychology*, 1954, **24**, 5-8.

VERNON, P. E. Environmental handicaps and intellectual development: Part II and Part III. *British Journal of Educational Psychology*, 1965, **35**, 1-22.

WALLACE, W. P., AND UNDERWOOD, B. J. Implicit responses and the role of intralist similarity in verbal learning by normal and retarded subjects. *Journal of Educational Psychology*, 1964, **55**, 362-370.

WALTERS, C. E. Comparative development of Negro and white infants. *Journal of Genetic Psychology*, 1967, **110**, 243-251.

WECHSLER, D. *Manual of the Wechsler Intelligence Scale for Children*. New York: Psychological Corporation, 1949.

WECHSLER, D. *The measurement and appraisal of adult intelligence*, 4th ed. Baltimore: Williams & Wilkins, 1958.

WHEELER, L. R. A comparative study of the intelligence of East Tennessee mountain children. *Journal of Educational Psychology*, 1942, **33**, 321-334.

WHITE, S. H. Evidence for a hierarchical arrangement of learning processes. In L. P. Lipsett and C. C. Spiker (Eds.), *Advances in child development and behavior*, Vol. 2. New York: Academic Press, 1965, pp. 187-220.

WILLERMAN, L., AND CHURCHILL, J. A. Intelligence and birth weight in identical twins. *Child Development*, 1967, **38**, 623-629.

WILSON, A. B. Educational consequences of segregation in a California community. In *Racial isolation in the public schools*, Appendices, Vol. 2 of a report by the U.S. Commission on Civil Rights. Washington, D.C.: U.S. Government Printing Office, 1967.

WILSON, R. S. Twins: Early mental development. *Science*, 1972, **175**, 914-917.

WISEMAN, S. *Education and environment*. Manchester: Manchester University Press, 1964.

WISEMAN, S. Environmental and innate factors and educational attainment. In J. E. Meade and A. S. Parkes (Eds.), *Genetic and environmental factors in human ability*. New York: Plenum Press, 1966, pp. 64-80.

WRIGHT, L., AND HEARN, C. B., JR. Reactive inhibition in normals and defectives as measured from a common performance criterion. *Journal of General Psychology*, 1964, **71**, 57-64.

WRIGHT, S. Statistical methods in biology. *Journal of the American Statistical Association*, 1931, **26**, 155-163.

YOUNG, M., AND GIBSON, J. B. Social mobility and fertility. In J. E. Meade and A. S. Parkes (Eds.), *Biological aspects of social problems*. Edinburgh: Oliver and Boyd, 1965.

ZAZZO, R. *Les jumeaux, le couple et la personne*, 2 vols. Paris: Presses Universitaires de France, 1960.

ZEAMAN, D. Learning processes of the mentally retarded. In S. F. Osler and R. E. Cooke (Eds.), *The biosocial basis of mental retardation*. Baltimore: Johns Hopkins Press, 1965, pp. 107-127.

ZEAMAN, D., AND HOUSE, B. J. The relation of IQ and learning. In R. M. Gagné (Ed.), *Learning and individual differences*. Columbus, Ohio: Merrill, 1967.

ZIGLER, E. Familial mental retardation: A continuing dilemma. *Science*, 1967, **155**, 292-298.

ZIGLER, E. The nature-nurture issue reconsidered: A discussion of Uzgiris' paper. Paper read at Conference on Sociocultural Aspects of Mental Retardation, Peabody College, Nashville, Tennessee, June 1968.

# Bibliography of Articles About 'How Much Can We Boost IQ and Scholastic Achievement?' by Arthur R. Jensen

ALBEE, G. W., *et al.* Statement by SPSSI on current IQ controversy – heredity *versus* environment. *American Psychologist*, 1969, **24**, 1039.

ALFERT, ELIZABETH. The promotion of prejudice. *Journal of Social Issues*, 1969, **25**, 206-211.

ANASTASI, ANNE. More on heritability: addendum to the Hebb and Jensen interchange. *American Psychologist*, 1971, **26**, 1036-1037.

ANASTASIOW, N. Educational relevance and Jensen's conclusions. *Phi Delta Kappan*, 1969, **51**, 32-35.

BAKER, GAIL L. Individualizing instruction for individual abilities: Heredity plus environment suggest a new approach. *Educational Leadership*, in press.

BENNETT, RUTH. A sociologist looks at the Jensen Report: Discussion of Rosedith Sitgreaves' paper, 'Statistics of the Jensen Report'. *New York Statistician*, 1971, **23**, No. 1, 5-7.

BENOIST, A. DE. Jensenismus: Tabu Rasse und IQ. *Junges Forum*, 1970, Nr. 6, 3-15.

BEREITER, C. The future of individual differences. *Harvard Educational Review*, 1969, **39**, 310-318.

BEREITER, C. Genetics and educability: Educational implications of the Jensen debate. In J. Hellmuth (Ed.), *Disadvantaged Child*, Vol. 3, *Compensatory education: A national debate*. New York: Brunner-Mazel, 1970, pp. 279-299.

BERUBE, M. R. Jensen's Complaint. *Commonweal*, 1969, **91**, 42-44.

BLOOM, B. S. Letter to the Editor. *Harvard Educational Review*, 1969, **39**, 419-421.

BODMER, W. F., AND CAVALLI-SFORZA, L. L. Intelligence and race. *Scientific American*, 1970, **223**, 19-29.

BONNOT, GERARD. L'intelligence se décide avant 4 ans. *L'Express*, pp. 26-27, 17-23, March, 1969.

BRACE, C. L., GAMBLE, G. R., AND BOND, J. T. (Eds.), *Race and intelligence*. Anthropological Studies, No. 8. Washington, D.C.: American Anthropological Association, 1971.

BRAZZIEL, W. F. A letter from the South. *Harvard Educational Review*, 1969, **39**, 348-356.

BRAZZIEL, W. F. Beyond the sound and the fury. *Measurement and Evaluation in Guidance*, 1970, **3**, 709.

BRAZZIEL, W. F. Perspective on the Jensen affair. *Childhood Education*, 1970, **46**, 371-372.

BROWN, F. G. The Jensen report: Review of the past, focus for the future. *Measurement and Evaluation in Guidance*, 1970, **3**, 18-24. Reprinted in: J. Hellmuth (Ed.), *Disadvantaged Child*, Vol. 3. New York: Brunner-Mazed, Inc., 1970, pp. 102-110.

BURGESS, JOHANNA, AND JAHODA, MARIE. The interpretation of certain data in 'How Much Can We Boost IQ Score and Scholastic Achievement?' *Bulletin of the British Psychological Society*, 1970, **23**, 224-225.

BURGESS, JOHANNA, AND JAHODA, MARIE. Reply to Professor Jensen. *Bulletin of the British Psychological Society*, 1971, **24**, 199-200.

BURNES, K. Patterns of WISC scores for children of two socio-economic classes and races. *Child Development*, 1970, **41**, 493.

BURT, C. Intelligence and heredity. *New Scientist*, May 1, 1969, pp. 226-228.

BURT, C. Correspondence (A reply to Burgess and Jahoda, *Bulletin*, **23**, 224-225). *Bulletin of the British Psychological Society*, 1971, **24**, 87.

BURT, C. Group differences in ability. *Educational Research*, 1971, in press.

CAMERON, H. K. The Jensen controversy. II. Cultural Myopia. *Measurement and Evaluation in Guidance*, 1970, **3**, 10-17.

CAMPBELL, P. B. The Jensen report. In *The Use, Misuse, and Abuse of Tests*. First Annual NEAMEG conferences on Measurement in Education. May 14-15, 1970, pp. 30-33.

CASS, J. Race and intelligence. *Saturday Review*, 1969, **52**, 67-68.

CATTELL, R. B. The structure of intelligence in relation to the nature-nurture controversy. In R. Cancro (Ed.), *Intelligence: Genetic and environmental influences*. New York: Grune & Stratton, 1971, pp. 3-30.

CAVALLI-SFORZA, L. Problems and prospects of genetic analysis of intelligence at the intra- and interracial level. In J. Hellmuth (Ed.), *Disadvantaged Child*, Vol. 3, New York: Brunner-Mazel, Inc., 1970, pp. 111-123.

COMER, J. P. Research and the black backlash. *American Journal of Orthopsychiatry*, 1970, **40**, 8-11.

CRONBACH, L. J. Heredity, environment, and educational policy. *Harvard Educational Review*, 1969, **39**, 338-347.

CROW, J. F. Genetic theories and influences: Comments on the value of diversity. *Harvard Educational Review*, 1969, **39**, 301-309.

DAVIS, R. H., MARZOCCO, F. N., AND DENNY, M. R. Interaction of individual differences with modes of presenting programmed instruction. *Journal of Educational Psychology*, 1970, **61**, 198.

DEUTSCH, M. Happenings on the way back to the forum. *Harvard Educational Review*, 1969, **39**, 523-557.

DEUTSCH, M. Organizational and conceptual barriers to social change. *Journal of Social Issues*, 1969, **25**, 5-18.

DREEBAN, R. Comments on Jensen. *Administrator's Notebook*. Midwest Administration Center, University of Chicago, 1969, **18**, No. 3.

EDSON, L. Jensenism, *n.*. Or the theory that IQ is largely determined by the genes. *New York Times Magazine*, pp. 10-11 +, August 31, 1969. Discussion, p. 4+, Sept. 21, 1969; p. 38+, Sept. 28, 1969.

EINHORN, H. J. Comment: On Hebb's criticism of Jensen, *American Psychologist*, 1970, **25**, 1173-1174.

ELKIND, D. Piagetian and psychometric conceptions of intelligence. *Harvard Educational Review*, 1969, **39**, 338-347.

ERZIEHUNG. Intelligenz – Bombe aus Berkeley. *Der Speigel*, No. 28, 1969, pp. 130-132.

EYSENCK, H. J. A critique of Jensen. *New Scientist*, pp. 228-229, May 1969.

EYSENCK, H. J. *Race, intelligence, and education.* London: Temple Smith, 1971. American edition: *The IQ Argument.* Freeport, New York: Library Press, 1971.

FEHR, F. S. Critique of hereditarian accounts of intelligence and contrary findings. *Harvard Educational Review*, 1969, **39**, 571-580.

FINDLEY, W. G., AND BRYAN, M. M. A note on Jensen and other new developments. Appendix A. In *Ability Grouping, 1970.* Center for Educational Improvement. University of Georgia, 1971, pp. 88-89.

FISHBACH, T. J., AND WALBERG, H. J. Weighted and unweighted means for estimation: A note on the Humphreys-Dachler and Jensen Papers. *Journal of Educational Psychology*, 1971, **62**, 79-80.

GAGE, N. L. IQ, heritability, race differences, and educational research. *Phi Delta Kappan*, 1972, **53**, 308-312. (a)

GAGE, N. L. Replies to Shockley, Page, and Jensen: The causes of race differences in IQ. *Phi Delta Kappan*, 1972, **53**, 422-427. (b)

GILLIE, O. Scientist attack illogical IQ theory. *Science Journal*, 1970, **6**, 9.

GOLDEN, M., AND BRIDGER, W. A refutation of Jensen's position on intelligence, race, social class, and heredity. *Mental Hygiene*, 1969, **53**, 648-653.

GOLDSTEIN, A. C. A flaw in Jensen's use of heritability data. *IRCD Bulletin*, 1969, **5**, No. 4. ERIC Information Retrieval Center on the Disadvantaged.

GORDON, E. W. Education, ethnicity, genetics and intelligence. *IRCD Bulletin*, 1969, **5**, No. 4. ERIC Information Retrieval Center on the Disadvantaged.

GORDON, E. W. Methodological problems and pseudoissues in the nature-nurture controversy. In R. Cancro (Ed.), *Intelligence: Genetic and environmental influences*. New York: Grune & Stratton, 1971, pp. 240-251.

GORDON, R. A. Comment: Concerning Hebb's criticism of Jensen and the heredity-environment argument. *American Psychologist*, 1970, **25**, 1172-1173.

GRUBER, H. E. How can we respond effectively? *IRCD Bulletin*, 1969, **5**, No. 4. ERIC Information Retrieval Center for the Disadvantaged.

HAMBLIN, R. L., BUCKHOLDT, D., AND DOSS, HARRIET. Compensatory education: A new perspective. *Toledo Law Review*, 1970, Nos. 2 and 3, Spring-Summer, pp. 459-499.

HAMMERTON, M. Race, morals, and research. *The Listener*, Jan. 28, 1971, pp. 99-101.

HEBB, D. O. A return to Jensen and his social science critics. *American Psychologist*, 1970, **25**, 568.

HIRSCH, J. Behavior-genetic analysis and its biosocial consequences. *Seminars in Psychiatry*, 1970, **2**, 89-105.

HUDSON, L. Nature, nurture: racialist comeback? *Times Educational Supplement*, 1969, **33**, July 4.

HUDSON, L. Intelligence, race, and the selection of data. *Race*, 1971, **12**, 283.

HUMPHREYS, L. G., AND DACHLER, H. P. Jensen's theory of intelligence. *Journal of Educational Psychology*, 1969, **60**, 419-426. (a)

HUMPHREYS, L. G., AND DACHLER, H. P. Jensen's theory of intelligence: A rebuttal. *Journal of Educational Psychology*, 1969, **60**, 432-433. (b)

HUNT, J. MCV. Has compensatory education failed? Has it been attempted? *Harvard Educational Review*, 1969, **39**, 278-300.

HUNT, J. MCV., AND KIRK, G. E. Social aspects of intelligence: Evidence and issues. In R. Cancro (Ed.), *Intelligence: Genetic and environmental influences.* New York: Grune & Stratton, 1971, pp. 262-306.

HUNT, M. The intelligent man's guide to intelligence. *Playboy,* Vol. 18, No. 2, Feb. 1971, 94-96, 106, 191-194.

HURST, J. G. The nature-nurture controversy – another view: A review of 'How Much Can We Boost IQ and Scholastic Achievement?' by A. R. Jensen. Unpublished manuscript. May 1969, pp. 2-129.

HYMAN, J. D. Communication: IQ and Race. *The New Republic.* 1969, **161,** 30-31.

IVANY, J. W. G. Resource letter EP-1 on educational psychology. *American Journal of Physics,* 1969, **37,** 1091.

JENCKS, C. Intelligence and race: What color is IQ? *New Republic,* Sept. 13, 1969, Nos. 10-11, Issues 2854-2855, pp. 25-29.

JORDAN, N. 'How Much Can We Boost IQ and Scholastic Achievement?' by Arthur R. Jensen: A critique of the paper and the problem. Unpublished manuscript. Institute for Defense Analysis, International and Social Studies Division. May 2, 1969, p. 38.

KAGAN, J. S. Inadequate evidence and illogical conclusions. *Harvard Educational Review,* 1969, **39,** 274-277.

KENEFICK, D. P. Has anyone seen my pertinent variable? *Mental Hygiene,* 1969, **53,** 657.

KEOGH, BARBARA K., AND MACMILLAN, D. L. Effects of motivational and presentation conditions on digit recall of children of differing socioeconomic, racial, and intelligence groups. *American Educational Research Journal,* 1971, **8,** 27-38.

LAMBERT, HAZEL M. Perspectives from Research. *Young Children,* 1969, **24,** 242-244.

LEDERBERG, J. Racial alienation and intelligence. *Harvard Educational Review,* 1969, **39,** 611-615.

LEWONTIN, R. C. Race and intelligence. *Bulletin of the Atomic Scientists,* 1970, **26,** 2-8. (a)

LEWONTIN, R. C. Further remarks on race and the genetics of intelligence. *Bulletin of the Atomic Scientists,* 1970, **26,** 23-25. (b)

LIGHT, R. J. Biometric issues in measuring the genetic component of human intelligence. *New York Statistician*, 1971, **22**, 3-8.

LIGHT, R. J., AND SMITH, P. V. Social allocation models of intelligence: A methodological inquiry. *Harvard Educational Review*, 1969, **39**, 484-510.

LIGHT, R. J., AND SMITH, P. V. Statistical issues in social allocation models of intelligence: A review and a response. *Review of Educational Research*, 1971, **41**, 351-367.

LINDSEY, R. A. Negro intelligence and educational theory. *Clearing House*, 1970, **45**, 67-71.

MCCONNELL, R. A. The Future revisited. *BioScience*, 1970, **20**, 903-904.

MAKINS, VIRGINIA. Interview with Arthur Jensen. *The Times Educational Supplement* (London), Sept. 3, 1971, p. 56.

MEAD, MARGARET. Sense – and nonsense – about race. *Redbook Magazine*, Sept. 1969, p. 35.

MERCER, MARILYN. Is your I.Q. really you? *Glamour*, Vol. 63, No. 2, pp. 212-213, 283-285.

MORRIS, F. L. The Jensen hypothesis: Social science research or social science racism. *Center Monograph Series*, No. 2. Center for Afro-American Studies, University of California, Los Angeles, 1971.

MOYNIHAN, D. P. Comment: Jensen not 'Must Reading' in the Nixon Cabinet. *Journal of Social Issues*, 1970, **26**, 191-192.

NEARY, J. Jensenism: Variations on a racial theme. *Life*, 68: 58B-58D+, June 12, 1970.

NEARY, J. Jensenism: Variation on a racial theme. *Life*. Discussions, July 4, 1970, p. 16A.

PLOTKIN, L. Negro intelligence and the Jensen hypothesis. *The New York Statistician*, 1971, **22**, 3-7.

RABINOWITCH, EUGENE. Jensen *vs.* Lewontin (a comment). *Bulletin of the Atomic Scientists*, Vol. 26, No. 5, pp. 25-26, May 1970.

RICHARDSON, K., SPEARS, D., AND RICHARDS, M. (Eds.), *Race, culture, and intelligence*. Harmondsworth, Middlesex, England: Penguin Books Ltd, 1972.

ROWAN, C. T. How racists use 'Science' to degrade black people. *Ebony*, Vol. 25, No. 7, pp. 31-40, May 1970.

RUBIN-RABSON, GRACE. Behavioral science *versus* intelligence. *Wall Street Journal*, p. 14, July 1, 1969.

SANUA, V. D. A critique of Jensen's article: 'How Much Can We Boost IQ and Scholastic Achievement?' Paper presented at the Professional Meeting of the New York Society of Clinical Psychologists, Inc., at Carnegie Endowment Center for International Peace, April 17, 1970, p. 42.

SAUNDERS, M. H., AND TESKA, P. T. An analysis of cultural differences on certain projective techniques. *Journal of Negro Education*, 1970, **39**, 109.

SCARR-SALAPATEK, SANDRA. Unknowns in the IQ equation. *Science*, 1971, **174**, 1223-1228.

SCRIVEN, M. The values of the academy (moral issues for American education and educational research arising from the Jensen case). *Review of Educational Research*, 1970, **40**, 541-549.

SHOCKLEY, W. Negro IQ deficit: Failure of a 'malicious coincidence' model warrants new research proposals. *Review of Educational Research*, 1971, **41**, 227-248. (a)

SHOCKLEY, W. Models, mathematics, and the moral obligation to diagnose the origin of Negro IQ deficits. *Review of Educational Research*, 1971, **41**, 369-377. (b)

SHOCKLEY, W. Dysgenics, geneticity, raceology: A challenge to the intellectual responsibility of educators. *Phi Delta Kappan*, 1972, **53**, 297-307. (a)

SHOCKLEY, W. A debate challenge: Geneticity is 80% for white identical twins' IQ's. *Phi Delta Kappan*, 1972, **53**, 415-419. (b)

SILCOCK, B. Race, class and brains. *London Sunday Times Weekly Review*, Feb. 1, 1970, pp. 49-50. (a)

SILCOCK, B. The case of the vanishing IQ gap. *London Sunday Times Weekly Review*, Feb. 8, 1970, p. 5. (b)

SITGREAVES, ROSEDITH. Comments on the 'Jensen Report'. *New York Statistician*, 1971, **22**, 1-2.

SNOW, C. P. How 'equal' are we really? *The Daily Telegraph Magazine*, No. 294, June 5, 1970, pp. 14-15.

STINCHCOMBE, A. L. Environment: the cumulation of effects is yet to be understood. *Harvard Educational Review*, 1969, **39**, 511-522.

SUDIA, CECELIA E. Minorities achieve the right to question achievement. *Children*, 1971, **18**, 155-157.

VAN DEN HAAG, E. Addendum to Jensen. *American Psychologist*, 1969, **24**, 1042.

VERHAEGEN, P. Reflexions an sujet de A. Jensen, 'Genetics, educability and subpopulation differences'. *Revue de Psychologie Appliquée*, 1972, in press.

VERNON, P. E. Genes, 'G', and Jensen. *Contemporary Psychology*, 1970, **15**, 161-163.

VOYAT, G. IQ: God-given or man-made? *Saturday Review*, 1969, **52**, 74-75. Reprinted in: J. Hellmuth (Ed.), *Disadvantaged Child*, Vol. 3. New York: Brunner-Mazel, 1970, pp. 158-162.

WATSON, P. How race affects IQ. *New Society*, 1970, **16**, 103-104.

WEYL, N. The Human 'Barometer'. *The Daily Telegraph Magazine*, No. 294, June 5, 1970, pp. 19-20.

WHITTEN, P., AND KAGAN, J. Stimulus-Response – Jensen's dangerous half truth. *Psychology Today*, 1969, **3**, 8.

WYSOCKI, B. A., AND WYSOCKI, A. C. Cultural differences as reflected in Wechsler Bellevue Intelligence (WBII) Test. *Psychological Reports*, 1969, **25**, 95.

ZACH, L. IQ test: Does it make black children unequal? *The School Review*, 1970, **78**, 249-258.

*Articles by Arthur R. Jensen*

JENSEN, A. R. Estimation of the limits of heritability of traits by comparison of monozygotic and dizygotic twins. *Proc. Nat. Acad. Sci.*, 1967, **58**, 149-156.

——. The culturally disadvantaged: Psychological and educational aspect. *Educational Research*, 1967, **10**, 4-20.

——. Social class and verbal learning. In M. Deutsch, I. Katz, and A. R. Jensen (Eds.), *Social class, race, and psychological development*, New York: Holt, Rinehart & Winston, 1968, pp. 115-174. (Reprinted in: J. P. DeCecco (Ed.), *The psychology of language, thought, and instruction*. New York: Holt, Rinehart & Winston, 1967, pp. 103-117.)

——. Social class, race, and genetics: Implications for education. *American Educational Research Journal*, 1968, **5**, 1-42. (Reprinted in H. F. Clarizio, R. C. Craig, and W. A. Mehrens (Eds.) *Contemporary issues in educational psychology*. New York: Allyn & Bacon, in press. (Reprinted in : I. J. Gordon (Ed.) *Readings in research in developmental psychology*. Glenview, Illinois: Scott, Foresman & Co., 1971, pp. 54-67.)

——. The culturally disadvantaged and the heredity-environment uncertainty. In J. Hellmuth (Ed.), *The culturally disadvantaged child*, Vol. 2. Seattle, Wash.: Special Child Publications, 1968, pp. 29-76.

——. Patterns of mental ability and socioeconomic status. *Proc. Nat. Acad. Sci.*, 1968, **60**, 1330-1337.

——. Another look at culture-fair testing. In *Western Regional Conference on Testing Problems*, Proceedings for 1968, 'Measurement for Educational Planning'. Berkeley, Calif.: Educational Testing Service, Western Office, 1968, pp. 50-104. (Reprinted in J. Hellmuth (Ed.), *Disadvantaged Child*, Vol. 3. New York: Brunner-Mazel, 1970, pp. 53-101).

——., AND ROHWER, W. D., JR. Mental retardation, mental age, and learning rate. *Journal of Educational Psychology*, 1968, **59**, 402-403.

——. How much can we boost I.Q. and scholastic achievement? *Harvard Educational Review*, 1969, **39**, 1-123. (Reprinted in *Environment, heredity, and intelligence*. Harvard Educational Review, Reprint Series No. 2, 1969, pp. 1-123.)
  *Congressional Record*, May 28, 1969, Vol. 115, No. 88, pp. H-4270-4298.
  Bract, G. H., Hopkins, K., and Stanley, J. C. (Eds.), *Perspectives in Educational and Psychological Measurement*, New York: Prentice-Hall 1972.

——. Reducing the heredity-environment uncertainty. *Harvard Educational Review*, 1969, **39**, 449-483. Reprinted in *Environment, heredity, and intelligence*. Harvard Educational Review, Reprint Series No. 2, 1969, pp. 209-243.

——. Criticism or propaganda? *American Psychologist*, 1969, **24**, 1040-1041.

——. The promotion of dogmatism. *Journal of Social Issues*, 1969, **25**, 212-217, 219-222.

——. An embattled hypothesis (interview). *Center Magazine*, 1969, **2**, 77-80.

——. Intelligence, learning ability, and socioeconomic status. *Journal of Special Education*, 1969, **3**, 23-35. (Reprinted in *Mental Health Digest*, 1969, **1**, 9-12.)

——. Jensen's theory of intelligence: A reply. *Journal of Educational Psychology*, 1969, **60**, 427-431.

——. *Understanding readiness: An occasional paper*. Urbana, Illinois: ERIC Clearinghouse on Early Childhood Education,

National Laboratory on Early Childhood Education, 1969, pp. 1-17.

——. IQ's of identical twins reared apart. *Behavior Genetics*, 1970, **1**, 133-148.

——. The heritability of intelligence. *Science & Engineering*, 1970, **33**, 40-43.

——. Race and the genetics of intelligence: A reply to Lewontin. *Bulletin of the Atomic Scientists*, 1970, **26**, 17-23. (Reprinted in D. Baer (Ed.), *Heredity and Society: Readings in Social Genetics*. New York: Macmillan, in press.)

——. Learning ability, intelligence, and educability. In V. Allen (Ed.), *Psychological factors in poverty*. Chicago: Markham, 1970, pp. 106-132.

——. A theory of primary and secondary familial mental retardation. In N. R. Ellis (Ed.), *International Review of Research in Mental Retardation*, Vol. 4. New York: Academic Press, 1970, pp. 33-105.

——. Hierarchical theories of mental ability. In B. Dockrell (Ed.), *On intelligence*. Toronto: Ontario Institute for Studies in Education, 1970, pp. 119-190.

——. Race and intelligence. *Psychology Today*, 1969, **3**, 4-6. (Reprinted in: Patricia C. Sexton (Ed.), *Problems and policy in education*. New York: Allyn & Bacon, 1970.

——. Can we and should we study race differences? In J. Hellmuth (Ed.), *Disadvantaged Child*, Vol. 3, *Compensatory Education: A National Debate*. New York: Brunner/Mazel, 1970, pp. 124-157. (Reprinted in: J. C. Grigham and T. A. Weissbach (Eds.), *Racial Attitudes in America: Analysis and Findings of Social Psychology*. New York: Harper & Row, 1971.

——. Parent and teacher attitudes toward integration and busing. Research Resume, No. 43, California Advisory Council on Educational Research, May 1970.

——., AND ROHWER, W. D., JR. *An experimental analysis of learning abilities in culturally disadvantaged children*. Final Report. Office of Economic Opportunity, Contract No. OEO 2404, 1970, pp. 1-181.

——. Statement of Dr Arthur R. Jensen to the General Sub-committee on Education of the Committee on Education and Labor, House of Representatives, 92nd Congress, second session. *Hearings on Emergency School Aid Act of 1970.* (H.R. 17846) Washington D.C.: U.S. Gov't Printing Office, 1970, pp. 333-342.

——. Controversies in intelligence: Heredity and environment. In D. W. Allen and E. Seifman (Eds.), *The Teacher's Handbook.* Glenview, Illinois: Scott, Foresman & Co., 1971, pp. 642-654.

——. Erblicher I.Q. -oder Pädagogischer Optimismus von einem an deren Gericht. *Neue Sammlung,* 1971, **11,** 71-76.

——. Selection of minorities in higher education. *Toledo Law Review,* 1971, Spring-Summer, Nos. 2 and 3, 403-457.

——. The role of verbal mediation in mental development. *Journal of Genetic Psychology,* 1971, **118,** 39-70.

——. Hebb's confusion about heritability. *American Psychologist,* 1971, **26,** 394-395.

——. A note on why genetic correlations are not squared. *Psychological Bulletin,* 1971, **75,** 223-224.

——. Do Schools Cheat Minority Children? *Educational Research,* 1971, **14,** 3-28.

——. Twin differences and race differences: A reply to Burgess and Jahoda. *Bulletin of the British Psychological Society,* 1971, **24,** 195-198.

——. The race × sex × ability interaction. In R. Cancro (Ed.), *Intelligence.* New York: Grune & Stratton, 1971, pp. 107-161.

——. Educability, heritability, and population differences. *Proceedings of the 17th International Congress of Applied Psychology,* 1972, in press.

——. The phylogeny and ontogeny of intelligence. *Perspectives in Biology and Medicine,* 1971, **15,** 37-43.

——. Heredity, environment, and educability. In L. C. Deighton (Ed.), *Encyclopedia of Education.* New York: Macmillan, in press.

——. A two-factor theory of familial mental retardation. *Proceedings of the 4th International Congress of Human Genetics*, 1972, in press.

——., AND HASKELL, E. Empirical basis of the periodic tables of human cultures. In E. Haskell (Ed.), *Full circle: The moral force of unified science.* New York: Gordon & Breach, 1972, Ch. 4.

——. Review of *Race, culture, and intelligence*, K. Richardson, D. Spears, and M. Richards (Eds.). *New Society*, 1972, **19**, No. 491, 408-410.

——. Educabilité, transmission héréditaire et différences entre populations. *Revue de Psychologie Appliquée*, 1972, **22**, 21-34.

——. A reply to Gage: The causes of twin differences in IQ. *Phi Delta Kappan*, 1972, **53**, 420-421.

——. The interpretation of heritability. *American Psychologist*, 1972, **27**, in press.

# Author Index

370

# Subject Index